9/09

NOV 03 2009

DEC 03 2010

MAY 0 3 2018

DATE DUE		

D1165712

Paul Was Not
a Christian

Paul Was Not a Christian

The Original Message of a Misunderstood Apostle

Pamela Eisenbaum

HarperOne
An Imprint of HarperCollinsPublishers

HarperOne

FIRST EDITION

Library of Congress Cataloging-in-Publication Data
Eisenbaum, Pamela Michelle.
Paul was not a Christian : the original message of a misunderstood
Apostle / by Pamela Eisenbaum. — 1st ed.
p. cm.
ISBN 978–0–06–072291–3
1. Paul, the Apostle, Saint. I. Title.
BS2506.3.E37 2009 *9/09*
225.9'2—dc22 *24.99* *34393* 2009009420
Ingram
09 10 11 12 13 RRD(H) 10 9 8 7 6 5 4 3 2 1

For Mark

Contents

Acknowledgments

I am a firm believer that scholarship is a corporate endeavor, not a solo enterprise. My debt to the scholars who have come before me is enormous, too many for me to name in entirety. But I would be remiss if I did not thank those who have played such a prominent role in helping me develop my thinking on Paul. The reader who looks to the notes at the end of this book will see that I am especially indebted to the work of four scholars: John Gager, Lloyd Gaston, Krister Stendahl, and Stanley Stowers. Without their pioneering work, this work would never have been possible. The same is true of three Jewish scholars who produced important scholarship on Paul: Daniel Boyarin, Mark Nanos, and Alan Segal. Their example inspired me to write this book. I thank all these scholars for their collegiality, support, and dialogue.

This book has taken me a long time to write. Over the years, I have shared parts of it with many of my colleagues, who have commented on my work and influenced it in various ways, but I must especially thank the colleagues who read parts of this manuscript as I was bringing it to completion: Neil Elliott, Dennis Haugh, Jonathan Klawans, Jeff Siker, and Amy Erickson. They read with great care, and in many cases they saved me from embarrassing errors. My long-suffering editor, Roger Freet, stuck with me when others would have given up and helped make this book more readable.

There are also organizations and institutions that have supported me in the writing of this book. The Association of Theological Schools

Theological Research Fellowship, sponsored by the Lilly Foundation, supported research and writing on work that fed into this book in 2001–02. The Association for Religion and Intellectual Life gave me the chance to participate in the Coolidge Fellows summer seminar in New York in 2004, where I was able to interact with a number of other scholars working on a variety of interesting projects. The summer also enabled me to spend time working in Lowe Library at Columbia University and Burke Library at Union Theological Seminary, where I was aided by the formidable reference skills of Seth Kasten.

I thank the faculty, students, and staff of the Iliff School of Theology, where I have taught for the past fourteen years. Iliff has always been a place supportive of the scholarly enterprise and I am extremely grateful. Many of my colleagues commented on this work, informally as well as formally in faculty colloquia. These conversations always resulted in the sharpening of my thinking. Deserving of special mention is Richard Valantasis, my colleague from 1999 to 2006. He supported me academically and personally throughout the development of this book. And I would be remiss if I did not mention the "Scribbling Women," who gave me the support, energy, and advice I needed to finish.

The students of the Iliff School of Theology played a very important role in the development of this book. In every class I taught on Paul, I learned a great deal from their questions and insights. I especially owe a debt to the doctoral students of the University of Denver/Iliff Joint Doctoral Program. They are among the best I have taught anywhere and it is my privilege to be their teacher. Several students at both the master's and doctoral levels served as my research assistants at various points in the process: Megan Ramer, Ann Dunlap, Derek Krebiel, Selena Billington, Mark Maxwell, and Eric Smith, who was there with me at the end, and who labored hard to track down bibliographical references.

Finally, I wish to acknowledge my family—both the Eisenbaums and the Georges—with the kind of profound appreciation that is hard to articulate. Quinn and Ryan, my stepsons, had to endure the length and intensity of my work on this project to an extraordinary degree; I thank them for their patience. Finally, no one is deserving of thanks more than my husband, Mark. He read the entire manuscript with his keen editorial eye, but more important, he created the loving and supportive environment that enabled me to write it. I could not have done it without you, Mark. I love you, and to you I dedicate this book.

I regret that Professor Stendahl died before the completion of this book. He was my advisor when I was at Harvard, and in some sense my journey with Paul began with him over twenty-five years ago. I will miss him.

> *Pamela Eisenbaum*
> *Denver, Colorado*
> *April 11, 2009*
> *Pesach, day 3*
> *Jubilee year dedicated to St. Paul, declared by Pope Benedict XVI*

Note to the Reader

All translations of Paul's letters are mine based on the Nestle-Aland twenty-seventh edition Greek New Testament, unless otherwise indicated. Translations from other parts of the Bible are from the New Revised Standard Version (NRSV), unless otherwise indicated.

I have tried to avoid the use of technical terms, but there are times when they were useful. In light of this I have provided a brief glossary at the end of the book.

Paul Was Not a Christian

Introduction

Once when visiting a large, wealthy, metropolitan church on Easter Sunday, I listened to a man give a testimony about his conversion to Christianity. He spoke of how he yearned for spiritual meaning and sought eagerly for religious truth throughout his life (he seemed to me to be on the young side of middle-aged) but was always disappointed with the answers given to him; that is, until recently, when he discovered Christ. Suddenly he realized his former life was a life of sin. Before his conversion, he explained, he had been Jewish. But now he had accepted God's unconditional loving act of grace in Jesus Christ and had given up the sin of Judaism.

Admittedly, I can no longer remember the details of the man's speech, which was rather lengthy, but I am certain he associated, if not equated, a life in Judaism with a life in sin. When he began to speak of his sordid past, I was expecting something more stereotypical—at least what I imagined to be stereotypical—of Christian testimonies in the American Protestant evangelical context. I thought he would say that he had been an alcoholic or a drug addict or had abused members of his family or had been obsessed with money and prestige and lived a vain, empty life, but he never mentioned any of these things. His description of his former, so-called sinful life sounded perfectly respectable to me. The mention of the words Judaism and sin in the same sentence came as a painful shock, to say the least.

As a Jew, the idea that Judaism is a flawed religion inherently linked to sin is deeply offensive. Unfortunately, this idea has been linked to the apostle Paul, but it really comes from a long history of Christian interpreters of Paul. While Christians of virtually every stripe, Catholic and Protestant, mainline and evangelical, now willingly accept that Jesus was a Jew, Paul is typically viewed as the first true Christian. The image of Paul as the first true Christian also requires him to be the first true convert to Christianity. The traditional story of Paul looks something like this: Paul was originally a zealous Jew who was persecuting the church, until something utterly miraculous happened: the resurrected Jesus appeared to him. This revelation led to Paul's conversion from Judaism to Christianity, from being a zealous Pharisee to being an unstoppable preacher of the gospel of Jesus Christ. Once converted, he realized the futility of Judaism, with its endless demands of the law, and rejected it.

Combining assumptions about Paul's biography with the theology of his letters as they understood them, Christian interpreters came to believe that Paul's conversion experience led him to articulate the doctrine of justification by faith, a doctrine that stands at the core of Christianity and, at the same time, constructs Christianity as the antithesis of Judaism, typically considered a religion of works. According to this view, Christianity correctly recognizes the inevitable failure of human beings to achieve righteousness and thus the necessity of accepting God's grace—in the form of Jesus Christ—while Judaism mistakenly puts its faith in the ability of human beings to achieve salvation through their own efforts. Christian theologians throughout the ages have varied as to whether they see Jews as merely misguided or willfully defiant, but there has generally been agreement that a theology that endorses "salvation by works" reflects a bad religion because it denies the grace of God. Thus, the man who described his conversion from Judaism to Christianity as a move from sin to grace had followed the traditional Pauline script to near perfection.

Because the negative image of Judaism is so closely linked to the apostle Paul, most Jewish interpreters of Paul have not had good things to say about him. However, my interest in writing a book on Paul began not out of spiteful resentment toward him, but because I passionately identify with his perspective on the world. Like Paul, I live as a Jew among Gentiles. Although I am Jewish, my scholarly expertise in the origins of Christianity landed me a teaching position in a Christian theological school. To be sure, not all my students are Christian and not all are studying for the Christian ministry, but many of them are. Although I never envisioned teaching in such an institution when I began my scholarly career, I now consider it a privilege. Being in a Christian institution has made me more self-consciously Jewish; remarkably enough, it has also contributed to my ability to see Paul as a Jew. Moreover, I have come to regard Paul as a Jew who wrestled with an issue with which many modern American Jews wrestle: how to reconcile living as a Jew with living in and among the rest of the non-Jewish world.

I think it safe to assert that this issue transcends the peculiar situation of modern American Jews. Stated generically, the problem to which I refer concerns the relation of particularity to universality. Anyone who wishes to maintain the particularity of his or her ethnic or religious identity without denying the validity of another's particular identity faces this problem. I think Paul reflected on this problem and ultimately developed some powerful insights on the subject, insights that have largely been overlooked because of the traditional image of Paul as a Christian. Unless one first recognizes that Paul was a Jew, both before and after his experience of Christ, and that he struggled with the cognitive and physical dissonance of being a Jew in a world with non-Jews, one cannot see how Paul confronted the problem of human difference. Thus, this book is an attempt to resurrect, if you will, Paul as a Jew in order to offer a constructive, alternative reading of Paul's letters that Christians, Jews, and perhaps others will find compelling.

I also write this book as a challenge to the portrait of Paul that has reigned for nearly two millennia. I intend to expose the bias embedded in the traditional portrait of Paul and the ways in which it has contributed to gross misrepresentations of Judaism and played no small role in the history of anti-Semitism. At the same time and just as important, I intend to demonstrate that I can explain Paul's letters compellingly and thereby construct a more credible and more persuasive portrait of Paul for readers interested in having a better grasp of Paul's life and work.

The image of Paul in this book portrays a man who, to paraphrase Krister Stendahl, was "called rather than converted."[1] In other words, Paul was called by God to fulfill a particular mission, one that was foretold in the Hebrew prophets: to bring knowledge of the one God—the God of Israel—to all the nations of the world. Paul believed that the recognition of the one God by Gentiles was necessary so that they might have a share in the world to come. Thus, Paul was not a *Christian*—a word that was in any case completely unknown to him because it had not yet been invented. He was a Jew who understood himself to be on a divine mission. As a Jew, Paul believed himself to be entrusted with the special knowledge God had given only to Jews. However, Paul also believed the resurrection of Jesus signaled that the world to come was already in the process of arriving and that it was time to reconcile non-Jews to God. Reconciling non-Jews to God also meant reconciling non-Jews to Jews, not because they were necessarily hostile to each other but because, if all people were potentially children of God, Jews and Gentiles must now be considered part of the same family; this entailed a new level of interaction and intimacy.

Contrary to prevailing opinion, I think Paul's theological orientation to the world can be used productively for thinking about religious pluralism. I hope to demonstrate this claim successfully in the pages that follow. Furthermore, I hope this book will enable Jewish as well as Christian readers to develop an appreciation for Paul's theological pluralism. Jews have typically portrayed Paul as the great betrayer of Judaism. I think this image is as much mistaken as the traditional Christian image. Viewing Paul as a Jewish heretic has resulted in nothing more than Jewish ignorance of an important theological resource. Given the history of Jewish-Christian relations, Jewish antipathy to Paul is no surprise. At the same time, the history of Jewish-Christian relations seems to me to warrant crossing the traditional boundary between the two faiths along with a refashioning of what constitutes Jewish and Christian identity in particular and interfaith relations in general. Just as the God of biblical history is a dynamic and not a static force, so, too, are our religious traditions.

Chapter

1

Was Paul Really Jewish?

Paul lived and died a Jew—that is the essential claim of this book. For some readers, the claim that Paul was a Jew is counterintuitive. Who could possibly be *more* Christian than Paul? For others, especially many scholars, Christian clergy, and lay devotees of Paul, the claim that Paul was Jewish is an entirely pedestrian observation. Sure Paul was a Jew; he himself said so (see Gal 1:13, 2:15). Virtually any book on Paul that one might pick up in a bookstore will tell you that Paul was Jewish. But it is usually only mentioned in passing, by way of introduction and background perhaps. In fact, Paul is overwhelmingly called Christian by people who write about him.

So, what exactly does it mean to read Paul as a Jew? In this book it means primarily three things: (1) Most basically, it means to take seriously Paul's religious identity as a Jew and not merely pay lip service to it. It means reading his letters with the working assumption that they were written by a Jew, specifically a Hellenistic Jew, that is, a Jew from the Greco-Roman era who speaks Greek and has been influenced by Greek thought and culture. (2) Reclaiming Paul as a Jew means to reclaim a historically plausible image of Judaism so as to combat the long history of Pauline interpretation that has bolstered Christian anti-Judaism. (3) Demonstrating Paul's Jewish world-view helps clarify much that is perceived to be inconsistent, contradictory, or just plain confusing in Paul's writings.

I have occasionally given lectures titled "Reading Paul as a Jew," and people have asked me about the title—"Does the phrase 'as a Jew' refer to Paul or to you?" "Both," I would say. I'm Jewish and Paul's Jewish—simple, right? Sort of. The religious labels we ascribe to people, institutions, and texts are more slippery than one might think, and religious identity is a more complicated question than at first it may seem. Let me explain.

While people intuitively think of the New Testament—of which Paul's letters are a significant part—as Christian, the vast majority of the twenty-seven documents that currently comprise the New Testament were written by Jews at a time before there was any such thing as Christianity. Because of the subsequent canonization of these texts, including Paul's letters, all these documents are now considered Christian. But in their own historical contexts, scholars think of them, or at least most of them, as Jewish sectarian literature. Paul clearly identifies himself as a Jew in his letters. Ironically, Paul is especially emphatic about his Jewish identity in Galatians, the letter often regarded as the most anti-Jewish of Paul's writings. He says that he is a Jew "by nature" or "by birth," as it is usually translated (Gal 2:15).[1] It is very important to stress that Paul does not use the designation "Jew" of himself as a label of his religious past. He speaks in the present tense; that is, Paul's self-identification is a description of himself at the time he wrote the letter to the Galatians. Interpreters have sometimes argued that when Paul calls himself a Jew, he means only that he is ethnically, and not religiously, Jewish. This is an incorrect view on several grounds. When Paul calls himself a Jew "by nature" in his letter to the Galatians, he contrasts it with another identity: he says he is not a "Gentile sinner." By speaking this way, Paul not only tells us who he is; he tells us who he is not. He says he is not a Gentile sinner—not simply not a Gentile; he is not a Gentile *sinner.* By so doing, Paul makes clear to us that the terminology of Jew and Gentile does not merely refer to one's ethnic or cultural heritage; the terms Jew and Gentile also refer to one's morality and one's disposition vis-à-vis God.

In terms of religious identity, Paul is representative of the Jews who produced the writings that now make up the New Testament. They were, to be sure, Jews who believed in Jesus, but they did not proclaim their religious identity as Christian. They thought of Jesus as the realization of classical Jewish hopes, and they thought of themselves as the true Israel or the faithful remnant of Israel, although those hopes were understood somewhat differently among different groups of Jews. This

description of the religious identity of New Testament texts in historical context makes them analogous to other Jewish sectarian writings
of the period, like the Dead Sea Scrolls. We have scores of Jewish texts
from antiquity, many of which reflect a sectarian perspective, that is, a
distinctive perspective on what it means to be Jewish. Sometimes this
perspective overlaps with other Jews' points of view; sometimes it is
idiosyncratic.

Thus, texts themselves do not inherently possess a static religious
identity. Paul's letters are appropriately called Christian because Christians chose to canonize them, and Christians continue to value them as
authoritative and incorporate them in their worship.[2] Complementarily,
Jews do not recognize them as authoritative and do not use them in
worship. From a Christian and a Jewish perspective, then, Paul's letters
are an essential feature of Christianity and thus a marker of Christian
identity.

But in the first century the letters could not possibly have functioned
as a marker distinctive of Christian identity. First, there is the obvious
reason that there was no such religious category "Christian." As far as
can be determined by historians, archaeologists, and biblical scholars,
there were no distinctively Christian institutions, buildings, or symbols
in the first century, and a few scholars believe that Christians did not
materially distinguish themselves until the late third or early fourth
century.[3] Beyond that, there were other believers in Jesus who were
not part of the Pauline circle; some of them even seemed to have opposed Paul. Thus, for the first several generations of believers in Jesus,
Paul and Paul's letters did not inform all Christians' belief in Jesus.
Most important, Gentiles of the Roman world who knew nothing of
Jesus—those whose practice today would fall under the loose category
of Greco-Roman religion—would have regarded the letters as Jewish
letters, because they were authored by a Jew, and they contain Jewish
language, imagery, and concerns.

If a Roman centurion had intercepted Paul's letter to the Romans,
he would have quickly spotted it as Jewish. Consider how the letter
opens: Paul says he is in service to someone named Jesus, which is the
Greek form of the Hebrew name Joshua, and this Jesus is descended
from the Davidic dynasty, the most glorious of the ancient monarchies
of Israel. And if the first few lines didn't tip off the centurion, when he
saw the language of Jew and Gentile—language Paul uses over and over

again in Romans (and elsewhere)—the centurion would know that this letter reflected a Jewish perspective on the world. For who else divides up the entire world into these two kinds of people, Jews and Gentiles, those who are Jewish and those who are not? It is certainly not how the Romans divide up the world: their operative categories were Romans and barbarians.

Moreover, Paul's letters would have been regarded as Jewish by other Jews of the time, including Pharisees. They might not have thought the letters contained correct views, and they might well have thought Paul a bad Jew, but a Jew nonetheless. The fact that Paul says he was subject to forty lashes (less one) five times from synagogical authorities (2 Cor 11:24) means that the synagogical authorities as well as Paul himself understood that he remained subject to Jewish authority. Similar to the illustration of the Roman centurion, Paul's letters would have been regarded as Jewish by other Jews because the writer was Jewish. Even if they never met him in person, other Jews of the first century would have recognized the author of these letters as Jewish because so many of the signature marks of Jewishness appear in them.

Modern readers of Paul tend to assume that Pharisees and other Jews would have considered Paul an apostate, a Jewish heretic who was no longer part of the Jewish community because of his belief in Jesus, and thus not really Jewish. In the context of the first century, however, Paul's belief in Jesus did not make him less Jewish. Belief in a messianic savior figure is a very Jewish idea, as can be demonstrated by a historical analogy. Only a half century after Paul wrote his letters, R. Akiba, one of the most revered of all rabbis of antiquity, believed that the Messiah had come in his day, only his name was not Jesus, it was Bar Kokhba. Not all Jews thought Bar Kokhba was the Messiah at the time, and after Bar Kokhba failed in his revolt against the Romans and died, it became clear that R. Akiba had been wrong.[4] But R. Akiba has never been judged a heretic, and his teachings continue to this day to be authoritative because they are preserved in the Mishnah and the Talmud. Thus, Paul's belief in Jesus would not have branded him a heretic—a pain in the neck perhaps, but not a heretic. So if we of the twenty-first century are willing to take account of the opinions of first-century persons such as Romans, Jews, and Paul himself, we must conclude that Paul lived and died a Jew, because his Jewish identity is represented in his letters. Even though, because Paul's letters have become essential to Christian tradition and self-understanding, in our contemporary context they are appropriately labeled Christian, in their own historical context this label would not have attached to them; it could not possibly have attached, since it did not yet exist. Rather, the teachings contained in the letters as well as their author would have been considered Jewish.

One point of clarification, however: it is obvious that Paul played a critical role in the development of Christianity and that his letters are regarded as an essential part of the Christian canon. I do not in any way wish to deny Christians their claim on Paul. But in this book Paul is unambiguously Jewish—ethnically, culturally, religiously, morally, and theologically.

Chapter

2

Paul the Problem

This study not only argues for the recovery of Paul's Jewish identity, but attempts to address several nagging problems that have dogged Pauline interpretation. These problems can be grouped under two general categories: problems of evidence and problems of interpretation. Problems of evidence refer to the status and credibility of historical sources relevant to the study of Paul. The most obvious example of this problem is the relationship between the Acts of the Apostles and Paul's letters. Some of Paul's autobiographical statements conflict with claims made about him by the author of Acts. Interpretative problems generally include any confusion readers experience when they confront Paul's letters. Interpretive problems grow in relation to the distance between the writer or speaker and the reader or hearer. Paul lived nearly two thousand years ago in a culture incalculably different from our own, and when he wrote his letters, he wrote them in ancient Greek to his contemporaries; he could not have imagined the vast modern audience he now enjoys. That there is a gap between what Paul likely intended to say and what we understand him to say should come as no surprise.

Problems of Evidence

Ultimately, problems of interpretation are more significant and pose a greater challenge than problems of evidence. Because problems of evidence can largely be resolved by acknowledging the limits of the historical sources, I will begin with discussion of this category and thereby clarify for the reader exactly which sources inform this study of Paul.

Acts Versus Paul's Letters

Most books on Paul, especially those that aspire to offer a biography of the historical Paul, rely heavily on the Acts of the Apostles to reconstruct Paul's life. There can be no doubt that Acts has played a central role in shaping the image of Paul in Christian tradition. The often-reproduced maps and chronologies of Paul's three tumultuous sea voyages found in so many study Bibles and textbooks are based on the stories of his travels as recounted in Acts.[1] The familiar story of Paul's conversion on the road to Damascus in which he collapses on the ground at the sight of the risen Jesus comes from Acts.[2] Although Paul speaks frequently of his travels and recounts in his own words his first encounter with Jesus in the first chapter of Galatians, the letters are not the source of the popular stories of Paul's travails in traveling or of his sudden roadside encounter with Jesus.

Because the book of Acts comprises a single, well-structured, chronological narrative, the events of Paul's life appear connected in a sensible order. By contrast, the bits of information in Paul's letters cannot be used to construct a tidy narrative of Paul's life. Furthermore, Acts is more entertaining reading than the letters. In Acts the apostle's life is an adventure story, complete with numerous chase scenes, last-minute escapes, murderous plots, stonings, courtroom drama, a shipwreck in which the ship is completely destroyed but all 276 passengers miraculously survive, throngs of people alternately enthused and violently agitated, whole towns thrust into chaos because of divided loyalties toward Paul and his companions, a cast of colorful supporting characters, including brutal tyrants (Herod), God-fearing centurions (Cornelius) and other officious Roman bureaucrats, synagogue officials (sometimes good, sometimes bad), wonder-workers, and—providing some comic relief—a few hapless individuals like Eutychus, who, having fallen asleep while listening to one of the apostle's less scintillating sermons, falls three stories out a window only to be quickly resurrected by Paul, who immediately afterward resumes the lesson.[3] Congruent with the letters, Paul is portrayed as a missionary preacher and teacher in Acts. But his speeches often come at dramatic moments in the narrative—

including passionate defenses of himself during trial—thus making the Paul of Acts a larger-than-life character and, ultimately, a more compelling figure for biography than the Paul who can be gleaned from the pieces of information in the letters.

Paul's speeches in Acts have a significantly different emphasis, as well as a different audience, than do his letters. Paul's primary self-identification in the letters is as *Apostle to the Gentiles.* The author of Acts, by contrast, does not consider Paul a true apostle—a term the author of Acts generally reserves for "the Twelve"[4]—but a prominent Jewish leader who was relentlessly but unjustly persecuted by other Jews as a result of his preaching in various and sundry diaspora communities. According to Acts, Paul's preaching career follows a consistent pattern: Paul always preaches in the synagogue whenever he first arrives in a new town, but the Jews repeatedly reject him. As a result, he ends up preaching to those outside the synagogue community, namely, Gentiles. To put the matter succinctly, the portrait of Paul that emerges from the narrative in Acts differs markedly from the image Paul projects of himself in his letters.[5] While the Paul of the letters understands his original commission from God to be the apostle whose preaching is dedicated to Gentiles, the Paul of Acts ends up preaching to Gentiles inadvertently, that is, only as a result of Jewish rejection of his message.

There are two basic reasons that Acts characterizes Paul differently than Paul characterizes himself. First, to state the obvious, Paul did not write Acts; someone commonly called Luke did, and he wrote it somewhere near the end of the first century or the beginning of the second while Paul wrote his letters in the middle of the first century.[6] Scholars debate whether Luke knew Paul personally—I think it unlikely—but even if they did know each other, we would expect Luke's perspective of Paul to differ from Paul's view of himself, just as we often perceive ourselves differently than others perceive us. For example, Paul's letters make obvious that letter writing was an important missionary strategy for Paul, yet Acts never once describes Paul composing a letter. Clearly, Paul the letter writer was not an important component of Paul's image for Luke in the composition of Acts.

Second, and more important, the genre and purpose of Acts are entirely different from those of Paul's letters. The author of Acts obviously had a different agenda than Paul had in writing his letters. Acts is not a biography of Paul.[7] No one would claim that Paul's letters constitute a biography either, but the difference is that Acts has traditionally been read as biography. Paul may be the most important character in Acts, but he is not the *subject* of Acts. Rather, Paul's actions are part of a grander narrative concerning the origins and development of "the church" at its earliest stages. Luke wrote Acts in order to provide a historical account of the first generation of Jesus' followers after the crucifixion. Paul wrote letters in order to continue his guidance and teaching among his followers. Because he was an itinerant missionary who established communities around the northeastern edge of the Mediterranean basin, he frequently could not be present when significant issues, questions, or conflicts arose. His letters substituted for his presence, enabling the apostle to offer guidance or encouragement to his followers at a distance. Thus, the genre and purpose of Paul's letters differ markedly from those of Acts.

Although there has been some debate about the literary genre to which Acts should be assigned, readers tend to regard Acts as a work of history.[8] A word of clarification is required, however, because scholars mean something different than lay people when they apply the term "history" to Acts. The criteria that inform the modern writing of history differ from those that informed ancient writing of history. Modern readers generally expect works of history to be reliable, accurate accounts of "what really happened." Thus, a historical work on the Civil War Battle of Gettysburg, for example, uses the historical record to capture as fully as possible the who, what, why, when, where, and how of the Battle of Gettysburg, with the goal being as accurate a correspondence as is achievable between "the facts" and the historical narrative in which those facts are presented.

By "the historical record" I mean the primary sources used by professional historians. The primary sources are the raw material out of which a coherent historical narrative is produced. In the case of Gettysburg, these may include official political or military documents, such as executive orders issued by President Lincoln, legislative acts passed by Congress, official and unofficial correspondence between various leaders with decision-making powers, letters and diaries of individuals who either participated in the battle or witnessed it, photographs, and material artifacts such as armaments or the personal articles soldiers carried. The list could continue. The historical context largely determines what constitutes the historical record. A Civil War historian has a lot more literary documents at his or her disposal than one whose expertise is in ancient Sumer.

The canons of modern history differ significantly from those of ancient history. Like modern historians, ancient historians, too, utilized sources in order to construct a narrative account that was faithful to the event or series of events under consideration. Unlike modern historians, however, ancient historians often favored oral sources over written ones. Written sources, to be sure, were utilized and incorporated into histories, but information obtained directly through person-to-person communication was considered more trustworthy than that obtained from a written source. Moreover, even though ancient historians, like modern historians, aspired to produce truthful accounts of past events, they did not operate with the concept of "facts" the way modern historians traditionally have. Indeed, I do not know of a word in ancient Greek that corresponds to the English word "fact." Thus, what counts as a faithful account of past events is measured by a different standard in antiquity than it is in modernity.

The reasons for the difference between the way ancient and modern societies report and preserve their pasts are complex and difficult to explain, but at least one reason is worth mentioning here for illustrative purposes: People in antiquity had few ways to record any given moment at the point when it occurred. There were no telephones, tape recorders, cameras, or video cameras; neither were there photocopy machines, computers, or fax machines; and since no such thing as journalism existed yet, people in antiquity did not typically take notes at important events. Thus, the gathering, retrieval, and cross-checking of data was an entirely different matter for ancient historians than it is for modern ones. For example, reporting who said what, when, and to whom would be a difficult thing to do accurately without the benefits of modern technology. Yet historical writings in the Greco-Roman period often contain the text of lengthy speeches given by key figures at key moments. How did ancient historians know what was said if they were not present (or even if they were)? We know from Thucydides, for example, the famous fifth-century BCE Greek historian who wrote *The History of the Peloponnesian War*, that ancient historians composed the speeches themselves.[9] There was no expectation to record the words spoken on a given occasion verbatim; rather, the author needed to convey what the figure would have plausibly said under the circumstances. From oral traditions about what sort of person he or she was, as well as oral reports about the circumstances in which they found themselves, the ancient historian composed a speech for that person on that occasion.

It is necessary to understand something about the writing of history in antiquity so as to recognize that Acts conforms to the ancient standards of writing history, not modern standards. We cannot expect, for example, that Paul's speeches in Acts contain Paul's exact words. Even though Paul's words appear with quotations marks surrounding them, they are not the equivalent of the president's State of the Union address as published in the *New York Times* or any other modern, respectable newspaper. Paul's speeches were composed for him by the author we call Luke. Paul's letters, on the other hand, contain the apostle's very own words, his thoughts, feelings, reflections, and theological and ethical teachings. The Acts speeches may be representative of certain kinds of public presentations Paul made; perhaps they are even true to Paul's character, but by modern standards they constitute a historically inferior source compared to Paul's letters.

My intention here is not to belittle Acts per se. Neither do I mean to imply that the information about Paul that comes down to us from Acts is of no historical value. On the contrary, Acts constitutes an undeniable part of the historical record that can be mined for information about the origins of Christianity generally, as well as some of its central figures like Paul, as long as it is used with an awareness of its literary tendencies and particular biases. (This is true of ancient and modern accounts of events.[10])

Precisely because of its genre as a work of history in the ancient sense, Acts is a very tricky source to use in terms of modern history. Ongoing debate about how to sift historical information from thematic and rhetorical elements in Acts means that using Acts to any significant degree would necessarily involve methodological complications that I prefer to avoid in this study. Thus, the stories and speeches in Acts play virtually no role in this study of Paul. The primary reasons for my exclusion of Acts are scholarly expedience—omitting discussion of Acts allows me to avoid the quagmire about its historical reliability—and a deliberate decision to construct a portrait of Paul based exclusively on the apostle's own writings. It is an extremely rare privilege to have direct access to the words of a figure from biblical history, never mind a figure as historically significant as Paul. I am most interested in Paul's self-understanding and the public image he projected of himself, the image that apparently led him to have such a successful career as the apostle to the Gentiles. Given this goal, Paul's letters necessarily trump other sources, such as Acts.

Disputed Letters

As one scholar has observed, ask students how many letters of Paul are contained in the Bible and you receive a wide variety of answers: seven? eight? ten? thirteen? fourteen?[11] Such divergent answers are not the students' fault; there are different ways to count Paul's letters, depending on what criteria you choose to use. The correct answer in this book is seven. They include the following: Romans, 1 and 2 Corinthians, Galatians, Philippians, 1 Thessalonians, and Philemon. Restricting myself to these seven letters is due to the credibility of these documents above all others as sources for the study of Paul. These texts are commonly known as the "undisputed epistles," which means that biblical scholars do not dispute their authenticity; all scholars agree these texts were authored by Paul. Since I am excluding Acts as well as the disputed epistles, these seven letters comprise the *essential* and, for the most part, the *only* primary documents that are—for the purposes of this study—reliable representations of Paul's religious identity and his religious and theological views.

What about Ephesians, Colossians, and 2 Thessalonians? Or how about 1 and 2 Timothy and Titus? These texts claim to be written by Paul, but scholars dispute their authenticity. To put it bluntly, many scholars, myself included, do not believe Paul is really the author of these letters.[12] According to this view, they are pseudonymous; that is, they are ascribed to Paul, but Paul didn't write them. That makes these texts historically unreliable for reconstructing Paul. While I will occasionally make reference to material from these six disputed letters for comparative or contextual purposes, my reconstruction of Paul does not depend on them. Although I consider these six documents of little use for understanding Paul himself and have therefore excluded them from the body of evidence used in my analysis, the reader deserves a word of explanation about why these letters are widely considered dubious.

Biblical scholars and other textual experts have two general categories for assessing the authenticity of texts: external evidence and internal evidence. External evidence refers to physical kinds of evidence about the various manuscripts containing the text under study as well as any other evidence that may help reveal how, when, and where the text originated.

For example, several important manuscripts of the text commonly known as Paul's Letter to the Ephesians do not specify "those in Ephesus" as the recipients. Variations in handwritten manuscripts are common (they will be discussed in more detail in the next section) and often attributable to scribal errors, but the quantity of early manuscripts that originally had no reference to the Ephesians indicates something is awry—the phrase "to those in Ephesus" was not part of the original text of Ephesians but was added later, which is one reason for the scholarly suspicion that Paul did not write Ephesians, a position held by the majority of New Testament scholars.[13] We cannot know with certainty the reason for this later editorial addition, but it appears that someone either wanted to connect the text with the city of Ephesus in particular and/or wanted to make it appear to be one of Paul's letters by naming a specific addressee, as is the case in all the undisputed epistles. Paul's name, however, consistently appears in ancient manuscripts as the sender of the letter ("Paul, an apostle of Christ Jesus by the will of God . . ."). One suspicious variant does not by itself make the case for pseudonymity. Evidence for pseudonymity works cumulatively.

A piece of external evidence often invoked to argue for the dubious nature of 1 and 2 Timothy and Titus, known collectively as the Pastoral Epistles, is their omission from what is likely the oldest manuscript of Paul's letters, Chester Beatty Biblical Papyrus II. Chester Beatty Biblical Papyrus II is a codex, that is, an ancient book, the entirety of which comprises an early collection of Paul's letters, which dates approximately to the year 200 CE. The codex includes all of Paul's undisputed letters except Philemon. Additionally, it contains Colossians, Ephesians, and Hebrews, but does *not* include 1 and 2 Timothy and Titus. Some have argued that the absence of the Pastorals from the Chester Beatty Papyrus is evidence that they were written pseudonymously a generation or more after Paul. Since the editor of Chester Beatty did not include these letters, it is possible to conclude that the editor did not know them or that the author chose to exclude them because he knew they were not authentic—in either case, we have evidence that Paul didn't write the Pastorals.

The situation, however, is a bit more complicated. Before there was a canonical New Testament, those who valued Paul's letters collected them together so as to preserve and disseminate Paul's teachings among a growing number of communities. Since there was no officially sanctioned list of letters until later (probably the fourth century), it is not surprising that there would be variation about what was included and what was excluded. Some scholars have argued, for example, that the absence of the Pastoral Epistles as well as Philemon indicates that the ancient editor of Chester Beatty Biblical Papyrus II deliberately chose not to include letters addressed to individuals, but rather only those addressed to communities (e.g., the Galatians, the Corinthians, etc.). Again, individual cases of external evidence do not by themselves make a case for pseudonymity.

Internal evidence must be given due consideration and evaluated together with external evidence. Internal evidence refers to aspects of the text itself—the style, form, and content—and whether those aspects comport with what we know of Paul from his undisputed writings, his life, his speech patterns, and his points of reference—that is, the people, places, and things that tend to preoccupy him, his style of expressing himself, and his theological ideas. Ephesians again provides a good example for illustrating how the evidence comes into play in disputing Pauline authorship of certain texts. There is little specific detail in Ephesians that allows us any insight into the circumstances that prompted Paul to write the letter. While scholars often debate the exact nature of the context underlying, say, Galatians, the text of Galatians provides a lot of concrete information about the specific situation that has given rise to the letter: Paul is the first missionary to have inspired people in Galatia to become followers of Jesus, due to some sort of infirmity that waylaid him in that region; since Paul left Galatia, other teachers have come there and taught in ways contrary to Paul's gospel; the other missionaries' teaching included an emphasis on circumcision, and that, more than anything else, seems to have aroused Paul's ire and prompted him to write the letter. Many more details could be highlighted from Galatians. This kind of specificity marks all the undisputed epistles. By contrast, Ephesians reads like a generic letter. Except for a couple of vague allusions to Paul's being in prison and mention of the name Tychicus near the end, nothing in Ephesians connects it to any particular context; there are no mentions of any particular circumstances, recent events, or specific issues—the kinds of things that make evident Paul's history with the community and his reasons for writing a letter. This generic nature is another indicator that the letter was not written by Paul.

By contrast, 1 and 2 Timothy and Titus are most definitely speaking to a particular situation, and they contain many specifics.[14] The problem is that some of the details do not match up well with what we know of Paul from other letters. However, they *do* seem to match the context of Christian communities that existed fifty-plus years after Paul's time. For example, the writer of the Pastorals presupposes the existence of church offices, such as bishop, elder, and deacon, in which lay authority to rule over the community.[15] This tripartite structure of authority appears in the writings of proto-orthodox figures of the second century, such as Ignatius of Antioch.[16] In 1 Timothy and Titus, the author writes to a person who has been ordained (i.e., Timothy or Titus) and to whom the authority to appoint others to church offices has been given.[17] Paul wrote to communities at large when he wanted to instruct people on how to resolve their conflicts, not to specially designated persons. While writings that come from the second century also reflect the existence of ecclesiastical offices, Paul's letters indicate that he had no interest in establishing institutionalized authority of this sort. Instead, Paul stressed that people had different gifts and talents, and thus he recognized that people could be assigned different roles and responsibilities in the church. Paul did not, however, establish a hierarchy nor did he ordain people to preestablished offices; rather he allowed people to evolve organically into certain roles.[18] Although Colossians, Ephesians and 2 Thessalonians make references to things that seem contextually out of place, the Pastorals contain *many* such instances—in addition to their discussion of ecclesiastical offices—making Pauline authorship of these texts most unlikely.

In addition to content, rhetorical and stylistic features bear on the question of authenticity. Although the magnitude of this problem is harder to recognize in the English translation than in the original Greek, a reader who compares the beginning of Ephesians, to take one example, with the initial verses of any of the undisputed letters will quickly realize that the sentences in Ephesians are extraordinarily long-winded. So long, in fact, that the relationship of the versification to the punctuation is odd and awkward to the English reader. Here, for example is Ephesians 1:7–10 in the NRSV:

> *In him we have redemption through his blood, the forgiveness of our trespasses, according to the riches of his grace that he lavished on us. With all wisdom and insight he has made known to us the mystery of his will, according to his good pleasure that he set forth in Christ, as a plan for the fullness of time, to gather up all things in him, things in heaven and things on earth.*

Long sentences are a common feature of ancient Greek writing, but Paul does not typically write this way. Although one can develop new habits of language in different stages of life, one's most fundamental speech patterns are unlikely to change in such a drastic way. Perhaps the best way to illustrate this point is by analogy with art and music. An aficionado of Mozart will typically develop the ability to recognize the signature traits of Mozart's musical composition and can often identify a piece of music as having been composed by Mozart, even if she has not previously heard it. Similarly, an expert on Picasso is expected to have the skills necessary to authenticate a work ascribed to Picasso, even while it must be acknowledged that a good forgery can sometimes fool even the best expert. The same applies to biblical scholars who have spent much time studying Paul's letters in Greek; Pauline scholars come to learn the marks of Paul's signature style. Paul typically wrote in a brash, almost staccato style characterized by ellipses, rhetorical questions, sarcasm, and impromptu arguments issued in response to complaints and inquiries from his followers. The stylistic resemblance of the seven undisputed epistles has long been acknowledged by Pauline scholarship, while the style of each of the disputed letters diverges to a greater or lesser extent from the family of undisputed texts.

Paul was also remarkably consistent about certain kinds of expressions, especially when they articulate key theological ideas. For example, when Paul speaks of the resurrection of the faithful or their ultimate salvation, he always speaks of it as in-progress or yet to come. Thus, he typically uses the future tense, as in Romans 10:9: "If you profess with your mouth 'Jesus is Lord,' and believe with your heart that God raised him from the dead, *you will be saved*;" or Romans 8:11: "If the spirit of the one who raised Jesus from the dead dwells in you, the one who raised Christ from the dead *will bring your mortal bodies to life* by the same spirit that dwells in you." But compare Ephesians 2:4–6: "God, who is rich in mercy, out of the great love with which he loved us, even when we were dead through our trespasses, *made us alive* together with Christ—*by grace you have been saved*—and *raised us up with him and seated us with him* in the heavenly places in Christ Jesus" (NRSV; emphasis added). Although Paul could have changed his mind about some things, it seems unlikely that he would shift from understanding believers as awaiting salvation to understanding them as already seated in glory with Christ, especially when the return of Christ and all the apocalyptic expectations that are believed to accompany the second coming remain unfulfilled. Paul believes he is living at the beginning of the end of time, but he also consistently indicates that the end time is far from complete. The language of unfulfilled expectation is pervasive throughout the undisputed letters, making implausible a spontaneous change of expression without a clear indication that some profound change of circumstance occurred. It is much more probable that someone other than Paul wrote Ephesians and the other disputed letters and that these authors were situated in a somewhat later time and used Paul's name to speak to new situations. In the case of the example just discussed, the language of having already been saved connects better, once again, with the proto-orthodox writers of the late first and early second centuries.

Like Ephesians, Colossians, 2 Thessalonians, and the Pastoral Epistles, it was once widely assumed that the Epistle to the Hebrews was authored by the apostle. Disputed by both ancient and modern scholars, the authenticity of Hebrews is no longer in question.[19] Rather, there is now unrivaled consensus that Paul did *not* write Hebrews. Indeed, Hebrews itself did not originally claim to be written by Paul. Early Greek manuscripts of Hebrews have no name attached to it. In other words, Hebrews circulated anonymously, and it is likely we will never know who the author of this text was.[20]

It is important that the reader recognize that modern scholars are not the only ones who have doubted the authenticity of some texts bearing Paul's name. In addition to Hebrews, ancient Christian interpreters disputed the authenticity of at least two other documents, the so-called Letter of Paul to Seneca and 3 Corinthians. These texts were *so* disputed by church authorities that they were never canonized.

Eventually, it became common knowledge that they were phony and therefore came to be regarded as forgeries, so that no scholar today would even attempt to defend them as Pauline. Thus, it is virtually a historical certainty that people produced and promulgated texts using Paul's name pseudonymously. In my view, such knowledge should lead readers to the realization that some of the letters attributed to Paul inside the New Testament canon are in all likelihood of dubious origins. Even if some or all of the disputed letters were written by Paul's disciples or by those who were part of a circle of followers who believed themselves faithful to the apostle's teachings, the disputed letters most likely do not reflect the direct, unmediated words of Paul.

With the exception of Hebrews—which need no longer be associated with the name of Paul—I will refer to the letters whose Pauline authorship has been seriously questioned as "disputed letters," rather than "forgeries." I do this largely because determining authorship is an inexact art, and it is therefore difficult to resolve the question of authorship with absolute certainty. Even if everyone were agreed that Paul did not write Ephesians, Colossians, 2 Thessalonians, and the Pastoral Epistles, interpreters could still argue—as they often have—that a disciple of Paul's wrote the letters and that they capture the spirit of Paul's thought and can therefore be regarded as part of the corpus of Paul's letters bequeathed to posterity. But such a strategy leaves the issue of the authorship of these letters too open-ended and ultimately irresolvable. The evidence against these texts is sufficiently strong that I cannot with any reasonable degree of certainty consider them part of Paul's written corpus.

Although all sorts of sources will be used in this study to fill out the larger world within which Paul wrote his letters, only Romans, 1 and 2 Corinthians, Galatians, Philippians, 1 Thessalonians, and Philemon count as primary sources about Paul. Ancient Jewish literature and Greco-Roman literature, as well as writings regarded as Christian, provide comparative and contextual data, but they do not provide direct, unmediated access to the details of Paul's life and the intricacies of his thought. Thus, the bulk of this book is necessarily concerned with the interpretation of the seven undisputed letters of Paul.

Problems of Interpretation

Problems of interpretation can arise whenever people try to communicate with one another. One of the disadvantages of written communication is that the author, even if still living, is often not readily available to answer questions of clarification. In most cases, the reader does not know the author personally or the author is unknowable, as in the case of documents written anonymously or by a committee. An illustration drawn from the work of literary critic Terry Eagleton highlights the problem of interpreting written texts. A sign posted in tube stations throughout London reads: "Dogs must be carried on the escalator."[21] To Londoners, the sign obviously applies only to people who have dogs with them; such persons must carry their dogs while riding on the escalator. But, as Eagleton cleverly points out, this string of words can convey other meanings. One could take the sign to mean that anyone wanting to ride the escalator must carry a dog; if one does not have a dog, it is not permissible to ride the escalator. Such misreading rarely occurs because most people who encounter these signs possess a set of shared assumptions within a common cultural context. Philosophers of language sometimes call these assumptions "cultural codes." Cultural codes always aid in the conveyance of meaning, but they usually work invisibly. Most people become conscious of such codes only when they are absent, such as when traveling in a foreign country with which one has no familiarity. Even if one has some knowledge of the language, the ability to grasp humor, irony, sarcasm, or even the appropriate form of addressing another person in certain circumstances challenges all but the most seasoned students of a culture and its language.

Ambiguity

Paul's letters challenge modern readers more so than other kinds of biblical literature, precisely because they are letters. In addition to the issue of cultural codes (broadly speaking) Paul's letters assume a kind of insider knowledge. With the exception of Romans, Paul's letters are addressed to people and communities with whom he is intimately acquainted. Both author and audience possess common knowledge about many things, things that Paul therefore can refer to without extrapolation because the information between them is taken for granted and can be assumed. The letters represent pieces of a larger conversation between Paul and his followers or, in some cases, his opponents. Modern readers can never be privy to the entirety of this larger conversation. In other words, reading Paul's letters is like reading other people's mail, except we only have a fraction of the correspondence. Paul surely wrote more letters than the ones that have been preserved—he himself refers to one such missing letter in 1 Corinthians 5:9. Moreover, we have access only to one side of the conversation, since no letters written to Paul from his congregants survived the ravages of history, even though we know that some of Paul's letters were prompted by letters he received from his followers.[22]

Those who are familiar with Paul have likely experienced the confusion that often accompanies the reading of his letters. Reading Paul can be difficult going. Paul's speech becomes seemingly convoluted in places, straining a reader's ability to follow his logic. Galatians 3 contains some of the most notorious passages. Here are a few verses from the NRSV:

> *Why then the law? It was added because of transgressions, until the offspring would come to whom the promise had been made; and it was ordained through angels by a mediator. Now a mediator involves more than one party; but God is one.*
>
> *Is the law then opposed to the promises of God? Certainly not! For if a law had been given that could make alive, then righteousness would indeed come through the law. But scripture has imprisoned all things under the power of sin, so that what was promised through faith in Jesus Christ might be given to those who believe. (Gal 3:19–22)*

Several questions arise from Paul's remarks here. What does it mean that the law "was added because of transgressions"? Standard commentaries will usually acknowledge the interpretive challenge of this particular expression and of Paul's logic in this section of Galatians generally.[23] In spite of the ambiguity, the typical explanation provided by commentators is that law (that is, Mosaic law) was given so as to hold in check the otherwise uncontrollable sinfulness of humanity.[24] Some commentators have claimed that the law was given with the explicit purpose of making the problem of sin worse.[25] Another interpretive option is that the law was necessary to abate the sinfulness of the Jews (or Israel, to use the ancient biblical term) in particular, not humanity in general. The assumption underlying this interpretation is that God did, in fact, give the Torah specifically to the Jews, and not to everyone, so when Paul says the law "was added because of transgressions" he must mean the transgression of Israel. (Another assumption underlying this reading in traditional commentaries is an anti-Semitic bias, namely that the Jews as a race are more prone to despicable behavior than other peoples; other peoples are able to discipline themselves, but the evil perpetrated by Jews required divine intervention to hold it in check.) Whether one accepts the first, second, or third interpretations, none of them does much to explain the remainder of the verse. Who is the offspring to whom the promise was made? The majority of scholars take the "offspring" to refer to Jesus.[26] Okay, for the sake of argument, let's say the identity of the offspring *is* Jesus; who then is the mediator? Most scholars I have surveyed say the mediator is Moses (though a few say it is Jesus), but who are the angels, and why is Paul compelled to mention them? Already it should be obvious that reading Paul can be like deciphering encoded messages.

Even if one comes to the point where one feels reasonably confident assigning definitions or specific referents to these words and phrases, like offspring = Jesus and mediator = Moses, connecting the various components quickly turns the decoded message into a logical conundrum. Why, for example, would Paul say that God bestowed the Mosaic law so as to control sin in v. 19 and then say in v. 22 that "scripture"—which contains the Mosaic law—"imprisoned all things under the power of sin"? In other words, while v. 19 sounds as though law helps people to cope with sin, v. 22 implies that God's law traps people under sin's power. Indeed, the thrust of this passage is often seen to lie with v. 22, especially when read in conjunction with certain other Pauline texts like Romans 7, where law and sin seem so closely linked. But this interpretive emphasis leaves (or should leave) readers with a difficult theological problem: Why would God give divine guidance that exacerbates the problem of sin, rather than relieve it? And, even assuming Christ provides ultimate relief from sin, why would God act so as to make sin worse in the first place? Does it really make sense to say that God's gift of Christ was a solution to a problem God caused in the first place?[27]

Most obtuse is the reference to angels, a mediator, and the oneness of God in the middle of this discussion on law, sin, and the promises of God. Again, much interpretive struggle and debate plagues this verse as scholars try to sort out what in the world Paul is talking about. Dozens, if not hundreds of different interpretive solutions have been proposed. Ultimately, there is nothing in the text itself that makes Paul's invocation of this material transparent in meaning. Galatians 3:19–22 is an excellent example for illustrating that modern readers lack the cultural codes necessary to fully understand the apostle. We must assume, however, that Paul expected his audience to understand him (whether they actually did or not). Surely Paul was not *trying* to be obtuse. However, as modern readers, we no longer possess the same set of cultural codes that Paul's intended audience had, at least not on an intuitive level, but we can work to recover them.

Even those Pauline proclamations that seem most straightforward and memorable can, upon a moment's reflection, become ambiguous. Take, for example, Galatians 3:28. In the NRSV it reads "There is no longer Jew or Greek, there is no longer slave or free, there is no longer male and female, for all of you are one in Christ Jesus." When Paul wrote these words, did he mean to suggest that these distinctions between people should be eradicated—and thus Christians should work to break down such barriers wherever they persist in society? Many Christian readers of Paul today, including scholars and students, take these words as a call for uncompromising equality. Justifiably, they understand Galatians 3:28 as evidence that Paul believed in equality between men and women and believed in the elimination of the institution of slavery and all other status distinctions. On the other hand, doesn't Paul's proclamation in Galatians 3:28 indicate that he takes these status distinctions for granted? In other words, Paul's purpose in Galatians 3:28 may not be to call for the elimination of such distinctions, but rather to reassure those with inferior social status and fewer privileges in society that these distinctions are irrelevant before God and irrelevant so far as salvation is concerned, even if they are an inevitable reality in human society. Galatians 3:28 has been used throughout history with equal vehemence by both those who seek political and social liberation for disadvantaged people and by those who wish to maintain the status quo.

Contradictions

It is not only interpreters, however, who offer diametrically opposed readings of Pauline literature. The second problem in reading the apostle's letters is that Paul sometimes appears to contradict himself. He makes statements about Jewish law that seem to be unequivocal condemnations. At other times, he expresses unmitigated praise for it. This can be illustrated by comparing the texts within each of the following pairs:

A. *We ourselves are Jews by birth and not Gentile sinners, yet we know that a person is justified not by works of the law but through faith in Jesus Christ . . . because no one will be justified by the works of the law. (Gal 2:15–16)*
B. *It is not the hearers of the law who are righteous in God's sight, but the doers of the law who will be justified. (Rom 2:13)*

A. *All who rely on the works of the law are under a curse; for it is written, "Cursed is everyone who does not observe and obey all the things written in the book of the law." (Gal 3:10)*
B. *The law is holy, and the commandment is holy and just and good. (Rom 7:12)*

A. *Those who are physically uncircumcised but keep the law will condemn you that have the written code and circumcision but break the law. (Rom 2:27)*
B. *Then what advantage has the Jew? Or what is the value of circumcision? Much in every way. For in the first place, the Jews were entrusted with the oracles of God. (Rom 3:1–2)*

A. *If it is the adherents of the law who are to be heirs, faith is null and the promise is void. For the law brings wrath; but where there is no law, neither is there violation. (Rom 4:14–15)*
B. *Is the law then opposed to the promises of God? Certainly not! (Gal 3:21)*[28]

Each of the A verses consists of an apparently negative statement Paul makes about law or those who observe the law; each of the B verses, a positive statement. Although I have taken these verses out of context by the way I have juxtaposed them, I have organized a sample of Paul's statements on law this way to illustrate the cumulative confusion that can result from reading Paul's letters with the intention of ascertaining his view of law.[29] Besides, Paul sometimes makes such seemingly contradictory statements within a few verses of the same letter, as illustrated by Galatians 3:19–22, discussed above, and by the third pair of texts where the selected verses from Romans occur in very close proximity to each other.

The contradiction in the first set of verses is perhaps most stark. Paul seemingly says in one place that justification is not possible by being Torah-observant (those who live by "works of the law") and, yet, in another place says that those who observe Torah ("the doers of the law) are in fact the ones who will be justified. From the second pair of texts, one might well ask why one who "relies on works of the law" is cursed if "the law is holy"? In the third pair of texts, Paul first condemns Jews who have the "written code," presumably the Torah, because they do not observe its commandments while simultaneously commending Gentiles who do observe them. In the next verse, however, he implies that one has an advantage simply by being Jewish, because God has entrusted Torah to them. In the final pair of texts, how can Paul say in one place that those who live by Torah render God's promises void, yet claim in another place that God's promises and Torah exist in theological harmony?

Any serious attempt to grasp Paul's views on Torah must grapple with the apparent dissonance that emerges when one takes on the entirety of Paul's corpus of letters. Although most experienced readers of Paul's letters acknowledge the challenge posed by such divergent statements, more facile interpreters too often read Paul with simplistic Reformation filters, by which I mean that they take note only of Paul's negative remarks on Jewish law, virtually ignoring the positive ones. As a result, some readers of Paul's letters do not experience any cognitive dissonance in their encounters with Paul. This is why it is helpful to juxtapose several seemingly incongruous claims Paul makes about law. When teaching introductory courses on Paul, I sometimes poll students with regard to their view of Paul's view of Jewish law—does Paul's theology affirm or negate the law? Without fail, the majority of students say Paul negates or devalues Jewish law. When I offer students a third

option—namely, does Paul think Jewish law had some, perhaps temporary, positive value but has been superseded by Christ?—the vast majority will select that option. When I ask them to justify this response, they
usually offer some version of the following explanation: One is justified
(or saved) by faith, rather than law, therefore Paul obviously devalues
law. At that point I usually highlight a text where Paul says something
unambiguously positive about law. My favorite is Romans 2:13, "For
it is not the hearers of the law who are righteous in God's sight, but
the doers of the law who will be justified." *Not the hearers but the doers
of the law will be justified.* Students are typically dumbfounded by this
statement. Many read it several times over thinking they have misread
it. Occasionally they ask if there has been a mistake made in the translation. It doesn't take long before students agree that the question of law
in Pauline theology is, well, complicated. I will attend to the problem of
Paul's view of Jewish law in chapter 12, but the first step in solving the
problem is the recognition that a problem exists.

The problem of Paul's seemingly incongruous statements is not restricted to the topic of law (although the problem is most severe in the case
of law). Paul's views on women appear contradictory at certain points,
as illustrated by comparing two statements from 1 Corinthians.

A. *The husband should give to his wife her conjugal rights, and
likewise the wife to her husband. For the wife does not have authority over her own body, but the husband does; likewise the husband does not have authority over his own body, but the wife does.
(1 Cor 7:3–4)*
B. *For a man ought not to have his head veiled, since he is the image
and reflection of God; but the woman is the reflection of man.
(1 Cor 11:7)*[30]

In the first text cited, Paul displays an egalitarian attitude: the husband, just like the wife, must cede to the desires of the spouse. In
1 Corinthians 11, however, Paul seems to operate with a hierarchical
framework that places men above women. Indeed, looking at the juxtaposition of statements like these, it is no wonder that Paul can be
variously praised or condemned for his views on women depending on
which texts strike a reader's fancy. Many feminist Christian readers have
argued that Paul held very progressive views concerning the status of

men and women in relation to each other. Evangelical interpreters, on the other hand, often appeal to Pauline texts to support a hierarchical gender framework within the family and church. Interpreters with strongly felt convictions can portray Paul either as progressive or conservative by appealing to select texts and either ignoring or downplaying those texts that stand in tension with the view of Paul that matches their agenda.[31]

Again, my purpose in highlighting Paul's seemingly incongruous claims about women is not to resolve this particular issue now, but to create an awareness in the reader (both of this book and of Paul's letters) of the dissonance the modern reader experiences when reading Paul. Reading Paul is like listening to a complex jazz composition—to the untrained ear it sounds like each musician is playing a different song, but to an aficionado, it is a sublime achievement. Paul was not a simpleton. His discussions on Jewish law, women, and many other matters related to theology and ethics are complex, and, as a result, they require study and patience. The reader who wishes to develop an appreciation for Paul must account for the undeniable discordance within his epistolary corpus. Many of Paul's most significant, most memorable statements stand in tension with other statements. How is it that Paul claimed that one cannot be justified by works of the law and yet also said—right there in Romans, the document that contains Paul's most profound, most influential discourse on the doctrine of justification by faith—that it is the doers of the law who will be justified? Any interpretation that does not make sense of both kinds of claims does not do justice to Paul.

Some Pauline scholars have become so frustrated with Paul that they have concluded the apostle's letters are riddled with such stark theological inconsistencies that to try to reconcile them would amount to little more than theological nonsense. Other scholars, especially those invested in constructing Paul's theology, take offense at the suggestion that Paul left an incoherent theological legacy. Most Pauline scholars take a kind of middle position. They deal with the problem of Paul's inconsistencies by using some kind of theory of human development. That is to say, Paul's theology developed over time, or he modified his thinking when confronted with new circumstances. To be sure, it is likely that Paul gained wisdom from his experience and may have modified or refined his position of this or that issue. But, since it is impossible to track how and why development occurred, such an attitude toward Pauline interpretation leaves the question of Paul's theological dissonance unresolved.

In my view, the claim that Paul does not make theological sense is mainly due to the inconsistencies between the traditional image of Paul that so dominates readers' imaginations and what Paul actually says in his letters. The traditional image of Paul carries with it rather limited expectations about what meanings can be plausibly derived from the apostle's writings. If Paul converted from Judaism to Christianity, and if the former is a religion of works based on Torah, while the latter is a religion of grace based entirely on faith in Christ, then it is difficult to imagine Paul writing in praise of Torah or articulating the privileges Jews enjoy or associating grace with Judaism. But, what often appears impenetrably complicated in Paul's writings may turn out to be rather simple if one starts with a different interpretive framework.

Chapter

3

How Paul Became a Christian

Before I make the case for understanding Paul as a Jew, I first need to explain how Paul came to be a Christian. Although a relatively small group of scholars, including me, has come to the point where Paul's Jewish identity appears blindingly obvious, most people—whether scholars, clergy, or laity; Jews, Christians, or others—see Paul as a Christian, and not just *a* Christian, but *the* Christian. Most modern readers regard Paul as so obviously Christian that to label him Jewish strikes many as counterintuitive. Who could possibly be *more* Christian than Paul? Since I expect many readers to respond to my claims about Paul with incredulity, I thought it would be helpful to demonstrate how Paul's Christian identity has been constructed through a centuries-long process. The reason readers encounter Paul intuitively as Paul the Christian has less to do with what Paul said in his letters than with how the memory of Paul and Paul's letters came to function in Christian history and theology.

Ancient Views of Paul

In the previous chapter, I gave some attention to the earliest sources that lay claim to the memory of Paul, namely, Acts and letters pseudonymously written in Paul's name. Those who produced these texts were either disciples of the apostle or his followers of subsequent generations who were committed to his life and teachings, even if they did not personally know him as a teacher. It is important to remember that these texts became fundamental to the traditional image of Paul. Most of the interpreters who became influential church authorities on Paul assume that Paul's corpus of letters includes the Pastoral Epistles and what scholars now call the deuteropauline epistles. That means, for example, that interpreters have traditionally assumed Paul promulgated the domestic ethics found in the household codes of Colossians and Ephesians. Even today, overwhelmingly, when evangelical Christian leaders preach about the roles of husbands and wives in the Christian household, and especially when they emphasize the subordination of the latter, they claim the authority for this view comes from Paul's teachings. But that claim depends almost exclusively on letters whose authority is now disputed by the majority of biblical scholars.

Interpreters have also assumed that the portrait of Paul in Acts dovetails with the material in his letters. The stories about Paul in Acts could be made to relate to information in Paul's letters in a variety of ways. Generally, however, it has been assumed that Acts complements, corroborates, and supplements whatever Paul said in his letters. Thus, the famous Council of Jerusalem of Acts 15 "matches" the meeting Paul describes in Galatians 2, such that it fills in—or fills out—the details of the same event.

Ancient interpreters knit together various traditions from various sources in order to form a coherent image of Paul.[1] In addition to the pseudonymous Pauline letters and Acts, other stories about Paul circulated and were preserved in written sources. Some of these sources were regarded as authoritative, and thus the stories contained in these sources were incorporated by the early church fathers into their discussions of Paul. For example, the First Letter of Clement, dated c. 100 CE, recounts the end of Paul's life as follows:

> Because of jealousy and strife Paul pointed the way to the prize for endurance. Seven times he bore chains; he was sent into exile and stoned; he served as a herald in both the East and the West; and he received the noble reputation for his faith. He taught righteousness to the whole world, and came to the limits of the West, bearing his witness before the rulers. And so he was set free from this world and transported up to the holy place, having become the greatest example of endurance.[2]

Although it is difficult to know with certainty the Pauline texts on which Clement might have based his claims, this summary description of the apostle's life evokes the memory of Paul mainly as an exemplary figure and less as one of the great doctors of the church. Clement's comments suggest that he knew extracanonical traditions about Paul's travels. Of course, Clement also surely knew Paul's Letter to the Romans, in which Paul reports his plan to go to Spain via Rome, though he says he is first going to Jerusalem (Rom 15:22–29). In any case, Clement's letter seems to be the oldest surviving account of Paul's death. Notably, 1 Clement is preserved in some important early manuscripts as part of the New Testament and was regarded as Scripture by some early Christian writers.[3]

Various extracanonical traditions about Paul's life (and death) began circulating widely in the second century. These traditions find their fullest recounting and are best preserved in two Christian apocryphal sources, the Acts of Paul, and the Acts of Paul and Thecla.[4] The former narrates Paul's martyrdom at the hands of Nero. Although these texts were recognized as forgeries in antiquity and thus considered dubious, some church fathers incorporate data about Paul's life from these apocryphal stories into their sermons and treatises. Thus, Paul's martyrdom becomes authoritative tradition, even though the story is not found in the canonical Acts. But detailing the various and sundry apocryphal traditions about Paul is not my goal here. Rather, I wish to make two points central to the construction of Paul in antiquity.

First, the portrait of Paul in Christianity, who he was and what he did, believed, and preached, developed over time through the accumulation of recounted memories and the subsequent writings of some very influential Christians of the first four centuries, who, in some cases, devoted countless hours to studying Paul's letters, so as to write commentaries and treatises on them and to preach on them to their communities. This cumulative tradition formed an image of Paul's person and thereby provided the interpretive framework within which Paul was read and understood. Put another way, a mental portrait of Paul was constructed by the devoted students of Paul's letters.

Second, Paul became critical to the most important debates in early Christianity. The New Testament canon itself indicates how central Paul was in the development of early Christianity. There are four canonical gospels, but thirteen letters bear Paul's name, in addition to another that tradition ascribed to Paul (i.e., Hebrews). That makes Paul the purported author of more than half the twenty-seven documents of the New Testament. In addition, most of Acts is given over to his story. It is not an accident that Paul came to dominate the New Testament canon. Rather, it seems to be due to the perception that Paul was critical to interpreting the gospel message. Jesus may be the core of the Christian message, but Paul became the key to unlocking that message. Indeed, the memory of Paul the man as well as the interpretation of his writings became the ground on which Christians fought some of their fiercest battles over doctrine and authority.

Paul's Exemplary Life

Although Paul was called an apostle, his story was quite different from the stories of other apostles. Unlike Peter, James, John, or the other apostles, Paul was not a disciple of the earthly Jesus, and therefore no mention is made of him in the gospels. The portraits of the twelve apostles, which, like Paul's, were constructed out of canonical and extracanonical traditions, portray them as followers of the earthly Jesus. Though admittedly faltering at times, they were loyal to Jesus from the beginning, even if they did not know the ultimate significance of his ministry until after their experience of his resurrection. In other words, the images of the Twelve were those of men who gradually evolved from disciples to teachers and miracle workers; they were men physically and spiritually close to Jesus. Their lives served as models of the virtuous life for Christians in the preaching and teaching of church tradition of subsequent generations. But none of the apostles within Jesus' circle proved to be as influential as Paul.

There were no doubt a variety of reasons that Paul's life became the paradigm for the Christian life generally. Perhaps because Paul came to know Christ only after Christ's death and resurrection, the apostle's life seemed to many Christians to resemble their own lives. Paul's experience of the risen Jesus could serve as a model for later Christians, who felt spatially and temporally removed from the human Jesus and the world he inhabited. Furthermore, Paul gave posterity a powerful legacy in the form of his letters. There is evidence that the letters were preserved partly because they provided his followers with a tangible way to remember their teacher. As one scholar has put it, Paul's letters functioned as "monuments" as much as "documents."[5] That is to say, the letters were physical objects that provided testimony to the memory of the apostle, memorials of the apostle's saintly life, a kind of textual relic, and this conceptualization may have played an important role in the canonization of Paul's letters.

There exists substantial evidence of widespread interest in both the letters and the person of Paul among a variety of Christians by the middle of the second century.[6] Although Paul's letters were not always foremost on the minds of early Christians, Paul's exemplary image was.[7] But as scholarship over the last half century has made clear, there were different "exemplary" images of Paul in circulation during the second and third centuries. Indeed, the battle over the apostle's legacy appears to have been a fierce one at times.

Although Paul's letters—originally written to individual communities to address their particular needs—appear to have been collected into one volume relatively early (perhaps as early as the turn of the second century), these early collections were not standardized.[8] In other words, early codices of the Pauline letters vary as to their contents, both in terms of which letters were included and the ordering of the letters. More important for our discussion at the moment, these early examples of the Pauline letter collection were not originally bound with Acts or, for that matter, any other writings that are now included in the New Testament. Indeed, there was no canonical New Testament yet in existence in the second and third centuries. To be sure, the gospels of Matthew, Mark, Luke, and John were widely known and in circulation, and so, too, were many other writings that eventually formed the New Testament. But these texts together had not yet coalesced to form a canonical whole—that is a fourth-century development. Moreover, many other Christian writings were in circulation as well. Thus, the literary and social context within which Paul's letters were read was neither monolithic nor homogeneous.

Until the New Testament was stabilized, admirers of Paul exercised choice in their selection of texts considered "Pauline," and thus the fabric that made up the intertextual web of materials laying claim to Paul's legacy was extremely varied. In other words, reading one set of Pauline letters—say, Romans, Galatians, and the Corinthian correspondence— creates a different impression of the apostle than if those letters are combined with the Pastoral Epistles in a single letter collection. While

1 Corinthians affirms the practice of celibacy for men and women and
lauds it as spiritually superior to marital life, the Pastorals deny the legitimacy of the celibate life, especially for women.[9]

In fact, the Pastoral Epistles may well have been written to counter
a rival image of Paul, one the author of those letters considered threatening and unfaithful to the "real" Paul. It appears that some members of the Pauline circle were women who abandoned conventional
forms of family life and embraced the ascetical life. The Acts of Paul
and Thecla recounts the story of a young Thecla, who, on the eve of
her marriage, abandons her betrothed so as to follow Paul, to whom
she displays undying devotion. Having heard Paul preaching from her
window (Paul is visiting a friend, Onesiphorus, who happens to live in
the house next door, where Paul pontificates regularly over dinner),
she is inspired to imitate the apostle by living the life of an itinerant
ascetic preacher. Although Thecla is the protagonist of this story, Paul
plays a key role, since it is his preaching of sexual renunciation that sets
the story in motion: "You must fear the one and only God and live a
chaste life."[10] Thus, Paul's mission and message differs significantly
from the canonical Acts; in the Acts of Paul and Thecla, Paul preaches
chastity as salvation. Thecla is portrayed as undaunted in her devotion
to Paul and possessed of unflagging commitment to live the chaste life
in the face of constant life-threatening persecution. She is indubitably
the heroine, eclipsing Paul in terms of faithfulness and bravery. But the
source of conflict in the story is not between Paul and Thecla. Rather,
the narrative tension derives from the visceral social and civic resistance to permitting women to choose a life of chastity and the authority that the chaste life bestows upon women. The climax of the story is
Thecla's baptism of herself in an act of desperation in the public arena
as she faces impending doom in a confrontation with hungry lions.
Divine intervention once again saves her life, whereupon she meets up
with Paul one final time, at which point he commends her to "go and
teach the word of God."[11]

The second-century church father Tertullian knew of the Acts of
Paul and Thecla and condemned it, for two reasons: he knew the author
to be a forger, and, like other proto-orthodox church fathers, Tertullian
opposed women having authority to teach (men) or to baptize. In his
treatise *On Baptism*, Tertullian makes himself perfectly clear:

But the woman of pertness, who has usurped the power to teach, will of course not give birth for herself likewise to a right of baptizing, unless some new beast shall arise like the former; so that, just as the one abolished baptism, so some other should in her own right confer it! But if the writings which wrongly go under Paul's name, claim Thecla's example as a licence for women's teaching and baptizing, let them know that, in Asia, the presbyter who composed that writing, as if he were augmenting Paul's fame from his own store, after being convicted, and confessing that he had done it from love of Paul, was removed from his office. For how credible would it seem, that he who has not permitted a woman even to learn with over-boldness, should give a female the power of teaching and of baptizing! "Let them be silent," he says, "and at home consult their own husbands."[12]

In this passage, Tertullian is able to impugn the authenticity of the Acts of Paul and Thecla while also voicing his opposition to women teaching and baptizing. Tertullian cites 1 Corinthians 14:32–33 ("let them be silent . . . and at home consult their own husbands") to support his argument that the Acts of Paul and Thecla is pseudonymous. Tertullian thus appeals to another text, one he considers to be genuinely Pauline, to demonstrate that the "real" Paul would never have condoned women having authority over men. Implicit in Tertullian's argument is a supreme confidence in his ability to judge what is authentically Pauline and what is not. Tertullian is certain that Paul would never have supported women in roles of ecclesiastical authority.

Although no scholars today would argue for the authenticity of the Acts of Paul and Thecla, the author who composed that text must have had a different mental image of Paul than Tertullian's. As Tertullian himself reports, when the presbyter who forged the text was caught, he said he did it "for the love of Paul." Presumably, he constructed his portrayal of Paul so as to be credible to other admirers of Paul. That means that other Christians believed that Paul would indeed have supported and even cultivated women as teachers and leaders among church communities. In short, there is clear evidence that different Christians had different, competing images of Paul and that one of the major points of contention in these competing images was Paul's attitude toward women.

To return to the Pastoral Epistles, there is compelling evidence that these letters were written in Paul's name to counteract the image of Paul being promulgated by the stories like those found in the Acts of Paul and Thecla.[13] They sought to provide the definitive description of Paul's life. The legacy that Paul left to posterity through his letters could never have functioned as a comprehensive manual capable of offering guidance on all matters relating to following Jesus. Paul's letters were generated by very particular sets of circumstances and written for very particular audiences. In most cases, he knew his audience personally and could draw on a cache of assumed common knowledge. But the letters came to have a life of their own, because people valued them, copied them, and shared them among other communities. As the audience for Paul's letters grew far beyond the immediate audience for whom Paul originally wrote, the letters' advice and teaching became less transparent. Regarding some subjects, it was as if Paul contradicted himself, or was at least ambiguous. An interpretive framework was needed—a lens that could guide readers' expectations of Paul.[14] Not surprisingly, that framework was Paul's life, as described in later texts. Even though there were differing images of Paul in the early church, eventually one biographical portrait of Paul came to dominate the collective consciousness of Christianity: Paul the convert. The seeds of this image can be found in the New Testament, though not so much in Paul's own writings as in Acts and the Pastoral Epistles.

According to the canonical order of the documents that make up the New Testament, Paul first appears in Acts 7:58 at the martyrdom of Stephen. Stephen has just finished a lengthy speech in which he mostly recounts the history of Israel but ends with a series of accusations against his Jerusalem audience: "Which of the prophets did your ancestors not persecute? They killed those who foretold the coming of the Righteous One, and now you have become his betrayers and murderers. You are the ones that received the law as ordained by angels, and yet you have not kept it" (Acts 7:52–53). Unsurprisingly, the audience becomes enraged at these words. At that moment Stephen has a vision of the heavenly Jesus, but the crowd rushes toward him, drags him out of the city, and stones him, at which point the text reads "And the witnesses laid their coats at the feet of a young man named Saul. . . . And Saul approved of their killing him" (7:58b, 8:1). So, Saul does not directly participate in the stoning, but he watches it with approval.

(That people leave their coats "at the feet" of Saul indicates that Saul held some kind of leadership position.) Leaving others to bury Stephen, Saul begins his infamous persecution of the church at this point in the narrative, "ravaging the church by entering house after house; dragging off both men and women" (8:3). The remainder of Acts 8 says nothing about Saul; instead the narrator turns attention back to Philip and the Jerusalem apostles, Peter and John, and their successful missionary efforts. Saul reappears in 9:1, where he is described as "breathing threats and murder against the disciples of the Lord."

After this reintroduction, the famous story of Saul's conversion is told. Within the course of ch. 9, all the following happens: Saul's dramatic encounter with Jesus, involving a flash of light, Jesus' voice, and Saul's being left blind for three days; Saul enters the city of Damascus, where he meets up with a disciple named Ananias, who has been instructed by Jesus to meet Paul; Ananias heals Saul of his blindness; Saul is immediately baptized; promptly following his baptism, he begins proclaiming Jesus as the Messiah in the synagogues of Damascus, which causes the local Jews to plot to kill him; luckily he escapes with the aid of "his disciples" who lower him in a basket through the city wall; he goes to Jerusalem to join the disciples; initially they fear him—they think he is faking his commitment because he had previously been such a zealous persecutor; eventually Barnabas convinces the apostles of Saul's sincerity, and thus he joins them in their preaching in Jerusalem; finally they send him off to Tarsus. Interestingly, the one thing that does not happen in ch. 9 that one would expect is the name change from "Saul" to "Paul"—that happens suddenly and without explanation in 13:9.

Unlike all the other apostles, Paul's story does not begin with his becoming a disciple of Jesus. Rather, Paul became an apostle only after Jesus' death, by virtue of an encounter with the risen Jesus. Therefore Paul does not enter the story of Christian origins before he becomes a follower of Jesus, as is the case with Peter and the other apostles, whose lives before Jesus are apparently irrelevant to subsequent Christian self-understanding. Both by Acts and his own account, Paul had been an enemy of Jesus' followers, and in his letters Paul himself acknowledges that he had been a persecutor of the church. Thus, Paul's turn toward Jesus was an about-face; in becoming a devotee of Jesus, he became the opposite of what he had previously been. This sinner-to-saint transformation became the paradigm of Christian conversion. Thus, the core of Paul's image in the traditional portrait of Paul is Paul's sudden and miraculous conversion. It is the key to understanding why Paul became the exemplar of the Christian life.

That Paul's conversion is central to the Lucan portrait of Acts is evident in that the story is told no less than three times in Acts. In addition to its being told in ch. 9, the story is put into the mouth of Paul himself during the course of two speeches in which Paul has to defend himself before accusing Jews (Acts 22:3–16; 26:9–18). In both of these speeches, consistent with the longer narrative version in ch. 9, Paul sets his encounter with the risen Jesus in the context of his having been an avid persecutor of the church. Also consistent with ch. 9, Paul's telling the tale of his conversion includes mention of the Jews turning against him; the persecutor, immediately upon conversion, becomes the persecuted. Indeed, from the time of his conversion to the "Way," there is virtually no time in which Paul is free from persecution by Jews, even as a few "good" Jews come to Paul's aid at points.

From a literary perspective, there is little doubt that Luke modeled many aspects of the portrait of Paul in Acts on the story of Jesus in the gospels. Paul's story in Acts revolves around Jerusalem much more so than it would seem from his letters, and it is the temple that becomes the site of the escalating conflict between Paul and the authorities. Paul is a traveling teacher-preacher who tries to persuade his own people (i.e., Jews—in spite of his identity as Apostle to the Gentiles) of the validity of his message. Among Jews, he inspires a few followers, but mostly he inflames adversaries, so that they want to destroy him. Perhaps most important, Jewish crowds and Jewish authorities are far more aggressive and far more threatening than Roman crowds and Roman authorities, just as is the case with Jesus as portrayed in Luke's gospel.

Thus already in the New Testament we see the beginning of literary and theological stereotyping of Jews as steadfastly opposed to any and all who believe in Jesus—and this stereotyping appears not just in the telling of the gospel story but in the story of Christian origins as recounted in Acts. Such stereotyping of Jews and Judaism in early Christian literature will eventually contribute to an essential component of Christian self-understanding that develops, namely, that Christianity represents what Judaism aspired to but could never attain. This sense of Christianity-as-Judaism-perfected turns into an understanding of Christianity as everything Judaism is not. The two religions are in

antithetical opposition. Therefore, the person who converts from Judaism to Christianity represents the worst kind of sinner turned into the
most glorious kind of saint.

Who better to represent the model Christian convert than Paul? But
Paul could not have served so well as a model if it had not been for Acts,
the Pastoral Epistles, and the development of a distinctively Western
Christian lens that made the experience of conversion central to Christian identity. If Christian tradition were solely dependent on the undisputed Pauline letters, it is difficult to imagine how the image of Paul the
convert could have been constructed in the first place. Paul does not use
the language of conversion of himself in his undisputed writings. He
never even uses the language of repentance in reference to himself. Paul
only uses such language to coax his Gentile followers to repentance.
To be sure, Paul refers to his having persecuted the church prior to his
encounter with the risen Jesus.[15] But this appears to be the only prior
behavior of which Paul feels shame. In all of his autobiographical reflections, Paul portrays himself as sinless. As he says of himself in Philippians 3:6: "As to righteousness that rests with Torah, I was blameless." In
2 Corinthians 11:22–23, when he feels driven by apostolic competition
in Corinth to compare himself to other teachers, he writes, "Are they
Hebrews? So am I! Are they Israelites? So am I! Are they descendants
of Abraham? So am I! Are they servants of Christ? Though I speak as
if I am mad, I am better [than they are]." He goes on to speak of the
many things he has endured, portraying himself as consistently, flaw-
lessly faithful, his virtue soundly in tact.

By contrast, 1 Timothy places the following words on Paul's lips:

> I am grateful to Christ Jesus our Lord, who has strengthened me,
> because he judged me faithful and appointed me to his service, even
> though I was formerly a blasphemer, a persecutor, and a man of vio-
> lence. But I received mercy because I had acted ignorantly in unbe-
> lief, and the grace of our Lord overflowed for me with the faith and
> love that are in Christ Jesus. The saying is sure and worthy of full
> acceptance, that Christ Jesus came into the world to save sinners—of
> whom I am the foremost. But for that very reason I received mercy,
> so that in me, as the foremost, Jesus Christ might display the utmost
> patience, making me an example to those who would come to believe
> in him for eternal life. (1:12–16, NRSV)

Casting himself as "foremost" among sinners, the Paul of the Pastoral Epistles styles himself as a convert, a man saved from his sin by the merciful intervention of Jesus Christ.[16] In distinction to Paul's own self-description in Galatians 2:15 as one of those who are "Jews by nature and *not* Gentile sinners," but congruent with the portrait in Acts, Paul's having been a persecutor of Jesus-followers is taken as representative of his entire former life, so that Paul is now deemed "foremost" among sinners. In sum, the portrait of Paul as the quintessential convert is established early on, but the image is not rooted in Paul's letters but in other sources.

Augustine

With the stabilization of the New Testament canon in the fourth century—ensuring that Acts and the Pastoral Epistles would be read synoptically with the other Pauline letters—the stage was set for Augustine, who may be credited more than anyone else with solidifying the image of Paul the convert in Christian tradition. Augustine himself is remembered as the convert par excellence—and for good reason. Augustine parlayed the experience of his own struggle to come to Christianity into a theological manifesto on Christian conversion in his spiritual autobiography, *Confessions.* With the help especially of Paul and the Psalms—often read synoptically as representing a single voice imploring God for deliverance—*Confessions* explores with remarkable candor the struggles of Augustine's inner self, especially the conflict that raged within him between pursuing the lofty life of the spirit and the meaner enticements of the flesh. In so doing, Augustine bequeathed to future generations the introspective conscience of the West that was to be the measure of religious, moral, and psychological authenticity. Most important to the discussion here, Augustine's influential interior dialogues concretized a particular reading of Paul's letters in which Paul's conversion is understood to be the key to his theology.

In Book 8 of *Confessions,* Augustine tells us that his momentous transformation occurred when he obeyed the voice that mysteriously told him to "pick up and read" and he subsequently opens at random to Romans 13: ". . . not in reveling and drunkenness, not in debauchery and licentiousness, not in quarreling and jealousy. But put on the Lord

Jesus Christ, and make no provision for the flesh, to gratify its desires" (vv. 13–14).[17] But truth be told, it is not Romans 13 that pervades the narrative about his conversion so much as it is Romans 7:

> For I do not do the good I want, but the evil I do not want is what I do. Now if I do what I do not want, it is no longer I that do it, but sin that dwells within me. So I find it to be a law that when I want to do what is good, evil lies close at hand. For I delight in the law of God in my inmost self, but I see in my members another law at war with the law of my mind, making me captive to the law of sin that dwells in my members. Wretched man that I am! Who will rescue me from this body of death? Thanks be to God through Jesus Christ our Lord! (vv. 19–25, NRSV)

These words are taken almost intuitively by modern readers as reflective of Paul's own inner struggles, which are taken to represent the struggles of all human beings. But were it not for Augustine, such ostensible intuitions would be rather dubious. Serious students of Paul's letters, both in antiquity and today, have often recognized and argued for other interpretive options. Origen, likely the greatest Christian biblical scholar of antiquity—who wrote his *Commentary on Romans* a century before Augustine—understood Romans 7 to be a form of speech-in-character, in which Paul takes on the voice of a person at different stages of moral development, seemingly assigning one stage to vv. 14–15 and another to 17–25.[18] Origen thought it impossible that Paul could be speaking autobiographically in Romans 7 because of v. 9: "I was once alive apart from the law." Because Paul was born and raised a Jew, there could never have been a time when Paul would describe himself as "apart from the law," in which he was no doubt reared. Therefore, Origen concludes, Paul must be speaking on behalf of others for pedagogical purposes.

Augustine, however, interpreted this text as reflective of Paul's personal struggles. He came to see his own experience and Paul's as basically the same, and he argued that Paul's experience of "doing the evil he does not wish to do" was illustrative of the nature of the human condition in the wake of Adam's fall. In spite of the apostle's extraordinary efforts to do good, he found that he could not do good. This is the human being living in the flesh, and the key sign of being mired in the flesh is sexual desire. Augustine reads Romans 7 as reflective of the conflict that he experienced between the "flesh" and the "spirit"; this is the view that informs *Confessions*.[19]

Augustine thought law is good in so far as it educates a person so that he can perceive sin and desire liberation from it. Through law comes a knowledge of sin and a knowledge of oneself as a sinner. This knowledge, however, does not enable one to be released from sin; rather, the awareness of sin brought about by law enables human beings simply to recognize their lowly lot and their sinful nature. According to Augustine, a person who, by his own accord, attempts to resist sin by conforming his will to God's law, will fail—that is not the purpose of God's law. The function of God's law is to teach human beings humility, not how to stop sinning. Therefore, says Augustine, rather than depend on one's obedience to law to correct one's sin, one must turn to God for help, and once one turns to God, one is *sub gratia*, "under grace."

> Therefore let the man lying low, when he realizes that he cannot rise by himself, implore the aid of the Liberator. For then comes grace, which pardons earlier sins and aids the struggling one, adds charity to justice, and takes away fear. When this happens, even though certain fleshly desires fight against our spirit while we are in this life, to lead us into sin, nonetheless our spirit resists them because it is fixed in the grace and love of God, and ceases to sin.[20]

The point is that Augustine's study of Paul and the interpretations he deduced from that study became thoroughly enmeshed with his understanding of his own religious transformation. Augustine saw his own conversion to Christianity mirrored in Paul's (alleged) conversion, and Paul's letters thereby became a window into the apostle's experience of transformation as well as a guide for those who aspire to be truly converted to Christianity.[21] Augustine was a religious seeker, one who was intensely self-aware about his spiritual quest. He recounts in *Confessions* the story of this quest, including the various stages he went through prior to his conversion to Christianity. Although baptized as an infant, Augustine strayed far from the orthodox Christianity of his mother (his father was not a Christian). At the age of eighteen he became a Manichean and was an adherent of Manichaeism for about a decade.

He subsequently became enthralled by the teachings of Neoplatonism. Thus, Augustine not only knew of other religious options, he explored some of those options for himself. With utmost seriousness and sincerity, he tried to conform his life to the teachings he found so compelling. Augustine wished to master his fleshly desires, and he explored various options in order to be cured. He was particularly concerned to overcome his struggle with concupiscence. By the time Augustine embraced Christianity, he could legitimately claim the status of a convert; he had self-consciously chosen Christianity, and this choice necessitated the explicit rejection of other religious options.

From Augustine's perspective, Paul was a kindred spirit. While the image of Paul the convert was already well formed by Augustine's time, Augustine elevated the significance of the apostle's conversion to an unprecedented degree, in large part because of the personal connection he felt with Paul. Just as Augustine was plagued by theological questions that Manicheanism could not adequately answer, so Paul was bothered by theological problems to which Judaism provided no satisfactory answers. Just as Augustine heard God calling to him through Paul's words in Romans 13, so Paul had heard God calling him through the words of Jesus (in Acts 9:20). Finally, the most obvious perceived commonality shared by Augustine and Paul is that both men found relief from their internal spiritual struggles through conversion to Christ. And while Augustine does not claim to have encountered a vision of the living Jesus at the time of his conversion, he believed his conversion was the result of divine intervention. From Augustine's perspective, both his and the apostle's conversions were the result of divine grace. Beyond the commonly perceived fact that Paul had "converted" from Judaism to Christianity, Augustine believed that Paul's words betrayed intimate knowledge of Paul's personal spiritual yearnings.

The fusion Augustine created between himself and Paul became the standard by which future religious experience in Western Christianity would be measured. Moreover, the kind of spiritual experience present in Augustine's *Confessions,* which was assumed to be the same kind of experience reflected in Paul's letters, became critical to Christian identity in general. The experience of conversion became foundational for Christian self-understanding. In the Western Christian imagination, conversion became a critical component of Christian religious experience, even though in the vast majority of cases, Christians were

Christians from birth and had thus not formally undergone a religious conversion at all. Conversion, in the Western Christian tradition, came to signify authentic religion, the immediate purpose of which is to control one's desire to sin. This does not happen by the individual's will, of course, but by pledging oneself to Jesus, who takes away one's sins.

Paul's Judaism was understood by Augustine, and therefore by Western Christianity after him, as an inferior religious option that Paul subsequently rejected when he became a Christian. Much of what Paul says in his letters was thereby construed as a critique of Judaism per se, because Paul's religious transformation was perceived to have involved the discovery of what was essentially wrong with Judaism. Embracing Jesus meant embracing Christianity, and embracing Christianity necessitated the concomitant rejection of Judaism, where Judaism is the stand-in for the wrong form of religious expression in general.

Augustine develops something known as the "doctrine of witness," which helped ensure a view of Judaism as a paradigm of the wrong kind of religion, though his was a more benevolent view of the Jews' wrongness than views of those who would come later. Augustine argued that Jews should be allowed to continue living as Jews within the realm of Christendom, though in an abject state; their continued existence served primarily two purposes: as witness and foil. First, because the Jewish Bible was essentially the same as the Christian Old Testament, and because Jews did not believe that Jesus was the Messiah foretold in Scripture, the Jews' preservation of Scripture was proof that Christians had not fabricated the prophecies of Jesus after the fact. Precisely because Jews were blind to the seemingly obvious prophecies of Jesus in their Scripture, they constituted an outside witness to the truth of Christianity.

Second, the Jews' disbelief in Christ, together with their determination to observe the "law" in a literal sense, meant that they stood outside the community of salvation. Their disbelief of Jesus meant, quite literally, that they had no faith at all. Instead, they busied themselves with performing "works of law," unaware that this gained them nothing. Since, for Augustine, salvation comes exclusively through faith—"saved by faith not by works"—the Jews were damned, and they didn't even know it, utterly blind to the love and grace of God.[22] Thus Jews and Judaism itself served as a foil to Christianity and a warning to Christians of the fate of those who lay outside the church.

Augustine rooted the doctrine of witness in Psalm 59:12: "Slay them not, lest at any time they forget your law; scatter them in your might."[23] In many ways, Augustine took these words literally. "Slay them not" meant that Christians should not kill Jews, although they were to remain in a state of degradation and humiliation as both a warning to Christians and a representation of their rejection by God. This argument effectively became policy for Christian leaders for centuries. But Augustine also took the later part of the psalm verse literally. Not only were Jews to be protected, but their observance of Jewish law was to be protected. Even though the observance of the law was of no benefit to them and their literal interpretation kept them blind to Scripture's true meaning, Torah observance enabled Scripture to be embodied as a living witness; the Jews served as "living letters of the law," speaking theological truth to the Christian faithful and the promise of salvation while also showing them the consequences that await the faithless.[24]

Augustine's connection of his conversion experience with Paul's and his reading of Judaism through that Pauline lens provide the foundations for subsequent interpretation of Paul. Because Augustine stands as the single most influential theologian in Christian history, his interpretation of Paul has reigned ever since.

Luther

In the thirteenth century, a Jew named Saul of Montpellier converted to Christianity. He took the name *Pablo Cristiani*, Paul Christian. He became a friar who, through public disputations with prominent Jewish leaders, was an active preacher to Jewish audiences in the hopes that they would convert. In contrast to Augustine's belief that evangelistic efforts should not be directed to Jews because Jews had to remain Jews in order to function as witness to the truth of Christianity, mendicant friars in the medieval period actively sought to convert Jews.

Although Luther's attitude toward the Jews famously shifted from benign in his youth to stridently hostile late in his life, he always prayed for the conversion of the Jews. He equated papists with Jews and saw both as the agents of the devil. Certainly Judaism had long been constructed in opposition to Christianity. Centuries of Christian preaching against the Jews, together with the now long-standing charges against

Jews that they understood themselves as actively persecuting Christians, just as they had persecuted Christ, had by this point ingrained a virulent form of anti-Semitism in Europe in the Christian population of which there was no precedent in antiquity. When the Protestant Reformation emerged in the sixteenth century, the charges that Jews killed Christian children, drank their blood, and baked it in matzah at Passover had been around for four hundred years.[25] Thus, it is no surprise that Luther saw Jews as the enemies of Christianity and preached that Jews were condemned to the flames of hell unless they converted to Christianity. For him, Paul was the ideal model of conversion, having turned from being a zealous Pharisee who persecuted the church to being its greatest evangelist.

Paul's life and writings had long been critical to Christian doctrine by the time Martin Luther came along. But more than anyone else, it was Luther who definitively established the framework for reading Paul that became so integral to Protestant identity. It was Luther who turned the concept of justification by faith into the gospel.

Like Augustine, Luther had a transformative experience that was sparked by his reading of the apostle, even though there are some differences. Luther's experience was not a conversion from one religious tradition to another. Rather it was a life-changing realization, and hence it is often referred to as a "discovery." Nevertheless, it was no less a significant event. The specific text that inspired Luther's discovery was not Romans 13, as it had been for Augustine; it was Romans 1:17: "For the righteousness of God is revealed in it from faith for faith, as it is written, 'The righteous one shall live out of faith.'" It would be only a slight exaggeration to say that from Luther's studious reflections on this one verse came the whole theology of the Reformation.

By his own account, Luther was tormented by the expression "the righteousness of God," because he believed it meant God's justice, which meant punishment for all sinners, and he was a sinner. Luther, "impeccable monk" that he was, "stood before God as a sinner with an extremely troubled conscience," believing that his good efforts to conduct himself in a manner pleasing to God would never be good enough.[26] He hated Paul for saying this, and he hated the idea that this wrathful God was coming to punish sinners. He feared that he would stand condemned to eternal damnation at the Last Judgment, which, like Paul, he believed was imminent.[27]

Luther reports that he meditated on Romans 1:17 night and day until it became clear to him the "righteousness of God" did not refer to God's own righteousness, that is, not as an attribute of God, but rather to righteousness that is imputed to the believer through faith. The Christian was the passive recipient of this righteousness; Christians did not become righteous as a result of their own good works. The key to unlocking "the righteousness of God" came from the verse from Habakkuk that Paul quotes: "The righteous one shall live out of faith."

> The expression "righteousness of God," said D. Martinus, used to hit my heart as a thunderbolt. For when under the papacy I read: "Deliver me in thy righteousness" [Psalm 31.1], . . . I immediately thought righteousness was the grim wrath of God, with which he punished sin. I hated St. Paul with all my heart when I read "the righteousness of God is revealed in the Gospel." But afterward, when I saw how it went on, that it is written, "The just shall live by faith," and also consulted St. Augustine on the passage, then I became glad, for I learned and saw that the righteousness of God is his mercy through which he regards us and keeps us just. Thus was I comforted.[28]

Elsewhere Luther makes clear that he comes to understand Romans 1:17 as meaning that it is a passive justice through which a benevolent God rectifies a person so that he or she may be saved. Luther says that "this phrase of Paul was for me the true gate to paradise."[29] And since Luther was a man who felt that Satan was always there ready to snatch him up, that kind of assurance came as a huge relief to his troubled conscience.[30] After all, it was out of fear that he turned from studying to be a lawyer to becoming a member of the Augustinian order. (He vowed to become a monk as a result of nearly being struck by lightening walking home one day.)

As Krister Stendahl has argued so powerfully, it is Luther's deeply troubled conscience that provided the structural foundation for the modern reading of Paul. Luther's internal struggle led him to make the question, "How can I find a gracious God?" of utmost importance in his reading of the Bible. According to Stendahl, Luther's question was the theological question of the day. "Penetrating self-examination reached a hitherto unknown intensity."[31] Paul's message, according to

Luther, that one is justified by faith in Christ, without works of the law, must have come as a tremendously comforting and liberating response. This was true for Augustine, but it seems even more so for Luther. Ultimately, it was more influential. Luther turned "the abstract question of a just God into an *existential* quest that concerned the *whole* human being, encompassing thought and action, soul and body, love and suffering. The search for salvation was not reserved for the intellect alone."[32]

While Paul had long been *the* apostle for Christian theologians by the time Luther came along, and Augustine was the most influential reader of Paul, Luther's reading of Paul went beyond what had come before in significant ways. In regard to salvation, Christian theology taught that, when Christians stood at the Last Judgment before Christ, they would be judged on the basis of the good works they had done. The righteousness that came from belief in Christ did not in and of itself make a person righteous; it created the foundation through which the Christian could become righteous. By contrast, Luther taught that righteousness was "already *now* . . . received through faith."[33]

What started Luther down the path of discovery and resistance to Rome was the controversy over the selling of indulgences. Indulgences had been standard practice of the church by the time of the initial rumblings of the Reformation, but they became an issue because their use by the church had become corrupt and self-serving. Properly speaking, indulgences were part of the church's system of repentance and forgiveness. They developed in order to mitigate what had been more severe punishments required as part of doing penance. One could receive an indulgence by special acts of fasting, prayer, retreat, or making donations, among other things. But by Luther's time, the church was actively cultivating the selling of indulgences in order to raise money for the building of Saint Peter's Basilica in Rome. Indulgences had become more of a method of fund-raising than a way to help individuals do penance for their sins; worse yet, indulgences had turned into salvation for a price.

In his 95 Theses, Luther protested this insidious abuse of indulgences. Given the situation, one can understand why the issues of sin, grace, forgiveness, repentance, and salvation became so critical to his thinking. It is in this context that Luther developed the doctrine of justification by faith, which he proclaimed as the central message of the Christian faith. One sees the utter centrality of justification in Luther's lectures on Romans and Galatians, but the idea is pervasive in his writings.

For the purposes of our discussion here, justification by faith may be summarized as follows: Law—by which Luther meant both the Mosaic law as well as law in general—was not the guide to living a life worthy of God. It was only designed to show human beings how hopelessly sinful they are. In his *Preface to the Old Testament*, he says:

> Therefore we see that these many laws of Moses were given not only to prevent anyone from choosing ways of his own for doing good and living aright . . . but rather that sins might simply become numerous and be heaped up beyond measure. The purpose was to burden the conscience so that the hardened blindness would have to recognize itself, and fell its own inability and nothingness in the achieving of good. Such blindness must be thus compelled and forced by law to seek something beyond the law and its own ability, namely the grace of God promised in the Christ who was to come. Every law of God is good and right, even if it only bids men to carry dung or gather straw. Accordingly, whoever does not keep this good law—or keeps it unwillingly—cannot be righteous or good in his heart. But human nature cannot keep it otherwise than unwillingly. It must, therefore, through this good law of God, recognize and feel its wickedness, and sigh and long for the aide of divine grace in Christ.[34]

Luther's working assumption, of course, was that original sin plagues human nature, hence humans cannot willingly do anything good. Law does not make human beings good, because even if humans follow the law, they do it unwillingly or for the wrong reasons. Thus they cannot truly be good. Stephen Westerholm puts it like this: "The law, like a mighty hammer, is meant to crush human self-righteousness and to drive human beings, made aware of their sinfulness, to seek mercy from the Savior."[35]

Once the Christians have accepted their failure to do anything to make themselves righteous in God's sight, they must reject seeing law as a tool to enable them to become righteous. Instead they must recognize their dependence on God and trust completely that God will do what one cannot do for oneself—God will make the believer righteous and effect salvation. Humans cannot draw themselves near to God, but God reaches out to human beings. This is evident through the incarnation of Jesus Christ. God, through Jesus Christ, makes righteous the one who has faith.

Paul's use of Abraham in Romans 4 provided Luther the perfect illustration of this theology. God called Abraham, and Abraham responded without a moment's hesitation. The patriarch thus demonstrated his complete faith in God, and the text of Genesis itself says that "he was reckoned righteous" by his faith (Gen 15:6 cited in Rom 4:3, 9; Gal 3:6). Paul goes on to explain that the Bible says this before Abraham was commanded to be circumcised, and Paul interprets this passage as meaning that Abraham was righteous before he did any "works." In other words, God judged him as righteous apart from his performing any commandments, i.e., circumcision, solely because of his complete and total faith in God.

According to Luther, this righteousness that God effects in those who believe in Jesus is in reality a kind of legal fiction because human beings are by nature sinners. Indeed, the believer in Jesus is just as much a sinner as a person who does not believe in Jesus. This idea is captured in Luther's famous phrase, *simul iustus et peccator,* "at the same time a sinner and justified." Indeed, law can continue to play the role of ongoing indictment, a constant reminder of one's sinful nature, even though it cannot effect goodness in people. The difference between the believer and the nonbeliever is that the believer has been effectively—if not in reality—made righteous before God through the sacrifice of Jesus Christ, and it is this righteous status ascribed to the believer that assures the Christian that he or she will avoid the wrath of God and be saved (see Rom 1:18). The righteousness that comes through Jesus Christ is, for Luther and for Protestant Christianity ever since, the result of God's grace. It is utterly undeserved, but God bestows this gift on the Christian nonetheless.

There is obviously a very close relationship between Luther's personal experience of God's grace and his coming to the doctrine of justification by faith through his reading of Paul. This experience resonated with others, to say the least, since it became the message of the Reformation and is the very definition of Protestant Christianity today, especially emphasized in the American context. While it has never been as central to Catholics as it is to Protestants, it is an important component of the Catholic faith. Indeed, Catholics and Lutherans came together to reconcile on this very issue and in 1999 produced the *Joint Declaration on the Doctrine of Justification.*

Justification by faith came to be seen as the central message Paul preached. In fact, justification by faith came to be understood as Christian gospel, and all the great Reformers adopted it, including John Calvin and John Wesley. It is the lens through which Paul has been read. In fact, Wesley himself was "converted"—or as he described it, felt his heart "strangely warmed"—while listening to Luther's Preface to Paul's letter to the Romans read aloud. (The preface served as an introduction to Paul's letter in Luther's translation of the New Testament.) It remains overwhelmingly the dominant Protestant paradigm of interpretation. But in the twentieth century another trajectory of interpretation began to emerge. Although initially ill formed and still very much a perspective in progress, it has evolved into the great challenge to the existing paradigm—a challenge on two fronts: that Paul did not reject his Jewish identity because Judaism was a religion of works, and that justification by faith is not the gospel Paul preached, both of which undergird the argument of this book.

4

Reading Paul as a Jew—Almost

Modern Jewish Interpreters of Paul

For most of the last two centuries, of course, it has been Christians who have been reading and interpreting Paul, not Jews. Nonetheless, starting in the late eighteenth century in Germany, Jews began reading, studying, and interpreting Paul. However, surprisingly little changed in terms of the image of Paul or the stereotypes of Judaism that Pauline interpretation perpetuated. A brief look at two influential Jewish thinkers who wrote extensively on Paul will illustrate the way in which Jewish scholars perpetuated the Christian Paul.[1] The German Jewish theologians Leo Baeck (1873–1956) and Martin Buber (1878–1965) were sophisticated and highly educated men. They both lived through the Holocaust, though under differing circumstances. While Buber became a Zionist and immigrated to Israel, Baeck stayed in Germany. Amazingly, he managed to survive Theresienstadt. Both men were well connected within both Jewish and Christian academic circles, had friends and colleagues who were Christian, and published their works in venues read by Jewish and Christian intellectuals of their day. Baeck and Buber wanted to offer an interpretation of Paul that would be credible to both Jews and Christians. Unfortunately, they were never able to transcend Jewish-Christian polemics; circumstances made it impossible.

Baeck devoted most of his intellectual energy to understanding the relationship between Judaism and Christianity. His first book, *The Essence of Judaism,* published in 1905, was a response to a book written by Adolf von Harnack in 1901, *What Is Christianity?* but its original German title was *Das Wesen des Christentums,* that is, "The Essence of Christianity." In 1938 Baeck published an essay titled "Romantic Religion"[2] in which he characterized Christianity as diametrically opposed to Judaism. Although Baeck saw strains of Judaism in Paul's writings, he viewed Paul as having left his Judaism behind, and in so doing, he became a "romantic." Baeck said there were essentially two types of religion, one classical, one romantic: Judaism corresponded with the former; Lutheran Christianity, or what he called "Pauline religion," corresponded to the latter. In Pauline religion, according to Baeck, the emphasis is on an otherworldly reality, which completely supersedes earthly reality, leaving everyday life devoid of any spiritual meaning. Baeck reasoned that romantic religion lacks the ethical component characteristic of classical religion and, thereby, causes its adherents to become utterly passive and ethically bankrupt:

> The salvation that comes through faith is in no sense earned, but wholly received. . . . God effects it, as Luther later explained the words of Paul, "in us and without us." Man is no more than the mere object of God's activity, of grace or damnation; he does not recognize God, God merely recognizes him; he *becomes* a child of redemption or destruction, "forced into disobedience" or raised up to salvation. He is the object of virtue and of sin—not its producer, its subject. One feels like saying: man does not live but is lived, and what remains to him is merely, to speak with Schleiermacher, the "taste of infinity," that is, the living experience; the mood and the emotional relation of one who knows himself to be wholly an object; the feeling of faith in which grace is present or the feeling of unbelief in which sin prevails.[3]

Here Baeck's understanding of Paul's theology is entirely mediated by Luther. Of course, his description of this form of religion reveals his negative assessment. When Baeck says that the person is "the object of virtue and of sin," he means that this Romantic form of religion, "Pauline religion," is one in which people are not understood as ethical beings, because they are not subjects who act, but rather are objects who are acted upon, either by God's grace or by sin, and thus they are not accountable for their actions.

In *Two Types of Faith*—purportedly written in Palestine in 1948 while the League of Arab Nations lay siege to the newly created state of Israel[4]—Martin Buber, like Baeck, argued that Judaism and Christianity represented two entirely different forms of religion, even if they were historically intertwined. But Buber did not explain the difference by appeal to Romanticism. Rather, the difference lies with Hellenism. "The Hellenistic Judaism of common coinage, as we know it for instance from the statements of Josephus on his mode of thinking . . . is satisfied to associate God with a power of fate, which causes the suffering of the righteous."[5]

Buber is not the first person to articulate the influence of Hellenism on Judaism before the time of Paul; he takes this idea from Protestant biblical scholars. But Buber articulates the significance of Hellenism in a way diametrically opposed to his Christian contemporaries. Buber highlights the Hellenistic notion of fate because, as he explains, the notion of fate—previously foreign to Judaism—helped to explain the seemingly interminable suffering Israel had endured for centuries and which seemed to have reached an unbearable level under Roman occupation. Such a situation caused some Hellenized Jews, like Paul, to develop the sense of a huge "abyss," as Buber calls it "full of wrath." Buber saw this idea reflected in the words of Paul: "For the wrath of God is revealed from heaven against all ungodliness and wickedness of those who by their wickedness suppress the truth" (Rom 1:18, NRSV). According to Buber, while Israel had previously enjoyed the love and protection of a God who had created human beings in God's own image and thus had no special need of reconciliation, now there seemed to be an unbearable enmity between humans and God. For Paul (and other Hellenistic Jewish writers), the fusion of Hellenistic fate with the Jewish belief in God created an enormous chasm between human beings and God and, thereby, a need for reconciliation.[6] Since humans were understood to be hopelessly under the power of fate, however, they can do nothing to effect reconciliation themselves; salvation from this grim situation must be initiated by God by some magnificent event of apocalyptic proportion. For Paul, it is the death of God's Son. Such is Buber's explanation of Paul's "justification by faith." Thus, Buber accepts the significance of

Hellenism for understanding Paul and Christian origins, but he views it as a theological malformation of Judaism.

Although Buber and Baeck were Jewish and read Paul from a Jewish perspective, they did not really offer a Jewish reading of Paul in the sense of seeing Paul's religious identity as Jewish. They had no interest in reclaiming Paul for the history of Judaism, nor did they develop an appreciation for the form of Judaism he represented. Rather, they took for granted the typical German Protestant understanding of Paul; they simply articulated the mirror image of that understanding. Buber and Baeck believed that Paul left his Judaism behind when he became a Christian (even if they have different explanations of how and why it happened). Thus they do not provide any insight into understanding Paul as a Jew in ancient Jewish context in spite of their own Jewish identity and their knowledge of Jewish sources. The only "Jewish" aspect of their reading lies in their *valuation* of Paul's Christian religiosity, not their interpretation of Paul himself. For Luther and German Protestants who followed in his interpretive path, Paul's theology represents the pinnacle of human religiosity; for Buber and Baeck it is the nadir. Buber and Baeck used Paul as a lens to critique Christianity, just as their Christian contemporaries used him to critique Judaism. Through Paul they argued for a view of Christianity as an eviscerated religion in which its adherents become hopelessly passive and incapable of living ethical lives. Given the circumstances in which Buber and Baeck lived, their views are not terribly surprising.

Richard Rubenstein, writing in 1972, summed up the typical Jewish view of Christian origins: "Jesus, yes; Paul, never!"[7] Rubenstein's pithy remark accurately captures a widely held view of Jewish-Christian history. Modern Jewish intellectuals made the case for a thoroughly Jewish Jesus but an equally strong case for seeing Paul as an apostate who forsook Judaism. In the development of Christianity, then, it is Paul who marks the break with Judaism, not Jesus. Jesus lived and died a Jew, but Paul became the first Christian. Thus Jewish interpreters of Paul tended to promote the view that Paul was the true founder of Christianity, a view first advocated by Nietzsche, and since followed by many others.[8] Joseph Klausner, another Jewish scholar writing in the first half of the twentieth century, articulated this view with great confidence:

It was not Jesus who created (or more correctly founded) Christianity, but Paul. . . . Jesus did not intend to found a new religion
or a new church; he only strove to bring about among his people
Israel the Kingdom of Heaven, and to do this as a Messiah preaching the repentance and good works which would result in the
politico-spiritual redemption of his people, and through them, of
all mankind. Not so Paul. He was the clearly self-conscious creator
and organizer of Christianity as a new religious community. He
made Christianity a religious system different from both Judaism
and paganism, a system mediating between Judaism and paganism
but with an inclination toward paganism.[9]

For Klausner, as for Buber and Baeck and virtually all other Jewish
readers, Christianity is not just different from Judaism; it is antithetical
to it. Thus, Klausner can confidently proclaim: "In spite of the fact that
the *foundations* of all the teachings of Paul are Jewish, his *own* teaching
is both the *contradiction of the Jewish religion* and the *rejection of the
Jewish nation*."[10] Now it was not only Christians who grounded their
understanding of Christianity and Judaism as essentialized religious
opposites in Paul; Jews did too.[11]

Unfortunately, the entry of Jewish scholars into the study of Paul
did not reveal much of the apostle's Jewish identity. Ironically, it served
only to reinforce the Augustinian-Lutheran understanding of Paul.
Although Buber and Baeck intended to offer a Jewish take on Paul,
one which tried to take seriously Paul's identity as a Jew, they largely
took the Christian reading and reversed it. Paul remained the site of
Christian-Jewish polemic.[12]

But things began to change in the second half of the twentieth century. As is the case in regard to so many things, the Holocaust was a
watershed. As theologians and scholars began to reflect on the past
from a post-holocaust perspective, some called for a critical reevaluation
of Christian anti-Judaism. At the center of this effort were a handful of
Protestant biblical scholars who pioneered something that would eventually be labeled the "new perspective" on Paul. Building on this work,
a few Jewish scholars began to offer their readings of Paul. It is only at
this point in the history of Pauline interpretation—within the last 40
years—that scholars began to locate Paul in his ancient Jewish context

with appreciation for Paul's Jewish identity. Without the contributions of these scholars, the present work would never have been possible.

The New Perspective on Paul

In a now famous essay titled "Paul and the Introspective Conscience of the West," Stendahl critiqued the Augustinian-Lutheran reading of Paul as being rooted in a kind of assumed correlation between Judaism and a generic form of religion characterized by works-righteousness. That is to say, Judaism was equated with a type of religion in which individuals are expected to "earn" their way to salvation. This religious system has no concept of divine grace and leaves an individual feeling hopelessly unable to measure up to the divine standard:

> The Reformers' interpretation of Paul rests on an analogism when Pauline statements about Faith and Works, Law and Gospel, Jews and Gentiles are read in the framework of late medieval piety. The Law, the Torah, with its specific requirements of circumcision and food restrictions becomes the general principle of "legalism" in religious matters. Where Paul was concerned about the possibility for Gentiles to be included in the messianic community, his statements are now read as answers to the quest for assurance about man's salvation out of a common human predicament . . . Paul's argument that the Gentiles must not, and should not, come to Christ via the Law, i.e., via circumcision, etc., has turned into a statement according to which all men must come to Christ with consciences properly convicted by the law and its insatiable requirements for righteousness.[13]

The Pauline doctrine of justification by faith is then touted as the cure—salvation is wrought by grace, not by works. Once the individual finds salvation "by grace through faith," she receives relief from the plague of the guilty conscience.

Stendahl revealed how the preoccupation with the inner psyche had led Christian interpreters to read their own problems as if they were Paul's problems. And because they misread the problems to which Paul was responding, they utterly missed the theological answers he provided as well. Put simply, Christians have been misreading Paul for centuries. Worse yet, this misreading of Paul was inexorably linked to the degraded conception of Judaism that had so often led to the worst manifestations of Christian anti-Judaism. Perhaps most important, Stendahl argued that justification by faith was not the eternal theological answer to a universal human problem, but a response to a particular situation involving the relationship between Jew and Gentile. James D. G. Dunn, who is credited with first coining the phrase "new perspective" to describe what was then an emerging new paradigm of Pauline interpretation, affirmed Stendahl's position: "Paul's doctrine of justification by faith should not be understood primarily as an exposition of the individual's relation to God, but primarily in the context of Paul the Jew wrestling with the question of how Jews and Gentiles stand in relation to each other within the covenant purpose of God now that it has reached its climax in Jesus Christ."[14]

Most important for modern readers to note is that Paul wrote to specific communities of believers, people with whom he usually had an intimate relationship.[15] Even within his own time, the audience Paul addressed was not the church universal, but specific churches. Although Paul sometimes instructed the addressees of a particular letter to share his thoughts with another community, Paul never envisioned the audience to whom he addressed his letters as "the church." If he never addressed Christians at large in his own time, then he certainly did not envision himself addressing Christians of all subsequent generations.

So whom did Paul address? New-perspective scholarship has emphasized the importance of realizing that Paul's primary audience was Gentile Jesus-followers. Essential to understanding Paul is recognizing the centrality of Gentiles, both in terms of his social world and in terms of his conceptual thinking. Paul repeatedly calls himself "Apostle to the Gentiles," and from everything we know of him from his letters, he consistently understood himself to have a mandate of preaching to Gentiles, in spite of a very different portrayal in Acts. As this book unfolds, I hope to demonstrate that understanding Paul's letters as specifically addressed to Gentiles is one of the most important keys to understanding Paul's mission, message, and identity as a Jew.

It may seem ironic to connect Paul with Gentiles while so doggedly labeling him a Jew. But understanding Paul as a Jew speaking to Gentiles can make all the difference in understanding what Paul wrote and why he wrote it. Take for example 1 Corinthians 7:19: "Circumcision is nothing and uncircumcision is nothing; but obeying the commandments of God is everything" (NRSV). In my experience of teaching Paul, most Christians read over this verse without noting anything strange or confusing about it. However, Jewish readers often pause over it. Once, a student of mine who also happened to be an ordained rabbi used this verse to argue that Paul could not have been "really Jewish" because, the rabbi reasoned, circumcision *is* one of God's commandments, so either Paul is not the Pharisee-trained Jew he claimed to be, or he is very confused in his thinking. The Christian students in the class responded to the rabbi in predictable ways, claiming either that Paul's point was that circumcision was not one of the *ten* commandments, or that it was not a moral commandment or ethical imperative like "Thou shalt not kill," and that it was those kinds of commandments that were really important.

For reasons I will explain later, none of these responses is satisfying, because each is predicated on the traditional Augustinian-Lutheran framework of Pauline interpretation. For now I simply want to use this verse to demonstrate that if one bears in mind that Paul is speaking to Gentiles, and that the teachings about Jewish law preserved in the apostle's letters are teachings about how Torah *is* and *is not* applicable to Gentiles, then Paul's reasoning begins to come clear. God did indeed command Abraham to be circumcised and to circumcise all the male members of his family. This biblical event becomes known later in Jewish tradition as the *berit milah*, the covenant of circumcision, and it is indeed regarded as one of God's most important commandments for most any Jew of Paul's time. But it is understood as a marker of Jewish identity and incumbent on Jewish males *only*. In other words, the commandment to circumcise applies specifically and exclusively to Jewish males, meaning it is not appropriate to circumcise Gentiles, for God did not and does not command Gentiles to be circumcised. When Paul says, "Circumcision is nothing and uncircumcision is nothing; but obeying the commandments of God is everything," he is not therefore claiming that circumcision is a meaningless ritual that can be ignored. Rather, Paul's point is that God does not require the same things of all people at all times. Priests, for example, had to obey a set of purity laws that did not apply to Israelites in general. Since only Jews are commanded to be circumcised, Gentiles are following the will of God by not being circumcised. I would paraphrase 1 Corinthians 7:19 as follows: "When Jews are circumcised and Gentiles remain uncircumcised, both are following the will of God, so neither group can claim superiority by virtue of the practice (or nonpractice) of circumcision."

In addition to the emphasis on Paul as the Apostle to the Gentiles, and to perceiving the ways in which the categories of Jews and Gentiles are absolutely essential to Paul's thinking, new-perspective scholars are committed to undoing the misconstrual of Judaism that has accompanied the traditional understanding of Paul, particularly in its Reformation and post-Reformation form. In contrast to Christianity, conceived by Christians as a religion of spirit, grace, and love, Judaism has been constructed as a religion of law, in which salvation must be earned and which produces adherents who legalistically calculate their accumulation of merit, brashly boast of their accomplishments, lack any notion of grace, and are devoid of genuine spiritual sentiment in their religious practice. This characterization of Judaism is a gross distortion, both in general terms and in the first century. Thus, any interpretation of Paul that promulgates or relies on such a view to draw conclusions about what Paul said should be repudiated. Instead, Paul's letters must be contextualized within a historically plausible reconstruction of first-century Judaism.

The scholar most influential in persuading New Testament scholars that their concept of first-century Judaism was a Christian fabrication that had no basis in reality was E. P. Sanders, whose 1977 book, *Paul and Palestinian Judaism*, devoted 428 of its 582 pages to a highly detailed and thorough study of Jewish literature produced between 200 BCE and 200 CE.[16] Sanders's study served to demonstrate that when Jewish literature was allowed to speak for itself, unaffected by the polemics of the New Testament and other early Christian writings, Judaism hardly appeared as the legalistic system of works-righteousness that Christian scholars had for so long assumed it to be. On the contrary, grace plays a critical role in the Jewish concept of God and God's relationship to Israel, God's chosen people.

Sanders identified a conceptual core for Judaism, which he labeled "covenantal nomism." This label was an attempt to capture Israel's understanding of itself as being in a special relationship with God, a covenanted relationship, wherein God bestows God's favor on Israel and in return expects Israel's loyalty. Israel expresses her gratitude to

God and demonstrates her loyalty by living within the terms of the covenant. In other words, the covenant, embodied in Torah, contains blessings and promises as well as commandments that God enjoins on Israel. The promises and blessings constitute God's side of the covenant, Sanders explains, while fulfilling the commandments constitutes Israel's side of the covenant.[17] In short, fulfilling God's commandments is the very manifestation of Israel's faith in God. Thus, the commandments accompany the covenant, but the performance of the commandments does not earn one membership in the covenant. On the contrary, performing the commandments is Israel's response to God's gracious initiative on Israel's behalf. More than an obligation, the fulfillment of God's commandments is a privilege, since it reflects Israel's special relationship with God, which Israel views as unique among the nations.

Within academic circles, Sanders's book is one of those rare works whose influence on subsequent scholarship is difficult to overstate. Not only did *Paul and Palestinian Judaism* inspire many responses by Pauline scholars, but it also exerted influence among scholars of ancient Judaism broadly speaking, which is a testament to its perspicacity and importance. Over the last twenty-five years, Sanders's reading of ancient Jewish literature has stood up remarkably well to analyses by later scholars as well as to new evidence that has emerged since he published the work. Ironically, Sanders's treatment of Paul was not nearly as insightful as his analysis of Jewish texts.

Sanders appealed frequently to Paul's "Jewish presuppositions" and "Jewish perspective" because the primary thrust of Sanders's argument was precisely to call attention to other scholars' anti-Jewish bias in reading Paul, owing to their ignorance of first-century Judaism except as negatively constructed by their mirror-reading Paul. But Sanders ultimately portrayed Paul as an extremely idiosyncratic Jew, completely out of step with the Judaism of the period, due to his semimystical encounter with the risen Jesus. Paul founded communities that distinguished themselves by "a separate entrance requirement (faith), a separate entry rite (baptism), and a separate social reality (the church)."[18] Paul's "Christianity" for Sanders therefore still ends up being a religious identity constructed in opposition to "Judaism." Although the terms of opposition are very different for Sanders than for traditional scholars, Pauline Christianity nevertheless constitutes the antithesis of Judaism. Sanders himself said that the only thing wrong with Judaism for Paul is that *"it is not Christianity."*[19] In sum, in spite of a sincere attempt to recapture Paul's Judaism, Sanders's Paul remains as Christian as the Augustinian-Lutheran Paul.

Nevertheless, Sanders's work has inspired many, many books and articles on Paul, some of which tried to utilize Sanders's reconceptualization of Judaism to reconceive Paul in such a way as to do justice to this newly discovered version of first-century Judaism. To be sure, those inspired by Sanders committed themselves to re-Judaizing Paul, to reading the apostle's writings as written by a real first-century Jew and former Pharisee who saw his world and his times through Jewish eyes. "Even as Apostle to the Gentiles, he still remained Paul the Jew, Paul the Israelite," proclaims James Dunn.[20] The intent was to do justice both to Paul and to Judaism so as to compensate for the distortions of the past. Reflecting on the impact of Sanders's work, Dunn says, "Nothing less became necessary than a complete reassessment of Paul's relationship to his ancestral religion, not to mention all the considerable consequences which were bound to follow for our contemporary understanding of his theology."[21]

This process of reassessment has been in progress a couple of decades. I see this study as building on the progress already made but also pushing it further. As we shall see later in the book, new-perspective scholarship still possesses a certain Christian bias in its understanding of ancient Judaism and thus in its understanding of Paul as a Jew. Paul's Damascus-road experience is seen as such a complete conversion from one religious perspective to another that Judaism is accordingly still constructed as the opposite of whatever it is that Paul is preaching. Paul may have been formed by Jewish tradition, but his experience of Jesus is interpreted to mean that he left the bounds of what can reasonably be called Judaism. As Mark Nanos has said, Paul is essentially portrayed as a bad Jew.[22] In the words of Jonathan Brumberg-Kraus, Paul is still conceived as a *goy*.[23] Although it may be more subtle, the opposition between Judaism and Christianity gets reinscribed in the reading of Paul. This is true of most recent Jewish interpreters too.[24]

At the same time, more and more sensitive and sophisticated ways of reading Paul have emerged that have begun to shift the entire

Augustinian-Lutheran complex of interpretation. These readings constitute more than a new perspective; they are radically new. Indeed they present a new paradigm for reading Paul. This radically new paradigm for reading Paul is the basis of this study.[25]

As part of the process of making a "complete reassessment of Paul's relationship to his ancestral religion," the reader must first possess a historically informed picture of late Second Temple Judaism. Otherwise, old assumptions are likely to operate implicitly or even subconsciously when we come to discussing Paul's concepts of sin, law, grace, and, most important, Judaism itself. The old Christian conception of Judaism must be replaced by a new one (which is not so much new as simply a picture consistent with Jewish sources of the period). While I have already mentioned a few characteristics of ancient Judaism in my discussion of the new perspective, a more systematic overview is in order, even if it must necessarily be simplified. Thus, what follows in the next chapter is an overview of the key components of late Second Temple Judaism.

Chapter

5

Paul's Jewish Inheritance

Like all religions, Judaism is historically dynamic. There are lines of continuity and discontinuity from Judaism in one epoch to Judaism in another. Judaism should not be confused with the society, culture, and religion of ancient Israel as reflected in most of the Hebrew Bible. There are important lines of continuity, both in terms of historical continuity and in terms of Jewish self-understanding. But it is awareness of the discontinuities that may best illumine what characterized postbiblical Judaism (roughly 200 BCE to 200 CE). In between Israelite religion and the classical age of rabbinic Judaism lies the variegated but vibrant Judaism of the Hellenistic and Roman period, commonly referred to as "Hellenistic Judaism."[1]

The Judaism of Paul's day began to take shape in the late third century BCE with the conquest of Alexander; this is the beginning of Hellenistic Judaism. (In fact, historians do not speak of "Judaism" at all until this period.) Politically speaking, the Hellenistic age ends with the coming of the Romans, when Pompeii's armies invaded Judea in 63 BCE. Culturally speaking, it lasted many more centuries—until the birth of Islam in the seventh century CE.[2] It is difficult to overstate the influence of Greek thought and culture on Jews and Judaism—it permeated virtually every aspect of Jewish life, and its effect continues until today. At one time, historians saw Paul as the great synthesizer of "Judaism" and "Hellenism," which led to the theological and ethical foundations of Christianity, and Judaism (that is, especially rabbinic Judaism) as rejecting Hellenism and retreating into isolation. This historical orientation was part of an overall Christian bias in scholarship in which Judaism was perceived to be a narrow religion, exclusivist and focused on its own particularity, as compared to Christianity, which was a universalistic religion that opened itself up to the world and all peoples. This understanding reinforced the opposition that had been created between Paul and the Judaism of his day. In recent years, as scholars have seen the way Hellenism pervaded every branch of Judaism, this view can no longer be sustained. In this chapter I will show how Paul's views are more similar to the views reflected in so many other Jewish authors of the Hellenistic age than they are different.

To enable the reader to envision the landscape of late Second Temple Judaism, I will highlight three components essential to grasping Judaism of this period, especially as most relevant to understanding Paul's Judaism: worship, Torah, and redemption. In the following chapter I will take up the question of Jewish identity in relation to Gentiles. Although this period in Jewish history is often thought of as an age of sectarianism, in which Jews fell into assorted subgroups like Pharisees, Sadducees, and Essenes, Jews of various sorts betray many similar ideas, attitudes, and practices about what constitutes Judaism.[3] I will therefore not focus on peculiar attitudes held by certain kinds of Jews but rather on what appears to be typical and commonplace, and, moreover, what will be most useful to the interpretation of Paul that follows in the subsequent chapters.[4]

God and Worship

It is practically a cliché to describe ancient Jews as monotheists in a polytheistic world, and, in spite of the term's lack of precision, monotheism still seems the best way to characterize the Jews' exclusive commitment to and worship of the one God, Creator and Sustainer of everything, but who cannot be "imaged" in any form. I will use the term *aniconic monotheism* to refer to the distinctive brand of Jewish monotheism of this period.[5] Aniconic monotheism is the signature mark of Judaism in the Hellenistic and Roman world, especially from the perspective of Jews themselves, though it is remarked on by Greek and Roman writers as well, sometimes with admiration.[6] Although there was no Greek or Latin word for monotheism as a peculiar form of religious piety, Hellenistic Jewish writers speak proudly of the oneness of God. Here is a description from the first-century Jewish historian Josephus, who is explaining how Moses, "the legislator," taught the people about the nature of God:

> To Him he [Moses] persuaded all to look, as the author of all blessings, both those which are common to all mankind, and those which they had won for themselves by prayer in the crises of their history. He convinced them that no single action, no secret thought could be hid from Him. He represented Him as One, uncreated and immutable to all eternity; and in beauty surpassing all mortal thought made known to us by His power, although the nature of His real being passes knowledge.[7]

Josephus goes on to say that all the great Greek philosophers, like Pythagoras, Anaxagoras, and Plato, among others, adopted the same essential conception of God, which of course they learned from Moses, who is portrayed as the first religious educator. The excerpt is from *Contra Apion*, a treatise Josephus wrote to defend Jews and Judaism against slanderous attacks on the antiquity and legitimacy of the Jews. It comes as no surprise then to find Josephus contrasting the Jewish conception of God with non-Jewish conceptions. They represent their gods "to be as numerous as they choose," says Josephus, "borne of one another and engendered in all manner of ways. They assign them different localities and habits, like animal species, some living underground, others in the sea."[8] Drawing on Homer's accounts of Greek mythology, Josephus demonstrates not only that these so-called gods are no models of morality (a complaint often made by Greek intellectuals of antiquity), but that they exercise no control over providence—neither in their own lives nor in the cosmos. Worse, new gods keep popping up, and new stories keep being invented; new temples are constructed while the old ones are left in disrepair. Such unconscionable neglect of tradition derives from ignorance of the one God and results in egregious impiety.

Jews, by contrast, possess knowledge of the "true nature of God," which they preserve accurately and worship appropriately. The Jewish God is the supreme God. Because God is a creator God, he relates to and cares for his creatures, but as God, he cannot be likened to them. Honor cannot be paid to God by creating images of his likeness—such "worship" is expressly proscribed. Even to conjure an image resembling a creature or created thing is to risk blasphemy. Josephus claims that worship of God is best expressed through living a virtuous life. However, the most literal conception of worship of God is represented by the temple cult in Jerusalem. The priests continuously conduct worship through offerings and sacrifices and safeguard the Torah, which means both literally observing the laws as divinely ordained as well as keeping archives of the Torah, but also genealogical and property records and presumably any other records necessary for adjudicating cases among the people so as to keep order.[9]

Interestingly, although Josephus writes *Contra Apion*, his last treatise, at about the turn of the second century CE, the temple had been destroyed thirty-some years earlier. Yet, Josephus speaks as if the priests are conducting their sacrificial services as he writes. The reader of *Contra Apion* would not know that the Jerusalem temple had been utterly destroyed and the sacrificial cult become extinct. Other writers speak of the temple and the temple cult similarly in the present tense. Scholars have long noted it but find satisfactory explanations lacking. It may be simply that writers of the late first and early second century CE assumed that eventually the temple would be rebuilt and sacrificial worship resume. After all, the first temple had been plundered and destroyed by the Babylonians five hundred years earlier, but rebuilding began a few generations later under the patronage of the Persians, who had defeated the Babylonians. Perhaps Josephus and others imagined a similar scenario, though he never speaks of such a hoped-for restoration.

In any case, worship—paying homage and giving glory to God—transpires ideally by designated priests who scrupulously perform all the appropriate sacrificial rites at the temple in Jerusalem. Sources indicate that Jews living abroad, as well as those living in the land, shared the idealization of the Jerusalem temple as the primary locus of worship of the one God. The vast majority of Jews, of course, could not literally participate in this form of worship; that is, they could not perform sacrifices in the temple, because they did not possess priestly status. Nevertheless, there were other ways that Jews looked to the Jerusalem temple for the worship of God, even if they experienced it vicariously. There were three major pilgrimage festivals where Jews from abroad would make their way to Jerusalem: Passover, Pentecost, and Tabernacles. To demonstrate their loyalty, they also paid one-half shekel annually to support the maintenance of the temple cult, thus ensuring that sacrificial offerings would continue unabated.

At the same time, however, admiration toward the temple in ancient Judaism is mixed with ambivalence, sometimes implicit, sometimes explicit. There is evidence that Jews of the Diaspora regarded synagogues as places of worship even if the Levitical sacrifices were not being offered in such synagogues. Historical evidence also indicates that Gentiles sometimes regarded synagogues as temples. Roman edicts seem to treat them similarly, while Gentiles antagonistic to Jews assume they can be desecrated by the same kinds of idolatrous images that can render the Jerusalem temple impure. Synagogues were called *proseuche*, "prayer houses," in Egypt and Asia Minor, presumably indicating that such places were used for some form of communal prayer, though the formalized liturgy associated with rabbinic Judaism was far from realized in the first and second centuries CE.

There were also some Jews who were critical of the temple establishment. The harshest critiques came not from the Diaspora but from Judean Jews and Jews living in the immediate environs of Judea (e.g., Galilee, Samaria). Many Jews had good reason to express displeasure: a goodly number of priests and high priests during the Hellenistic era were corrupt or tyrannical or both, and many of them were responsible for horrible civil violence.[10] But in addition to these eruptions of grotesque impiety, evidence from the Dead Sea Scrolls has demonstrated that some Jews who were priests themselves and/or those who tended toward elitist forms of piety abandoned the temple and organized themselves into a holy congregation of priests, equivalent to the sanctuary. In other words, they viewed their own desert community as the real temple, the place where God dwelled with the people. Whatever the reason—conflicts over rights to the high priesthood or perhaps differences of opinion about ritual practice—the Jews who wrote some of the texts from the Dead Sea believed the Jerusalem temple had either become defiled or it did not possess the adequate degree of holiness to ensure proper worship of God. Instead, this desert community maintained a degree of holiness that allowed it to function as if it were the temple. They regarded themselves as the true keepers of God's covenant, the trusted interpreters of Scripture—able to adjudicate any and all matters of ritual and ethical practice—and their communal meals were equivalent to the sacrificial offerings consumed by priests in the holy sanctuary as prescribed by Torah.[11]

In short, while the temple is of central importance to Second Temple Judaism, that importance was mostly symbolic for the majority of Jews. Its significance had become relativized even before the Romans destroyed the temple in 70 CE. In practice, Jews who were not priestly nobility or who did not live in Jerusalem or its environs, would have had virtually nothing to do with the temple in practice except during pilgrimage festivals, but even then, there is good reason to believe that many Jews living far from Jerusalem did not go up to Jerusalem during the festivals—many would not have had the resources or the leisure time to go on pilgrimage.[12]

In the literature of the period, Jewish worship of God was spoken of mostly in negative terms, that is, in polemics about how *not* to worship God. Jewish sources repeatedly express horror at idolatry and exhort Jews to avoid any semblance of it. Jews must abstain from the worship of any object, animal, or person, and the prohibition against idolatry must be guarded at all costs. Both Josephus and Philo report that when Gaius Caligula attempted to erect a statue of himself in the Jerusalem temple, Jews were in an uproar and on the verge of revolting. Fortunately, Gaius was assassinated and the crisis averted. The worship of God alone, best demonstrated by the abhorrence of all forms of idolatry, is consistently the single most important marker of true piety from the ancient Jewish perspective.[13] As Philo exhorts, "Let us, then, engrave deep in our hearts this as the first and most sacred of commandments, to acknowledge and honour one God Who is above all, and let the idea that gods are many never even reach the ears of the man whose rule of life is to seek for truth in purity and guilelessness."[14]

When Jewish writers want to lampoon Gentiles, they ridicule the worship of deaf and dumb idols, especially the worship of animals by prostration to images of animals—Egyptians were notoriously foolish and debased in the eyes of Jews precisely because they appeared to worship animals. In the Wisdom of Solomon, a text also produced by an Alexandrian Jewish author writing about the same time as Philo, the plagues God visited upon the Egyptians are ascribed not merely to their persecution of the Hebrews, but to their idolatry.[15] Paul expresses a similar sentiment in the first chapter of his letter to the Romans. In another passage, the Wisdom of Solomon describes with merciless irony an idol maker who has just completed his handiwork:

> *He takes thought for it, so that it may not fall, because he knows that it cannot help itself, for it is only an image and has need of help. When he prays about possessions and his marriage and children, he is not ashamed to address a lifeless thing. For health he appeals to a thing that is weak; for life he prays to a thing that is dead; for aid he entreats a thing that is utterly inexperienced; for a prosperous journey, a thing that cannot take a step; for money-making and work and success with his hands, he asks strength of a thing whose hands have no strength. (Wis 13:16–19)*

Idolatry is the Jewish equivalent to the Christian concept of original sin in that it is the first and primary cause of every other sin. Hence tirades against idolatry in Jewish sources portray idolatry as inevitably leading to every other kind of sin and debauchery: "For the worship of idols . . . is the beginning and cause and end of every evil" (Wis 14:27).

Yet, during the Hellenistic and Roman periods, Jewish writers treat their Gentile neighbors' worship of other gods with increasing tolerance (even if condescension). Many writers, especially those in the Diaspora, reflect on how Jewish forms of belief and practice can be conceptually reconciled with other forms of religiosity. For example, an author from third- or second-century-BCE Alexandria equates Moses with the god Hermes, because both are perceived as having a similar function, namely, transmitting oracles from the divine to the human realm.[16] Herod the Great spent lavishly on the construction of Greek buildings, including pagan temples. While Josephus approves of this kind of magnanimity, he faults Herod for not showing comparable generosity toward Jews. Josephus nevertheless touts Jewish religious tolerance by praising Herod's son Agrippa, who was highly regarded for his scrupulous observance in religious practice and for the generosity and honors he paid toward Gentiles and Jews alike.[17] Elsewhere Josephus claims that Moses forbade Jews to "deride or blaspheme the gods recognized by others, out of respect for the very word 'God.'"[18] Philo says virtually the exact same thing.[19]

Of course, what may be most important for modern readers to understand is that while Jews proudly portrayed themselves as uncompromising worshippers of one God and one God only, that did not mean Jews did not recognize the existence of other divine or semidivine beings. In fact, the literary history of this period indicates that there was an explosion of thinking about angels. While stories of God sending intermediaries to earth to carry out the divine will appear in Jewish Scripture, angelic figures usually remain unnamed, and not much attention is paid to them as figures in their own right. In contradistinction to biblical stories, the apocryphal and pseudepigraphical literature produced in the Hellenistic and Roman periods engages in all sorts of angelological speculation.[20] One text found among the Dead Sea Scrolls is an elaborate liturgical text that describes the worship of God by the heavenly host, whose members are often called *elohim* or *elim*, literally meaning "gods."[21] Sometimes called "The Angelic Liturgy" or "Songs of the Sabbath Sacrifice," the text describes the liturgy performed on each Sabbath for the first quarter of the solar year.[22] In Jewish angelology of the period, an elite group of seven archangels regularly appear, and they take on more significance as individuals who play key roles in the lives of humans.[23] For example, in the apocryphal book of Tobit (second century BCE), when Tobit prays for healing from blindness, God sends the angel Raphael to answer Tobit's prayer (as well as the prayer of Sarah, Tobit's daughter-in-law to be, who is afflicted by a demon that has caused the seven men to whom she has been wed to die on their wedding night). Raphael, incognito as a distant relation, accompanies Tobit's son Tobias on a journey that consumes most of the narrative; his true identity is revealed only at the end.[24]

My point in describing the emphasis Jews placed on aniconic monotheism is for the purpose of anticipating later discussion of Paul's investment in the same kind of theological emphasis. Paul reveals in his letters that he possesses the same kind of stereotype of Gentiles as idolaters. His recognition of Jesus as "Lord" did not alter his singular devotion to the one God. To be sure, Paul is reaching out to Gentiles with his message about the death and resurrection of Jesus, but this message is of a piece with his profound concern to rescue Gentiles from their idolatry.

Torah and Election

"Torah" can be used in different ways in Jewish texts and tradition and thus can be translated by different English terms. The most commonly used English equivalent is "law," sometimes capitalized as "Law." To be sure, "law" is one important component of Torah. But Torah can also refer more precisely to the first five books of the Bible: Genesis, Exodus, Leviticus, Numbers, and Deuteronomy. In a modern Jewish context, Torah refers to a single scroll containing all five books, though in Paul's time the five books were most likely on separate scrolls but thought of as a collection. Modern Christians, too, think of these books as forming a special unit within the Bible; in a Christian context it is most commonly known as the Pentateuch, though that label did not exist in Paul's time. Less precisely, Torah is sometimes used as a synonym for all of Scripture. Paul himself sometimes used it this way.

In spite of the semantic variation, the best way to capture the range of meanings contained in the word "Torah" in English is to understand it as teaching or instruction, that is, God's instruction. Indeed, there is actually more narrative than there are commandments in Genesis through Deuteronomy, and the stories were viewed as a source of divine instruction just as much as the legal portions. Moreover, while Torah refers to the text (or set of texts), Torah is also the manner of living that binds the Jewish people to God. To speak of "keeping" Torah means more than simply preserving the texts in their material form; it means to study and teach it diligently, to live by its principles, and to use it in the adjudication of disputes within the community. To put it succinctly, Torah is more than a written text; it is a way of relating to God. The essence of Torah as embodied in the people of Israel is captured by the words of the *Shema*, which come from Deuteronomy:

> *Hear, O Israel! The Lord is our God, the Lord alone. You shall love the Lord your God with all your heart and with all your soul and with all your might. Take to heart these instructions with which I charge you this day. Teach them to your children. Recite them when you are at home and when you are away, when you lie down and when you rise up. Bind them as a sign on your hand and let them serve as a frontlet on your forehead; inscribe them on the doorposts of*

your house and your gates. (Deut 6:4–9, author's translation based on JPS [Jewish Publication Society translation])

What may be most important for modern Christian readers to understand is that Torah constitutes the covenant between God and the people. Not only do the people have obligations toward God, but God, too, makes promises that constitute God's obligations toward the people. The covenantal form of Torah is best seen in Deuteronomy, which is mostly composed of Moses speaking for God, reviewing Israel's history up to that point, and then recapitulating the "law" as revealed at Sinai. Moses concludes the recitation of the law with these words:

> *The Lord your God commands you this day to observe these laws and rules; observe them faithfully with all your heart and soul. You have affirmed this day that the Lord is your God, that you will walk in His ways, that you will observe His laws and commandments and rules, and that you will obey Him. And the Lord has affirmed this day that you are, as He promised you, His treasured people who shall observe all His commandments, and that He will set you, in fame and renown and glory, high above all the nations that He has made; and that you shall be, as He promised, a holy people to the Lord your God. (Deut 26:16–19, JPS)*

This passage reveals the way in which the people willingly assent to the commandments God has given them. At the same time, God affirms his commitment to fulfilling the promises he has made to the people. It is a contract mutually agreed to and which carries with it responsibilities and consequences for both parties. To be sure, there are serious consequences for violating God's law—spelled out in graphic detail in Deuteronomy 27–28. Most awe-inspiring is the list of curses, which concludes, "'Cursed be anyone who does not uphold the words of this law by observing them.' All the people shall say, 'Amen!'" (Deut 27:26). To be cursed in antiquity was a frightening thing. But there are also glorious rewards and assurances of well-being given in the blessings that are enumerated, as well as a reiteration that Israel is God's favored people (see Deut 28:1–14).

The relationship that God establishes with Israel through the covenant is unique among the nations. This idea is sometimes known as the concept of election; Israel is God's chosen people, and there is a close connection between the concepts of Torah, covenant, and election. The laws that God bestows on Israel are not understood as a liability, but as a gift, the result of Israel's favored status. Moses tells the people that the laws that he has been charged to teach the people will result in Israel's being esteemed by all the other nations. "For what great nation is there that has a god so close at hand as is the Lord our God whenever we call upon Him? Or what great nation has laws and rules as perfect as all this Teaching (Torah) that I set before you this day?" (Deut 4:7–9, JPS).

There is an unresolved tension already present in the Torah between a conceptualization of God as God of the whole world and God as the God who favors Israel. While elaborating on the prohibition against idolatry, Moses tells the people:

> *When you look up at the sky and behold the sun and the moon and stars, the whole heavenly host, you must not be lured into bowing down to them or serving them. These the Lord your God allotted to other peoples everywhere under heaven; but you the Lord took and brought out of Egypt . . . to be His very own people. (Deut 4:19–20, JPS)*

This text is an attempt to reconcile the issue of how the one and only creator God is also the God who elected Israel as the chosen people.

Many of the commandments that comprise the Torah are regulations designed for the sole purpose of demonstrating Israel's special status among the nations. As such, these laws are applicable only to Israel. The most obvious of these are the dietary and purity laws (see Lev 11–15). The conclusion to the catalogue of forbidden and permitted foods in Leviticus 11 makes clear that these laws pertain to Israel alone: "For I am the LORD your God; sanctify yourselves therefore, and be holy, for I am holy. You shall not defile yourself with any swarming creature that moves on the earth. For I am the LORD who brought you up from the land of Egypt, to be your God; you shall be holy, for I am holy" (Lev 11:44–45). The refrain, "you shall be holy, for I am holy" appears, with slight variations, many times throughout the legal portions of the Torah, especially those dealing with cultic observances. It is a kind of summary statement of the *function* of the covenant between God and Israel—to render Israel as elect among the nations. As God instructs Moses to tell the Israelites: "Now therefore, if you obey my voice and keep my covenant, you shall be my treasured possession out of all the peoples. Indeed, the whole earth is mine, but you shall be for me a priestly kingdom and a holy nation" (Exod 19:5–6). Israel has a specially consecrated status as *a priestly kingdom and a holy nation* that other peoples do not share. Israel's sanctification is unique; she alone among the nations is holy. But Israel's election as a holy nation also obligates it in unique ways. Greater proximity to God requires a greater degree of holiness, and holiness is maintained through the purity regulations specified in Torah. Just as the priests within Israel are beholden to a higher standard of purity than are ordinary Israelites, so Israel as a nation is obligated to uphold a higher standard of purity than other peoples.[25] If Israel fails to uphold the required standard of purity, not only does she violate the covenant, but she risks losing her holy status and thus contact with the divine presence.[26]

The concept of purity/impurity in Judaism is too complex to discuss here in detail, but it is important to understand that there are different kinds of impurity, the primary distinction being between moral and ritual impurity.[27] Ritual impurity should not be equated with sin; it is caused by natural, unavoidable conditions experienced by human beings, which are usually temporary, such as menstruation or contact with the dead (burial). Moral impurity, on the other hand, is contracted by heinous immoral acts, namely idolatry, sexual immorality, and the spilling of innocent blood. It is long-lasting and in some cases permanent. It cannot be relieved by rites of purification but only punishment (including exile or exclusion) and atonement. We will see Paul's aberration for things that cause moral impurity later. Especially relevant within the context of this book, moral impurity is enjoined upon everyone, Jew and Gentile alike, while ritual impurity is enjoined on Israel alone.[28] Furthermore, because ritual purity regulations are not incumbent on Gentiles, there is no moral condemnation of Gentiles for not observing purity regulations.

Ritual purity regulations simply ensure that Israelites, who bear greater proximity to God than non-Israelites, do not allow certain defiling conditions to accumulate and thus cause the divine presence to depart. Thus, when an Israelite male ejaculates, he is required to wash himself as well as all the materials that had contact with his semen; he must then wait until evening to reassume the status of "pure." If the man ejaculates inside a woman during sexual intercourse, both of them are considered "unclean," and both are required to bathe and wait until evening before returning to a state of purity (see Lev 15:16–17). While in their state of uncleanness, they are prohibited from certain activities that would bring them into greater contact with the divine, like making an offering in the temple. But, assuming the Levitical laws pertaining to sexual intercourse have been observed (see Lev 18), there is nothing immoral or bad about sexual intercourse between a man and a woman. There is nothing inherently bad about semen. Nevertheless, a genital flux poses a potential danger to holiness. The exact reason why Israel associates genital fluxes with impurity remains something of a mystery, though it may have something to do with threatening the integrity of the divine-human boundary. In any case, there is no prohibition against sexual intercourse or ejaculation in general. Most purity regulations, in fact, pertain to things that would be impossible to prohibit, like menstruation and skin disease.

The tension between God as a universal deity and God as the benefactor of Israel in particular is mostly implicit in Israelite Scripture, but it increasingly became an issue that needed to be explicitly addressed in the literature of the late Second Temple period as well as in rabbinic literature. The special relationship between God and Israel is understood to have been initiated by God, hence the designation "chosen" people. Some biblical texts make explicit that God's election of Israel and deliverance from Egypt was not due to any particular merit on Israel's part:

> It was not because you were more numerous than any other people that the LORD set his heart on you and chose you—for you were the fewest of all peoples. It was because the Lord loved you and kept the oath that he swore to your ancestors, that the LORD has brought you out with a mighty hand, and redeemed you from the house of slavery, from the hand of Pharaoh king of Egypt. Know therefore that the LORD your God is God, the faithful God who maintains covenant loyalty with those who love him and keep his commandments, to a thousand generations. (Deut 7:7–9)

While postbiblical Jewish writers sometimes pondered *why* God chose Israel to be his people and offered different reasons as explanation, Jewish literature of the first century is consistent in the assumption *that* Israel has been specially chosen by God and that the status of "chosenness" results from God's benefaction toward Israel. A famous story from an early rabbinic text known as the *Mekhilta* illustrates that Israel's election is due to God's initiative and not Israel's merit.

> *I am the Lord Thy God* (Exod 20:2). Why were the ten commandments not said at the beginning of the Torah? They give a parable. To what may this be compared? To the following: A king who entered a province said to the people: May I be your king? But the people said to him: Have you done anything good for us that you should rule over us? What did he do then? He built a city wall for them, he brought in the water supply for them, and he fought their battles. Then when he said to them: May I be your king? They said to him: Yes, yes. Likewise, God. He brought the Israelites out of Egypt, divided the sea for them, sent down the manna for them, brought the quails for them. He fought for them the battle with Amalek. Then he said to them: I am to be your king. And they said to him: Yes, yes.[29]

This story implies not that *Israel* had to earn God's blessings, but that *God* had to earn Israel's favor! Of course, it is difficult to escape the perception that in electing Israel, God seems to have acted arbitrarily, perhaps even capriciously. Some ancient Jewish writers wanted to find reasons so as to justify having been chosen to receive the divine law—probably because they were uncomfortable with the arbitrary nature of election.[30] Indeed, why should God have bestowed favor on Israel as God's chosen people, when God created the whole world and all its inhabitants?

Overwhelmingly, however, Jews did not perceive an irresolvable conflict between "grace" and "works" that would plague Christian theologians of later centuries. Jewish writers repeatedly speak of the necessity of righteous deeds and assert that righteous deeds merit rewards (often in this life, not just the next one), while acts of wrongdoing merit punishment. Just as frequently, they assert that God is gracious, merciful, and forbearing toward human beings who are in actuality incapable of being worthy of God's affirmation. This latter sentiment is found frequently in the Psalms of Thanksgiving, a text found among the Dead Sea Scrolls. Many of these psalms are poignant expressions of humility before God.

I give you thanks, Lord, because you have taught me your truth, you have made me know your wonderful mysteries . . . with the abundance of your compassion with the depraved of heart. Who is like you, Lord, among the gods? Who is like your truth? Who is just before you when he goes to court? No spirit can reply to your reproach, no host can stand up against your anger. All the sons of your truth you bring to forgiveness in your presence, you purify them from their offences by the greatness of your goodness, and by the abundance of your compassion.[31]

The writer of this psalm is the antithesis of the stereotype of the self-righteous Jew. Here we see a pious Jew of antiquity who does not understand himself as having constantly to earn God's favor, but rather he acknowledges in humility that his own justification comes by the grace of God. Disobedience and the failure to fulfill all the commandments perfectly do not imply dismissal from the covenantal community, as long as repentance is expressed and there remains a freely willed desire to participate in the covenant. Similarly, Israel's suffering or humiliation at the hands of enemies does not imply that God has abrogated the covenant and the promises God made to Israel. Ancient Jewish writers tended to attribute the lugubrious conditions that afflicted Israel at various times to God's discipline—punishments inflicted on the people so as to reestablish the equilibrium of the covenant and restore them so that they may again reflect their status as the elect. Just as Israel's prophets interpreted the destruction of the first temple by the Babylonians as punishment for Israel's sins, so, too, Josephus, who wrote a history of the infamous Jewish war with Rome (66–70 CE), interpreted the destruction of the second temple as God's punishment for Israel's wrongdoing. In neither case, however, is this punishment interpreted as God's withdrawal from the covenant with Israel. To be sure, such calamitous events are a sign of divine *displeasure*, but not of divine *disfavor*. One of the most striking texts that illustrates this theology of suffering occurs in 2 Maccabees. In a digression from recounting the persecution and violence leading up to the desecration of the temple by the Seleucid ruler known as Antiochus IV Epiphanes, the author addresses the reader directly:

Now I urge those who read this book not to be depressed by such ca-
lamities, but to recognize that their punishments were designed not

*to destroy but to discipline our people. In fact, it is a sign of great
kindness not to let the impious alone for long, but to punish them immediately. For in the case of the other nations the Lord waits patiently
to punish them until they have reached the full measure of their sins;
but he does not deal in this way with us, in order that he may not
take vengeance on us afterward when our sins have reached their
height. Therefore he never withdraws his mercy from us. Although he
disciplines us with calamities, he does not forsake his own people. Let
what we have said serve as a reminder; we must go on briefly with the
story. (2 Macc 6:12–17)*

I will revisit this passage later, because it is important for understanding some of Paul's comments about the accumulation of sin in Romans
and Galatians. For now it is enough to note the way in which punishment is understood as a sign of God's favor toward Israel.

Such an understanding arises out of the context of covenantal theology, by which I mean that God's having made the covenant with
Israel was an act of grace—Israel did not earn it—but Israel's response
was expressed by the faithful observance of the commandments, which
were an integral part of the covenant. It is what Sanders was trying to
convey by his description of the conceptual core of Judaism as "covenantal nomism." The covenant between God and Israel is understood
to be eternal; it cannot be abrogated because in principle God cannot
break God's promises—a sentiment powerfully expressed also by Paul
in Romans 11. That the covenant endures forever is itself perhaps the
greatest indicator of the profound role grace plays in the theology of
ancient Judaism.

There can be no doubt that ancient Judaism, like modern Judaism,
placed an emphasis on what one was supposed to do, not on what one
was supposed to believe. That is not to say that ancient Judaism had no
beliefs or belief system. It is simply to say that many if not most Jewish
writers of antiquity understood themselves to possess a set of traditional
customs and laws to which they were bound and the observance of
which they took as an expression of their faithfulness to God. Thus,
the faith-works dichotomy so familiar to modern Christians was not a
functioning conceptual distinction in ancient Judaism—nor, I dare say,
was this bifurcation part of the conceptual world of early Christianity.
After all, it is not as if the early followers of Jesus possessed no ethical

standards or that leaders like Paul did not have expectations about what constituted appropriate behavior for those who were "in Christ."

Conceptually speaking, Torah implied the idea of covenantal theology and referred to the way of life to which Israel was required to adhere. When most Christians hear the term "Torah," they think of the latter— that Judaism means living according to the teachings of the Torah, and not without good reason. The choice of the English "law" to translate the Hebrew *torah* is partly the result of Jewish scribes of the third century BCE in Alexandria, who chose the term *nomos* for *torah* when they translated Hebrew Scripture into Greek. The Greek word *nomos* has a different semantic range than does the Hebrew *torah*. The overall sense of *nomos* is similar to the English concept of law; in fact, Greek *nomos* and the English "law" are more similar to each other than either is to *torah*. That Greek-speaking Jews chose to use *nomos* as the equivalent for Torah should not be taken as an indication of a lack of spiritual fervor or that Jews were becoming more "legalistic" in the postbiblical period. It is likely that Hellenistic Jews found *nomos* the most appropriate or natural equivalent because it expressed a quality highly valued throughout the Mediterranean at the time. Both the Greeks and the Romans placed a very high value on ancestral tradition and the rule of law. That Jews described Torah as an ancient constitution, which they cherished, carefully preserved and protected, and to which they strictly adhered, indicates they were presenting themselves as a society that was credible and comprehensible to Greek and Roman rulers, elites, and intellectuals. Ancient Jewish writers also portrayed Torah not just as one particular constitution, but as one founded on universal principles and in which the noblest ideals of human communal life are embodied. Torah contains the ultimate system of morals and values because its origin is divine; it was given to the ancient Israelites by God via Moses. Moses is frequently referred to as *nomothetes*, "lawgiver," by Josephus, because he is the one to whom God gave the law and the one who instructed the people in its precepts.[32] Thus Moses is credited with establishing for the Jewish people a functioning constitution embodied in the Torah. It is no surprise that Moses, as the "lawgiver of the Jews," is the most well-known figure among non-Jews, since the Greeks admired such persons and lionized their own lawgivers as heroes.[33]

In diametric opposition to the stereotype of Jews as legalistic and obsessed with technical matters of law that made no real ethical difference,

Hellenistic Jews characterized their devotion to Torah as a form of morality to which they imagined other peoples aspired or should aspire. Already by the second century BCE, Jews writing in Alexandria saw such marked similarity between Hellenistic values, customs, and practices, and the practice of Torah by Jews, that they were compelled to explain what they saw as the essential sameness of Judaism and Hellenism. Aristobulus believed that virtually the entire body of Greek philosophy depended on Jewish Scripture for all its critical insights. He claimed that both Pythagoras and Plato studied Torah; the latter was an especially devoted student who also lived by its precepts.[34] As Erich Gruen has said of Aristobulus, "all of Jewish law was constructed so as to underscore piety, justice, self-control, and the other qualities that represent true virtues—i.e., the very qualities subsequently embraced and propagated by the Greeks."[35] Although few writers go as far as Aristobulus, the characterization of Jewish law as the expression of virtues to which any human being could or should aspire is an idea expressed in numerous Jewish texts of the era.

To be sure, Jews sometimes produced documents that were concerned with highly technical matters of law, matters that usually involved peculiarly Jewish stipulations regarding purity and that reflect internal arguments among Jewish elites. Examples of such texts appear among the Dead Sea Scrolls. A document known to scholars by the shorthand label 4QMMT, which appears to be a letter written by the priestly leader(s) of the Qumran community to other Jewish authorities in Jerusalem, contains reiterations, clarifications, and explications about certain laws applicable mainly to priests. Regarding some laws, the author(s) appear to be disputing practices they view as too lenient an interpretation of law. To an outsider, what is at stake in these disputes is not self-evident and could appear trivial or obtuse. To take one example: Torah teaches that contact with a corpse causes impurity. Priests therefore are commanded to avoid such contact except in the case of close relatives, for the rites of mourning themselves seem to constitute "contact." The author of 4QMMT asserts that contact even with dry bones—skeletal remains after the soft tissue has decomposed—is the equivalent of contact with a corpse. The author of 4QMMT also advocates for a broader zone of holiness in and around the temple than was currently in practice at the time—the implication being that purity laws pertaining to the temple were not properly in force in the view of the author of 4QMMT.

4QMMT's interest in the finer points of purity is no more an indication of legalism than is a proposed piece of legislation indicative of a general tendency of Americans to obsess about every jot and tittle while missing the "spirit" of the law. The concerns addressed by 4QMMT are the kinds of concerns typical of priestly classes charged with ensuring the maintenance of proper ritual. Indeed, most of Jewish literature produced during the Hellenistic period does not resemble 4QMMT but addresses a broader audience. Furthermore, a preoccupation with purity is not peculiar to Jews or Judaism. Purity rules and rituals governed Greek and Roman temples, and juridical discussion and debate would sometimes ensue over whether purity was being properly maintained—this is especially the case in times of crisis. There is no reason to think that Jews were more preoccupied with law, either in theory or in practice, than comparable cultures to which they may be likened.

Consider the example of 1 Maccabees, a historical chronicle that recounts the religious persecution by the Seleucid ruler Antiochus IV Epiphanes and the successful revolt led by the Maccabees to defend the religion of their ancestors. Mattathias, patriarch of the Maccabean family, inspires the people with the following battle cry: "Let everyone who is zealous for the law and supports the covenant come out with me!" (1 Macc 2:27). Subsequent to this rallying cry, the text describes an early battle that is lost as a result of observance of the proscription against fighting on the Sabbath. This incident leads Mattathias to make a proclamation that fighting on the Sabbath is necessary to preserving the covenant (see 1 Macc 2:40–41). From that point on, the text reflects no tension about fighting on the Sabbath; it is simply assumed as necessary. A similarly mixed message characterizes 2 Maccabees as well. While 1 and 2 Maccabees both stress an uncompromising attitude about Jewish identity being dependent on strict Torah observance, compromises are made, sometimes because they are necessary—as with fighting on the Sabbath—but sometimes the text recounts accommodations to Hellenistic culture that implicitly contradict precepts of the Torah for which no reason is given and over which no theological angst is apparent.

Because the corpus of Hellenistic Jewish literature is vast, generalizations are necessarily oversimplifications. Nevertheless, the vast majority of Jewish literature produced during the Hellenistic and early Roman periods avoids discussion about picayune matters of Jewish law. Rather, it tends to portray Jewish law either as the embodiment of universal ethical principles or as preservation of ancient customs and traditions. The stereotype of Jews as preoccupied with legal minutia—much of which derives from the portrayal of the debates between Jesus and the Pharisees in the Gospels—is belied by the literary sources of the period. Texts like 4QMMT are the exception in the prerabbinic period, not the norm; they reflect religious virtuosos who in many ways foreshadow the rabbis and rabbinic discourse of later centuries.

Because scholars have too often assumed that the strict observance of Jewish law stands behind any and every text that is in some way defending Judaism against outside influence, they often perceive reference to the observance of specific commandments where in fact there is none. In the first chapter of Daniel, for example, Daniel resides at the palace of the Babylonian king Nebuchadnezzar, because he has been specially selected to be one of the king's wise men. These men are afforded every courtesy, which includes royal rations of food and wine. The narrative tells us, however, that "Daniel resolved that he would not defile himself with the royal rations of food and wine" (Dan 1:8).

In most annotated editions of the Bible and commentaries on Daniel, commentators explain that Daniel refuses to eat the royal rations because he keeps kosher.[36] Daniel would rather die of starvation than violate Jewish dietary laws. Yet, while Daniel says he does not want to defile himself by eating what is offered, exactly what he fears will cause defilement is not at all clear. The text does not identify the kind of food offered to Daniel and his friends except to call it "royal rations." The working assumption of modern interpreters is that the food must be some kind of meat that is forbidden. But if that is the case, then why does Daniel not ask for some other kind of meat? Why ask for vegetables? The dietary laws of Leviticus 11 are hardly an affirmation of vegetarianism. And what about the wine? Wine is not forbidden, so why can't Daniel drink it?

Another interpretation, however, is possible, even probable. What is really at stake is not any specific commandment or set of commandments about food. If there is danger of violating any law, it is *the law* on which the Israel's covenant with God is predicated: "You shall have no other gods before me." Consumption of the king's food and wine is not in and of itself a problem. Daniel cannot eat the food or drink the wine because the meat—whether it comes from a cow or a pig is irrelevant—has been ritually slaughtered in the context of the Babylonian royal court. That is to say, the meat (or a portion of it) has been sacrificed to another god. It may even be that it constitutes an offering to the king himself (ch. 6). Similarly, the wine is likely perceived to be a libation (5:2–4). All the subsequent stories about Daniel as the great wise man, seer, and counselor to the Babylonian royal court revolve around the issue of idolatry—either in the form of worshipping idols at the command of the king or worshipping the king himself. Thus, the refusal by Daniel and his friends to partake of the "royal rations" in the first chapter of Daniel constitutes the first instance of their unwillingness to worship anyone or anything that is not the God of Israel, or the Most High God, as God is called in Daniel. To have eaten those royal rations would have been the equivalent of worshipping either the god(s) of Nebuchadnezzar or the king himself.

The current scholarly consensus assumes that the scrupulous observance of dietary laws constituted one of the essential foundations of Judaism from the second century BCE.[37] This assumption derives largely from the old habit of projecting rabbinic discussions found in the Mishnah, Talmud, and other collections of rabbinic teaching, which are often of a very technical nature, into an earlier period when, in fact, our evidence for any widespread preoccupation with the details of the laws of *kashrut* is pretty slim.

Jewish dietary laws, of course, were not invented in the rabbinic period but have biblical origins—the foundational text being Leviticus 11. But, interestingly, biblical narrative rarely mentions food as an issue; there is not a single story in which the violation of dietary laws causes conflict in a biblical story or where the neglect of such commandments is specifically named as one of Israel's egregious sins—the kind that cause the prophets to issue judgment oracles and subsequent divine punishment.[38] The Hebrew story of Esther, for example, does not ever raise the question of whether Esther ate only proper Jewish food while she lived in the Persian king's palace. She eats the food given to her by the royal official without hesitation, just as she graciously receives other gifts and beauty treatments offered to her.[39] Similarly, Jehoiachin, a king of Judah who reigned briefly before being taken into captivity in Babylon, is said to have been given a daily portion of food from the Babylonian king Evil-merodach, the successor to Nebuchadnezzar, who apparently bestowed royal hospitality upon Jehoiachin, which the latter graciously received.[40] Among canonical texts, then, Daniel's refusal to eat food offered to him by a Gentile is the exception rather than the rule.

To be sure, outside the biblical canon in the Jewish literature of the Hellenistic period, we find more stories where avoidance of Gentile food is explicitly mentioned.[41] But it is usually mentioned only briefly or in passing; it is generally not the focus of the narrative, and, like Daniel, when the issue of food does crop up, it is not about scrupulously following a complex system of permitted and prohibited foods, but of ensuring that one does not risk eating food offered to idols, because that would constitute a violation of the first commandment, not because it would be a violation of the Levitical laws.

Moreover, what is true of dietary practices is true of other practices prescribed by Torah. Jews did not understand being Torah-observant to mean they were to attend to every jot and tittle, as if every individual prescription represented a divine imperative of the highest order. Jews wanted to live in accordance with Torah, because they believed doing so enabled them to live a righteous life in accord with God's will. As Josephus says, "Him we must worship by the practice of virtue; for that is the most saintly manner of worshipping God."[42] One of foremost experts on extrabiblical Jewish literature, George Nickelsburg, has spoken out strongly against the Christian stereotype of "postbiblical" Judaism's being a legalistic perversion of biblical religion. After surveying a representative sample of the vast array of Jewish literature of this period, including many of the texts I have mentioned in this discussion, Nickelsburg claims, "these texts make relatively little mention of individual commandments of the Torah and the variety of ways in which they might be interpreted and the variety of ways in which they might be applied or modified."[43]

Redemption

Ancient Judaism is not what one would call a religion of salvation. This is perhaps the most fundamental misconception that informs the Christian view of ancient Judaism. With very few exceptions, Judaism does not focus its attention on personal salvation. Furthermore, Judaism does not articulate the issue of salvation as a question about whether one is saved by works or by faith. In fact, the idea that one follows the commandments because of the desire to attain rewards is often condemned. Performing God's commandments should be done out of love for God, not because one wishes to achieve salvation. An early rabbinic commentary on Deuteronomy offers this caution:

> "To love the Lord thy God."—Lest you should say, "I shall study Torah so that I may be rich and so that I may be called Rabbi and so that I may receive a reward in the world to come," Scripture says: "To love the Lord thy God." All that you do, do only from love.[44]

Christians assume that personal salvation is the fundamental question of religion—*all* religion. Salvation is so central to Christianity that Christian theologians even came up with a name for the study of salvation: "soteriology." Therefore, Judaism has typically been evaluated in terms of how salvation is conceptualized and how an individual achieves salvation.

With very few exceptions, there is no notion of eternal life, no resurrection of the body, and no expectation that reward and punishment will be administered after death in the Hebrew Bible.[45] In ancient Israel, divine rewards and punishments come in the form of blessings and curses in this life. Rewards bestowed upon Israel include rain so as to make the land fertile and productive, many children, and great wealth.

There was, however, a conception of redemption or salvation in biblical literature, but it was not something bestowed in the next life or the next world. The biblical paradigm for redemption is the Exodus; redemption is freedom from slavery in Egypt. In prophetic texts, it is salvation from the oppression and violence of various enemies, for example, Babylon, the Seleucid dynasty, and Rome; repossession of the land after exile; and, in some texts, the glorification of Israel in the form of triumph over enemies (rather than just freedom from them).

Then, sometime in the second century BCE, belief in life after death begins to emerge in Jewish texts, or at least in some Jewish texts. By Paul's time, the idea is common, though there are those who reject the idea. The writer of Sirach, an apocryphal Jewish text dated to the early second century, explicitly denies that any kind of postmortem existence awaits human beings.[46] Although no texts written by the Sadducees survive, texts produced by others, including the Gospel of Matthew, tell us that the Sadducees did not believe in life after death. Among those who did believe in life after death, some believed the soul was immortal, that upon the death of the body, the soul returns to its celestial home. But belief in the resurrection of the body did become increasingly common. Many apocalyptic texts envision an end-time resurrection of the dead. Sometimes it is only the righteous who are raised, while presumably the wicked remain permanently nonexistent. Most texts, however, envision the resurrection of everyone, the righteous and the wicked. This resurrection is followed by a final judgment in which the righteous are rewarded with eternal life and the wicked are condemned. Significantly, the Pharisees and subsequently the rabbis embraced the idea of bodily resurrection.

In both the biblical period and later, salvation is primarily envisioned in communal rather than individual terms. A new creation is born from which an idyllic age emerges. Sometimes the focus is exclusively on Israel, that is to say, in some texts Israel triumphs over her enemies, and the people (re)inherit the land. Redemption is imagined in concrete terms. "The twelve tribes are restored, the people gathered back to the Land, the Temple and Jerusalem are renewed and made splendid, the Davidic monarchy restored: God's kingdom is established."[47] There is complete cessation of violence, justice prevails, and Israel lives in peace and prosperity.

Sometimes redemption is envisaged more broadly and the idyllic age involves all of creation. The images that inform this vision for a new age will be familiar to many: people will beat their swords into ploughshares, and the lion will lie down with the lamb. Thus there are biblical traditions that begin to move toward the idea of redemption as a whole new world, but essentially it is conceived in this-worldly terms. But in most Jewish literature produced after the biblical age, redemption is something that comes in "the world to come," as it is called in rabbinic literature.

The traditional Christian understanding of Jewish soteriology is that salvation is earned through "works." God keeps a ledger in which each person's good deeds are weighed against his bad deeds (sins). If a person has more good deeds than bad, he or she earns eternal life, imagined as a blissful existence in the presence of God. If bad deeds outweigh the good, he or she must suffer eternal punishment. Thus salvation in Judaism is imagined as a merit system, which is measured on a quantitative scale. If at the time of death one has performed more acts of righteousness than sins, one is saved.

Yet, contrary to long-standing stereotypes, ancient Jews did not have a peculiarly excessive interest in law; they did not preoccupy themselves with picayune legal details while neglecting more serious ethical matters. Thus, the idea that Judaism is a religion in which one is "saved by works" is not an accurate characterization. Although there are a few scattered references in early Jewish texts to the image of a ledger that God keeps to which every individual will ultimately be accountable, it is just that—an image meant to encourage people to act righteously, not a doctrine of salvation.

The view of Judaism as a religion in which one is "saved by works" carries with it several other misconceptions about Judaism. Of most significance, it denies the important role of grace and repentance in Judaism. Grace not only plays a role in early Jewish thinking about salvation, it plays a critical role. Because Israel has been elected by God to be God's own possession, and because this election is gratuitous—Israel did not earn her special status with God, as we saw earlier in our discussion about Israel's understanding of God—God's special relationship to Israel is predicated on grace, not merit. Israel participates in the covenant as a people, and participating in the covenant grants the people of Israel a privileged status that is ongoing. As E. P. Sanders argued thirty years ago, the vast majority of Jewish sources from the time of Paul understand that participation in the covenant *is* salvation.[48]

The importance of grace is especially manifest in the idea of the "merit of the fathers." This is the idea that all the people of Israel benefit from the extraordinary righteousness of the patriarchs, especially Abraham. God expressed his love for Abraham by making promises of blessing, promises of land, numerous progeny, etc., promises that extend to Abraham's entire family, including future generations. God tells Abraham to "Look toward heaven and count the stars, if you are able to count them. . . . So shall your offspring be" (Gen 15:5, JPS). The biblical narrator immediately follows up God's words with this: "And because he put his trust in the Lord, He reckoned it to his merit" (Gen 15:6, JPS). (The NRSV reads "And he believed the LORD; and the LORD reckoned it to him as righteousness" [Gen 15:6]—this is an important verse for Paul [Rom 4:3; Gal 3:6], which we shall look at later.) Based on comments like this, later interpretations of Abraham hold him up not only as extraordinarily righteous, but as one whose righteousness overflowed to the benefit of those counted as his descendants. Long before the covenant at Sinai, God made a covenant with Abraham *and* Abraham's descendants:

> "I will maintain My covenant between me and you, and your off-spring to come, as an everlasting covenant throughout the ages, to be God to you and to your offspring to come."
>
> God further said to Abraham, "As for you, you and your off-spring to come throughout the ages shall keep My covenant." (Gen 17:7–9, JPS)

God is therefore gracious to Abraham's descendants, the people of Israel. It matters not that they sometimes go astray. As described earlier, God may manifest displeasure or disfavor and punish Israel, but God does not reject Israel. The covenantal bond God established with Israel through his commitment to Abraham is eternal. The merit of the fathers is expressed in different ways, but the concept is always tied to an understanding of God as gracious. Here is one expression of it from the prophet Micah:

> Who is a God like You,
> Forgiving iniquity
> And remitting transgression;
> Who has not maintained His wrath forever
> Against the remnant of his own people,
> Because He loves graciousness!
> He will take us back in love;
> He will cover up our iniquities,
> You will hurl all our sins
> Into the depths of the sea.
> You will keep faith with Jacob,
> Loyalty to Abraham,
> As You promised on oath to our fathers
> In days gone by. (Mic 7:18–20, JPS)

However, grace does not exclude the importance of repentance. In both biblical tradition and later, the posture of humility is a constant theme. Part of being humble is to recognize one's shortcomings, faults, and sins, and, as a consequence, to repent and seek forgiveness. Anyone who makes a sincere effort at repentance can be assured of forgiveness by God and therefore assured of a share in the world to come. The Torah describes an elaborate process of repentance and forgiveness. Indeed, this is precisely the purpose of many sacrificial laws; they are designed to atone for sins so as to return a person to good standing before God.

Ironically and in spite of this, these prescriptions for seeking atonement for sin were seen as "acts" of repentance from the traditional Christian perspective of Judaism, and thus they constituted more "works." Although Christian scholars sometimes noted there were passages in Jewish texts that undermined this stereotype of Judaism—for example, those that refer to the merit of the fathers—they tended to ignore or relativize them. R. H. Charles, a very well respected scholar in his day, provides an excellent illustration of the traditional Christian perspective of Jewish soteriology:

> Every good work . . . established a certain degree of merit with God, while every evil work entailed a corresponding demerit. A man's position with God depended on the relation existing between his merits and demerits, and his salvation on the preponderance of the former over the latter. The relation between his merits and demerits was determined daily by the weighing of his deeds. . . . But as the results of such judgments were necessarily unknown, there could not fail to be much uneasiness, and to allay this doctrine of the vicarious righteousness of the patriarchs and saints of Israel was developed . . . [that a] man could thereby summon to his aid the merits of the fathers, and so counter balance his demerits.
>
> It is obvious that such a system does not admit of forgiveness in any spiritual sense of the term. It can only mean in such a connection a remission of the penalty to the offender, on the ground that compensation is furnished, either through his own merit or through that of the righteous fathers.[49]

From this quotation, it sounds as though Jews would have been in a constant state of hopelessness and anxiety regarding their salvation. It is no wonder that Paul's proclamation of justification by faith came as a huge relief to this oppressive form of religion. But the idea that early Judaism (or later Judaism, for that matter) promulgated the notion of salvation by works is a Christian misunderstanding. Salvation is not conceived as something earned, but something graciously granted to all who enjoy participation in the covenant. As Sanders sums up, "If there is a doctrine of salvation in Rabbinic religion, it is election and repentance."[50]

The question that then must be asked is whether redemption includes only Israel, or to put it another way, only those who stand within the covenant. Moreover, is it only those who remain in good standing within the covenant who will be redeemed at the end of history? Just how inclusive is the vision of redemption? As with biblical tradition, the rabbis most often focus on Israel when discussing the world to come. That is to say, early rabbinic texts are mainly concerned about the redemption of Israel; they address what happens to non-Israelites only infrequently. Unsurprisingly, these texts assert that all Israel will ultimately be redeemed by God. In rabbinic terms, "All Israelites have a share in the world to come."[51] A similar sentiment can be found in virtually every ancient Jewish text that addresses the question of eschatology, from the prophetic literature of the Bible to the postbiblical apocalyptic literature, from the Dead Sea Scrolls to the Greco-Jewish literature of the Apocrypha, as well as to Paul himself, who also claims, "all Israel will be saved" (Rom 11:26, NRSV).

The question is, *Who is Israel?* Traditionally Christian readers of Paul assumed that, when Paul claimed all Israel will be saved, he did not mean the Jews of his day who claimed to be descendants of Abraham. Such readers believed Paul was speaking of *them*, that is to say Christians, followers of Jesus, who understood themselves to be the spiritual descendants of Abraham. There is every reason to interpret Paul, however, as saying exactly the same thing as the rabbis. We will look at this issue later. In the meantime, let us consider what other texts say.

Like Paul in Romans 11:26, most Jewish texts do not specify exactly who Israel is; they assume readers know. However, the issue is sometimes explicitly addressed. The mishnaic tractate *Sanhedrin* states that all Israel is included in the future redemption, but then it goes on to list some exclusions:

All Israelites have a share in the world to come, for it is written, The people also shall be all righteous, they shall inherit the land for ever; the branch of my planting, the work of my hands that I may be glorified (Isa 60:21). And these are they that have no share in the world to come: he that says that there is no resurrection of the dead prescribed in the Law, and [he that says] that the Law is not from Heaven, and an Epicurean.[52]

This text continues on, with certain rabbis identifying more exclusions and refining the kinds of exclusions already named. The list is concerned to name those kinds of people that could conceivably be included in the collective identity of "Israel" but seemingly do not deserve to inherit the world to come. For example, in this context, an Epicurean does not refer to a Gentile, but is rather a generic name for a heretic, someone who had once been a Jew, a part of Israel, but has now renounced that status. Indeed, that is perhaps the most significant point to be made about this text (and others like it). The list of those who do not have a share in the world to come is not a list of people who have simply committed certain sins or who have committed too many sins, as the traditional Christian perspective of Jewish soteriology would have it. The list is illustrative of the kinds of people who have opted out of being part of Israel. To be an Epicurean is to opt out of Israel explicitly and deliberately; to deny the resurrection of the dead is to deny that God's promises to the patriarchs will be fulfilled and thus to deny redemption altogether; and to deny the divine status of the Torah is to deny the covenant that defines the relationship between God and Israel. The naming of exclusions is not a naming of bad Israelites; it is a naming of those who are no longer a part of Israel.

There is another important point illustrated by this example from the Mishnah. As is typical of early rabbinic texts, this text does not address whether the nations (Gentiles) who are not now and never have been part of Israel are included in the world to come. In other words, the list marks a kind of boundary of who constitutes Israel; it does not say anything about the fate of non-Jews. Put another way, to claim that all Israel is saved is not implicitly a claim that the world to come will be populated exclusively by Israelites. So the question is, Are Gentiles part of redemption? Do they have a share in the world to come?

As Paula Fredriksen points out, most biblical texts fall into one of two categories. "At the negative extreme, the nations are destroyed, defeated, or in some way subjected to Israel."[53] At the other extreme, all nations participate in the final redemption, known as the Day of the Lord, envisioned as all the nations converging on Jerusalem along with Israel, in order to worship the God of Israel, the one God. Such imagery is found in several prophetic books. This well-known text from Isaiah provides a nice example:

> *In days to come the mountain of the LORD's house*
> *shall be established as the highest of the mountains, and shall be raised*
> *   above the hills;*
> *all the nations shall stream to it.*
> *Many peoples shall come and say,*
> *"Come, let us go up to the mountain of the LORD, to the house of the*
> *   God of Jacob;*
> *that he may teach us his ways and that we may walk in his paths."*
> *For out of Zion shall go forth instruction, and the word of the LORD*
> *   from Jerusalem.*
> *He shall judge between the nations, and shall arbitrate for many*
> *   peoples;*
> *they shall beat their swords into plowshares, and their spears into*
> *   pruning hooks;*
> *nation shall not lift up sword against nation, neither shall they learn*
> *   war any more. (Isa 2:2–4 = Mic 4:1–3)*

Zechariah offers a similar vision:

> *The inhabitants of one city shall go to another, saying, "Come, let us go*
> *to entreat the favor of the LORD, and to seek the LORD of hosts: I myself*
> *am going." Many peoples and strong nations shall come to seek the LORD*
> *of hosts in Jerusalem, and to entreat the favor of the LORD. Thus says*
> *the LORD of hosts: In those days ten men from nations of every language*
> *shall take hold of a Jew, grasping his garment and saying, "Let us go*
> *with you, for we have heard that God is with you." (Zech 8:21–23)*

Many other biblical texts illustrate a vision of redemption inclusive of Gentiles. And let us be clear: the Gentiles referred to are not converts.

That is to say, they are not people born Gentile who convert to Judaism in this world and then enjoy life in the next world together with Israel. Such individuals would already be considered part of the corporate identity of Israel prior to the eschaton. To be sure, the nations are described as coming to worship the God of Israel in Jerusalem, and thus they are pictured as renouncing their own gods. But this transformation of Gentiles has not happened prior to the moment of redemption; it occurs as part of God's act of redemption.

Following in this prophetic tradition, many postbiblical texts also reflect a broadly inclusive vision of salvation, in which Jew and Gentile participate in the new creation. The book of Tobit, a text found in the Apocrypha, serves as another example: "Then the nations in the whole world will all be converted and worship God in truth. They will all abandon their idols, which deceitfully have led them into their error; and in righteousness they will praise the eternal God. . . . Those who sincerely love God will rejoice, but those who commit sin and injustice will vanish from all the earth" (Tob 14:6–7).[54] In rabbinic literature, one can find similar imagery. One of the oldest and most important Jewish prayers, the Alenu, articulates this hopeful vision of the world to come:

> We hope, therefore, Lord our God, soon to behold thy majestic glory, when the abominations shall be removed from the earth and the false gods exterminated; when the world shall be perfect . . . , and all humankind will call upon thy name. . . . May they bend the knee and prostrate themselves and give honor to thy glorious name. May they all accept the yoke of thy kingdom.[55]

The reader may still wonder, is this not conversion? The simple answer is no. To become a Jew requires that one be born of a Jew (and not have renounced that Jewish identity by worshipping another god or gods) and/or that one undergo certain ritual acts, of most importance, circumcision. (At this point in Jewish history, what, if any, ritual act a woman had to undergo is not clear. Male-specific rituals and commandments are the norm.) As we will see clearly in the next chapter, Gentiles who worship or even respect the one God that Israel acknowledges are regarded as righteous Gentiles, not as Jews. Circumcision is what distinguishes a Jew from a Gentile. Yet, as Fredriksen says, Christian interpreters "routinely slip from seeing the eschatological *inclusion* of Gentiles as meaning eschatological conversion. This is a category error. Saved Gentiles are *not* Jews."[56] Gentiles are human beings, created by God, and in the image of God, but Jews and Gentiles are fundamentally different kinds of people. To anticipate the conclusion of this book, God created the world as a multiplicity of things and sentient creatures. To respect the plurality of creation is a recognition of the divinely ordained order of things; it is to recognize and respect God's preeminent reign over creation.

Just as the lion lies down with the lamb, so the Jew and the Gentile come together in peace and harmony. To envision the world to come as a time of peace among all the peoples of the world is to envision a world where there still exists many different peoples, for there would be no significance to the image of peace if in the world to come there is only one nation. To be sure, that this vision of a world redeemed includes everyone worshipping the one God is a reflection of the fact that this is still a Jewish vision of redemption—as opposed to a Hindu or Buddhist vision. Nevertheless, it is a broadly inclusive image of life in the next world.

6

Who Is and Who Isn't a Jew?

Because Paul is famous for his outreach to Gentiles, and because that outreach is perceived to constitute a move away from the exclusionary attitude that characterized traditional Judaism, it is important to consider what the ancient sources tell us about Jews' attitude toward Gentiles. Some readers may be surprised to learn just how open many Jews were to non-Jews.

Biblical and Second Temple texts represent differing attitudes toward Gentiles. Some construct Jews and Gentiles as two absolute categories of persons and between which there is an impermeable boundary; some express vitriolic hostility; some recognize various forms of kinship between Jews and other nations; and some barely make a distinction between Jew and Gentile at all. One scholar has argued that differing attitudes toward Gentiles, especially with regard to Gentiles' access to Jewish identity—through conversion, intermarriage, etc.—may be the single greatest factor that led to the sectarianism of the late Second Temple period.[1]

At the same time, while recognizing that there was a plurality of attitudes toward Gentiles at this time, I intend to demonstrate that certain attitudes were more typical throughout most of antiquity than other attitudes. Specifically, while ancient Jewish authors display an air of superiority toward non-Jews—the kind of mentality that virtually all peoples have of themselves vis-à-vis outsiders—they do not regard Gentiles as anathema, a source of pollution to be avoided at all costs. Overwhelmingly, Jewish texts from antiquity, both biblical and postbiblical, do not demonize and excoriate Gentiles simply because they are Gentiles. On the contrary, the most vituperative rhetoric among Jews is directed at other Jews. The Jews of biblical antiquity perceived some degree of permeability in the Jew/Gentile boundary, otherwise conversion to Judaism—a development most likely of the second century BCE—would never have been conceivable.

Perhaps the best way to undo the traditional perception that Jews of antiquity were hostile toward Gentiles is to begin with the observation that Jews did not regard Gentiles as inherently "unclean."[2] In most of the literature of this period, Gentiles were not regarded as defiled or in a permanently degraded state of impurity; neither were they a source of defilement to Jews. This is a simple observation, but it requires repeated emphasis because, in my experience, people tend to receive this information with disbelief; at the very least, it strikes them as counterintuitive. So here it is again: *Gentiles were not susceptible to ritual impurity, and Jews did not contract impurity by contact with Gentiles.* Leviticus and other portions of Torah devote considerable attention to detailing the various ways a Jew incurs ritual impurity, yet contact with Gentiles is never mentioned as a source of such impurity.[3] Moreover, the rabbinic system of purity and impurity, which, following the tradition of the Pharisees, elaborated and extended biblical purity laws, accepts as a basic premise that Gentiles are not intrinsically impure according to *Torah law.*[4]

Wherever a stipulation is embedded in a section of Torah explicitly addressed to the Israelites (e.g., Lev 12:1: "The LORD spoke to Moses, saying: Speak to the people of Israel . . ."), the rabbis infer this to mean that Gentiles are excluded from the obligations contained therein.[5] The rabbis' reasoning is consistent with the widespread premise of Jews in antiquity that Israel was uniquely chosen by God and that the covenant was the expression of this uniqueness. It is no surprise, then, that the covenant includes laws that enable Israel to demonstrate her unique status by prescribing special obligations that do not apply to other nations. Only those who are party to the covenant are obligated to observe these special laws. Thus Gentiles are exempt and there is no expectation that Gentiles observe these laws or even that they *should* observe these laws. One could even argue that it would be inappropriate for Gentiles qua Gentiles to undertake such observances, unless, of course, they convert to Judaism.

As discussed in the previous chapter, these special obligations have virtually nothing to do with morality. Instead, their intent is to ensure Israel's special status as God's "treasured possession" and her sanctity (Deut 7:6). Because Gentiles are not party to the covenant, they have never been sanctified or consecrated to God, and thus they are in no danger of a close encounter with the divine, so to speak, so they cannot be at risk of ritual impurity.[6] Put another way, the susceptibility to ritual impurity correlates to sanctity. The greater the degree of sanctity, the greater scrupulousness is required in observing purity. That is why the priests are obligated to observe more extensive purity regulations than ordinary Israelites. Similarly, less is required of Gentiles than of ordinary Israelites. That Gentiles are not susceptible to ritual impurity is strikingly illustrated by texts from the Mishnah in which the rabbis explicitly note that bodily fluids like menstrual blood and semen that flow from Gentiles are *clean*, following Torah law, while the same bodily discharges from Israelites are *unclean*. That is to say, the former are not susceptible to impurity, which makes them intrinsically pure; the latter are susceptible to impurity and thus required to follow the laws of purity. Consider the following *halakhic* assertion: "If a Gentile woman discharged semen from an Israelite it is unclean. If an Israelite woman discharged semen from a Gentile, it is clean."[7] Hayes explains, "In other words, the Israelite semen retains its defiling capacity within a Gentile woman, whereas the Gentile semen does not acquire the capacity to defile within an Israelite woman."[8] In a later discussion, we shall see how Paul employs a parallel form of reasoning in discussing marital unions between "believers" and "nonbelievers."

To be sure, there are numerous ancient Jewish texts that limit relations between Jews and outsiders. One would be hard-pressed to find any well-defined group of people that does not regulate the way in which its members and outsiders interact. Boundaries must be somehow defined and maintained in order for a social group to exist at all and for its members to have any sense of group identity. Of course, what has received the most attention from commentators traditionally are those texts that severely restrict relations with outsiders and which do so in ways that are expressly hostile and seemingly xenophobic. More often than not, however, expressions of hostility and laws proscribing interaction with outsiders are directed to specific groups or kinds of Gentiles and reflect particularly charged historical or theological situations.

Severe proscriptions are usually directed at Gentiles who are either Israel's enemies or people perceived as immoral or, most often, both.

Take for example, Deuteronomy 7:1–6, a *locus classicus* for illustrating Jewish xenophobia:

> *When the* LORD *your God brings you into the land that you are about to enter and occupy, and he clears away many nations before you—the Hittites, the Girgashites, the Amorites, the Canaanites, the Perizzites, the Hivites, and the Jebusites, seven nations mightier and more numerous than you—and when the* LORD *your God gives them over to you and you defeat them, then you must utterly destroy them. Make no covenant with them and show them no mercy. Do not intermarry with them, giving your daughters to their sons or taking their daughters for your sons, for that would turn away your children from following me, to serve other gods. Then the anger of the* LORD *would be kindled against you, and he would destroy you quickly. But this is how you must deal with them: break down their altars, smash their pillars, hew down their sacred poles, and burn their idols with fire. For you are a people holy to the* LORD *your God; the* LORD *your God has chosen you out of all the peoples on earth to be his people, his treasured possession.*

To be sure, there is no way to make this text nice. It calls for the annihilation of the nations, *goyim*, of the land, the land that God is now giving to Israel. What must be noted, however, is that God's command here applies specifically to the seven nations of the land, not all the nations of the world. The peoples of the land, whom God condemns to destruction at the hands of the Israelites, are not destroyed simply because they are Gentiles. There is nothing inherently impure, immoral, or otherwise defective to the point of deserving condemnation that characterizes all other nations in general. Moral impurity results from accumulated sinful behavior intolerable to God (i.e., idolatry, sexual immorality, and bloodshed), whether the sinners are Jew or Gentile, and it potentially defiles individuals and whole groups in some cases. Notably, it defiles the land (and all that is associated with it), which apparently renders a place uninhabitable by God.

That the condemnation of the peoples of the land does not apply generally to all Gentiles is made plain later in Deuteronomy. In giving instructions on conduct in warfare, God tells Israel that it may take the women, children, livestock and other booty of the enemy to enjoy at will (see Deut 20:14). A clarification then follows that delimits the allowance of booty: "Thus you shall treat all the towns that are very far from you, which are not towns of the nations here. But as for the towns of these peoples that the LORD your God is giving you as an inheritance, you must not let anything that breathes remain alive. You shall annihilate them" (20:15–17; cf. 13:12–17). Booty from the peoples of the land is banned because the land and everything in it has become polluted through accumulated moral impurity.

Furthermore, there are numerous laws in the Torah that explicitly include non-Israelites, most frequently those pertaining to the *ger*, the resident alien, a Gentile who dwells long-term within Israel. For example, while the dietary laws of Leviticus 11 do not extend to resident aliens, the prohibition against consuming anything while its blood remains in it does (see Lev 17:10–14). The stated rationale, "For the life of every creature is its blood . . . ," as well as the punishment "whoever eats it shall be cut off," indicates that this is a form of moral impurity, and it is therefore an ethic that applies to all peoples. A similar pattern can be observed in the laws regulating sexuality in Leviticus 18: "You shall keep my statutes and my ordinances and commit none of these abominations, *either the citizen or the alien* who resides among you . . . otherwise the land will vomit you out for defiling it, as it vomited out the nation that was before you" (vv. 26–28; emphasis added).

Many laws of Torah have as a presumption that Jews and Gentiles live and work together. In the same chapter of Leviticus that says, "You shall love your neighbor as yourself" (Lev 19:18), it also says, "You shall love the alien as yourself" (Lev 19:34; cf. Exod 10:19). There are even stipulations allowing non-Israelites participation in festivals and cultic life.

An alien who lives with you, or who takes up permanent residence among you, and wishes to offer an offering by fire, a pleasing odor to the LORD, shall do as you do. As for the assembly, there shall be for both you and the resident alien a single statute, a perpetual statute throughout your generations; you and the alien shall be alike before the LORD. You and the alien who resides with you shall have the same law and the same ordinance. (Num 15:14–16)

This text gives the impression that virtually any cultic rite in which an Israelite can participate a *ger* may participate as well, though such participation is voluntary.

A few texts even indicate that undergoing circumcision did not necessarily turn one into an Israelite (see Exod 12:48). In ancient Israel there does not seem to have been as much emphasis on circumcision as *the* marker of identity compared to later, during the Maccabean period, when circumcision becomes the distinguishing marker of Jewish identity for males. By Paul's time, circumcision is often mentioned by non-Jewish writers as the distinguishing mark of Jewishness, in spite of the fact that ancient ethnographers were aware that other "barbarian" peoples practiced circumcision.[9] Still, rhetoric must be distinguished from reality. As Shaye Cohen has convincingly argued, since circumcision is applicable only to half the population, and since people in antiquity did not generally appear in public nude, it is difficult to imagine that circumcision ever served as a useful way to distinguish a Jew from a Gentile in antiquity.[10]

The question must be raised concerning whether and in what ways a *ger* in ancient Israel was distinguishable from an Israelite. If a *ger* observed the Sabbath, participated in cultic life by making sacrificial offerings to the God of Israel, and (if male) was circumcised, how could one differentiate a resident alien from an Israelite? I suspect that, at least in many cases, one couldn't. It is no surprise, then, that the Hebrew word *ger* in rabbinic literature comes to mean "proselyte," i.e., someone who has converted to Judaism. In sum, the laws of Torah as well as numerous biblical stories indicate the political, social, and religious incorporation of non-Israelites into Israelite society to varying degrees, in some cases extending to full assimilation.

What was true in ancient Israel is likely only more true in the Hellenistic period. After the Babylonians destroyed the first temple and Jews went into exile, some of whom never returned, and diaspora communities emerged, the permeability of boundaries between Jew and Gentile only increased. Cohen has shown that Jews of the Hellenistic period were, quite literally, indistinguishable from Gentiles. Cohen surveys a vast array of ancient literature, looking for all the characteristics he can think of that would make a Jew recognizably Jewish—e.g., physical features, language, clothing, names, occupations, etc.—and concludes that none of these things served as indicators of Jewishness.[11] So how did you know a Jew in antiquity when you saw one? Ultimately, Cohen says, you didn't. However, you could reasonably infer that a person was Jewish in two ways: First, a person was likely to be Jewish if he or she kept company with other Jews. That is, if he or she appeared to be socially integrated into the Jewish community. Second, a person was likely to be Jewish if seen engaging in certain practices typical of Jews, like abstention from pork and Sabbath observance. Such inferences, while reasonable, would be no guarantee of someone's Jewish identity, however, because "Gentiles often mingled with Jews and some Gentiles even observed Jewish rituals and practices. As a result, these reasonable conclusions would lead you to label some Gentiles as Jews."[12] The reverse confusion was also possible: a Jew could be mistaken for a Gentile if he or she did not regularly interact with a (discernable) Jewish community or if not visibly observant. I suspect that there were almost as many varying degrees of observance in antiquity as there are today. As we shall see when we discuss the Pharisees in the next chapter, there would be no reason for groups like the Pharisees to exist if Torah observance was uniform among the Jewish population.

I highlight the intangibility of the boundary between Jew and Gentile because it is generally assumed that Jews were not only easily distinguished from others but that Jews' preference for their own kind was extreme. Jews, in other words, kept to themselves, avoiding as much as possible interaction with non-Jews. Indeed, Jews in antiquity developed a reputation for their unwillingness to mingle with other peoples. This reputation is evident in the New Testament. In Acts 10:28, Peter reportedly says to some new non-Jewish friends, "You yourselves know that it is unlawful for a Jew to associate with or to visit a Gentile; but God has shown me that I should not call anyone profane or unclean." This social exclusivity appears in a few other texts of the Second Temple period. The book of Jubilees, an apocryphal work that rewrites biblical history with a view toward the liturgical cycle of feast days, is often cited as evidence that Jews strenuously avoided interaction with non-Jews.

And you also, my son Jacob, remember my words, and observe the commandments of Abraham, your father: Separate yourself from the nations, and eat not with them. And do not according to their works, and become not their associate; for their works are impure and all their ways are a pollution and an abomination and uncleanness. They offer their sacrifices to the dead and they worship evil spirits, and they eat over the graves and all their works are vanity and nothingness. (22:16)[13]

This text appears to confirm what Peter says in Acts and does so with a more strident tone. A few texts from Qumran are sometimes cited as evidence of Jews' desire to keep themselves separate and distinct from all other peoples.[14] It should come as no surprise that such texts also demonstrate strong abhorrence of intermarriage.

However, contrary to popular belief, there is no categorical ban on intermarriage to be found among the laws of the Torah. While intermarriage with the peoples of the land is, along with all other forms of contact, absolutely forbidden in Deuteronomy 7 (quoted above), Deuteronomy 20:10–14 expressly permits marriage to a foreign woman taken captive in war, even prescribing the appropriate procedures for transforming her into a legal wife. Only priests, for whom a whole set of special marriage laws obtain, are subject to a law requiring endogamy (see Lev 21:13–15).[15] Although biblical texts often demonstrate a clear preference for endogamy (e.g., the patriarchal narratives in Genesis), nearly as many indicate marriages were contracted with foreign women and that through such marriages foreign women were assimilated into Israel.[16]

During the postexilic period, however, a strain of Jewish tradition emerged that, in distinction to the integrationist approach of the earlier biblical period, condemned all forms of exogamy. Jubilees and 4QMMT advocate a view in which Israel's "seed" is itself pure and must not be mingled with the seed of Gentiles, because Israel's seed is holy—it has been set apart from the nations; it has been specially consecrated to God and is therefore holy and wholly different from the nations. Jubilees' polemic against miscegenation relies on a literalist interpretation of Exodus 19:5–6, where God declares that Israel shall be a kingdom of priests and a holy nation.[17] Exodus 19:5–6 was never intended as a demand for every Israelite to function literally as a priest, since the book of Exodus itself makes a clear distinction between priests and lay Israelites. Genealogical status mattered for priests but not for ordinary Israelites. But works like Jubilees and 4QMMT reflect a broadened priestly perspective, one that extended and enhanced the ideas of purity and holiness as they pertained to Israel's collective identity. This genealogical purity had to be maintained in order for Israel to maintain her holy status and her covenantal bond with God. The only way to maintain it was by prohibiting Jews from marrying Gentiles under *any* circumstances.

Such a vision of genealogical purity precludes the possibility of a Gentile assimilating into Israel through marriage (as was evidently possible in ancient Israel) or of conversion. If Gentiles come from a wholly different seed from which Israel must remain separate, then it does not matter if an individual Gentile abandons idols in favor of exclusively worshipping the God of Israel. If the concept of the "holy seed" is the core determinant of Jewish identity, what Gentiles do and don't do becomes irrelevant. For the authors of Jubilees and 4QMMT, there is an impermeable boundary between Jew and Gentile.[18]

But this understanding of Jewish identity does not represent the majority view among Jews of antiquity. In fact, it is likely that writings like Jubilees and 4QMMT are reactionary responses to the very thing they seek to prevent: a high degree of permeability between Jew and Gentile resulting in the incorporation of Gentiles into the Jewish community to varying degrees. Although we do not possess evidence of a standardized procedure for conversion to Judaism before the rabbinic period, there is evidence that Gentiles could be and in fact were converted to Judaism and that such people were entitled to marry Jews and, ultimately, to become full-fledged members of Israel. Furthermore, there were other options besides conversion for Gentiles who were attracted to Judaism. Not only was the boundary between Jew and Gentile in antiquity permeable, but the boundary itself is best conceived of not as a finite linear border but as a group of successive bands or fields representing varying degrees of porosity.[19]

In *Contra Apion*, Josephus extols the virtues of Jewish history, customs, and institutions against the calumnious claims made by some Gentile writers. One such charge is that Jews swear an oath before God and all heaven and earth "to show no good will to a single alien, above all to Greeks." In refuting this charge, Josephus first appeals to the similarities between Jews and Greeks: "we are severed more by our geographical position than by our institutions, with the result that we neither hate nor envy them." Indeed, continues Josephus, many Greeks "have agreed to adopt our laws; of whom some have remained faithful, while others, lacking the necessary endurance, have again seceded."[20] He goes on to argue that the Jewish constitution embodies the very highest ideals of human justice, and he details some specific areas of Jewish law to illustrate this. In discussing laws governing human relations, Josephus returns to the treatment of aliens:

> To all who desire to come and live under the same laws with us, he gives a gracious welcome, holding that it is not family ties alone which constitute relationship, but agreement in the principles of conduct. On the other hand, it was not his pleasure that casual visitors should be admitted to the intimacies of our daily life.[21]

"Not family ties alone" determine membership in the Jewish *ethnos*, but "agreement in principles of conduct." Thus Josephus explicitly recognizes the porosity of Jewish society, both in terms of legal structures and in actual practice.

For Josephus and other Jewish Hellenistic writers, Judaism and Jewish society is marked not so much by peculiarity as by the ability to embody the highest values of the ideal human community—at least as it was envisioned by the people who formed the *oikoumene* (the common "civilized" habitation) of the Greco-Roman world. Indeed, Josephus insinuates that Jews are the only ones who have actually realized the ideal human society through their constitution, whereas most other political philosophers may have drafted admirable proposals for such constitutions (like Plato), but their societies have been unable to embody those ideals.[22]

By the time of Josephus, Philo, and Paul, a tradition had already been established of conceptualizing the Jewish people as bound by—and bounded by—a single ideal *politeia*. *Politeia* is a common Greek term often translated "constitution," by which is meant "way of life." It can also be translated "citizenship." The books of Maccabees and the Letter of Aristeas provide evidence that sometime during the Hasmonean period Jewish identity was reconceptualized; it began to break away from dependence on geography and genealogy and instead became dependent on the notion of belonging to a common *politeia*. *Politeia* is very much a Hellenistic concept, in which the identity of a "people" is not determined by either geography or ethnicity (though these aspects may still play a role) but rather by its *politeia*.

Before Jewish writers appropriated their strategy, Hellenistic writers redefined what it meant to be Greek. Isocrates (436–338 BCE) said that being Greek was not a matter of birth or nature, but of common thought and education.[23] Jewish Hellenistic writers reflect the same kind of understanding of being Jewish. In other words, for most Jews of the late Second Temple period, to be a Jew meant that one regarded oneself as a citizen of the Jewish *politeia,* and that *politeia* was enshrined in the Torah.

A community defined by a *politeia* functions with more permeable boundaries than does a community defined by geographic borders or by genealogical descent. One may become a citizen simply by adopting the ways of the *politeia.* Thus, individuals and sometimes whole communities once considered barbarian became "Greek" or "Roman," as the case may be, including some Jews.[24] If Jews could become Greeks, why couldn't—why shouldn't—Greeks become Jews?[25] By appropriating the Greek model of *politeia,* Judaism became a cultural option analogous to, but clearly distinct from, Hellenism.[26] Geography and genealogy continued to play some role in conceptualizing Jewishness, but these factors ceased to be either necessary or sufficient conditions for determining membership in the Jewish community.[27] The concept of the Jewish *politeia* worked well in a situation where large numbers of Jews lived in diaspora communities, some of which had existed for generations and had consequently become a prominent presence in their respective locations.[28]

The dispersal of Jewish communities around the Mediterranean and the prominence of some of them obviously caused increased interaction between Jews and non-Jews. There is no way to acquire accurate figures, but significant numbers of Gentiles took an interest in Judaism. Toward the end of *Contra Apion* Josephus waxes effusively on the widespread influence of Jewish customs, beliefs, and laws.

[T]hroughout the whole world . . . our laws . . . have to an ever increasing extent excited the emulation of the world at large.

Our earliest imitators were the Greek philosophers, who, though ostensibly observing the laws of their own countries, yet in their conduct and philosophy were Moses' disciples, holding similar views about God, and advocating the simple life and friendly communion between man and man. But that is not all. The masses

have long since shown a keen desire to adopt our religious observances; and there is not one city, Greek or barbarian, nor a
single nation, to which our custom of abstaining from work on the
seventh day has not spread, and where the fasts and the lighting of
lamps and many of our prohibitions in the matter of food are not
observed. Moreover, they attempt to imitate our unanimity, our
liberal charities, our devoted labour in the crafts, our endurance
under persecution on behalf of our laws. The greatest miracle of
all is that our Law holds out no seductive bait of sensual pleasure,
but has exercised this influence through its own inherent merits;
and as God permeates the universe, so the Law has found its way
among all mankind.[29]

Josephus no doubt speaks hyperbolically; the statement that "there
is not one city . . . to which our custom of abstaining from work on
the seventh day has not spread . . ." cannot be taken literally. Interestingly, however, Philo says virtually the same thing, even though both
literarily and geographically he writes in a different context.[30] Although
historians must take account of the exaggerated rhetoric and apologetic
motives of Jewish writers like Philo and Josephus, the widespread influence of Judaism among non-Jews to which they give testimony is supported by other kinds of evidence.[31]

The Roman satirist Juvenal, for example, is famous among historians
for his laments about the corrupt influence of Judaism and other foreign
cults on Roman tradition. He complains caustically about some unfor-
tunate fellow Romans "who have had a father who reveres the Sabbath,"
and who worships "nothing but clouds and the divinity of the heavens."
It is clear that Juvenal is speaking about Jewish practices performed by
Romans and the ill-fated consequences for the future children of Rome.
For he continues, "In time they [the children] take to circumcision.
Having been wont to flout the laws of Rome, they learn and practice
and revere the Jewish law. . . . For all of which the father was to blame,
who gave up every seventh day to idleness."[32]

Stories in Hellenistic Jewish literature about Gentiles who convert to
Judaism appear frequently. A Jewish novella roughly dated to the first
century BCE known as *Joseph and Asenath* recounts the story of how the
daughter of an Egyptian priest came to marry the famously prudish
Joseph.[33] Part of Joseph's meteoric rise to power in Egypt entails Pha-

raoh's giving "Asenath daughter of Potiphera, priest of On" to Joseph as a wife (Gen 41:45). Asenath is the mother of Ephraim and Manasseh, whom Jacob blesses and effectively adopts, thereby reckoning them among the eponymous ancestors of the tribes of Israel. The biblical narrative reveals no anxiety about Asenath's being a foreign woman. She is mentioned in Genesis only in passing; no details about the nature of her marriage to Joseph are given. Later interpreters, however, saw a potential interpretive problem in an ancestral matriarch of Israel being an Egyptian. *Joseph and Asenath* addresses the problem by filling the gap in the biblical story with a romantic tale in which Asenath "converts" to Judaism by dramatically foreswearing idols and pledging her exclusive devotion to the God of Israel. Her transformation is marked by prayer and mystical experiences, rather than standardized rituals as later Jewish law would require.

There is substantial evidence that "theological conversion" was recognized by many Jews in antiquity as a *kind* of conversion or—recognizing the potential confusion in using the word "conversion"—a legitimate religious orientation appropriate to Gentiles. A transformation from polytheism and idolatry to aniconic monotheism was understood as an acknowledgement both of the truth of Judaism and of religious truth generally. Philo speaks of "all who spurn idle fables and embrace truth in its purity, whether they have been such from the first or through conversion to the better side have reached that higher state."[34] To be sure, Philo goes on to explain further that these "proselytes" do become members of the Jewish commonwealth (*politeia*), and this entails leaving behind their former family and friends. But, interestingly, Philo makes no mention of circumcision as a necessary ritual marking the transformation to the "higher state"—not in *Special Laws*, or in any other treatise, in spite of several references to proselytes in Philo's works.[35] Indeed, elsewhere Philo seems to speak of proselytes as if they are not physically but only spiritually circumcised.[36]

In addition to mixed marriage and conversion, another way to gauge both Jewish openness to Gentiles and Gentile interest in Judaism is to explore the category of "God-fearers." The Greek term *theosebes*, usually translated "God-fearer" or "God-worshipper," as well as equivalent expressions,[37] became in the late Hellenistic period a designation used of Gentiles who were regarded as pious by Jewish standards. Of course Jews had long used versions of the same expression in Hebrew and Greek to describe the piety of other Jews. The "fear of God" is a common expression in biblical literature, used to designate the virtue of piety to which all Jews should aspire, and it continued to be used with respect to other Jews in Jewish Hellenistic literature.[38] But in the Hellenistic period, "God-fearer" becomes a common way for Hellenistic Jewish writers to speak of favored Gentiles. It is doubtful that there were precise requirements that had to be met for any given Gentile to be called a "God-fearer," but generally it refers to Gentiles who were either respectful of the Jewish God or of the Jewish community or both.

Scholars long debated whether "God-fearers" constituted a category of persons with a recognized status of some sort—in other words, Gentiles who, though not proselytes or converts, had some kind of standing in the Jewish community—or whether "God-fearer" was simply a way for a Jew to pay a non-Jew a compliment for demonstrating reverence to the Jewish God or for an act of patronage that benefited the Jewish community. An important inscription recently discovered in the ancient city of Aphrodisias has tipped the scales in favor of seeing God-fearers as Gentiles who had gained some sort of official or semiofficial recognition in at least some Jewish communities in Greco-Roman antiquity.[39] Moreover, calling a Gentile "God-fearing" in some cases signaled that such a person had been transformed from being an idolatrous worshipper of many gods to an aniconic monotheist—in other words, a person who had undergone a theological conversion that Jews valued and recognized.[40] But Aphrodisias in particular provides an important piece of evidence attesting to the fact that in some cities of the Greco-Roman world, Jews recognized certain Gentiles and honored them with a label that had theological and/or social significance to the Jewish community, even if the term was not used with categorical precision.[41]

Some think of the God-fearers as a social category in between the simple binary taxonomy of Jew and Gentile that we assume typically informed the Jewish outlook on the world, but this conception is not helpful. The Jews of antiquity did indeed make a fundamental distinction between Jew and Gentile. Such a distinction was probably essential to the preservation of Jewish identity, especially in the Diaspora. Paul himself is testimony to the perduring power of this binary division of humanity for Jews, even the most urbane ones. What I wish to stress is the way in which Jews of the Diaspora—or at least many parts of the

Diaspora—were integrated into the social and civic life of the cities in which they dwelled. Similarly, Gentiles could be active participants in synagogue life. The Gentiles regarded as God-fearers are best thought of as the Jewish Hellenistic equivalent of the *ger*, the resident alien of ancient Israel. Like the *ger*, the God-fearer acquires standing in the Jewish community and could be socially integrated into the Jewish community without being completely subsumed into the corporate identity of Israel.

Jewish communities managed to maintain their distinctive identity, but the maintenance of that identity did not require physical and social separation from Gentiles. Evidence of diverse kinds continues to point to Jew-Gentile interaction of virtually every sort one can imagine: through business transactions in the marketplace, involvement in politics on both the local and imperial levels (the latter as evidenced by long-standing connections between the Herodian family and the imperial household), as well as through social, cultural, and religious points of contact in which Jews and Gentiles mutually influenced one another.

Sabbath observance provides a good example. Evidence from several sources leads us to believe that Jewish communal gatherings on the Sabbath involved the public reading and study of Torah and that Gentiles were sometimes present for these gatherings—or, even if not present, Gentiles could potentially be exposed to Jewish teachings since Sabbath gatherings in some places had a high enough public profile. We have already mentioned Josephus's claim in *Contra Apion* about the widespread observance or partial observance of the Sabbath by non-Jews as well as Jews all around the Mediterranean. To that piece of evidence, we may add related comments Josephus makes in his other works, comments made by Philo, as well as the familiarity with the Sabbath among Roman writers.[42] Besides Juvenal (quoted earlier), the poets Horace and Ovid attest to pervasive Sabbath observances among Gentile *plebs*.[43]

But the clearest evidence for the presence of Gentiles in synagogues on the Sabbath, and that these Gentiles were sometimes referred to as God-fearers, comes from Acts, which contains numerous references to these pious Gentiles.[44] In one scene, Paul addresses a synagogue audience in Pisidia Antioch on the Sabbath as "You Israelites and others who fear God" (Acts 13:16). Two other examples from Acts are worth highlighting:

As Paul and Barnabas were going out, the people urged them to speak about these things again the next sabbath. When the meeting of the synagogue broke up, many Jews and devout converts[45] followed Paul and Barnabas, who spoke to them and urged them to continue in the grace of God.

The next sabbath almost the whole city gathered to hear the word of the Lord. (Acts 13:42–44)

The same thing occurred in Iconium, where Paul and Barnabas went into the Jewish synagogue and spoke in such a way that a great number of both Jews and Greeks became believers. (Acts 14:1)

The use of the term "devout converts" in the first excerpt is vague. It could be that the writer of Acts has in mind full-fledged converts. But "devout converts" could be simply an imprecise equivalent for God-fearers, that is, Gentiles who are involved in Jewish life in some way but have not (or not yet) undergone conversion, which for a man most likely meant circumcision (cf. Philo's reference to "uncircumcised proselytes" above). Given what follows in v. 44—that the whole city gathered to hear Paul on the following Saturday—as well as the frequency with which Acts refers to God-fearing Gentiles, I suspect it is the latter. The second excerpt does not use any of the usual "God-fearer" terms, but simply refers to Greeks being present in the synagogue at the time of Paul's sermon. When paired with "Jews," "Greeks" clearly means Gentiles. Paul uses it that way (see Gal 3:28; Rom 1:16). Many other texts from Acts could be highlighted to illustrate the presence of Gentiles in synagogues and that Gentiles were routinely exposed to Jewish preaching and teaching. Acts simply takes for granted the presence of Gentiles in and around diaspora synagogues.

Interaction with Gentiles did not in most instances create the kind of anxiety that has traditionally been assumed for the Jews of antiquity. The vast majority of Jews saw themselves as part of the *oikoumene*, the collection of peoples who made up the "inhabited world" living around the Mediterranean basin. Jews were not merely reactive but also proactive in finding productive Hellenistic avenues to pursue Jewish objectives. Jews translated their Scriptures into Greek, thus producing what we now know as the Septuagint, surely one of the most influential text collections in Western history. While the primary motivation for the

Septuagint may well have been that many Jews had lost Hebrew and now spoke Greek as their primary language, it had the added benefit of making Jewish tradition, history, and law available to a non-Jewish audience, and of this Josephus and Philo and others were very proud. As Eric Gruen observes, Jews in many ways saw diaspora communities not as groups of victimized Jewish exiles but in terms more analogous to how the Romans viewed their colonies. Like Rome, Jerusalem was the "mother city" (literally, *metropolis*); it was the geographic center toward which Jews felt great loyalty.[46] But Jews who lived abroad also became attached to the places in which they dwelt, and they could take on the identity of those localities without feeling any less Jewish. As Josephus says, "All persons invited to join a colony, however different their nationality, take the name of the founders. . . . Our Jewish residents in Antioch are Antiochenes, having been granted the rights of citizenship by its founder, Seleucus. Similarly, those at Ephesus and throughout the rest of Ionia bear the same name as indigenous citizens, a right which they received from Alexander's successors."[47] In the wake of the devastating effects of modern colonialism, it may seem problematic, but some Jews saw those diaspora communities as satellites enabling the spread of Judaism throughout the human community. In light of this "outreach" to Gentiles in diaspora communities, Paul's mission need not be seen as such a novel invention.

Thus, the image of Jewish communities dedicating themselves to maintaining impregnable ramparts and walls of steel so as to keep themselves segregated from the rest of humanity is both historically false and insidious in its stereotyping of Jews and Judaism. Therefore Paul's interaction with Gentiles should not be seen as the radical step it is typically perceived to be.

Chapter

7

The Flexible Pharisees

One often hears that ancient Judaism of the late Second Temple period was the age of sectarianism.[1] There were different schools of thought, typically referred to as sects: Sadducees, Pharisees, and Essenes among other groups, each of which claimed to represent "true" Judaism. That there were indeed such groups is beyond historical dispute. Several sources speak of the three groups just named, and some occasionally mention other Jewish groups that were distinctive in some way or other.[2] What is questionable is the extent to which each of these groups represents a "sect" that construed itself in opposition to other Jewish groups.[3] The Sadducees, for example, could simply be a label for those of priestly descent who view themselves as somehow connected with the temple establishment in Jerusalem. In other words, it is probably not the case that *any* Jew could elect to be a Sadducee on the basis of shared commitments or that the Sadducees saw themselves as anything other than religious elites who claimed certain entitlements. So the Sadducees were likely an exclusive club, but were they a sect?[4] In the case of the Essenes, sources lead us to believe that Essenes sometimes lived apart from other Jews and followed a highly disciplined ascetic lifestyle; and at other times they lived among other Jews, married, and had families. Were all Essenes, then, sectarian, or just some?

We have thus far focused on features of ancient Judaism in general, rather than the peculiar beliefs and practices of distinctive groups of Jews. But there is one "brand" of Judaism that is necessary to explore further. Paul says in Philippians 3:5 that he once styled himself a Pharisee "with regard to Torah," and Acts identifies Paul as a Pharisee as well. Later interpreters have made much of Paul's identity as a former Pharisee, because the Pharisees were presumed to espouse peculiar sectarian ways; specifically, they were judged to be intensely attached to Torah, down to the most minute details.[5] Because Paul's embrace of Jesus was supposedly attended by a rejection of Torah, Paul's "conversion" is made all the more dramatic by his having been a Pharisee. The following discussion, therefore, is an effort to illumine as much as historically possible the Pharisees and the extent to which they should be regarded as sectarian, as a way of better filling out the picture of Paul's Jewish identity. As we shall see, it may be best to think of the Pharisees as a party rather than a sect, because they engaged the wider society more than their reputation gives them credit for.

We have the following sources from which we can learn about the Pharisees: rabbinic traditions about the Pharisees; passages in the writings of Josephus; stories from the Gospels and Acts; and some texts of the Dead Sea Scrolls, which, like the Gospels, tend to portray the Pharisees in an unflattering light. In addition, we have Paul's letters. Paul and Josephus are the only two men who claim to have been Pharisees and whose writings were preserved for posterity; they then stand as the only firsthand witnesses to Pharisaic Judaism, and the extent to which they can be said to represent Pharisaism is difficult to determine. Historians must proceed with caution by using the literary evidence cumulatively and comparatively.

The Pharisees emerge sometime during the Second Temple period, becoming a significant force during the Maccabean era. Josephus portrays them as a political party of sorts who wield considerable power with the populace and, consequently, act as either the agents of the Hasmonean rulers or are treated as enemies. Chronologically speaking, Josephus places the earliest significant role played by Pharisees during the reign of John Hyrcanus (134–104 BCE). According to Josephus, the Pharisees are very influential initially in the court of Hyrcanus, who is said to have followed Pharisaic teachings on Jewish law. However, the malicious intrigues of a few, particularly a Sadducee named Jonathon, managed to create enmity between Hyrcanus and the Pharisees, effectively removing them from court. Hasmonean hostility toward the Pharisees continued through the reign of Hyrcanus's son, Alexander Jannaeus.[6]

After Alexander's death in 76 BCE, an unusual thing happened in the history of Israel: a woman became sovereign. Her name was Alexandra Salome, Alexander Jannaeus's widow. In spite of the fact that Alexander had two adult sons, Josephus claims the Hasmonean king bequeathed the kingdom to her on his deathbed.[7] Although Josephus's two accounts of Alexandra Salome's rise to power differ in the details, in both cases the Pharisees play a key role.[8] In stark contrast to her husband, Alexandra Salome favored the Pharisees, and as a result they became politically powerful and influential during her reign. Their political influence appears to have waned again with the rise of Herod the Great (73 BCE–4 BCE), though Josephus is not explicit about the role played by Pharisees in Herod's court.

Just how much political influence the Pharisees were able to wield, and exactly by what means, is in historical actuality very difficult to gauge. Within the substantial corpus of Josephus's writings, discussion of the Pharisees as a political party is confined to a handful of episodes. For example, while Josephus indicates that the Pharisees were crucial to the successful reign of Alexandra Salome, there is scant mention of specific ways in which they exercised their political will. Moreover, on the few occasions when Josephus labels someone a "Pharisee," their identification as such seems either incidental to the narrative or the relevance of that information is not made explicit. Because one of Josephus's primary interests as a historian of the Jewish people is to recount the stories of political leaders, including detailing all sorts of political intrigue and the fates that each leader met, we might have expected to learn more about individual Pharisaic leaders and the way in which they exercised their power. Unfortunately Josephus simply does not provide that information. Thus, we can only make inferences based on what he tells us, together with what is reported in the other sources.

The Pharisees were likely influential with a broad segment of the population, because, in addition to Josephus, other ancient authors coming from vastly different perspectives perceived them as powerful and felt threatened by them. The Pharisees are no doubt best known from the Gospels, where they are usually portrayed negatively as malicious opponents of Jesus.[9] The Gospels are responsible for the popular image of the Pharisees as spiritually vapid hypocrites who tout their exacting knowledge of Torah while flouting the "spirit" of divine law in their ethical practices. Hostile polemic against the Pharisees is most palpable in the Gospel of Matthew, which, not incidentally, is also considered the most "Jewish" of the gospels. Matthew places in Jesus' mouth an entire speech, unparalleled in the other gospels, devoted to the condemnation of the Pharisees:

"Woe to you, scribes and Pharisees, hypocrites! For you lock people out of the kingdom of heaven. For you do not go in yourselves, and when others are going in, you stop them. Woe to you, scribes and Pharisees, hypocrites! For you cross sea and land to make a single convert, and you make the new convert twice as much a child of hell as yourselves. . . . Woe to you, scribes and Pharisees, hypocrites! For you tithe mint, dill, and cummin, and have neglected the weightier matters of the law, justice and mercy and faith. It is these you ought to have practiced without neglecting the others. . . . Woe to you, scribes and Pharisees, hypocrites! For you clean the outside of the cup and of the plate, but inside they are full of greed and self-indulgence. You blind Pharisee! First cleanse the inside of the cup, so that the outside also may become clean." (Matt 23:13–15, 23, 25–26)

Of first importance to note is that the essential sin of the Pharisees is hypocrisy. On more than one occasion, Matthew says that what the Pharisees teach is basically right and good; the problem is that they do not practice what they preach: "The scribes and the Pharisees sit on Moses' seat; therefore, do whatever they teach you and follow it; but do not do as they do, for they do not practice what they teach" (Matt 23:2–3). And Jesus says in the Sermon on the Mount: "For I tell you, unless your righteousness exceeds that of the scribes and Pharisees, you will never enter the kingdom of heaven" (Matt 5:20). Two observations can be gleaned from these examples: the Pharisees are considered by Jesus' followers to be authorities—for they sit "on Moses' seat"— when it comes to the teaching of Torah. At the same time, Matthew would not critique the Pharisees so severely if the Pharisees were not perceived to be powerful and influential with many of the same people whom Matthew wishes to influence.[10] Thus, while the Pharisees are frequently listed as one of the "sects" of Jews during this period, they hardly kept to themselves. In distinction to the Essenes who retired to the Judean desert in order to live exclusively with others of the same sect, the Pharisees of the Gospels appear engaged in the political and religious life of the Jews of Judea and its environs.[11] They have certain practices and credentials that distinguish them from others, but they do not as a general principle separate themselves from other Jews.[12] Like Jesus, they preach in the marketplace and teach in the public square and seem to have been received with popular appreciation, at least by some segments of the population. It is no coincidence that Jesus' debating partners are usually Pharisees and only very rarely Sadducees (Essenes are never mentioned in the New Testament). In reality, Pharisees as a group probably had little or no political power, in the sense of playing a legally sanctioned role in governing Judea and related territories, at least not during the Herodian period. However, it is likely that some individual Pharisees held high-status positions as midlevel functionaries or advisors in the administration of the Jerusalem temple. While the extent of the Pharisees' role in conspiring to kill Jesus is no doubt exaggerated in the Gospels because of the hostility between leading Pharisees and leading Jesus-followers after the Jewish revolt (66–70 CE), claims of Pharisaic involvement are plausible because the Pharisees were perceived as powerful by other groups who were vying for power.

Texts found among the Dead Sea Scrolls also express hostility toward Pharisees.[13] While that hostility is expressed very differently than in the Gospels, some of the reasons for that hostility appear similar to the motivations of some followers of Jesus. Because the perspectives of the writers of the Dead Sea Scrolls and the writers of the Gospels are so utterly different, claims made about Pharisees common to both are likely to be historically reliable.

The most important overlap between the Scrolls and the Gospels in their critique of the Pharisees is that they are too quick to interpret precepts of the Torah in such a way as to compromise their integrity. Put another way, some of the Pharisees' views were more flexible, more accommodating and, in some cases, considered to be too lenient by other Jews, including some followers of Jesus. Although readers of this book are much more likely to have familiarity with the portrayal of the Pharisees in the Gospels than in the Scrolls, I suspect that it may come as a surprise when I say that the gospel writers view the Pharisees as too *lenient*—a surprise precisely because the Christian stereotype of the Pharisees is that they are legalistic and literalistic, following every precept of the Torah to an exacting degree. As part of that picture, they are assumed to be "conservatives" when it comes to Judaism generally and

Torah observance in particular. But, ironically, it is their reputation for being highly preoccupied with the technicalities of Torah observance that also leads to the perception of them as hypocrites. The Pharisees' intricate knowledge of Torah enables them to twist and turn the law in their interpretations so that they end up defying the law while making it seem as if they are heeding it—this is precisely the critique that the Gospels and the Scrolls share. That is why Jesus says that "unless your righteousness *exceeds* that of the scribes and Pharisees, you will never enter the kingdom of heaven."

Contrary to popular opinion, followers of Jesus advocated for a more "conservative" position on some points of law than the Pharisees did. Their respective views on divorce as recorded in the gospels of Matthew and Mark serve as an excellent illustration of Pharisaic flexibility in comparison to the conservatism of Jesus' followers. The debate on divorce begins with Pharisees posing to Jesus the question of whether divorce is permissible. Jesus responds by conceding that the Mosaic law permits divorce (see Deut 24:1–4) but then says this law was merely one of compromise because of the people's "hardness of heart." For it was not always so, says Jesus, quoting Genesis, "God made them male and female. For this reason a man shall leave his father and mother and be joined to his wife, and the two shall become one flesh" (Mark 10:6–8).[14] Ultimately then, it is not permissible to separate what God has joined. Divorce is forbidden—no exceptions, at least according to the Markan version. In Matthew an exception is made for "unchastity" (Matt 19:9). In other words, divorce is permitted if one's wife has committed adultery. In sum, the debate on divorce portrays Jesus' teaching as strict and the Pharisees as holding too lenient a position with regard to marital law (even when the Pharisees' position comports with the words of Moses!).

We find a similar condemnation of those who take too permissive an attitude toward marriage in the Dead Sea Scrolls. In a document commonly called the Covenant of Damascus, which includes extensive discussion of the proper rules for living in perfect accord with Torah, a critique of other teachers, here nicknamed "the builders of the wall," are collectively condemned as "fornicators" because "they take two wives in their lives," a clear violation of God's law because the "principle of creation" is that "male and female he created them" (Gen 1:27).[15] To be sure, the text is not explicit that this is a situation of divorce; it could apply to those who have been widowed and who marry again. However, given the citation from Genesis 1:27, it seems that the author of this text has in mind divorce and advocates a position similar to the one taught by Jesus. The important point is that the teaching of Jesus and the Scrolls take a position stricter and less flexible with regard to conjugal law than the position ascribed to the Pharisees.

One of the ways in which scholars know that the teachers here being criticized are Pharisees is that a few lines later in the same document another marital practice is condemned, that of niece marriages: "And each man takes as a wife the daughter of his brother and the daughter of his sister. But Moses said: 'Do not approach your mother's sister, she is a blood relation of your mother' (Lev 18:13). The law of prohibited marriages written for males applies equally to females, and therefore to the daughter of a brother who uncovers the nakedness of the brother of her father, for she is a blood relation." For the Scrolls community, the prohibition specified in Leviticus 18:13 is understood in more generalized terms as prohibiting men from marrying the children of their brothers and sisters, that is, their nieces. The ruling is stated in polemical terms, making it clear that other Jews permit these kinds of marriages (indeed, this appears to have been a common practice). Because rabbinic sources preserve traditions about the Pharisees, and because those traditions indicate that Pharisees permitted niece marriages, it seems likely that the Covenant of Damascus is referring to Pharisaic teachings and those who follow them. Although there is no teaching of Jesus preserved in which Jesus condemns Pharisees for niece marriages, the Covenant of Damascus helps provide a broader understanding of how and why other Jews—Jews who do not believe in Jesus and whose polemics are not motivated by the belief that the Pharisees were involved in the death of Jesus—condemned Pharisaic practice. The Pharisees are regarded as too permissive when it comes to the interpretation and application of Torah to marriage and divorce.[16]

While the Scrolls community condemned Pharisaic *halakhic* leniency, those who laid claim to the Pharisees' legacy, the rabbis, evince no embarrassment at their reputation for leniency. Rabbinic traditions about the Pharisees, those of which we can be reasonably certain date to Pharisaic times (i.e., before the destruction of the temple in 70 CE and which are therefore likely to be contemporary with Paul), recite *halakhic* teachings that frequently reflect a permissive stance—permissive, that is, relative to what was commonly expected or to what other authorities taught.[17] Take for example the following saying, found in the Mishnah:

> R. Yosi b. Yoezer of Zereda testified that the Ayil-locust is clean, and that the liquid [that flows] in the shambles [in the Temple] is not susceptible to uncleanness; and that he that touches a corpse becomes unclean. And they called him 'Yosi the Permitter.'[18]

To a reader who has never before been exposed to the Mishnah, this excerpt may be obtuse, so allow me a few explanatory remarks. Yosi b. Yoezer may just be the earliest named Pharisee in history. He stands first in the famous chain of Pharisaic leaders preserved elsewhere in the Mishnah[19] and can therefore be dated to as early as the second century BCE. Yosi's teaching is comprised of three *halakhic* rulings, each of which pertains to a question of ritual purity. Of most importance, each of Yosi's rulings is considered a permissive interpretation of Torah observance. Unfortunately, the third ruling is an enigma, but I will briefly discuss the first two of Yosi's rulings.[20]

First, Yosi declares that a certain type of locust is clean. By declaring it clean, he means either that it is eatable, or that such locusts do not transmit uncleanness inside the temple precincts. The dietary laws of Leviticus forbid the eating of all winged insects with the notable exception of locusts, certain types of locusts being subsequently specified in Leviticus 11:22. There are, however, several varieties of locusts, and questions must have arisen as to whether or not all kinds of locusts are permitted or just some kinds. In other words, one can interpret Leviticus 11:22 as giving examples of the varieties of locusts, all of which are permitted, or as a rule that permits only those types of locusts specified in the text. Leviticus does not specifically name the Ayil-locust as one of the permissible locusts, but Yosi obviously felt the Levitical law was broad enough to include it. With regard to the problem of locusts in the temple, Yosi's ruling may simply mean that a locust that hops or flies from something unclean to something clean does not transmit uncleanness and thus defile the clean vessel.

Yosi's second ruling concerning liquids that are not susceptible to uncleanness is more complicated. Yosi rules that flowing liquids within the temple precincts, liquids like blood (due to incessant slaughtering) and water cannot conduct ritual impurity from one thing to another (or from one place to another). The reader may recall from the earlier discussion (ch. 5) that some kinds of impurity are contagious; some are not. Some substances transmit impurity; some do not. The specific situation envisioned here is one in which a liquid, say water, flowing from a ritually clean vessel or purified space, like an altar, flows into something that is ritually unclean, like an ordinary vessel—does the liquid transmit the uncleanness *back* to the clean vessel? Yosi says no, liquid streams cannot become contaminated from flowing into unclean vessels. Thus, the clean vessels that originally contained the clean liquid cannot be made unclean when their contents spill onto something impure. Yosi's opinion on liquid streams is particularly useful for illustrating the leniency of the Pharisees because, unlike the two other rulings, in this case we have access to the opinions of Yosi's opponents from other sources.

For reasons that are not entirely clear, the issue of whether or not a flowing stream of liquid is capable of transmitting impurity appears to have been hotly debated. Traditions preserved elsewhere in rabbinic literature attest that the Sadducees held the opposite opinion, namely, that streaming liquid is susceptible to uncleanness, and that this particular issue marks one of the key distinctions between Pharisees and Sadducees.[21] Even more interesting is that an important document preserved among the Dead Sea Scrolls raises the same issue and renders an opinion in keeping with the Sadducean view: "Concerning streams of liquid, we have determined that they are not intrinsically pure. Indeed, streams of liquid do not form a barrier between the impure and the pure. For the liquid of the stream and that in its receptacle become as one liquid."[22]

The quotation comes from the document known to Scrolls scholars as 4QMMT, a text I have already mentioned several times. It contains several other teachings like this one that appear to be ruling on some finer points of Torah observance, points that obviously did not enjoy a consensus. Every opinion contained in 4QMMT reflects a stricter interpretation of Torah within the range of available options. The vast majority of scholars think the group responsible for the Scrolls was a subset of the Essenes, not Sadducees, though it appears that on some matters of Torah interpretation the Dead Sea sect and the Sadducees held similar views—views that represent a more stringent perspective than the Pharisees'. Reflecting on Yosi's saying from the Mishnah, Jacob Neusner offers a nice summary statement comparing the different levels of strictness that different groups of Jews advocated:

So Temple authorities applied a stricter rule than did the Pharisees: The locust could receive uncleanness, and purity rules did pertain to the liquids in the Temple slaughterhouse—a considerable inconvenience. The Temple in all respects must be inviolable, and the sanctity rules applied as strictly as possible. This indeed later characterized the priestly Sadducees' view of the purity laws. They saw the laws as strict, but affecting only the Temple. The Pharisees interpreted those laws leniently, but regarded them as applicable everywhere, even in connection with common meals. The Essenes were equally strict but kept the laws only in their commune, where it was relatively easy to do so.[23]

For the person who wishes to understand Paul in historically accurate terms, it is essential to have a historically accurate understanding of Pharisees. The Christian tradition constructed its image of the Pharisees on the basis of the polemical portrait of them in the Gospels and on the assumption that Paul was an ex-Pharisee who rejected everything for which Pharisees stood when he converted to Christianity. The Pharisee came to symbolize all that is religiously and ethically incorrect. So successful was this construction of Pharisaism that it is enshrined in the commonplace usage of the English word group. According to *Merriam-Webster's Collegiate Dictionary* (11th ed.), a Pharisee, when capitalized, is "a member of a Jewish sect of the intertestamental period noted for strict observance of rites and ceremonies of the written law and for insistence on the validity of their own oral traditions concerning the law;" when not capitalized, the label can be applied to anyone considered to be "pharisaical." To be "pharisaical" is to be "marked by hypocritical censorious self-righteousness." A synonym given for "pharisaism" is "hypocrisy."

The reputation of Merriam-Webster notwithstanding, I hope by now it is clear that, while the Pharisees were "noted for strict observance of rites and ceremonies of the written law," they do not constitute the "right wing" of Jewish society. On the contrary, many of their contemporaries criticized them for being too flexible in interpreting prescriptions of Torah. In other words, through their oral traditions they subordinated Torah to human needs and desires and were therefore considered self-serving. In short, the Pharisees were criticized for not being adequately faithful to Torah, which was considered by *all* Jews to be divine law.

The difference between the Pharisees/rabbis and their critics is that the former understood their flexibility in Torah observance as comporting with the divine will. Put another way, they interpreted Torah in a way they considered faithful to the "spirit" of the law.

While the Gospels may not demonstrate much understanding or sympathy for the Pharisaic perspective on the world, much of their critique resembles the criticisms of other Jews. The Gospels and the Scrolls both portray the Pharisees not as faithful guardians and interpreters of Torah but as hypocrites. Stories in the Gospels of the Pharisees' fastidious behavior are intended to show that while the Pharisees can "talk" Torah, they only use it for their own purposes. That is why Jesus in Matthew's gospel warns his followers that unless their righteousness exceeds that of the scribes and Pharisees, they will be shut out of heaven.

Gospel writers tend to blame the Pharisees' compromising interpretation of Torah on their following the "traditions of their ancestors," *instead of* Torah. For the gospels of Matthew and Mark especially, it is precisely because the Pharisees follow the traditions of their ancestors that they do not follow the (written) Torah scrupulously—that is the essence of the gospel critique. A lengthy episode in Mark 7 illustrates this perspective. The opening verses of the chapter set the scene for the debate that will follow:

> *Now when the Pharisees and some of the scribes who had come from Jerusalem gathered around [Jesus], they noticed that some of his disciples were eating with defiled hands, that is, without washing them. (For the Pharisees, and all the Jews, do not eat unless they thoroughly wash their hands, thus observing the tradition of the elders; and they do not eat anything from the market unless they wash it; and there are also many other traditions that they observe, the washing of cups, pots, and bronze kettles.) So the Pharisees and the scribes asked him, "Why do your disciples not live according to the tradition of the elders, but eat with defiled hands?" (7:1–5)*

When the Pharisees ask Jesus why he and his disciples do not follow the "traditions of the elders" but eat with hands defiled, Jesus retorts with a saying from Isaiah, "This people honors me with their lips, but their hearts are far from me; in vain do they worship me, teaching human precepts as doctrines" (vv. 6–7, quotation from Isa 29:13). He then says to the Pharisees, "You abandon the commandment of God and hold to human tradition" (v. 8). The debate is not concluded at this point, but it is Jesus who introduces the next point of contention with a similar comment: "You have a fine way of rejecting the commandment of God in order to keep your tradition!" (v. 9). Thus, Jesus sets the Pharisees' appeal to the "traditions of the elders" in opposition to proper observance of Torah.

Of course, that was not the Pharisees' perspective. To be sure, the Pharisees seemed to have distinguished themselves from other groups of Jews by the value they placed on these "traditions of the elders." They cherished these traditions, and they felt charged to preserve them with care so as to pass them on to future generations. But the Pharisees also saw these traditions as necessary for fulfilling the precepts of the Torah. They recognized that many commandments were not adequately spelled out in Scripture. There was a need for more precise instructions on many matters. While Leviticus appears to many modern readers as excessively detailed about the causes of ritual impurity, for example, and the rites of purification necessary to remove that impurity, the person who tries to put them into practice will quickly realize all that is left unspecified. By their appeal to the "traditions of the elders," the Pharisees and later rabbis gave credibility to the kinds of auxiliary instruction that spelled out Torah observance with greater precision.

Josephus says that the main distinction between the Pharisees and the Sadducees derives from the Pharisees' appeal to these "traditions" as authoritative:

> [T]he Pharisees had passed on to the people certain regulations handed down by former generations and not recorded in the Laws of Moses, for which reasons they are rejected by the Sadducaean group, who hold that only those regulations should be considered valid which were written down, and that those which had been handed down by former generations need not be observed.[24]

Unlike the gospel writers, Josephus represents the Pharisees' reverence for their elders' teaching positively. Never does Josephus give the slightest hint that the elders' teachings compete with the teachings of Torah. On the contrary, the Pharisees are consistently described by Josephus as the most exacting and accurate interpreters of Jewish law, as excelling their fellow Jews in terms of piety and observance, and that they were the leading "school" of the nation, enjoying great popularity with the masses.[25] Indeed, Josephus's overall portrait of the Pharisees is far more flattering than that of the Sadducees: "[The Pharisees] are . . . extremely influential among the townsfolk; and all prayers and sacred rites of divine worship are performed according to their exposition." When holding priestly office, even the Sadducees submit to the teachings of the Pharisees, "since otherwise the masses would not tolerate them."[26]

Josephus also provides evidence of certain beliefs that characterize the Pharisees and that distinguish them from other groups. They believe in life after death and that a person's postmortem existence corresponds to the quality of his or her ethical life in the flesh: if one were righteous, one is rewarded with an easy passage to the next life; if one were wicked, one is subjected to eternal punishment.[27] In this regard the Pharisees hold views similar to the Essenes but quite different from the Sadducees, who reject any notion of life beyond the grave. Josephus also says that the Pharisees believe in divine providence, but not at the expense of free will. Put another way, individuals bear responsibility for the choices they make and thus have a measure of control over their lives, but providence is also at work in a complementary sense. This "middle way" distinguishes the Pharisees from the Sadducees, on the one hand, who think everything that happens is determined solely by human action, and from the Essenes on the other, who claim that nothing whatsoever happens unless it is in accord with fate.

The beliefs that Josephus claims characterize the Pharisees largely comport with claims in New Testament texts: the Pharisees highly valued the study of Scripture and devoted themselves to it; they saw themselves as the keepers and teachers of ancestral traditions not written down in Scripture; they believed in the resurrection of the dead; and they seemingly believed in angels and spirits capable of guiding human lives.[28] Moreover, the Pharisees were not sectarian in the sense of being a withdrawn subgroup of Israelite society, such as the Essenes who dwelt at Qumran. Rather, they were a socially engaged reformist group who wished to exercise leadership among Jews regarding the faithful practice of Judaism.[29] Instead, they maintained their property and familial and social relations and at least some were well-respected teachers. They cultivated relationships with political powers like the Hasmoneans, the Herodians, and eventually the Romans, so as to influence the general population to live out the ideals of Judaism as they defined them, but the Pharisees as a group did not constitute a political party or governmental body. Some Pharisees held influential and powerful positions in society, though it appears that simply being a Pharisee did not guarantee access to high social or political status. In short, Pharisees had a measure of power in first-century Jewish society but not quite as much power as some New Testament texts would lead one to believe. The Pharisees were a voluntary association whose members shared a common vision of an ideal Jewish society, and in various ways they committed themselves and their resources to achieving that vision. Relative to the Sadducees, however, the Pharisees were far less exclusive, and relative to the Essenes, they were far less sectarian. They lived out their ideals not in seclusion, but in the midst of Jewish society and in cooperation with the larger Hellenistic society of which they were an integral part.

There is one area of divergence between Josephus and New Testament texts that also happens to be an area of convergence between the New Testament and rabbinic traditions about the Pharisees: attention to laws pertaining to purity, tithing, agriculture, and Sabbath observance. Because these two disparate bodies of evidence overlap in this regard (in spite of completely different valuations of these interests), it is likely that the Pharisees of the first century did in fact give special attention to these matters. Christian readers are no doubt familiar with the controversy stories of the Gospels in which Jesus and the Pharisees debate the validity of certain practices on the Sabbath and whether certain dietary practices related to ritual purity are necessary. We have already discussed a debate between Jesus and Pharisees in Mark 7, which explained that the Pharisees "do not eat unless they thoroughly wash their hands . . . and they do not eat anything from the market unless they wash it; and there are also many other traditions that they observe, the washing of cups, pots, and bronze kettles." Although this text and its parallel in Matthew, as well many other controversy stories that could be cited, portray such ritual practices negatively—at best they are unnecessary; at worst they contravene the spirit of Torah—the Pharisees themselves understood them as acts of genuine piety and faithfulness.

The Pharisees believed the laws of Torah that applied to the priests who were responsible for maintaining the cultic practice of the temple were applicable to all of Israel. Pharisaic piety, in other words, is rooted in a democratized understanding of cultic piety, reflecting a kind of "priesthood of all believers" vision for Israel. The Pharisees pursued God's command that "You shall be for me a priestly kingdom and a holy nation" (Exod 19:6) to its fullest extent. As one scholar has said, "The Pharisees thus arrogated to themselves—and to all Jews equally— the status of the Temple priests, and performed actions restricted to priests on account of that status. The table of every Jew in his home was seen as being like the table of the Lord in the Jerusalem Temple. Everyone is a priest, everyone stands in the same relationship to God, and everyone must keep the priestly laws."[30] Of course the obligation to assume priestly forms of piety did not mean that the Pharisees ritually slaughtered animals at home, so as literally to imitate the temple cult in their personal domicile. No, but they emulated the way the priests ate their food in the consumption of ordinary meals at their own ordinary tables. Priestly food is food that has been consecrated to God by following certain ritual processes (like washing the vessels and utensils used for the food as well as one's hands) that render the food "pure" or "clean." The Pharisees' concern to eat their meals in a state of ritual purity was a way of consecrating themselves and their food to God. It was a way of sanctifying an ordinary human activity, like eating, as performed by ordinary people.[31]

This understanding of ritual purity, however, is not a view typical of the ordinary first-century Jew.[32] On the contrary, it is a distinctly Pharisaic view. Thus, when gospel writers criticize the Pharisees for placing so much emphasis on ritual purity, they may well reflect the understanding of the "average" first-century Jew—eating food in a state of ritual purity is an obligation of the priests and is irrelevant to everybody else. Furthermore, since most people presumably did not have the leisure time to study Torah, they were likely ignorant of the arcane laws pertaining to ritual purity, at least in the finer points of detail. Even if the gospel writers' perspective is not typical, the important point is that the Pharisees' preoccupation with purity, especially as it pertains to dietary laws, is not representative of a general Jewish attitude in the middle of the first century.

Furthermore, it is not clear how the observance of purity in regard to eating common food would have played out beyond the land of Israel, that is, in the Diaspora. Tithing and agricultural laws, which for the Pharisees effectively functioned as dietary laws,[33] would not have obtained or at least would not have obtained in the same way. Rabbinic traditions about the Pharisees lead us to believe that the Pharisees were located primarily in Israel. Yet the two people who claim to be Pharisees whose writings are preserved are Jews of the Diaspora: Josephus and Paul. While Josephus was born and raised in Israel, the first time he uses the label "Pharisee" of himself occurs relatively late, in the biographical treatise appended to the *Jewish Antiquities* and commonly known as the *Life*. Josephus wrote the *Life* in order to defend his reputation, which had been attacked by those who questioned his role during the revolt against Rome. In spite of the fact that he gives an account of the three Jewish schools (Pharisees, Sadducees and Essenes) in his first major work, the *War*, which recounts the history of the revolt, and mentions that a few other key figures that he dealt with during the revolt were Pharisees, he never says he is a Pharisee. Thus, scholars rightly wonder whether he really was a Pharisee, or whether it simply became expedient for him to claim the title at a much later point in life. For our purposes, it does not matter whether Josephus *really* was a Pharisee or whether he misrepresented the point at which he became a Pharisee; it only matters that he believes he can use the label credibly of himself after he has dwelt in Diaspora—more specifically, the city of Rome—for more than twenty years. While in the land, dietary practices may have marked off the Pharisees from other Jews, the evidence from Josephus indicates otherwise, since he makes no mention of such practices as distinctive of the Pharisees.

All of this evidence concerning the Pharisees should help us shine new light on Paul's claim that he had once been a Pharisee. The typical portrait of the Pharisees has been essential to the classical portrait of Paul the Christian. The apostle's former life as a Pharisee serves as the foil for his subsequent life as a Christian after his conversion. But if the image of the Pharisees as legalistic prigs is false, then we cannot characterize Paul as having converted from this alleged brand of Judaism into something that is its opposite. Perhaps Paul had a more flexible view of Torah to start with, and thus perhaps his seemingly "looser" interpretations of various commandments derive from his training as a Pharisee. In other words, it is not necessary to see his Damascus road experience as the point of origin for the apostle's more creative interpretations of Scripture. His more adaptive teachings on Torah as apostle to the Gentiles were most likely learned while he was a Pharisee.

Chapter

8

Paul the (Ex?)-Pharisee

Virtually all studies of Paul begin with the story of Paul's "conversion," the Damascus road experience in which Paul has a vision of the heavenly Christ. This moment in Paul's life is *the* moment—the moment that completely transformed both Paul and history. For it is through Paul's conversion that the gospel is preached to all the nations. In other words, it is Paul's conversion that leads to the (potential) conversion of the world. No wonder, then, that scholars and poets frequently speak of it in the most dramatic terms. A recent book on Paul begins as follows: "Paul. Two thousand years after he was born his name still conjures up a conversion that changed his own and every Christian life forever."[1] Through this magical, mystical encounter with the risen Jesus, Paul the Jewish Pharisee and persecutor of the church became Paul the Christian apostle. The story of Paul's conversion has since become emblematic of the key moment that is the foundation of every Christian life.

Given its significance to Christian tradition, Paul's conversion easily ranks as the most essential fact of nearly every biographical portrait of Paul. But if it were not for Acts, would this so-called fact be so prominent? Would subsequent readers of Paul's letters have been able to determine that Paul converted? Although some scholars see implicit reference to Paul's conversion experience everywhere in the Pauline corpus, most modern scholars, when pressed, will acknowledge that Paul does not have much to say about his supposed conversion.[2] Interpreters offer various reasons to explain why Paul is not compelled to reflect on this momentous event more often; the most common reason being that in his initial contact with potential believers Paul would have preached about his experience at length and thus he did not need to rehearse it in any detail; it could simply be assumed. In any case, the vast majority of commentators assume Paul's conversion is the experiential foundation on which all of his teachings are based. Paul's conversion is to Pauline scholarship what the Big Bang is to physics: the thing itself is an enigma, but somehow it is supposedly the explanation for everything else.

In recent years, some scholars have challenged this view. Krister Stendahl makes a compelling case for understanding what happened to Paul as a prophetic call rather than a conversion.[3] Paul's description of his encounter with the risen Jesus in Galatians 1 is reminiscent of the description of certain Hebrew prophets at the time of their call by God. The first "word of the Lord" to come to Jeremiah says the following: "Before I formed you in the womb I knew you, and before you were born I consecrated you; I appointed you a prophet to the nations" (Jer 1:4–5). Compare Galatians 1:15–16: "But . . . God, who chose me while in my mother's womb and called me through his grace, thought it right to reveal his Son in me, so that I might proclaim him among the nations."[4] The notion of being specially chosen—chosen even before birth—to speak on God's behalf is obviously common to both Jeremiah and Paul. Stendahl argues that those passages in which Paul speaks of the experience typically called his "conversion" are really about Paul's call to a new vocation, namely, as Apostle to the Gentiles.

In his 1990 book, *Paul the Convert*, Alan Segal argues that Paul could properly be called a convert not because he converted from Judaism to Christianity, as has been traditionally assumed, but because his mystical encounter caused him to switch from being a Pharisee to being a believer in Jesus. Perhaps a modern analogy might be a Catholic man who had been given a Jesuit school education, which he took seriously and which led to his contemplating becoming a priest, but who later experienced some sort of mystical transformation (which he described as being "born again"), and this resulted in his becoming a leading member of a charismatic Pentecostal church.

In short, even though scholars have raised questions about the traditional understanding of Paul's encounter with the risen Jesus, most scholarly interpreters as well as laypersons still perceive this moment as a moment of religious conversion. I believe that the language of conversion in regard to Paul is confusing and misleading precisely because it inevitably seems to imply either that Paul converted from Judaism to Christianity (in spite of Segal and others who have tried to update the conversion model) or that he converted from a bad form of religion to a good one. In my view, Stendahl's language of "call" better captures Paul's Damascus road experience, especially as Paul himself describes it,[5] but one must also account for the way in which Paul sometimes speaks of having given up his past life.

Although there are clues to grasping Paul's understanding of his religious experience throughout his letters, there are only two texts in which Paul provides any substantial reflection on the development of his religious identity: Galatians 1:11–17 and Philippians 3:2–9. In both of these texts, Paul contrasts his earlier and later life. Not surprisingly, both of these texts are foundational to the image of Paul the convert, though only Galatians 1:11–17 includes Paul's description of the Damascus road encounter with the risen Jesus. However, the very same Galatians passage is foundational to those who see Paul as having been called rather than converted.

I want you to know, brothers and sisters, that the gospel proclaimed by me is not a gospel according to human knowledge. For I did not receive it from a human being, nor was it taught to me, rather it came through a revelation of Jesus Christ. For you heard of my earlier life in Judaism, how intensely I was persecuting the church of God and trying to destroy it, and how I progressed in Judaism beyond many of my own age among my people, because I was especially eager for my ancestral traditions. But when God, who chose me while in my mother's womb and called me through his grace, thought it right to reveal his Son in me, so that I might proclaim him among the nations, I did not immediately consult with flesh and blood, nor did I go up to Jerusalem to those who were apostles before me, but I went off to Arabia and later I returned to Damascus. (Gal 1:11–17)

Standard English translations commonly render the Greek phrase that I have translated "earlier life in Judaism" as "former life in Judaism."[6] Both are acceptable ways to render the Greek text. The difference between them may seem too subtle to arouse much attention among English speakers, but "former" in this context betrays a bias toward seeing Paul as having jettisoned his Jewish identity after the revelation of Christ. "Former life in Judaism" makes it sound as if Judaism is not something with which Paul identifies any longer, whereas "earlier life in Judaism" is ambiguous. "Earlier" could imply that Paul has left Judaism behind as a result of the revelation, or it could simply be that Paul is referring to an earlier time in his life as a Jew, before he believed in Jesus. The first interpretation comports with the traditional understanding of this passage as the story of Paul's conversion, while the second interpretation reflects the reading of this passage as the story of Paul's call by God to become Apostle to the Gentiles. The former stresses discontinuity between Paul's experience before and after Jesus, while the latter emphasizes continuity.

In Galatians Paul highlights essentially two things that characterize his "earlier life in Judaism": his persecution of the church and his advanced education in Judaism. Although his verbiage is somewhat different, Paul emphasizes those same two things in Philippians 3:2–9. To most readers, the juxtaposition of these two things reinforces the idea that it is precisely Paul's devotion to Judaism that caused him to persecute believers in Jesus. Put another way, being a zealous Jew requires that one also exhibit hostility to Christianity. The working assumption is that Judaism and Christianity are diametrically opposed to each other. That assumption then leads inevitably to seeing Paul's experience of the risen Christ as a religious conversion. Since Judaism and Christianity are mutually exclusive religious options, Paul's acceptance of Christ means a concomitant rejection of Judaism.

Many anachronistic assumptions are made when reading Paul's text in this way, most significantly that there exists something called "Christianity" to which Paul had the option of converting. At this point in history, however, Christianity does not yet exist as a separate and distinct religion.[7] That Christianity begins as a sect of Judaism has been repeated often enough that it is practically a truism. Yet few people have actually absorbed the historical implications of this statement. If Christianity began as a sect of Judaism, then we must think of it as a form of Judaism in the early period. (At what point in history it came to constitute a separate and distinct religion is something of a historical enigma that currently preoccupies some historians of antiquity. But I know of no scholars writing today who would claim that Christianity was *not* a sect of Judaism in Paul's time.) After all, Paul was part of the first generation of believers, since he was a contemporary of Peter, James, and others who were "apostles before him." Besides, as I will discuss below, while Paul uses the expression "earlier life in Judaism" here, he typically speaks of his Jewish identity in the present tense.

Instead of seeing Paul's commitment to and advancement in Judaism as the cause or necessary corollary of his persecution of the church, a better explanation of why Paul mentions these two things together can be found within the context of Galatians. In this first chapter of Galatians, Paul is defending the validity of his mission and message, which he felt had been threatened. One of the ways he defends what he has preached to the Galatians is to emphasize that it comes from a divine and not a human source. He mentions his studies in Judaism in conjunction with his persecution of the church to demonstrate that whatever he learned from his teachers in those days, he could not possibly have learned anything about Jesus because he was persecuting believers in Jesus at that time. Furthermore, he could not have learned it from the other apostles because he did not go up to Jerusalem until much later, and even then he did not show himself to the communities of believers in Judea; he visited only Peter and James. Thus, while Paul refers to his reputation as an educated man ("I progressed in Judaism beyond many of my own age . . ."), the rhetorical stress of the passage is on Paul's not having had any human teachers who taught him the gospel, because he received it by divine revelation.[8] Paul's claim to having experienced divine revelation is important not because it was a conversion, but because it reminds his Galatian congregants of his apostolic authority.

Like Galatians 1:11–17, Philippians 3:2–9 is a much-discussed passage by interpreters trying to unravel Paul's transformation from zealous Pharisee to pious Christian. It overlaps with Galatians 1 in the mention of Paul's persecution of the church and his advanced education in Judaism, though Philippians is helpfully more specific than Galatians about certain aspects of Paul's Jewish background:

Beware of the dogs! Beware of those who do evil! Beware of those who cut wrongly into flesh. For we are the circumcision, we who worship in the spirit of God and boast in Christ Jesus and do not put confidence in the flesh. Although I might also have confidence in (my) flesh. If anyone else thinks he has confidence in (his) flesh, I have more, circumcised on the eighth day, by virtue of belonging to the people of

> *Israel, from the tribe of Benjamin, a Hebrew born of Hebrews, with regard to Torah—a Pharisee, with regard to zeal—a persecutor of the church, in terms of the righteousness attained by (the practice of) Torah—I was blameless. But whatever gains had accrued to me, these I now count as loss because of Christ. Even more, I count all things as a loss, on account of the surpassing knowledge of Christ Jesus as my Lord, for whose sake I have suffered the loss of everything and consider it as rubbish, in order that I may gain Christ, and be found in him, not having my own righteousness derived from (the practice of) Torah, but one that derives from the faith of Christ, righteousness that is from God because of faith.*

In vv. 5–6, Paul uses several labels in order to stress emphatically his Jewish identity: circumcised on the eighth day (as biblically prescribed in Genesis 17), an Israelite, a Hebrew, and a Pharisee—the last being particularly significant, as this is the only time Paul uses this designation of himself. As in Galatians, he mentions being a persecutor of the church, which, in conjunction with his Jewish credentials, raises the question of whether Paul understands his earlier Jewish identity as precluding any form of commitment to Christ and the church. To the typical modern reader, the linking of persecution of the church with Jewish credentials in Paul's description of himself ostensibly insinuates that Jewish identity and Christian identity are mutually exclusive. One cannot be committed to Christ and a Pharisee at the same time.

This reading, however, has more to do with modern assumptions than with what Paul says. To be sure, in both Galatians and Philippians Paul's mention of his past persecution of the church is embedded within descriptions of his Jewish identity. Readers reasonably assume that Paul would be ashamed of his persecution of the church since becoming a believer in Jesus. The mistake people make, however, is then to assume that, whatever other past activities get listed along with persecution of the church, these must be activities of which Paul is also ashamed. Paul's life before Christ is a life wholly and irredeemably marked by sin; *ergo* Paul's commitment to Judaism and Jewish practice that forms such a huge part of his earlier life is seemingly inherently linked to a sinful past life of which Paul is ashamed. Being schooled in the "traditions of his ancestors," being circumcised, and being a Pharisee are associated with the flesh and sin, and thus Paul feels shame about these qualities that characterize his former life. Paul's life after Christ is marked by religious activities that bring redemption; it is a life lived in Christ, a life characterized by the appropriate kind of religious zeal, a life about which one can therefore rightly boast. Paul's life is summed up in two totally discontinuous phases: before Christ and after Christ. This bifurcated image of Paul's life is, quite simply, another way of describing the dominant image of the apostle as Paul the convert discussed in chapter 3.

However, if one brackets the traditional image of Paul the convert and the assumptions that instinctively accompany it, it is possible to read these texts as evidence for at least as much continuity in Paul's self-understanding as discontinuity. Indeed, notice Paul's use of the present tense: "For *we* are the circumcision . . ." The context of the passage from Philippians is similar to the one that gave rise to his letter to the Galatians: it seems that Paul has rivals who tout certain kinds of credentials that purportedly give them status as teachers or community leaders—credentials concerning their Jewish background and education. Paul claims that he, too, has these credentials; he, too, can claim a privileged status on the basis of his Jewish ancestry, his devotion to Jewish tradition, and his knowledge of Torah. With the possible exception of "Pharisee," all the labels in the Philippians passage appear to be descriptions that characterize Paul at the time he wrote his letter to the Philippians; they are not *merely* characterizations of his *earlier* life.

Quite the contrary, Paul's use of various Jewish labels of himself is almost always in the present tense. He uses the same labels he uses in Philippians in several other places, for example, Romans 11:1: "I myself am an Israelite, a descendant of Abraham, a member of the tribe of Benjamin," and 2 Corinthians 11:22: "Are they Hebrews? So am I! Are they Israelites? So am I! Are they descendants of Abraham? So am I!" As is the case in Philippians and Galatians, what most often triggers Paul to spell out his Jewishness through these various identity markers is the perceived need to reassert his authority over other leaders who are either directly challenging him or who are held in esteem because of their Jewish credentials. Paul wants to show that he has the same credentials as they have. In any case, he *is* a Hebrew; he *is* an Israelite; he *is* a descendant of Abraham—all these things are no less true of Paul as a follower of Jesus than they were before his encounter with Jesus. Significantly, not long after the revelation of Christ near Damascus described in Galatians 1, Paul pointedly reminds the Gentile Galatians that he is a Jew: "We ourselves are Jews by nature and not Gentile sinners" (Gal 2:15).[9]

Even the label Pharisee is not really used as a description of a former self: "With regard to Torah—a Pharisee," he says in Philippians 3. Paul uses this label in order to assert that he is a skilled interpreter of Torah by virtue of having studied with Pharisees, and in this sense Paul's use of "Pharisee" is part of the description of the apostle's current identity. As discussed in the previous chapter, the Pharisees were known for several things, but one of the most important was their devotion to the study of Torah, and they were considered the virtuosos of Torah interpretation. To claim that one had spent time in the company of Pharisees is the ancient Jewish equivalent of bragging about having had an Ivy League education.

In addition to boasting of their Jewish ancestry, Paul's rivals had claimed expertise in Torah, which must have impressed members of Paul's community at Philippi, and he wanted to remind them that, whatever scriptural competence the *other teachers* had, they probably did not have the kind of expertise *Paul* had. Since Philippians is the only time Paul uses this label of himself in his letters, it is unlikely that he still considers himself a Pharisee, in the way, say, he considers himself an Israelite or a descendant of Abraham, but it still represents a constitutive part of his current religious identity. Contrary to the long-standing tradition of interpretation, "Pharisee" as Paul uses it in Philippians is *not* meant to symbolize the religious opposite of being "in Christ."[10]

To follow the Ivy League analogy further, a person who has graduated Harvard may still consider himself or herself "a Harvardian," but such a designation does not in this case mean that one is currently a student in residence at Harvard. Rather, it designates one's alumnus/na status and probably that one feels shaped by that particular institution. In other words, using the label "Harvardian" to evoke an association with Harvard, even if it is a prior association, can still be an appropriate way of describing some aspect of one's identity. When it comes to Torah, Paul signals that he has studied with the best and brightest by his use of the label "Pharisee."

Being circumcised, a descendant of Abraham, and a Pharisee—these qualities or accomplishments are still a fundamental part of Paul's identity, just as is evidently true for the rival teachers who inspired Paul periodically to invoke them as a reminder to his audience. The frequency with which Paul engages in one-upmanship with other leaders and teachers who circulate among Christ-believing communities indicates that Jewish identity carries with it a certain cachet. That Paul and Paul's rivals share claims to Jewish ancestry and an advanced degree in Torah means that Jewish identity is, in fact, a status marker recognized within at least some early communities of Jesus-followers.

It is important to note that the rhetorical force of Paul's argument in Philippians 3 depends on recognizing that the identity markers Paul uses are indicators of status, not of shame. If Paul is sincere—and I see no reason to think he isn't—when he says he counts all his Jewish privileges and credentials as a loss, then they must be things people ordinarily count as valuable. If Paul considered his past life one of sin and degradation, then he would not call giving up that life a loss; on the contrary, giving up *that* kind of a life would count as a gain. Claiming the special status of being an Israelite, a descendant of Abraham and having achieved Pharisaic training in Torah—these are things of value. They are not shameful things; they are honors. They are status symbols, and not superficially so, but the kinds of things that are appropriately recognized as good, desirable, and honorable, at least to Jews. They are the kinds of things people brag about, not the kinds of things that cause embarrassment. To put the matter in extremely simple terms, Paul is not claiming he has given up bad and shameful things for Jesus. On the contrary, he has given up good and honorable things. What Paul is saying in Philippians 3 is that he no longer values such claims to status, because they pale in comparison to being a follower of Jesus.

Paul's point in Philippians is not terribly complicated or subtle: people should not be impressed by claims to privilege and status, especially when such claims allow some people to wield special forms of influence in the human realm. Although Paul typically specifies only Jewish status markers, his argument applies to human status symbols generally. My working assumption is that Paul and the vast majority of his rivals never held any kind of status that would be recognized by Romans—at least not by Romans who had no appreciation for Jews and Judaism. Since Paul's community of origin was Jewish, and since most other Christ-following teachers in this early period were also of Jewish origin and who furthermore revered a figure who was an Israelite, the primary field of status reference was Jewish. Hence Paul's virtually exclusive use of Jewish status labels to describe himself: circumcision,

Hebrew lineage, being morally "blameless," and learned in Scripture. Paul almost surely never held any kind of status that would have been recognized by non-Jewish communities. In spite of Paul's claims to being a Roman citizen in Acts, there is no indication in his own writings that Paul ever held any Roman honors or privileges. Some scholars, in their attempts to reconcile Acts with the letters, maintain that Paul's silence on the matter in his letters does not mean he was not a Roman citizen. Such scholars rightly point out that my claim that Paul was not a Roman citizen constitutes an argument from silence, and is thus not well founded. To be sure, arguments from silence must be used with great care. But because Paul so often refers to his past accomplishments, credentials, and the positions of status he achieved, one would certainly expect that, if Paul had ever achieved the status of Roman citizen, he would have referred to it, and he would have referred to it precisely in a context like that of Philippians 3 and similar passages, where questions of his authority and status were raised by others and Paul was defending himself. Holding Roman citizenship would only reinforce Paul's point more strongly that all such "fleshly" honors are rubbish in comparison to the glories of knowing Christ.

In sum, while there are elements of discontinuity between Paul's past and present, Paul's understanding of himself as a Jew is not one of them. Superficial and decontextualized readings of Paul's letters have neglected to take adequate account of the polemically charged rhetoric of the passages from Galatians and Philippians.[11] In both the Galatians and Philippians texts, Paul is arguing about status and authority with rival teachers whom he perceives as a threat to his authority and whom he believes have attacked or at least tried to diminish his status as a teacher and preacher. In neither case does Paul's response reflect embarrassment about his Jewish identity generally or his elevated accomplishments in Jewish learning. In Galatians 1, the reference to his advanced Jewish education is merely the foil for contrasting the ways in which he acquired knowledge: he learned Torah and ancestral traditions through human teachers, but Paul's knowledge of Christ came through a revelation from God, not from human teachers.

Philippians 3 does not narrate the experience of revelation, but it provides an expanded description of Paul's formation as a member of the learned Jewish elite of his day. Like Galatians, the description of Paul's Jewish credentials in Philippians 3 does not reflect any shame or embarrassment on Paul's part. Paul wishes to demonstrate that, while he can lay claim to having as elevated a status in Jewish learning as his rivals, such claims to status are ultimately of little value. Status claims are about nothing more than posturing and vanity. Moreover, the rhetoric of Philippians 3 is designed to cause Paul's rivals to feel shame not for being Jewish but for having made so much of their Jewish status. Paul never rejected his Jewishness (presumably, neither did the rival teachers). There is no evidence that Paul's Jewish identity is any less robust, or any less intact after his encounter with the risen Jesus than it was before.

Of course, there are ways in which Paul contrasts his earlier and later life. Paul had a life-altering experience when he encountered the risen Jesus. I am in no way claiming that this event wasn't significant in Paul's life. On the contrary, it is the most significant event of his life, the turning point that made him the Apostle to the Gentiles and the second most important man in Christian history. But acknowledging that Paul's experience on the Damascus road was life-changing does not make it a conversion from one religion to another, as is often the perception today. Furthermore, in historical terms, calling Paul's encounter with Jesus a conversion has little explanatory value.[12]

The apostle's mystical encounter with the risen Jesus cannot be used as the key to understanding Paul. It's not the key for two reasons: First, precisely because it was a personal religious experience of an extraordinary nature, it is not describable by means of rational explanation according to the canons of historical scholarship. It is a unique mystical moment in the apostle's life, and what was mystical for Paul must remain merely mysterious for everybody else. Let me make clear that I am not a cynic who denies that such religious experiences are possible and thus intend to argue Paul never experienced the risen Jesus. He obviously experienced something that led to his becoming Apostle to the Gentiles, but we cannot use the experience itself as a key to understanding, because it is the nature of personal religious experience to be fundamentally unknowable, especially when it occurred in the distant past. In my view, such experience is therefore not an appropriate object of historical investigation. What is appropriate to investigate, and what most concerns me in this study of Paul, are the consequences of whatever it was that happened or that Paul believed happened.

Second, Paul barely makes mention of his so-called conversion in his letters. In other words, Paul himself does not tend to appeal to the Damascus road experience to explain what it means to believe in Jesus. Within the entire corpus of undisputed epistles, only twice does Paul make any notable mention of it: in Galatians 1 and Philippians 3.[13] In those cases, as we saw, Paul appeals to his Damascus road experience in order to defend his credibility as an apostle. His rhetorical posture in both texts is defensive; his apostolic authority has been undermined, or at least he perceives it to be under threat. In any case, outside of these two texts, a careful reader of Paul's letters is hard-pressed to find references to Paul's supposed conversion. In fact, Paul never even uses the language of "conversion" of himself. He never calls himself a "proselyte for Christ," and he never refers to his belief in Jesus as a form of *metanoia*, literally "repentance," a common label for someone who has traded an old degenerate life for a newly reformed one.

Of course, many interpreters claim to see Paul's conversion experience everywhere in the letters, because the image of Paul the convert has been the lens through which Paul's letters have been read.[14] For example, Romans 7:7–13 has been seen as the most important testimony to Paul's supposed conversion, even though most interpreters before Augustine and many interpreters today do not think Paul speaks autobiographically in this passage. (I will discuss Romans 7 in more detail in chapter 13.) But if we jettison that image of Paul the convert (or at least try to bracket it for now), then it becomes difficult to find many instances where Paul refers to it and nearly impossible to find texts that actually indicate Paul's theological dependence on this supposedly foundational event.

To be sure, the passages discussed from Galatians and Philippians are genuine examples of Paul speaking autobiographically of his religious experience. Moreover, one cannot deny the language of discontinuity present in those texts; Paul clearly contrasts earlier and later stages of his life. Other than the obvious transition from being hostile to Jesus to becoming a follower, the biggest difference between the earlier and later Paul is that he went from being a persecutor of the "church of God" to being a victim of persecution. In fact, it is the issue of persecution that is most in need of explanation if we are to debunk the notion that Paul underwent a conversion.

Why did Paul the Pharisee persecute the church in the first place? What was offensive about it? What was so problematic about Jews and god-fearing Gentiles believing in Jesus? Why did Pharisees or synagogue officials feel it was necessary to punish these people? The usual starting assumption is that Jews simply were hostile to Jesus, and thus they acted in hostile ways toward his followers. Just as Jewish leaders had to get rid of Jesus, so they endeavored to stamp out his followers. Not only does this view neglect to explain the actual reason for the hostility, but it reflects many deeper assumptions, such as: Christianity existed in the first century; being Christian was defined by belief in Jesus; and that Judaism and Christianity were religions in diametrical opposition to each other. With these as working assumptions, it appears as though Paul's persecution of Jesus-followers while he was an active Pharisee hardly needs explaining. But belief in Jesus as the Messiah or as some other divine messenger or savior is a very Jewish idea. If Jewish leaders didn't persecute Akiba and other Jews when they proclaimed Bar Kokhba the Messiah a century later, why would they persecute those who proclaimed Jesus the Messiah? Jewish leaders may not have liked the idea, but it is a big leap from disagreement or dismissal of an idea to hostility and persecution.

Modern scholars who recognize that the traditional account does not actually explain Jewish persecution of the early church have attempted to provide more creative explanations. Most often these explanations articulate some critical aspect of early Christian belief or practice that would have crossed the threshold of tolerance among more mainstream Jews. One common explanation is that Jewish leaders would have found the idea of a *crucified* Messiah deeply offensive. The proof text for this is Galatians 3:13, which itself is a citation of Deuteronomy 21:23: "Cursed is everyone who hangs on a tree." According to this line of thinking, crucifixion was not just a shameful death, it was a death cursed by God.[15] Thus, proclaiming a crucified Messiah would have been utterly outrageous and offensive.

The problem with this explanation is that there was no such belief in ancient Judaism.[16] The passage from Deuteronomy refers to a person who has been executed on account of a capital offense; the reason for the curse is the offense, not the manner of execution. In any case, being hung on a tree in Deuteronomy refers not to the execution itself, but to what is done to the body *after* the criminal has been executed—it is displayed as a warning to others. Given the horror of crucifixion, Jews at the time of Paul may well have described being crucified as a curse, but such a description was likely meant to indicate that such a person was a victim, not a villain, and victims of crucifixion typically invoked sympathy rather than scorn from other Jews.[17] If, on the other hand, an instance of crucifixion were perceived to be deserved, then, like Deuteronomy, the curse would refer to that person's having been condemned as a criminal and thus cursed by God on account of his or her illicit action(s). In sum, it is implausible that Jewish authorities would have been so deeply offended by the idea of Jesus having been crucified that they would have persecuted his followers. That they would have found the notion of a crucified Messiah weird seems likely, but there is no reason to think they would have punished those who adhered to that idea simply because it was weird.

Another explanation has recently become popular among scholars influenced by the new perspective: that there was competition for Gentile converts among different groups of Jews and that conflicting ideas about how Gentiles could be integrated into Israel led to hostility. The specifics of this explanation vary somewhat from one scholar to another, but the critical feature is Paul's attitude toward Gentiles; Gentiles constitute the axis around which Paul turns from persecutor to persecuted. Even before his encounter with Christ, so the argument goes, Paul was a Jewish missionary—on behalf of Pharisaic Judaism, that is—and consistent with the Pharisaic point of view, he advocated that male Gentiles must first be circumcised if they wish to be full-fledged members of Israel and that as proselytes they must understand that they are as much obliged to keep Torah as any native-born Jew. In sum, Paul and other Pharisees objected to the way some members of the Jesus movement were making Jewish converts, and that was why they persecuted Jesus believers.[18]

Those who advocate this explanation argue that more than just a violation of Torah is at issue, however; the situation would have provoked a sociological crisis. For if Jewish followers of Jesus were making converts in a way that significantly deviated from the norm, they risked blurring the boundary between Jew and Gentile. The integrity of Israel would have been perceived to be at stake. In other words, Jewish identity itself was being threatened, and this would constitute a serious enough threat to account for Jewish persecution of the Jesus movement, explaining both why Paul persecuted the church and why he himself was persecuted.

Although this explanation has its merits, the idea that Jews, including Pharisees, would have so objected to the inclusion of Gentiles sans circumcision also has its problems. As we've seen in earlier discussion, Jews of antiquity were not as exclusivist as they have been made out to be. Although there were a few such groups (such as the community who lived at the Dead Sea), Jews were no more exclusivist than other ethnic groups and perhaps even less so, given the evidence of Gentiles' participation in synagogues and their interest in Jewish practice.

I think the reason for persecution is much simpler: Jesus had been executed a criminal by Rome because he was perceived to be a political threat. He had aroused multitudes with his preaching of the kingdom of God; he criticized the temple establishment in Jerusalem, which bore allegiance to Rome and through which Roman colonial power was maintained; and he seems generally to have been a regular disturber of the peace. For his followers to carry on in his name would no doubt have been threatening to those who did not wish to perturb the Romans further, as was the case for most Jewish authorities, religious and political, and for any Jews who had a interest in the status quo or least did not want a rebellion.[19] From what we can glean from sources, the Pharisees would likely have been among those who accepted or at least tolerated Roman colonial rule.[20] If believers in Jesus persisted in calling Jesus "Lord" and "Messiah" and proclaiming "the kingdom," it is easy to understand how other Jews who wished to avoid the ire of Rome would want to suppress such subversives. Apparently, one way to exercise some control over Jesus-followers was through synagogue discipline, specifically, by administering the forty lashes less one. This scenario seems to me the most historically plausible way to explain why Paul persecuted the early church while he was a Pharisee. As several scholars have recently demonstrated, when Paul subsequently went around proclaiming Jesus as Lord, his message was anti-Imperial.[21] Thus, Paul turned from persecutor to persecutee because he turned from having a complacent attitude toward the Romans to preaching a message of defiance.

According to new-perspective views, Paul is still viewed as someone who does a 180-degree turn about some critical aspect of Jewish identity—what was once rejected with hostility is now embraced with love—only instead of an about-face over Jesus-the-crucified-Messiah, as is the case for traditional interpreters, for new-perspective scholars Paul's change of heart revolves around Gentiles. John Dominic Crossan and Jonathon Reed pithily capture this view when they assert that Paul "converted *not from Judaism to Christianity*, of course, *but from violent opponent and persecutor of pagan inclusion to non-violent proponent and persuader of pagan inclusion.* That which he persecuted *for* God was exactly that to which he was called *by* God."[22]

I suspect that Paul's attitude toward Gentiles did change after his encounter with the risen Jesus, but I do not think it was necessarily a sudden 180-degree turn. That is to say, I do not think we should speak of Paul's "conversion" over Gentiles anymore than we should speak of his conversion over Jesus. Rather I think the role of Gentiles in Paul's thinking evolves over time.[23] Indeed, it is more likely that Paul had given some significant measure of attention to Jew-Gentile interaction, especially since being a Pharisee did not require one to live in seclusion from Gentiles. Evolution, rather than conversion, is not only historically and psychologically more plausible, it has the added advantage of giving Paul credit for theologically reflecting on his experience and by that process having thoughtfully developed his ideas. His experience of Jesus is an extremely important event that accelerates that evolution, but that is quite different from understanding that experience as a conversion.

As a Pharisee, before his encounter with the risen Jesus and all that that implied, Paul may have been concerned about purity regulations, and this would have limited his contact with Gentiles. But we must also remember that most Jews did not observe purity laws in such strict terms; purity regulations were, after all, intended primarily for priests, since they were the ones responsible for performing the rites of sacrifice and other rituals that mark the worship of God. Contrary to popular belief, Gentiles (and women for that matter) were not considered inherently impure, even by the strictest Pharisees. Pharisees did not think that there was an existential state called Gentile-ness, possessed by all Gentiles and which rendered them permanently and irredeemably impure. Impurity is caused by exposure to impure substances or by involvement in certain sinful actions. Idolatry tops the list of activities considered sinful. Gentiles are, by definition, people who worship other gods. Since a given Gentile may at any given time have engaged in an idolatrous act (a sacrifice, a prayer, swearing an oath—any of these are idolatrous if the name of another god is invoked), they are *potentially* impure, and contact with them may render a Jew impure. Jews' avoidance of Gentiles is due, therefore, to their desire to avoid contact with anything that supports or might support idolatry, lest the Jew seem to have done something to support the worship of another god. If, however, one could be sure that a Gentile was not engaged in any idolatrous activities, one would presumably be free to interact with him or her. Because the Gentiles who comprise the membership of Paul's churches have already renounced idolatry, there is no reason for Paul to be concerned about contact with them—*even if he were still a Pharisee!*

In any case, Pharisees concerned themselves with much more than purity regulations. They speculated about the world to come and engaged in serious study of Torah. All these things: purity and how it regulates contact with others most likely to be ritually impure, speculation about the end of time, and Torah—all these are things that would not only preoccupy your typical Pharisee, these are things that continue to occupy Paul after his encounter with Jesus. To be sure, Paul is not a typical Pharisee after his encounter with Jesus—he changes his mind about some important things, like the significance of Jesus and, consequently, what time it is in history. The experiences he has, however, alter the constellation of his theological universe, but the universe itself remains intact. But if people rely on conversion as the most essential event in Paul's life, they sever the apostle from the very arena that can make Paul intelligible in historical context.

Having been educated as a Pharisee, Paul was a deep thinker. His preternatural ability to think theologically is obvious to those who have studied his letters. Indeed, in his letters Paul frequently articulates the theological, ethical, and social reasoning underlying his teachings, partly because his congregants have written to him posing questions and sometimes even challenging him about what he has taught them. Thus the vast majority of what we have in Paul's letters is Paul justifying his claims and his behavior as an apostle. While some of what he says may seem complicated or even obtuse to modern readers, the vast majority of Paul's writing is comprised of arguments and explanations in defense of his theological position. Understanding the logic of why Paul believes as he does is essential to understanding Paul. I don't mean logic of the immutable, mathematical sort. I mean the logic of ancient Judaism. Every religious tradition has an internal logic that gives it coherence. The way Paul channeled his own religious experience into the mission with which God charged him can be explained within the theological universe that is first-century Judaism.

Here's what I think happened in a nutshell: Paul's experience of the risen Jesus leads him to move up the apocalyptic clock. Jewish literature of Paul's day clearly indicates that resurrection of the dead is something that is associated with the final judgment and the end of history. Resurrection was not something that was supposed to happen one individual at a time; it was envisioned as a collective experience that marked the end of time and the final reckoning of the wicked and the righteous. Seeing the risen Jesus—whatever form that took—caused Paul to revise his understanding of the moment in history of which he was part. Once he believed the end of time was much closer than he had previously thought, he necessarily had to revise his understanding about some other things, most importantly, the Gentiles. One of the most powerful beliefs associated with the end times is that all the nations—that is, all the Gentiles—would flock to Zion in recognition of the one, true God, the God of Israel, renouncing once and for all other gods. It is the vision of a monotheist's utopia. Through Israel's prophets, God foretold this new age:

> *Turn to me and be saved, all the ends of the earth! For I am God, and there is no other. By myself I have sworn, from my mouth has gone forth in righteousness a word that shall not return: "To me every knee shall bow, every tongue shall swear." (Isa 45:22–23)*

In my view, it is this utopian vision that inspired Paul to translate his faith in Jesus into his charge as Apostle to the Gentiles. As a result, he could no longer concern himself with the kinds of purity regulations that preoccupied many Pharisees (assuming that he was so preoccupied to start with), because turning the Gentiles from idolatry to the knowledge and worship of the one, true God trumps any need to separate the spheres of Jew and Gentile. The utopian monotheist vision requires gathering different peoples together, not their separation.[24]

Chapter

9

A Typical Jew

Paul called himself a servant of Jesus Christ, proclaimed the cosmic significance of Jesus' death and resurrection to people whom he had never met, and encouraged them to become part of a community "in Christ." There are numerous ways in which the apostle's letters reflect typical Jewish attitudes, beliefs, and biases, but his Jewish identity has been obscured by years of interpretive tradition. In order to recover Paul's Judaism, it takes a bit of effort, though not as much as you might think. When one knows what to look for, Paul's Jewish perspective is everywhere throughout his letters. In what follows, I intend to demonstrate the strains of continuity in Paul, in other words, the way in which he remained a typical Jew even after his experience of Jesus.

Prejudices

One of the easiest ways to perceive how thoroughly Jewish Paul was is through his biases, the kinds of things that Paul so takes for granted that he betrays not the slightest doubt about their self-evident truth whenever such things come up. I consider Paul to have been a thoughtful and original theological thinker, as well as a cultural critic, but he is also a human being who, like everybody else, has a limited perspective on the world.[1] His perspective is limited by who he is, a Jew whose historical context is the Greco-Roman world, and he holds certain biases based on that identity, some of which are rather distasteful. Even his openness to Gentiles had limits. In his biases toward others, Paul is a typical Jew.

In 1 Thessalonians, regarded by most scholars as Paul's earliest letter, Paul never once refers to his Jewish education (unlike Galatians, Philippians and 1 Corinthians) and never once cites from Jewish Scripture (which he does in most of his letters). But in many ways Paul speaks to his Gentile charges like a typical Jewish teacher of the first century. In speaking of the Thessalonian congregation's high reputation, Paul lauds their "faith in God," by reminding them of how they "turned from idols to God, so as to serve a living and true God." This description of turning to serve a living and true God is standard language—almost cliché—to describe Gentiles who have come to appreciate the wisdom of Jewish monotheism. As discussed in chapter 5, idolatry is the quintessential flaw of the Gentile, and the abandonment of idolatry is the *sine qua non* of being a righteous Gentile in the eyes of a Jew.

When speaking to and about "Gentiles," the terminology conjures images of idolatry. In speaking to the Corinthians about spiritual gifts, Paul refers to their past life: "You know that when you were Gentiles, you were enticed and led astray to [serve] speechless idols" (1 Cor 12:2). That Paul associates the Gentile manner of life with idolatry is most obvious in Romans:

> *Though they knew God, they did not glorify him as God or give thanks to him, but they became confused in their thinking, and their senseless minds were dimmed. Claiming to be wise, they became fools; and they exchanged the glory of the immortal God for images resembling a mortal human being or birds or four-footed animals or reptiles. . . . They exchanged the truth about God for a lie and revered and worshipped the creature rather than the Creator. (1:21–25)*

And ignorance is no excuse for idolatry. For, as Paul explains in Romans 1, although Gentiles did not have the benefit of Torah, God was knowable. "Since his creation of the world, that which is invisible can be perceived intelligibly, both his eternal power and divine essence, through the things he has made" (1:20). Romans makes clear that idolatry is not just a sin; it's a sin of cataclysmic proportion. The wrath of God that Paul expects to be unleashed upon the world soon is due to this willful idolatry (see 1:18).

According to the Jewish view of the world, idolatry is the sin that leads to all other sins. The Wisdom of Solomon, an Alexandrian Jewish text virtually contemporary with Paul, sums up the connection between idolatry and sin rather matter-of-factly: "For the worship of idols . . . is the beginning and cause and end of every evil" (Wis 14:27). Paul demonstrates that he associates Gentiles with sin by the way he casually and almost incidentally equates being a Gentile with being a sinner: "We ourselves are Jews by nature and not Gentile sinners." (Gal 2:15) Compare the Wisdom of Solomon:

> *Then it was not enough for them to err about the knowledge of God. . . . For whether they kill children in their initiations or celebrate secret mysteries, or hold frenzied revels with strange customs, they no longer keep either their lives or their marriages pure, but they either treacherously kill one another, or grieve one another by adultery, and all is a raging riot of blood and murder, theft and deceit, corruption, faithlessness, tumult, perjury, confusion over what is good, forgetfulness of favors, defiling of souls, sexual perversion, disorder in marriages, adultery, and debauchery. (Wis 14:22–26)*

"Sexual perversion" here literally means "alteration of generation," that is to say, nonprocreative sex. Sexually immoral behavior in particular seems to go hand in hand with idolatry, for it is almost as characteristically "Gentile" as idolatry itself. "For the idea of making idols was the beginning of fornication" (Wis 14:12). It is not terribly surprising, then, that when Paul makes his tirade against idolatry in Romans 1, he, too, associates it with "sexual perversion":

> *They exchanged the truth about God for a lie and revered and worshipped the creature rather than the Creator. . . . For this reason God gave them up to degrading passions. Their women exchanged natural intercourse for unnatural, and in the same way also the men, giving up natural intercourse with women, were consumed with passion for one another. (Rom 1:25–27, NRSV)*

This text is important today for many Christian denominations debating the acceptability of same-sex practice. To be sure, Paul does not look upon it favorably. What is often missed, however, is the context of this passage. It is crystal clear from Romans 1 that what Paul is speaking against is the sin of idolatry. The "degrading passions" are the by-product of idolatry, and Paul's mention of it is almost incidental—the result of an instinctive Jewish association between idolatry and "unnatural" sexuality, which itself derives from nothing more than the Jewish stereotype of Gentiles in antiquity. Paul's tirade against idolatry in Romans 1 ends with a long list of vices: "they were filled with every kind of wickedness, evil, jealousy, malice. Full of envy, murder, descension, deceit, craftiness . . ." and it goes on (Rom 1:28–32). Its resemblance to the list from the Wisdom of Solomon quoted above demonstrates once again that Paul's perspective is a typically Jewish one. Jewish attacks on Gentile idolatry, frequently vicious and extreme, are commonplace and predictable. That is to say, they reflect Jewish stereotypes of Gentiles, and that stereotype includes the idea that Gentiles are prone to sexual licentiousness. In Pauline terms, Gentiles are weak in the flesh.

So when Paul exhorts the Thessalonians about living a life pleasing to God, it's no surprise that the first specific instructions he mentions concern appropriate sexual behavior: "For this is the will of God, your sanctification: that you reject sexual licentiousness. Know that each of you is to control his own body in holiness and honor, not in the passion of desire, like the Gentiles who do not know God" (1 Thess 4:3–5). Once again, Paul reveals his typical Jewish stereotype of Gentiles, as sexually unrestrained. In fact, he equates "the passion of desire" with Gentiles, "Gentiles who do not know God," which is a way of emphasizing that Gentiles are by nature idolaters. Interestingly, this comment almost makes it sound as if Paul's audience at Thessalonica is not made up of Gentiles. Of course they *are* Gentiles. Indeed, it is likely that Paul used the expression "the Gentiles who do not know God" so as to make a distinction between his Gentile followers, who know God, and the rest of the Gentiles, who do not.

God, Ethics, Purity, and Sex

Paul's ethical teachings basically fall into two categories: conventional teachings that are so generic there isn't anybody in Greco-Roman society who would find them objectionable, and those teachings that the apostle derives directly from his religious perspective. Those in the first category don't require much explanation. It encompasses those portions of Paul's letters where he says things like: avoid gossip, contentiousness, selfishness, drinking to excess, late-night carousing, slovenly behavior, and the like. On the positive side, he exhorts his congregants to be gentle, kind, peace-loving, forgiving, possessed of self-control, and the like. These kinds of teachings are the ancient equivalent of recommendations one finds in ethical campaigns directed to the American public. "Don't drive drunk" would be an example of this kind of teaching. Is there anyone who would argue against such an imperative? Anyone who would seriously argue that drinking and driving is a good idea? Imperatives like "Don't drive drunk" and "avoid gossip and carousing" reflect the ethical values shared among all or virtually all members of society. When Paul offers ethical advice of this sort, it shows he holds certain views that are conventional in Greco-Roman society generally, so conventional, in fact, they could just as well be the teachings of a high-born Jew in Alexandria, a low-born Pharisee in Jerusalem, a Roman senator, a slave in Caesar's house, a worshipper of Artemis, or a priest in the cult of Isis.

The second category, those ethical teachings that derive directly from Paul's religious perspective, are the teachings capable of revealing the way in which Paul maintained a Jewish value system throughout his life. Paul's belief in Jesus did not lead him to adopt a radically new system of values. It led him to tweak his existing one, but the essential principles of a recognizably Jewish value system are still intact. Perhaps one could say that even Paul's tweaking of his Jewish tradition was itself indebted to a Pharisaic ethos, which tended toward flexibility in certain interpretations of Torah because of a desire to accommodate new circumstances as they arose.

One of the most important core Jewish values that Paul maintained throughout his life is an unambiguous commitment to a monotheistic theology. We have already discussed how Jews understood themselves to be fundamentally different from Gentiles because Jews devoted themselves exclusively to the one God, whose transcendence of all created things meant that this God could not be represented in any form whatsoever, while Gentiles were marked by the worship of many gods, who were represented by many forms and images. In concise terms, Jews were worshippers of the one, true, living God, and Gentiles were idolaters. At the same time, Gentiles who shunned idolatry were commended by Jews. Thus, Gentiles are in principle redeemable; they have the capacity to recognize God, and, in fact, it seems many did by the Roman period. As we saw when discussing Josephus and Philo, there was a tension between an ingrained association between Gentiles and idolatry on the one hand and a belief that Gentiles (who, like Jews, owe their existence to God) have the same potential to lead virtuous lives devoted to God. Paul's letters reflect the same basic assumptions about Jews and Gentiles.

Paul's monotheism is so thoroughgoing and so important for understanding the nature of his mission to the Gentiles that the bulk of the next chapter is devoted to it. What I wish to address here is the way in which Paul utilizes the closely related concepts of holiness and purity to mediate God's presence among the community of believers.

As discussed in more detail in chapter 5, biblical holiness may be defined as the space within which God can dwell. Since God's power is so awesome, contact with it is extremely dangerous. Holiness enables God's presence to be felt among God's people and facilitates human contact with the divine through safe means. Although not frequently emphasized by interpreters, Paul regularly addresses his congregants as *hagioi,* usually translated "saints" or "holy ones."[2] Creating a space for the divine presence requires the construction and maintenance of boundaries that separate what or who is holy from what or who is common. Hence, when God says to Israel "You shall be for me a priestly kingdom and a holy nation" (Exod 19:6), holiness is the distinguishing feature that makes Israel both different from other nations and able to mediate between God and humanity. In Leviticus 20:26 this point is made explicitly: "You shall be holy to me; for I the Lord am holy, and I have separated you from the other peoples to be mine." Calvin Roetzel makes the point that this long-standing tradition of holiness is foundational to Paul's thought. "Paul followed a well-marked trail in his association of deity and identity. His mode of address presumed a community of 'holy ones' that in some sense knew what it was and what it was for."[3] In the salutation of 1 Corinthians, Paul addresses his audience as follows: "To the church of God that is in Corinth, *to those sanctified* through Jesus Christ, called to be *holy ones*, along with all those who in every place call on the name of our Lord Jesus Christ . . ."[4]

When Paul uses the language of holiness and sanctification of his addressees, he is not merely complimenting them for believing in Jesus. He is reinforcing the idea that they form a community of holiness, so that the Spirit of God may dwell among them. There is a very close connection between holiness and spirit—hence Paul's frequent use of the phrase *pneuma hagion*, "Holy Spirit" (e.g., Rom 15:13; 1 Cor 6:19), though Paul often uses "Spirit" and "Holy Spirit" interchangeably, as equivalent ways of describing the presence of God dwelling among the community of believers.

As many interpreters have observed, Paul likens the community of believers to the temple. First Corinthians 3:16–17 is often cited to illustrate this idea: "Don't you know that you are God's temple and that God's Spirit dwells among you? If anyone destroys God's temple, God will destroy that person. For God's temple is holy, as are you." The Jerusalem temple was conceived of as God's dwelling on earth or, to put it more theologically, the place where God's presence intersects the human realm. That is why maintenance of the temple's sanctity was absolutely critical. Similarly, God's Spirit is present within the Pauline community of believers, thus sanctity must be an essential quality of the community.

Paul's comments are often interpreted to mean that the community is the functional equivalent of the Jerusalem temple, and, in many ways, that is exactly right. If the primary function of the temple is to mediate the divine presence, then any assembly of worshippers functions similarly. Unfortunately, most Christian interpreters move beyond perceiving an analogical equivalence between the temple and community of Christ-believers to interpreting Paul as asserting that the church has superseded the temple and the entire cultic enterprise. Jonathan Klawans argues that scholars of early Christianity generally have tended to read all forms of cultic language, namely, the terminology of sacrifice, purity, and holiness, as an implicit critique of actual cultic practice.[5] But, as Klawans argues, Paul's use of the imagery of the temple and cult is almost always positive and productive. Indeed, Paul's use of the language of purity and sanctity, and his likening of the community of believers to the temple, is typical of the tendency among so many Jews of this era "to expand the realm of holiness"; it reflects a practice of *imitatio Templii*, in which "channeling the sanctity" of the temple into other forms of worship functions as no more a critique of the temple than the monastic practice of *imitatio Christi* functions as a critique of Jesus.[6] Like groups of Pharisees who ate their otherwise ordinary meals in a state of ritual purity, the Qumran community who ate their communal "pure food" like temple priests, the rabbis who translated the sacrificial system of the temple into a liturgical cycle or prayer-offerings, and sundry Jewish communities of the Greco-Roman period who viewed their synagogues as sacred precincts, Paul's cultic language does not imply any critique of the Jerusalem temple. On the contrary, it is a sign of the tremendous power of the temple and the cult and the awe it inspired among Jews spread far and wide. It is also a sign of social and theological developments about the nature of God's presence. In any case, there is nothing in Paul's letters that indicates any radical deviation from the Jewish orientation to the temple cult in this period of Jewish history.

Christian believers enter into the state of holiness or sanctification (holiness and sanctification render the same Greek word, *hagiosmos*) upon baptism, thus being granted privileged access to the Spirit of God individually and communally. In contrasting "holy ones" (*hagioi*) with "unrighteous ones," Paul says to the Corinthians "Rather you were washed, you were sanctified, you were made righteous in the name of the Lord Jesus Christ and in the Spirit of our God" (1 Cor 6:11). But once baptized into the body of Christ, believers have a responsibility to maintain a state of purity in their individual bodies or selves. This means individuals must behave in such a way as comports with their sanctified status; if they don't, they threaten the sanctity of the community. That is to say, if they violate the boundaries that maintain holiness, they risk the abandonment of God's presence, which, of course, impacts the entire community of believers.

Paul's teaching on sexual ethics toward the end of 1 Thessalonians constitutes one of the best illustrations of the theological system that connects purity, holiness, and the presence of the Spirit:

> *This be the will of God,* your sanctification: *that you reject sexual licentiousness. Know that each of you is to control his own body in* holiness *and honor,*[7] *not in the passion of desire, like the Gentiles who do not know God; nor should you overstep and take advantage of a brother or sister in this matter, because the Lord is an avenger in all these things, just as we spoke to you earlier and solemnly warned you. For God did not call us for* impurity, *but for* holiness. *Therefore, anyone who rejects this [teaching] rejects not human [authority] but God, who gives his* Holy Spirit *to you.* (1 Thess 4:3–8)

I have highlighted in the quotation all the words related to holiness, as well as the mention of "impurity," *akatharsia*.[8] While the terminology of holiness can apply both to God and human beings, the terminology of purity applies almost exclusively to human beings. Purity works in conjunction with sanctity, but it is not its equivalent. Regulations and rituals related to purity construct and maintain boundary markers of persons, objects, temporal units, and spaces, so as to preserve a sanctified state and thus facilitate the divine presence. In 1 Thessalonians 4:3–8, Paul reminds his newly converted followers that a state of sanctity is foundational to their new life. When the Thessalonians "turned from idols to God, so as to serve a living and true God," they were consecrated to God, that is to say, they were sanctified and thus can now experience the Spirit of God.

The privilege to enter into holiness is both a gift from God and a responsibility for the Thessalonians. Earlier in his letter, Paul says the Lord "establishes the hearts" of the faithful as "blameless in holiness" (1 Thess 3:13). The "Lord" in 3:13 appears to be Jesus, and thus it seems that Jesus functions as a kind of mediator of holiness, thereby making it possible for humans to experience the Spirit of God. But maintaining the state of holiness also depends on human action. Purity describes that arena of human action in which people are held accountable for honoring the state of sanctity that God has consecrated to them. Formerly, the Thessalonians were Gentiles "who did not know God" and thus could not be known by God either, which is to say they were deprived of the privilege of sanctity. They lived lives marked by moral impurity because of their sexual practices and various other activities associated with idolatry. This moral impurity meant they were not only unfit for any contact or communion with God, but that they were in a state of desecration or abomination and ultimately would be subject to God's condemnation in the final reckoning of the world.

As discussed in chapter 5, recent scholarship has identified two kinds of purity/impurity evident in ancient Judaism, ritual impurity and moral impurity. Ritual impurity pertains to certain human conditions that render an Israelite or Jew impure, which consequently put such a person temporarily at one level removed from sanctity, that is, God's presence. Ritual impurity is contagious to other members of Israel, but it only poses a danger to the sanctity of the community if it is not properly handled. The primary purpose of the system of ritual purity/

impurity appears to have been to regulate the boundaries between the divine and human realms, and, analogously, to maintain the boundaries between Israel and the nations, since Gentiles were not obliged to follow the laws of ritual purity.[9]

In contrast to ritual impurity, all people are expected to maintain a state of moral purity, and sin is a critical factor in distinguishing moral from ritual impurity. Moral impurity, however, does not refer to impurity incurred from the violation of just any ethical imperative. It is associated with particular kinds or categories of sin. In biblical literature, moral impurity pertains specifically to three kinds of egregiously sinful behavior: idolatry, sexual immorality, and bloodshed.[10] These immoral activities cause a severe form of defilement that, in marked distinction to ritual impurity, cannot be remedied by performing the relatively simple rites of purification prescribed in Leviticus 12–15. Moreover, unlike other kinds of ethical violations, these kinds of sins cannot be addressed by restitution or routine rituals of atonement. Rather, moral impurity can only be relieved by some extraordinary form of atonement that usually involves a severe punishment, possibly including exile or expulsion.

Most significant to the study of Paul is the frequent association between sexual immorality and defilement of a grievous nature. In the context of both biblical tradition and Jewish Hellenistic writings, Paul's frequent appeal to the language of purity/impurity when addressing the issue of sexuality is hardly unexpected. Yet its significance is frequently overlooked, or there is confusion about how Paul uses purity language.[11] Note the catalog of vices in Galatians 5:19–21: "Now the works of the flesh are obvious: sexual immorality (*porneia*), impurity (*akatharsia*), licentiousness, idolatry, sorcery, enmities, strife, jealousy, anger, selfishness, dissensions, factions, envy, drunkenness, carousing, and things like these." A quick glance at these verses indicates that this text is a conventional vice catalogue typical of Greco-Roman rhetoricians of all stripes. However, Paul's Jewish spin is evident in the first four terms of the list: *porneia* ranks first among the "works of the flesh," followed by *impurity, licentiousness,* and *idolatry.* This can hardly be a coincidence, given how frequently Paul makes the association among *porneia,* impurity, and idolatry. In the passages from Thessalonians and Romans discussed above, we have seen the way in which this tripartite group of concepts functions almost as a default setting for the apostle. The mere mention of one leads almost inevitably to the mention of another and just as often to the mention of both others.

Paul frequently uses purity language in distinctly Jewish ways in reference to moral questions with the precise intention of marking a boundary around the community of Christ-followers. First Thessalonians 4:3–8 is an excellent illustration of Paul's creative redeployment of God's charge to Israel that she be a "holy nation," the Lord's own possession and thus separate from other nations. The Thessalonian congregation is, as we have said several times, made up of Gentiles, like all of Paul's congregations. How are these Gentiles going to be distinguished from other Gentiles? Paul answers that they will be marked by their sanctity: "For this be the will of God: your sanctification" *not* like "the Gentiles who do *not* know God." This charge is analogous to Moses' charge that Israel will be a holy nation. Instead of ritual purity functioning to distinguish God's sanctified people from other peoples, as in biblical tradition, Paul uses moral impurity to make the distinction.[12] Paul puts this boundary in place not merely by imputing to the Thessalonians the qualities of sanctification and holiness, but by teaching his followers to regulate certain key behaviors that render their individual bodies "pure," whereby they ensure the state of sanctity required for the divine presence in the midst of the corporate body. Sexual behavior in particular appears to function this way.

Paul's use of the concept of moral purity is most obvious in the Corinthian correspondence. It is no mere coincidence that Paul addresses several questions that have been raised in the Corinthian community concerning sexually inappropriate behavior. First Corinthians 5:1–13 is exemplary of the need to have some grasp of the concept of purity as Paul understands it, without which it would be virtually impossible to understand the text. Paul begins with a statement of outrage: "It is widely reported that there is *porneia* among you—the likes of which is not found even among the Gentiles—a man is living with his father's wife!"[13] His response strikes many readers as harsh and intolerant. Unlike other issues Paul is forced to address in his letters, he does not mince words or resort to more oblique rhetorical strategies to argue his point of view. Rather he pronounces an immediate judgment "in the name of our Lord Jesus," which he instructs the community to proclaim publicly the next time they gather together: "You are to hand this man over to Satan for the destruction of his flesh in order that his spirit might be saved on the day of the Lord."

Although there is some dispute about the exact nature of the circumstances to which Paul refers when he says a "man is living with his father's wife," it is fairly clear sleeping with one's stepmother constitutes incest.[14] Sexual sins are not simply legal infractions remedied by restitution or rituals of atonement. These are sins that cause serious defilement, and this defilement extends beyond the sinner: it potentially pollutes the space and the community in which God's presence dwells. As discussed earlier, biblical law stipulates that individuals who commit sins that are morally defiling may be subject to capital punishment or banishment so as to protect the sanctity of the community. When Paul instructs the Corinthians to hand this man over to Satan, Paul is instructing them to expel him from the community. What exactly is meant by "destruction of his flesh" is debated by scholars, but it seems that Paul is expressing some kind of hope for the individual's ultimate salvation on judgment day. In the meantime, the primary intent of Paul's judgment is not the condemnation of the offending party but the protection of the community. To be sure, we may also assume it functioned as a punishment for the man. But Paul does not specify any conditions for his reinstatement. Paul's condemnation of this man is analogous to the biblical *karet* punishment: he is being "cut-off" from the community, the punishment for sexual immorality. That the focus of Paul's concern is the community and not the individual sinner becomes obvious a few verses later:

> *I wrote to you in my letter not to associate with sexually immoral persons—not at all meaning the immoral of this world, or the greedy and robbers, or idolaters, since you would then need to depart from the world. But now I am writing to you not to associate with anyone who calls himself brother or sister who is sexually immoral or greedy, or is an idolater, reviler, drunkard, or robber. Do not even eat with such a person. For what have I to do with judging outsiders? Is it not insiders whom you are to judge? God judges outsiders. "Drive out the wicked person from among you."[15] (1 Cor 5:9–13)*

Even though Paul names several sins beyond sexual immorality here, the issue to which he responds in this section of his letter and the overall context of 1 Corinthians make clear that the dominant issues Paul addresses are sins related to worship and sex, and it is these two arenas of human action through which Paul's Gentile followers define themselves over against other Gentiles. In fact, that may be one reason these two kinds of sin, idolatry and sexual immorality, coalesce into one essential, cosmic sin of defilement. For biblical tradition itself made a similar distinction. The Canaanite nations were driven out of the land because they had committed abominable acts through which they had defiled the land. Other people from other nations, however, who are not guilty of moral impurity may live among the Israelites.

Paul's teaching that one cannot associate with a sinner within the community of believers, but one can associate with such a person if that person is not a member of the community, strikes many modern Christian readers as counterintuitive. Indeed, the counsel found in most subsequent Christian tradition is just the opposite. One may always associate with other Christians—that Christians are sinners is to be expected; that's why the church, which saw itself as the mediator of the forgiveness of Jesus Christ, exists in the first place. This particular aspect of Paul's teaching, namely that one cannot associate with immoral persons inside the church, while it is okay to do so outside the church, is one of the most obvious signs that Paul is thinking in terms of Jewish moral purity and pollution and not just moral-ethical terms.

In moral-ethical terms, sin is defined by the action itself. Such an attitude is reflected in a slogan I have often heard repeated by modern evangelical Christians: "Love the sinner, hate the sin!" It doesn't really matter who commits the sin; it is the particular act that constitutes the sin. If a man sleeps with another man's wife, it does not matter who the man is, baptized Christian or not—it constitutes adultery. The sin of adultery, which many modern Christian churches would regard as a very serious matter, would not, however, be perceived as putting the church community in danger of defilement. There is no perceived need, therefore, for modern Christian churches to expel one of its baptized members for adultery.

By contrast, Paul regards certain sins not in the moral-ethical terms commonplace among modern American Christians but rather in terms of moral purity/impurity. When a system of moral purity is operative, sexual sins in particular cannot be separated from the sinner or from the religious community to which the sinner belongs. The reason that an insider who commits such sins is more dangerous than an outsider is because the former entered into a sanctified state when he or she was baptized. As already noted, Paul frequently calls his Gentile charges "holy ones." As was the case for the Israelite priests, those who possess a greater degree of sanctity also live with a greater risk of defilement. That a traditional concept of moral impurity is the principal guiding factor in the apostle's responses to the Corinthians becomes explicit in 1 Corinthians 6:15–20:

> *Do you not know that your bodies are members of Christ? Shall I therefore take the members of Christ and make them members of a prostitute? God forbid! Do you not know that whoever is united to a prostitute becomes one body with her? For it is said, "The two shall be one flesh." But anyone united to the Lord becomes one spirit with him. Flee sexual immorality! Every sin that a person commits is outside the body; but the sexually deviant one sins against the body itself. Or do you not know that your body is a temple of the Holy Spirit among you, which you have from God, and that you are not your own? For you were bought with a price; therefore glorify God in your body.*

Unlike the excerpt from 1 Corinthians 5, here it is not clear that Paul addresses one particular individual who is sleeping with a prostitute, or whether this was a pervasive problem among male members of the Corinthian church. Ultimately, it doesn't matter whether it was one person or ten: sexual immorality has certain properties of contagion. The defilement of one person's body defiles the corporate body of believers. The close connection between an individual body and the corporate body of the assembly is evident by the way Paul slips seamlessly from speaking about an individual's body in vv. 15–18 to speaking of the body of believers in vv. 19–20.[16] As Klawans says, "in the second temple period, references to the moral defilement of the sanctuary by sexual sins becomes commonplace."[17] Because the assembly of believers was the equivalent of the sanctuary, Paul's vigorous concern for monitoring sexual behavior may be seen as a reflection of the Hellenistic Jewish preoccupation with moral purity and impurity.

The last text I wish to highlight on this subject is the seventh chapter of 1 Corinthians, where Paul famously deals with marriage and celibacy. Interpretations of 1 Corinthians 7 were enormously influential for determining later Christian practice. The chapter as a whole is beyond the scope of our discussion, but Paul's comments regarding marital relations between believers and nonbelievers again reveals the way in which Paul reflects mainstream Jewish thinking of his day with regard to community boundaries.

> *To the rest I say—I and not the Lord—that if any believer has a wife who is an unbeliever, and she consents to live with him, he should not divorce her. And if any woman has a husband who is an unbeliever, and he consents to live with her, she should not divorce him. For the unbelieving husband is made holy through his wife, and the unbelieving wife is made holy through her husband. Otherwise, your children would be unclean, but as it is, they are holy. But if the unbelieving partner separates, let it be so; in such a case the brother or sister is not bound. It is to peace that God has called you. Wife, for all you know, you might save your husband. Husband, for all you know, you might save your wife. (1 Cor 7:12–16, NRSV)*

Paul's teaching here is usually taken by interpreters to apply to the case of a married man or woman who "converts" to Christ and whose spouse remains "unconverted." Should the believer divorce the spouse or remain in the marriage? Virtually all interpreters assume Paul's teaching here reflects a concession with regard to intermarriage, which in this case refers to marriage between a baptized member of the community and an outsider. In other words, Paul did not countenance marriages undertaken between believers and nonbelievers; rather, he addresses a situation of existing marriages but where one party has joined the Christ community. Indeed, a bit further on in the same discussion Paul says that a widow is free to remarry if she wishes but "only in the Lord," and this is taken to mean that she must marry a fellow believer.

Paul's language in 1 Corinthians 7:12–16, however, indicates that he did not consider marital relations between a believer and nonbeliever threatening to the sanctity of the community.[18] This view stands in marked contrast to the situations described by Paul in chs. 5 and 6 of the same letter, one of which was incest, the other concerning members of the community having sex with prostitutes; both of these Paul regards as not only immoral but morally defiling. The sexual sins addressed earlier in the letter pose a serious danger to the sanctity of the community—why isn't that the case here? If a believer persists in marital relations with an unbeliever, why doesn't that cause the same kind of defiling contagion to the individual and thus the corporate body of believers? And how is it that Paul regards the children of such a union as holy? Usually the contagion of impurity works the other way round. Contact between persons or things "unclean" and "clean" causes the clean to become unclean. Here, Paul says, what would otherwise be "unclean" is "holy."

While the vast majority of interpreters take no account of the way in which purity may be operative in Paul, those who do so tend to see Paul as making a radical departure from the traditional understanding of purity in Judaism; some even see evidence that Paul has dispensed with the notion of ritual impurity altogether. In my view, ritual impurity is generally not pertinent to Paul because he is working exclusively, or almost exclusively, within a Gentile context—something I will say more about below. There are some points, however, where one can see a kind of overlap between moral and ritual purity, which sometimes happens in other Jewish literature or with certain arenas of human behavior, one of which is sexuality.[19] Both in the Bible and in Pharisaic Judaism, some sexual behavior is regulated by ritual purity laws, and some by moral impurity laws. General speaking, appropriate sexual conduct within the confines of marriage is regulated by a system of ritual purity, not moral purity. Sex between husband and wife while the wife is menstruating causes ritual, not moral, defilement. In other words, a violation of that sort may be a sin, but it does not constitute a sin on the order of sleeping with your mother. Ultimately, the point is that the questions raised about marriage and divorce in Corinth have led Paul to a discussion about appropriate sexual practices in relation to marriage, and that causes him to make a shift toward assessing the situation in terms of ritual impurity. Here Paul demonstrates a characteristically Pharisaic mode of argumentation in the way he addresses the question as well as in the leniency he demonstrates in rendering a judgment.

Paul's Pharisaic leanings have already been revealed in 1 Corinthians 7 in the way Paul handles the matter of divorce. First, Paul manifests a considerably more lenient position regarding divorce than Jesus, whose teaching Paul refers to earlier in the chapter, but he gives consideration to several special situations, which probably reflect real-life circumstances. In distinction to Jesus, Paul shows himself to be much more of a pragmatist. Second, Paul's position regarding appropriate marriage partners is in principle the same as the position held by Josephus, Philo, the rabbis, and Torah itself, namely, that one does not need to marry someone who is of the same "race." In other words, suitable marriage partners are not determined by genealogy, but by *politeia*, that is, whether they share the same way of life as part of a common community.

First Corinthians makes clear that the real threat of pollution entering the body of believers comes from the moral impurity that is contracted by sexual sins. It is the sexually sinful behavior of those inside the community that poses the greatest threat. When Paul rails against sex with prostitutes in 1 Corinthians 5, it is not because the actual physical contact with the bodies of prostitutes causes defilement. It is the sexually licentious behavior of community members that causes the defilement and potential degradation of the communal body of believers. Paul is thinking in terms of moral impurity. *Acts* of sexual immorality pollute the community. Moral impurity bears properties of contagion, but its contagion does not spread through ordinary physical contact the way menstruation does for example. That form of contagion is characteristic of ritual impurity. Moral impurity affects or "infects" the sanctified community by the immoral actions of community members, especially when the community takes no action to constrain the guilty person or persons. Thus, sinful behavior becomes a source of moral impurity when there is a significant quantity of sinful activity being tolerated or perhaps even indulged.

Paul's ultimate concern is not so much about protecting the individual husbands or wives as it is with protecting the body of believers, including the children who belong to it. Put another way, Paul is mapping the boundaries of the Christ community as they pertain to Gentiles. Those boundaries require both definition and flexibility. For Paul, Gentiles believing "in Christ" retain some measure of likeness to other Gentiles, if for no other reason than that they retain a genealogical connection to them; to state the obvious, they do not have Jewish parents.[20] Indeed, I suspect that the relationship between genealogy and the definition of communal boundaries is the heart of the matter in 1 Corinthians 7:12–16. For v. 14 in particular, the question driving Paul's response is, what is the status of the offspring of mixed marriages? Later rabbinic law took up this question with great enthusiasm, envisioning all manner of marginal offspring and then attempting to define the status of such offspring in relation to the Jewish community. Of course, it is precisely in dealing with marginal cases of religious and ethnic identity that communal boundaries can be defined.

Paul's flexibility in his attitude toward nonbelieving spouses and the offspring of mixed marriages is not the radical step away from Pharisaic Judaism that it is often portrayed as. Rather, it is congruent with the strain of first-century Jewish thinking regarding kinship matters that became most influential.[21]

To summarize: In concert with the dominant tradition among Hellenistic Jews, Paul put greater emphasis on religious and moral principles in defining membership in the sanctified people of God than on ethnic origins and genealogical status. But he also utilized the concept of purity to construct boundaries for his community and regulate contact with outsiders. Paul's community boundaries were no wider, nor more narrow, than the boundaries constructed by most other Jews, including the rabbis, but the lines of demarcation were different.

Scripture and Tradition

It is not uncommon to hear Pauline scholars say that Paul "thought with Scripture." By that they mean that Paul was steeped in Jewish Scripture.[22] We have already seen that Jewish writers like Josephus and Philo bragged that all Jewish people knew their laws, not just a few elites, because the Scriptures were regularly read aloud. Indeed, the public reading of Scripture seems to be the primary reason Jews gathered on the Sabbath. Josephus and Philo no doubt exaggerate greatly, but the habit of gathering weekly to hear the Scriptures read makes it likely that a vast number of Jews, including those who were illiterate by modern standards, had some degree of familiarity with the contents of the Torah. We may at least claim that the general population of Jews was better educated about their ancestral laws and traditions than most of the other peoples around the Mediterranean, including the venerable Greeks and Romans, who possessed no mechanism to facilitate similar kinds of public readings to the masses.[23]

But there were also elite Jews, like the Pharisees and those who lived at Qumran, who pursued the study of Scripture with great intensity.

Because Paul identifies himself as having been a Pharisee, we know the apostle's scriptural literacy was, at the very least, above average. As discussed in chapter 8, Paul's claim of being a Pharisee is a shorthand way of claiming he had an advanced degree in Torah. The evidence from Paul's letters validates the claim. Paul shows familiarity with many different parts of Scripture. But more significant to understanding Paul's traditional engagement with the Scriptures is the general attitude he displays toward them, his facility and creativity in interpretation, and the way in which he relies on Scripture to validate his various arguments, especially his mission as Apostle to the Gentiles. The Pharisees were known for precision and accuracy in their knowledge of Scripture, but they were also known for incorporating nonwritten traditions into their interpretive work and for the creative way they put Scripture in dialogue with contemporary circumstances.

Paul refers to Scripture with a few different expressions, but the one most significant for the subject of this book is *nomos*. In English, *nomos* is translated "law," sometimes capitalized as "Law." It became the standard term used to translate the Hebrew word *torah* among Hellenistic Jews. The apostle's use of *nomos* for Torah comports with the traditional usage of Greek-speaking Jews. Paul does not regard the Torah—whether in the broad or the narrow sense—as simply the ancient written law code of the Jews. The sacred writings that collectively later become the Hebrew Bible contain the story of God's creation of the universe, the narrative of God's election of Israel, and the stories of the patriarchs and the kings, not to mention the Psalms and the poetic oracles of the prophets. It also included a set of laws given to Moses at Sinai. Thus, Jews of antiquity, including Greek-speaking Jews like Paul, regard Torah as that which constitutes the sum of God's revelation to God's people. It is important for the modern reader to bear this in mind when reading Paul's letters. Because virtually all English translations render *nomos* as "law," it can mislead readers into thinking that Paul uses the term to refer only to the Mosaic law, or to the "legal portions" of a modern Old Testament, or just to Jewish ceremonial laws, or, more abstractly, to any form of legalistic thought and practice. This mistake can lead to bigger mistakes and serious misreadings of Paul.

One of those bigger mistakes is to think Paul, as a follower of Jesus, did not hold the Torah in the same high esteem as Pharisees and other learned Jews did. It's not that Christ is necessarily seen to be the antithesis of Torah (though this has been the view of some Christians), but that Christ has now superseded the Torah. That Paul thinks Torah and Scripture have been exceeded by Christ is not merely a long-standing assumption among Christian readers; it has become a truism, repeated so often as "obvious" that it is almost impossible to consider any alternatives. Thus, readers assume that Jewish Scripture already has effectively become the "Old Testament" for Paul, divested of its authority because of the coming of Christ. Its only purpose is to point to Jesus as the Christ.

Nothing could be further from the truth. Paul always treats Israel's sacred texts with reverence and respect, and he frequently appeals to them as a source of divine authority. He calls them "the oracles of God" and says they "have been entrusted to the Jews" (Rom 3:2), a privilege enjoyed by Jews alone. In Romans 13:8–10 he invokes the great commandment to love one's neighbor as oneself and then appeals to the Mosaic law—he explicitly names four of the ten commandments—as the means to fulfilling God's will that human beings love one another. Just as Jews and Christians of subsequent generations came to regard their Bibles as God's Word and, as such, the authoritative guide to living one's life in accord with God's will, so Paul esteems the Scriptures of Israel as God's Word and holds himself and his followers accountable to it.

The modern reader must remember that there was no such thing as the New Testament in the first century. For that matter, there are no distinctly Christian writings that have the status of Scripture in the first century. When Paul refers to Scripture—whatever term he uses—he is referring exclusively to Jewish sacred writings, roughly the equivalent of what Christians would later come to call the Old Testament. Although the boundaries of the Jewish canon were not firmly fixed in the mid-first century, there was widespread agreement about the sacred status of many of the same texts that today comprise the Hebrew Bible, and the texts to which Paul appeals as Scripture were the same texts most any first-century Jew would recognize as having divine authority.[24] The point is that Paul does not regard either the Torah proper or the Scriptures of Israel generally as the "Old Testament."[25] It is not a designation that would have made any sense to Paul in reference to Israel's

Scriptures. The label "Old Testament" would not have made sense to anyone in the first century as a description of Jewish sacred writings. The bottom line is that Scripture for Paul always refers to a collection of unambiguously Jewish sacred texts, that he uses the terminology of law (*nomos*, which may also be translated "Torah") as a synonym for the Scriptures, and these sacred writings are no less authoritative for the apostle after his encounter with Jesus than they were before it.

In chapter 2, "Paul the Problem," I highlighted several passages in which Paul purportedly makes condemnatory remarks in relation to Torah (or "law"), passages that therefore would seem to support the traditional reading that Paul rejected or at least seriously devalued Torah in favor of Christ. I will address these passages and others that present a similar challenge in detail in chapter 12. But it may be helpful to anticipate that discussion a bit here. Whenever Paul seems to speak negatively of Torah, he is not, in fact, condemning the Torah *per se*. Let me state the matter emphatically and categorically: Paul *never* condemns Torah. Neither does he devalue, diminish, or degrade it; it remains the Word of God and the means through which human interpreters may discern the will of God. Paul's infamous remarks are always condemnations of non-Jews adopting Torah observance. When Paul says, "If it is the adherents of the law who are to heirs, faith is null and the promise is void. For the law brings wrath" (Rom 4:14–15), or when he says that "all those who rely on the works of the law are under a curse" (Gal 3:10), his comments are directly aimed at Gentiles, because his letters are explicitly addressed to Gentiles.[26]

In extremely simple terms, Paul objects to the appropriation of the Mosaic law by Gentiles, whether that appropriation is motivated by Gentiles who express a heartfelt desire to undertake Torah observance or because of some sort of coercion by other Jewish teachers. There is not a single instance in which Paul condemns circumcision or food laws or any other specifically Jewish laws *as practiced by Jews* (whether those Jews follow Jesus or not). Every single derisive remark about circumcision, for instance, is a condemnation of any endeavor by Gentiles to circumcise. Paul reserves his condemnations for the non-Jews and/or their Jewish teachers who believe Gentiles must subject themselves to Torah and become Jews in order to become part of eschatological Israel. According to Paul, for Gentiles to attach themselves to Torah after Christ's death and resurrection is to doubt the promises of God most concretely.

Total trust that God always delivers on God's promises is as close to a definition of faith in Paul's writings as I can imagine.

The narrow meaning of Torah that Paul sometimes uses represents the covenant God made with Israel at Sinai. There is a close connection between the Torah as revealed at Sinai and the concept of the election of Israel as chosen among the nations. At the same time, Israel's election was intended to be in the service of the whole of creation. God is the creator of the universe, and all the nations are ultimately accountable to God. Knowledge of God's will is therefore desirable and expected of all human beings. Naturally, then, Torah as Scripture, that is, a witness to God's plan, speaks to all the nations (= Gentiles). But Torah also contains stipulations that pertain exclusively to Israel in her role as a mediator between God and the nations, that is, Israel as a priestly kingdom and holy nation. The stipulations that enable Israel to function in this role are obligatory for Jews but not for other peoples. While Gentiles may become Jews through conversion, which is expressed through a commitment to live according to Torah, the revelation of Jesus as Christ and the apocalyptic point of view that Paul adopted as a result led him to believe that it was no longer necessary or appropriate for Gentiles to become Jews. In order for God to be recognized and glorified as God of the whole world on the "Day of the Lord," the various nations of the world must gather *as the nations*. In other words, it is necessary that Gentiles remain Gentiles on the Day of the Lord, when the God of Israel is shown to be the one God of the world.[27]

Paul understands his mission as Apostle to the Gentiles in these terms. For Paul, the promised blessings that characterize the new age that dawns with the Day of the Lord dovetail with the promise that God made to Abraham in Genesis that all the nations would be blessed through him, and those promises are about to be fulfilled. Though God's plan was revealed long ago in the Scriptures, the nations remain largely ignorant of God and of the divine plan that is unfolding. The Apostle to the Gentiles is, therefore, God's agent with the express mission of bringing to the nations the message that the moment is here and that by the grace of God they have been given a special dispensation through Christ. All they have to do is have faith.

Faith in what, you may ask?

Chapter

10

A Radical Jewish Monotheist

As the great New Testament scholar Nils Dahl argued, Paul's theology and his sense of mission cannot be separated, though many Pauline scholars have tried.[1] Ultimately, however, one cannot understand Paul's particular theological vision without also gaining insight into Paul's self-understanding as Apostle to the Gentiles, and one cannot understand Paul's mission as Apostle to the Gentiles without also having some understanding of the theological principles that motivate that mission.[2]

One must recognize that Paul did not write a systematic theology. One cannot extract from the corpus of Paul's letters a set of essential or even well-defined distinctly "Christian" doctrines (of course, later Christian theologians grounded their doctrines in Paul or wrote systematic theologies based on the Pauline corpus). Paul's letters are *occasional* in nature. That is to say, they are letters, written to address particular issues, questions, situations, etc.; they are not treatises or essays on abstract theological topics.[3] The question is, if Paul did not write a systematic theology, can one identify a coherent message from reading his letters? Along with Christiaan Beker, I believe the answer is yes and that the framework that provides this coherence is Jewish Apocalyptic. Jewish Apocalyptic "constitutes the heart of Paul's gospel, inasmuch as all that is said about Christ refers to that process of salvation which will imminently climax in the *regnum Dei*," by which Beker means the final, triumphant reign of God that not only marks the climax of history but inaugurates the messianic age.[4]

If asked to explain the essence of Paul's mission as Apostle to the Gentiles, a traditional reader of Paul's letters would say that Paul's mission was to preach the gospel, the core content of which is the death and resurrection of Jesus, so as to persuade the Gentiles hearing the gospel to have faith in Jesus Christ and so find salvation on judgment day. (One presumably demonstrates one's faith simply by believing the truth of the claim itself and by being baptized "in Christ."[5]) Typical readers would also say that the theological convictions that really mattered to Paul derived from the revelation of Jesus that led to his conversion. To put the traditional view into its standard anti-Jewish polemic, the primary theological conviction motivating Paul's apostolic mission is that Jesus has replaced Torah as the key to salvation; consequently, Jews no longer have any special standing, but all have equal access to God through Jesus (and only Jesus), hence the need to launch a comprehensive mission to the nations.

The reader of this book will not be surprised to learn that the understanding of Paul's missionary theology summarized in the previous paragraph is not the one advocated in this book. On the contrary, *that* version of Paul's missionary theology is closely linked to the traditional paradigm of Paul as a convert from Judaism to Christianity. According to the traditional view, Christ is seen to be so central to the missionary program that any classical Jewish beliefs Paul may have held are either inconsequential to his mission as Apostle to the Gentiles, or they have been rejected in light of the Damascus road experience. To put it simply, Christ is the heart of Paul's life and thought. Christ is also the goal of his mission as Apostle to the Gentiles.

In contrast to the traditional view, I assert that the most important theological force motivating Paul's mission was a thoroughgoing commitment to Jewish monotheism and how to bring the nations of the world to that realization as history draws to a close.[6] In simple terms, Paul is motivated by his faith in God, whom he believes has charged him with a prophetic mission to Gentiles. Christ is an essential part of the prophetic message, but Christ is not the primary cause from which we can explain all subsequent effects that manifest themselves in the apostle's life and work; God is. In theological terms, Paul's theology is fundamentally not *christocentric*; it is *theocentric*. Inspired by the fundamental conviction of aniconic monotheism, best captured by the *Shema*, the closest thing Judaism has to a creed: "Hear O Israel, the Lord is our

God, the Lord is One" (Deut 6:4), and the knowledge that God's final reckoning with the world was imminent, Paul passionately took up the task of proclaiming to the nations the oneness of God.

In classical Jewish terms, the God of Israel and the God of the Universe were always one and the selfsame God, but now it was time for the nations to acknowledge and glorify God, and this God alone, or else face the wrath of God. The tension between divine particularity, manifest in God's special covenant with Israel, and divine universality, manifest in God's role as Creator and Sustainer of the universe— the One God who providentially oversees all the workings of human history—would be eschatologically resolved in the final reckoning, and the messianic age would begin.

The figure of Abraham provided Paul with an excellent starting point for taking his message of monotheism to the nations. While the narrative details differ significantly for Abraham in Genesis 12 and Paul in Galatians 1, their biographies share a similar pattern. Both are called by God to a purpose that will not merely benefit themselves or their immediate families but all (at least potentially) nations or peoples. Both Paul and Abraham become alienated from their communities of origin as a result of this divine commission. In Abraham's case, God literally calls him away from his family and kin, and, as is familiar to Jews and Christians, Abraham never lives to see the establishment of his family in the land that God promised. Instead, his life is marked by nomadism in the extreme. Except for the cave of Machpelah, which Abraham buys from a Hittite prince as a burial plot for Sarah, Abraham never does possess the land of promise; he spends most of his life residing in Canaan and its environs as a resident alien.[7] "A wandering Aramean was my father" became the refrain of remembrance of the patriarch (Deut 26:5). God's promises about the country that Abraham was to inherit were disappointingly deferred. In Paul's case, God's call results in his alienation from the more conventional Jewish community in which he was presumably raised and, implicitly, from the kind of insulated life of strict Jewish observance that marked the ideal communal life of the Pharisees. Like Abraham, God's call of Paul resulted in his living an itinerant life among people who were not his kin.

Even more important than the text of Genesis for understanding how Abraham helped shape Paul's religious identity is the portrait of Abraham popular in Paul's time. Just as is the case today for modern readers, a well-developed tradition of interpretation existed in antiquity that tended to guide the way in which ancient readers understood Scripture. Biblical figures like Abraham especially tended to capture the imagination of interpreters. As a result, many extrabiblical stories and interpretive traditions were produced and functioned in tandem with Genesis to create an image of Abraham, an image that was both drawn from ancient readers' study of Genesis and, complementarily, that became part of their working assumptions when they approached the stories of Abraham in Genesis.

One important example of this popular interpretive tradition is that Abraham's call in Genesis 12 is taken to reflect a break with his family of origin, a break rooted in his discovery of God and consequent rejection of idolatry. Stories abound among the works of ancient Jewish authors about the events that underlie the call of Abraham in Genesis 12:1–3: "And the child [Abraham] began to realize the errors of the land—that everyone was going astray after graven images and after impurity . . . and he separated from his father so that he might not worship the idols with him."[8] Such stories functioned as putative explanations of Abraham's blind obedience to a command that required him to abandon his mother and father. These stories likely originated out of a need to explain such terse and enigmatic biblical texts, but they also took on a life of their own, perhaps because of their explanatory power in making sense of the text.[9] Eventually, Abraham was considered not just the first person who responded faithfully to the call of the God of Israel; he became known as the first monotheist in human history. As Josephus tells us,

> He thus became the first person to argue that there is a single God who is the creator of all things, and that whatever any of these other things contribute to the good of the world, they are enabled to do so at His command, and not by any inherent force of their own. . . . Because of these ideas the Chaldeans and the other people of Mesopotamia rose up against him, and having resolved, in keeping with God's will and with His help, to leave his home, he settled in the land of Canaan.[10]

The very same logic that claims Abraham as the forefather of Israel presumes that Abraham underwent some kind of religious transformation during the course of his life. Abraham could not have been born to Jewish parents, because there weren't any Jews at the time of his birth. If Abraham became the first Hebrew/Israelite/Jew by responding to God's call, then he must have been something else first. In other words, Abraham did not start life as a monotheist; he *became* a monotheist. (For the Jews of antiquity who passed on traditions about Abraham, Judaism and monotheism would have been seen as virtual equivalents. Furthermore, while modern scholars appropriately distinguish between Israelite religion and Judaism, the Jews of postbiblical antiquity did not—they saw an unbroken thread of continuity between themselves and the people spoken of in Scripture as Israelites or Hebrews. In other words, while it may be anachronistic to call Abraham a "Jew," the "Jews" of the Hellenistic era did not know that and thus thought of Abraham as the first Jew.) Many versions of Abraham's discovery of monotheism emphasize the patriarch's rejection of idolatry as the critical step in Abraham's turn toward God.[11] Therefore, it is not surprising that both Philo and Josephus consider Abraham not just the patriarch of Israel but the first proselyte, for Abraham was originally a Gentile, a Chaldean to be precise. Furthermore, many ancient exegetes, including Josephus and Philo believed that Abraham came to monotheism through his precocious study of the stars, since the Chaldeans were famous for their skill at astronomy. In some strains of postbiblical tradition, the Israelite patriarch excels not only in the science of astronomy but in wisdom and virtue generally, such that he becomes the mentor and teacher of other peoples like the Phoenicians and Egyptians.[12]

Just as Abraham is considered the quintessential hero whose divine call leads him to abandon his old way of life and wander among foreign peoples who receive the benefit of his wisdom, so Paul can understand himself as fundamentally Jewish and yet transformed by his religious experience into someone who must live among other peoples, namely, Gentiles, in order to teach them about the foolishness of idols and the wisdom of worshipping the one true God. Thus, although he remains Jewish, Paul no longer lives among Jews, partly because his call to go to the nations requires this of him, and partly because of the hostility toward him on the part of at least some Jews and Jewish authorities.

The modern reader should not, however, misunderstand the parallel between Paul and Abraham. Paul's experience should not be construed as a reversal of Abraham's: Abraham went from Gentile to Jew; Paul does *not* go from Jew to Gentile. Paul is not an antitype of Abraham; he is a new Abraham.[13] Conceptualizing Paul as the new Abraham is really more an eschatological fulfillment of Abraham's divine purpose. Paul sojourns and gives instruction to the nations, just as Abraham did. Moreover, God assigned Paul a critical role to play in bringing about the transformation from the old era to the new one. When God invades your life and assigns you a mission, it's disruptive! But it was not a rupture in his religious identity as a Jew. The critical disruption for Paul was the realization of what time it was in history.

God at the Center of Paul's Thought

Paul's monotheistic theology not only provides evidence of his ongoing identity as a Jew, but it is essential to understanding his theological vision generally and the reasons for his mission. Strangely, Pauline scholars as a whole have not commented much on this. I suspect that Christian interpreters have taken it for granted—the working assumption being that Christianity, like Judaism, was and still is a monotheistic faith, so of course Paul was a monotheist. As James Dunn observes, "Paul's convictions about God are all too axiomatic. Because they were axioms, Paul never made much effort to expound them. They belong to the foundations of his theology and so are largely hidden from view."[14] But without calling attention to this aspect of Paul's thought, one is liable to miss critical aspects of his message and mission.

On the other hand, from the perspective of outsiders to the Christian tradition, Paul has sometimes been ridiculed for having abandoned monotheism. Such ridicule is part of a more general theological critique, advanced for centuries by Muslims and Jews, against the Christian doctrine of the incarnation, namely that God became human, and the notion of a triune God, namely that God is three-in-one, Father, Son, and Holy Ghost. To reduce a long tradition of theological dialogue and debate to one sentence, Muslims and Jews believe that devotion to Christ renders the Christian claim to monotheism misguided at best and idolatry at worst, while Christians see no contradiction between their affirmation of the oneness of God and the doctrine of the Trinity.

But, to once again reiterate a point made several times already in this book, Christianity does not yet exist as an independent religious system in Paul's time. Paul is not operating with the doctrine of the incarnation as it was defined in the Council of Nicea (CE 325) or the Christian doctrine of the Trinity as it was hammered out in the Council of Chalcedon (CE 451). At the same time, Paul's letters already reflect a surprisingly high Christology that appears to anticipate later orthodox views. That is to say, Paul's letters manifest a belief in Jesus' divinity that came to characterize the full-out identification between Jesus and God of later official Christian doctrine. Jesus is clearly a divine figure of unique status in Paul's letters, and this has led many historians to conclude that devotion to Christ as developed by Paul must have come from outside—that is, non-Jewish—influences.[15]

It is therefore not difficult to understand how Paul's passionate belief in Jesus, along with the concentrated focus on Jesus that mark the apostle's letters, could lead some readers to believe that Jesus has displaced the God of Israel as the one to whom Paul (and other believers associated with the Pauline circle) now pledged allegiance. Indeed, some Christians read Paul exactly that way: the second century Roman bishop Marcion (85–160 CE) believed the God whom Jesus represented was a completely different God from the God of Israel. Of course, Marcion and later Gnostics with similar ideas were dubbed heretical by proto-orthodox and orthodox Christians.

As Larry Hurtado has observed, devotion to Jesus among early believers as attested in New Testament writings did not evolve into a separate Christ cult. Hurtado argues that devotion to Christ developed within a Jewish monotheistic framework and that that framework is at least partly responsible for the constraints maintained by proto-orthodox Christians, constraints that kept devotion to Jesus from developing into a "separate cultus devoted to Jesus as a new second god."[16] Furthermore, Paul's letters provide the earliest extant evidence of the way devotion to Jesus arose from within the context of Jewish monotheism.

Hurtado has identified four convictions held by early followers of Jesus, all of which are well attested in Paul's letters and about which there is no evidence that Paul differed in any significant way from other leaders in the Jesus movement.[17] In other words, these convictions were likely what the earliest generations of believers held in common and what helped to bind them as a community. I wish to cite them here because they characterize in summary form the significance of Jesus for Paul and the way in which that significance can be fully grasped only within the context of classical Jewish convictions about God. According to Hurtado these convictions are manifest in the formulaic sayings that scholars generally agree represent citations of common "Christian" tradition of the earliest strata.

> (1) that God had released Jesus from death, so that it really is Jesus, not merely his memory or influence, who lives again; (2) that God bestowed on Jesus uniquely a glorious new form of existence, immortal and eschatological bodily life; (3) that Jesus has also been exalted to a unique heavenly status, thus presiding by God's appointment over the redemptive program; and (4) that those who were given these special encounters with the risen Jesus were divinely commissioned to proclaim Jesus' exalted status and to summon people to recognize in his resurrection/ exaltation the signal that the eschatological moment of redemption has arrived.[18]

Every one of the convictions Hurtado has identified are convictions about Jesus, yes, but each of them is linked to convictions about God that derive from Jewish tradition. In Paul's letters the resurrection of Jesus proclaims something important about Jesus, to be sure, but its primary function is as testimony to the power of God and as a signal that the dawn of the eschatological age has arrived. Moreover, being an apostle involved understanding oneself as part of the eschatological program of redemption. Proclaiming the gospel meant also making known to the world that the eschatological age was about to dawn.

I will return to the specific role of Christ in Paul's thought, but first I wish to highlight for the reader some exemplary texts from Paul's letters that illustrate Paul's continuing devotion to God, the one and only God, the God of Israel, Creator and Sustainer of the universe.[19] For Paul never compromises the singularity and universality of God by his devotion to Christ. Nor does Paul the apostle of Jesus Christ deny the special relationship God has with Israel. On the contrary, it is the creative tension between universality and particularity that characterized Jewish monotheism in the Greco-Roman period that enabled Paul to interpret his religious experience of the risen Jesus into a call from the God of Israel to become an apostle to the nations, whose mission was to proclaim the coming reign of God.

The theocentric character of Paul's thought is evident in a number of ways throughout his letters. First and most obvious is the staggering amount of God language present in them. According to Dunn, the word "God" appears 548 times in the Pauline corpus (153 in Romans alone), not counting the number of times God is referred to by pronouns or by other titles. Using Romans as an example, Dunn points out that the "attentive reader cannot but be struck by the steady sequence of genitive phrases" that mark its opening chapter: "gospel of God," "son of God," "beloved of God," "the will of God," "the power of God," "the righteousness of God," "the wrath of God," "the glory of God," and the list continues.[20] These phrases occur frequently in the other epistles, though not with the same density they appear in Romans. It is worth noting that Paul uses the phrase "gospel of God" almost as often as he uses the phrase "gospel of Christ."[21] Even in places where one might expect Paul to use Christ language, he opts for God language. When referring to the community of believers as "church" (*ekklesia*), Paul often describes them as "the church(es) of God" and only rarely "church(es) of Christ."[22]

Second, while it was the Son of God who has been revealed "in" or "through" Paul, it is clearly God who called Paul and gave him his commission as an apostle (see Rom 1:1; 1 Cor 1:1; Gal 1:15). God's primacy, in other words, is evident by the way in which Paul attributes virtually everything that happens in the entire cosmos to God's agency. There are many descriptive appellations of God that make clear God is fully in charge of the unfolding of history: it is "God who judges the world" (Rom 2:2; 3:6), "God who shows mercy" (Rom 9:16; Phil 2:27), "God who justifies" (Rom 4:5; 8:33), "God who quickens the dead" (1 Cor 15:22, 36, 42),[23] "God who predetermines [or predestines] events" (Rom 8:29–30; 1 Thess 5:9), "God who makes and fulfills promises." It is the will of God that determines everything and to which everything is subject. It is not surprising, then, to find Paul making such frequent mention of the will of God, whether it is past events to which he is referring, future events, or in his petitions to God. Of course, such an attitude is consistent with the image of God as Creator and Sustainer of the universe.[24]

Third, words of prayer and worship are exclusively directed to God. Paul's letters usually include what is called a "Thanksgiving," so-called because Paul gives thanks to God for the joys and successes of his congregants. "I give thanks to God in every remembrance of you, in every one of my prayers" (Phil 1:3).[25] The thanksgiving usually occurs right after the greetings at the beginning of a letter. But Paul is inspired to turn to God to offer thanks or in other expressions of prayer at several points in his letters. These prayerful expressions, too, are always directed to God.[26]

To be sure, Paul oftentimes offers words of thanks or praise or supplication *through* Christ, but it nevertheless remains clear that God is the one to whom the words are addressed. Romans 7:25 provides a succinct example: "Thanks be to God through Jesus Christ our Lord." In at least two texts, Paul makes explicit that the exalted Christ performs a mediating function between humans and God. One appears in 2 Corinthians: "For in him every one of God's promises is a 'Yes.' For this reason it is through him that we say the "Amen," to the glory of God" (2 Cor 1:20).[27] The other is from a famous passage in Romans: "Who will bring charges against God's elect? God is the one who justifies! Who is there to condemn? Christ Jesus is the one who died, and yet he was raised, and it is he who is at the right hand of God and who intercedes for us" (Rom 8:33–34).

To be sure, Paul sometimes speaks of Jesus in ways that sound strikingly similar to ways he describes God. Most obvious is that Paul's favorite title for Jesus is *kyrios* "Lord." The title appears in the epistolary greetings, as well as in prayers, hymns, and confessions. In other words, *kyrios* appears in formulaic expressions that reflect common pre-Pauline tradition of the earliest generation of believers. For example, in Romans 10:9, Paul appeals to a common confession or profession of faith among believers: "If you confess with your lips Jesus as Lord and believe in your heart that God raised him from the dead, you will be saved."[28] The most memorable and magisterial instance of this early "Christian" confession is found at the end of the famous hymn in Philippians 2:6–11: "At the name of Jesus every knee should bow . . . and every tongue confess Jesus Christ as Lord" (vv. 10–11). More than other titles, *kyrios* is the one that "denotes the Lord Jesus Christ's special status and dignity."[29]

"Lord" was a common way for Jews in antiquity to refer to God already by Paul's time. In Hebrew Scripture, God is referred to by several epithets, including "Lord." But this particular designation for God may have become more theologically freighted by Paul's time. The Hebrew word *adonai*, which literally translates "Lord" or "my

Lord," was probably substituted in public readings of Scripture whenever God's name appeared in the text. Scholars often refer to the divine name as the tetragrammaton because it was composed of four consonants, represented in English as YHWH. While the oldest (i.e., pre-Christian) extant copies of the Septuagint write out the divine name in Greek or Hebrew letters, there is evidence from Aramaic sources, as well as from Philo and Josephus, that Jews did not pronounce the name, but instead spoke the word *kyrios*.[30] Thus, there is a close association between the divine name and *kyrios* or "Lord." Scholars often point to this close association when they wish to stress how astonishing it is that Paul used *kyrios* as a title for Jesus.

At the same time, the word *kyrios* is the ordinary Greek word for a human lord or master. Caesar was commonly called *kyrios* (among many other titles), but the term can also be used on a very small scale to refer to any household patriarch in relation to other members of his household. *Kyrios* was also used in the Roman period in reference to certain popular deities, such as Aesclepius, for example.[31] Some scholars have suggested that Paul's use of the title *kyrios* for Jesus derives exclusively from these kinds of Hellenistic uses. The attempt to constrain the sphere of influence to (non-Jewish) Greek and Roman usage is partially due to the incredulity of other scholars that Paul could have used the *kyrios* title of Jesus if it was such an important title for God. For wouldn't the profession of faith that "Jesus is Lord" threaten the exclusivist claim to the oneness of God that characterizes Judaism? If we follow this line of logic, Paul cannot be the learned Pharisee he claims to have been—he really was more "Greek" than "Jewish," because he appears ignorant of the thoroughgoing nature of Jewish monotheism.

Alternatively, I suggest that Paul's preference for the term *kyrios* in reference to Jesus was for the purposes of expedience. As Apostle to the Gentiles, Paul designed his message for the non-Jewish polytheistic world. By repeatedly referring to Jesus as Lord, Paul was trying to instill in his Gentile audience the kind of loyalty required of those who have now chosen to devote themselves to the One God, especially since there were many gods in Greco-Roman society, and people were accustomed to paying homage to more than one. For Gentiles, proper worship of one god did not necessarily imply that one needed to abstain from worshipping all others. Paul's proclamation of Jesus as Lord was likely an essential first step in enabling Gentiles to comprehend the kind of theological exclusivity demanded by Jewish monotheism. (The use of *kyrios* for Jesus could also have been a challenge to the Lordship of Caesar, and therefore a critique of Roman imperial ideology.)

In 1 Corinthians Paul displays just this sort of expedient disposition. In the midst of his discussion of the pitfalls of idolatry, he says the following: "We know . . . that 'there is no God but one.' Even if there may be so-called gods, whether in heaven or on earth—just as there are many gods and many lords—yet for us there is one God, the Father, from whom are all things and for whom we exist, and one Lord, Jesus Christ, through whom are all things and through whom we exist" (1 Cor 8:4–6). Here Paul acknowledges that within the larger social context within which his charges dwell, there are many who are called "god" or "lord," but, whatever the existential status of those gods and lords, ultimately and cosmologically, there is but One, to whom his followers pledge their allegiance. It would be a mistake, I think, to interpret Paul as saying here that no other gods or lords exist. On the contrary, Paul is referring both to chimerical beings that in reality (or in Paul's view, anyway) don't exist (like idols) *and* to earthly and supernatural powers that really do exist but are nevertheless subservient to the One. As N. T. Wright says, "The pagan pantheon cannot simply be dismissed as metaphysically nonexistent and therefore morally irrelevant. It signals an actual phenomenon within the surrounding culture that must be faced and dealt with, not simply sidestepped."[32]

In recent years, several scholars have commented in regard to 1 Corinthians 8 that it is astonishing that Paul invokes the *Shema*—thus unequivocally embracing traditional Jewish monotheism—and then unself-consciously uses it as the basis on which to defend the lordship of Christ. Scholars find Paul's use of the *Shema* particularly astonishing in this case precisely because it appears that Paul is bifurcating the *Shema*, making it thereby applicable to both God and Christ, which admittedly seems a rather odd use of the proclamation of the oneness of God.[33] From a Christian point of view, this reading of 1 Corinthians 8:4–6 makes it look like a momentous turning point in the development of a distinctly Christian theology. From a Jewish point of view, this interpretation of 1 Corinthians 8:4–6 sounds like Paul puts the *Shema* to blasphemous use.

But this reading of 1 Corinthians 8 represents, in my view, either a misreading or perhaps simply an overreading of what Paul is saying.

Because God in ancient Judaism was understood as a creator God, God maintains an ongoing relationship with creation, including individual created beings. God acts in history. That is to say, God did not just create human beings; God continually interacts with them as well. Because God is God, however, God's involvement with people requires mediation, and this mediation often takes the form of specially chosen humans in biblical literature. We could name many such figures from the biblical narrative: Abraham, Moses, Aaron, Joshua, etc. Sometimes God sends angels out from the heavenly realm to achieve his purposes on earth.

In the late Second Temple period, there was a marked proliferation of angels and other semidivine figures. Stories abound in pseudepigraphic literature in which archangels such as Michael or Raphael are sent by God in response to a person's petition (e.g., Tobit) or simply to carry out a task in accordance with God's will (*Testament of Abraham*). Alternatively, God sometimes brings up human beings to heaven so that they might return to earth to report what has been revealed to them. Much extracanonical literature of this period utilizes the genre of "apocalypse," which literally means "revelation." Apocalypses usually recount how a specially chosen figure has been exalted to heaven and what that one has seen of the heavenly realm(s). Such a figure functions as an intermediary between the human and divine realms. The books of Enoch, which appear to have been enormously popular in some circles in antiquity—perhaps even considered authoritative on a par with other prophetic writings by the Qumran community—portray Enoch as the prophetic visionary extraordinaire. The elaborate imaginings of Enoch as a highly exalted figure derive from Genesis 5:24, where it says Enoch was translated to heaven, and thus it was presumed that he never suffered death.

The point is that even as Judaism progressed toward a more serious degree of monotheism through the Second Temple period, Jewish imagination simultaneously envisioned a growing number of intermediaries and exalted figures. These intermediaries were not only envisioned as part of the heavenly host, but sometimes certain roles traditionally thought of as belonging to God were ascribed to them. Enoch, for example, is sometimes portrayed as the eschatological judge who will separate the wicked from the righteous at the final judgment. In other

texts, a similar role is ascribed to Adam or Abel. But as long as these figures were understood as God's agents, carrying out God's will, they do
not seem to have threatened monotheism as most Jews understood it.

One mediating figure that has a uniquely exalted status and was
clearly not human, but was no mere angel either, is Wisdom. Wisdom
is divine knowledge personified as a woman; "Lady Wisdom" figures
prominently already in Proverbs 8. But in much Hellenistic Jewish literature, reflection on the figure of Wisdom increases dramatically. For
Wisdom (or the Logos, which is a transgendered Hellenized incarnation
of Wisdom[34]) becomes the primary agent of creation and the cosmic
mind that continuously orders creation. In the Wisdom of Solomon,
a text produced by Alexandrian Jews and roughly contemporary with
Paul, Wisdom is described as "the fashioner of all things" (7:22), "an
associate in [God's] works" (8:4), through whom God "formed humankind" (9:2). Wisdom is . . .

> *The breath of the power of God,*
> *and a pure emanation of the glory of the Almighty; . . .*
> *For she is a reflection of eternal light,*
> *a spotless mirror of the working of God,*
> *and an image of his goodness.*
> *Although she is but one, she can do all things,*
> *and while remaining in herself, she renews all things;*
> *in every generation she passes into holy souls*
> *and makes them friends of God and prophets;*
> *for God loves nothing so much as the person who lives with wisdom.*
> *(Wis 7:25–28)*

Scholars have long observed the similarities between the figure of
Wisdom and some early reflections on the figure of Jesus, especially
the first chapter of the gospel of John. Though the connections are
observed less often in Pauline scholarship, there are scholars who have
argued for the influence of Wisdom traditions in Paul in general, and
in 1 Corinthians 8 in particular.[35] My concern is not so much to establish particular lines of influence as it is to emphasize that highly
exalted figures do not threaten the monotheistic religious system that
characterizes Judaism in this period. On the contrary, such figures serve

to reinforce its fundamental principles. Indeed, Jewish monotheism of the Greco-Roman period incorporated intermediary figures precisely to ensure the absolute oneness of the one God.

Recall the confessional formula of 1 Corinthians 8:4–6:

For us there is one God, the Father,
from whom are all things and for whom we exist,
and one Lord, Jesus Christ,
through whom are all things and through whom we exist.

When Paul and other early followers of Jesus avowed or confessed Jesus as their Lord, it was not meant as a polemic against Jews who had a wrongheaded conception of God because they didn't believe in Jesus. Neither was it meant as an attempt to position Christ as an alternate god in place of other pagan gods. Rather, Paul uses the formula "One God, . . . One Lord" to stress both the oneness of God and that all of creation belongs to that one God, who has one agent, the Lord Jesus Christ, capable of enacting the will of God. In other words, the oneness of the lordship of Christ points toward the oneness of the Father God from which everything and everyone was created. Just as Lady Wisdom in the excerpt quoted from the Wisdom of Solomon extends into all things, touching every generation of humankind, she is "but one." Jesus Christ functions similarly; Christ the one Lord is capable of reconciling all of humankind, all the nations, to God, because Christ's lordship is not only one; it is higher than all other spheres of sovereignty governed by all the other "lords." While the nations have had various lords to whom they have given loyalty, by relinquishing those allegiances in favor of an exclusive and singular allegiance to Christ as Lord, they participate in the redemptive process that reconciles all peoples to God, and, as I shall argue in the next chapter, the various nations become reconciled to one another because they become part of one divinely ordained family— they become descendants of Abraham.

Thus the fact that *kyrios* was a term closely associated with the God of Israel does play a role in its becoming a key title for Christ. But this development is not so terribly scandalous to traditional Jewish monotheism as many scholars think. After all, there are plenty of terms that can be used of both God and humans without compromising the essential oneness of God. The Greek term *doxa*, usually translated "glory" when the subject is God, is often the same word that is translated "honor" when the subject is a man.[36] Ultimately, I suspect the wide range of connotations associated with *kyrios* influenced the development of this title as central to the figure of Jesus Christ.

Because of the similarity of language used in relation to Jesus and God, it is easy to miss the care that characterizes Paul's speech most of the time and that functions to distinguish between Jesus and God. There are certain things, for example, that Paul would never say of Jesus. Most obviously, Paul never refers to Jesus as *theos*, "god."[37] It may be, in fact, that *kyrios* dominates as a title for Jesus precisely so as to keep clear the distinction between God, who is almost always referred to as *theos*, and Christ.[38] As already mentioned, words of worship are not directed to Christ; they are directed to God through Christ. Confessing Jesus as Lord does not constitute worship or adoration on a par with God.[39] To be sure, Christ is often part of the content of prayers or words of praise, but that is different from being the object of worship. Even in texts that exemplify a strikingly high Christology—so high it appears as if Paul anticipates the Trinitarian doctrine of the fourth century in which Jesus is a coequal part of the Godhead with the Father—a more careful reading reveals the way in which the apostle maintains a distinction between God and Christ and the way in which the latter is always subordinate to the former.

The text scholars most frequently point to when wanting to demonstrate just how godlike is Jesus is an early hymn that appears in Philippians 2:6–11. Its concluding lines read as follows:

Therefore God exalted him
and granted him the name that is above every name.
so that at the name of Jesus every knee should bow,
of things in heaven, things on earth, and things under the earth,
and that every tongue confess the Lord Jesus Christ,
to the glory of God the Father. (vv. 9–11)

There is no question that Jesus is highly exalted here. The imagery suggests the whole cosmos recognizes Jesus Christ as Lord and submits to his authority. Yet, two aspects of this passage should dissuade interpreters against any reading that conflates Jesus and God or conflates veneration of Jesus with worship of God: First, it is God who exalts

Jesus; God remains unquestionably in charge. The same is true of Jesus' resurrection—that, too, is an act of God, not an act of Jesus. Whenever Paul refers to the resurrection of Jesus, he consistently says either that God raised Jesus from the dead, or he refers to the event using the passive voice, "Jesus was raised from the dead," with God implied as the subject.[40] Second, the exaltation of Jesus serves the purpose of glorifying God the Father. As is said so often in Hebrew Scripture, God acts so as to glorify or magnify God's name, so that all will know that God is God. As Paul says elsewhere, "do everything for the glory of God." As long as veneration of Jesus points to God, it is not a threat to God or to the foundation of Jewish monotheism; it is all done to the glory of God.[41] As Dunn says of hymns like Philippians 2:6–11 where Jesus seemingly forms the content of the worship: "they are not addressed *to* Christ, but give praise to God *for* Christ."[42]

Modern readers tend to assume that Paul's own religious devotion was directed toward Christ. Once again, this assumption derives, at least partly, from the Paul-the-convert paradigm. Paul's conversion meant that the postconversion Paul turned toward belief in Jesus Christ as his Lord and Savior. It's not that readers think Paul stopped believing in God or replaced the God of Israel with Jesus, but they do assume that Christ became the focus of the apostle's religious energy and that Paul preached the necessity of belief in Christ, without whom one could presumably never know God or be known by God.

Confessing Jesus Christ as Lord and Savior becomes the *sine qua non* of Christian faith. While it is nearly impossible to define the essence of any religion—that which defines a particular religion regardless of the various historical and cultural incarnations it undergoes over time— some sort of veneration of Christ seems to mark virtually every variety of what we commonly call Christianity. Even as the status of Christ in relation to God may differ among a seemingly infinite number of denominations, as well as proper forms of worship, sources of authority, the ethical implications of being Christian, etc., Christ is always somehow part of the picture. And for the dominant Christian tradition, whether Orthodox, Roman Catholic, or Protestant, Christ is no mere prophet or enlightened founder; Christ is a manifestation of God. At some point, believing in Christ became the essential and only correct way for Christians to believe in God. Thus, to confess one's faith in Jesus as Lord became the same thing as confessing faith in God. To name God specifically in prayers, benedictions, etc., in other words, became redundant.

All this is baggage that a Christian reader of Paul's letters has but that Paul himself did not have. A shift in devotional focus from God to Christ may have already begun with other New Testament writers, but these writers come at least a generation after Paul.[43] As noted by many scholars, Paul carefully distinguished between Jesus and God and did not worship Jesus as if he were a god, nor does the apostle treat Christ as the equivalent of God, the use of similar language notwithstanding. Rather, confessing Jesus as Lord was supposed to point people toward God; it was not meant to distract people from God nor to complicate the unitary nature of God. One misunderstands Paul if one misses this point.

The Faith *of* Versus the Faith *in* Jesus Christ

One of the clearest and perhaps most shocking ways to demonstrate that Paul maintained a clear distinction between Jesus and God in terms of religious devotion is that when Paul exhorts his charges to faith, it is not to faith in Jesus; it is to faith in God. This assertion surprises modern readers for a couple of reasons. In some cases Paul explicitly refers to Jesus' resurrection when he exhorts his followers to have faith. Given modern Christian assumptions about a triune God, a superficial look at such texts will cause a reader to misread what Paul says. For example, the apostle in Romans 4:24 says that righteousness will be reckoned "to those who believe in *the one who* raised Jesus our Lord from the dead." Obviously "*the one who*" refers to God, even though the word "God" (*theos* in Greek) does not appear in the text. Thus, the belief of which Paul here speaks is unequivocally directed toward God.[44] Nevertheless, Paul makes mention of Jesus' resurrection as a description of the God in whom one should have faith. Paul's tendency to refer to God as the *God who raised Jesus* indicates that the phrase functioned as an explanatory epithet that was helpful in distinguishing Paul's God—the one, true, living God—from all the other gods floating around in Greco-Roman culture.[45] But there are other obstacles that hinder readers' ability to see Paul's devotional focus on God—obstacles that create difficulties even for very attentive readers.

English translations have rendered certain phrases in such a way as to obscure what Paul is and is not saying about having faith in God and Jesus. Exposing the problem in this case requires a bit more effort from the reader. However, it is extremely important to the thesis being proffered in the present book, and so, in my judgment, it is worth the effort. I therefore beg the reader's indulgence.

The term "faith" appears a lot in Paul's letters. Certainly for interpreters within the traditional framework (though not *only* them[46]), faith is the center of Paul's gospel. In particular, since the Reformation, "justification by faith" was perceived to be the theological essence of Paul's writings, and implicitly it became for many Protestant Reformers the essence of Christianity itself. Properly speaking, justification by faith refers to the process by which a Christian receives salvation. In discussions of Paul's use of the phrase "justification by faith," interpreters tend to focus on explaining what justification is. If they take up the meaning of "faith," they tend to explain the why, not the what. In other words, commentators will explain to readers *why* Paul emphasizes faith, especially as opposed to its alternative: works. But commentators generally do not feel compelled to explain *what* this faith is. Rather, they assume everyone knows what Paul refers to whenever he speaks of faith. So what is the nature of the faith by which one is justified? Generally speaking, the assumption is that the "faith" in the formula "justification by faith" is a shorthand way of speaking of the faith a believer has in Christ. Since faith in Christ is essentially what makes a Christian a Christian, one is justified—and thus assured of salvation—by being baptized into Christ, thus demonstrating one's faith in Christ.

Before addressing what Paul specifically means when he uses the phrase "faith in Christ," a word about Paul's understanding of faith per se, for it is markedly different from modern notions. Modern Jews and Christians tend to think of "faith" as a synonym for "belief," where it means ascent to a particular belief in something over a claim of skepticism. When a modern Christian proclaims, "I believe in God," this profession of faith is implicitly or explicitly a claim of theism over atheism. "I believe in God" means "I believe in the existence of God." We live in a post-Enlightenment era where a scientific perspective on the world dominates and poses a threat to religious belief. Atheism is a viable option for the modern Western world more than ever before. By making professions of faith, those who are theists are professing a belief that others do not share and that our scientific culture causes us to doubt.

For Paul, and for the majority of his contemporary Jews, this kind of doubt is not the issue. Jews took the existence of God for granted; it was not a debatable point. Paul's use of the term *pistis* is more akin to our word for "trust" or "faithfulness." It has connotations of loyalty, devotion, and commitment. When the apostle speaks of having faith in God, he means devoting oneself completely to God and trusting in God's promises. When Paul speaks of Abraham's faith in Romans 4, he is speaking of the patriarch's commitment, trust, and devotion. Moreover, it certainly includes one's mental disposition as well as behavior. As we shall discuss shortly, by using the term *pistis*, Paul is not distinguishing between faith and works as it is usually understood, as if being faithful entailed only thinking certain thoughts, and "works" meant only doing things without actually having any faith. In light of Paul's more holistic understanding of the word, it is sometimes appropriate to translate *pistis* in Paul's letters as "faithfulness" precisely because it captures these dimensions of the Greek term better. The rendering of *pistis* as "faithfulness" is important to the issue of the relationship between "faith" (or "faithfulness") and Jesus.

If I ask my Christian students, What does Paul mean by faith? Faith in whom? Faith in what? The answer is "faith in Christ." Sometimes they answer "faith in God." When pressed, they will usually add that Paul has a particular understanding of faith in God that necessarily includes faith in Christ, since Christ is the only legitimate means by which a person can gain access to God. To reiterate the point in simpler terms, to believe in God within a Christian context means also believing in Christ. The question is, does my students' articulation of this long-standing Christian assumption about faith comport with what Paul means by faith, or do subsequent Christian readers impute to Paul an understanding foreign to his way of thinking?

When modern readers read almost any English translation, they will come across several passages in which Paul ostensibly speaks explicitly of faith in Christ (or Jesus or God's Son, etc.). However, every instance in which the phrase "faith *in* Christ" (or its variants) appears in the undisputed letters would be better translated "faithfulness *of* Christ."[47] In the Greek text that underlies the English there is no preposition between the nouns "faith" and "Christ."

The two nouns form what is called a genitive construction. "Christ" or its equivalent (e.g., Son of God, Lord) appears in the genitive form. Like German and Latin, the Greek language conveys the various grammatical parts of speech by adding prefixes and suffixes and thus altering the form of nouns and verbs. (By contrast, English for the most part relies on word order.) In Greek, there are four cases: nominative, genitive, dative, and accusative. The nominative case generally indicates the subject of a sentence, the dative an indirect object, and the accusative the object of the verb. The most common way to render a Greek noun in the genitive case into English is with the preposition "of," and it denotes belonging or gives more specific definition to whatever noun or phrase it stands in relation to. One could muster any number of examples from ancient Greek literature generally or the Pauline literature in particular to illustrate this. The expression "the righteousness of God" in Romans 3:21 looks like this in Greek: δικαιοσύνη θεοῦ. The second word in transliteration is *theou*, God, in the genitive case (the nominative form is *theos*). For that reason, virtually every English translation renders the phrase "righteousness of God." The same type of grammatical construction underlies "faith of Jesus Christ": πίστις Ἰησοῦ Χριστοῦ; written in transliteration it would read as follows: *pistis iesou christou*. *Pistis* means "faith" or "faithfulness" and the *ou* endings on "Jesus" (*ies-*) and "Christ" (*christ-*) indicate the genitive case. Thus, the most literal translation of *pistis iesou christou* is "faithfulness *of* Jesus Christ." The choice of the preposition *in* to convey this kind of genitive construction is by no means a self-evident choice. Far from it. Nevertheless, the phrase is consistently rendered "faith *in* Jesus Christ" in English translations.[48]

Why don't English translations render the phrase as the "faithfulness of Jesus Christ"? The historical answer is that the tradition of English translation has been deeply influenced by the debates that defined the Reformation. Martin Luther's German translation has been especially influential here. He translated the phrase so that it had to be read as a subjective genitive. For example, in Romans 3:22 Luther rendered *pistis iesou christou* as *den Glauben an Jesus Christus*, and by so doing, he removed the ambiguity present in the Greek text, so that it clearly meant "faith *in* Christ."[49] Another answer has to do with the general perspectival nature of all knowledge. To date, virtually all translators of New Testament texts have been Christians. As we now know, "faith in Christ" became the essence of the Christian faith itself. Muslims, Christians, and Jews can all speak of their "faith in God" but only Christians profess "faith in Christ." In spite of the impressive critical acumen of scholarly translators, they possess a Christian perspective that is itself the cumulative product of centuries of Christian reflection, so it is understandable that they conflate their own Christian beliefs with Paul's. In this instance, the problem is exacerbated by the common assumption that Paul deserves the credit for being the first to proclaim the necessity of having faith *in* Christ.

Of course, even if we translate the phrase literally as "faith of Christ," there remains grammatical ambiguity, because there are two basic ways to understand the relationship between the genitive noun and the words it stands in relationship to. These two ways are referred to in technical terms as the objective genitive and the subjective genitive. If *pistis christou* is an objective genitive, Christ is understood to be the *object* of "faith," hence the reason for translating the phrase "faith in Christ." If, however, *pistis christou* is a subjective genitive, it is translated "faithfulness of Christ" because the "faithfulness" refers to Christ's faithfulness—"Christ" is the subject of "faith" in this case.

A similar ambiguity can arise in English and will help to illustrate the issue. Take the following sentence: *For the love of God and country, I will do my duty.* This is an example of an objective genitive. *Love* is directed toward *God and country*. Put another way, *God and country* are the object of *love*. Let us consider another sentence: *Without the support of family and friends, I never would have finished this book.* This is an example of a subjective genitive. *Support* is not directed toward *family*; rather, *support* describes or modifies what the *family* has done for the speaker of the sentence. In both of these examples, there is little room for confusion because the context restricts the possible meanings. But if the context is ambiguous, or if no context is provided, as with an isolated phrase like "the love of God," then either meaning is possible. The *love* may be directed *toward God* (an objective genitive) or the *love is God's* (a subjective genitive). In essence, one can only assess whether the phrase *pistis iesou christou* is an objective or a subjective genitive by examining it in context.

There are strong grammatical and theological reasons for the subjective genitive reading that can be seen by looking at it carefully in context. Although we will discuss Romans 3:21–22 in more detail in chapter 13, it provides an excellent example here for illustrating why the subjective genitive is the better reading. As expected, the NRSV translates the text using the preposition "in":

> *But now, apart from law, the righteousness of God has been disclosed, and is attested by the law and the prophets, the righteousness of God through faith in Jesus Christ for all who believe.*

Compare my translation, which uses "of" as well as "faithfulness":

> *Now, however, apart from the Torah, the righteousness of God has been made manifest to which the same Torah and the prophets gave witness; [namely,] the righteousness of God [which has come] through the faithfulness of Jesus Christ for all those who are faithful.*

Certainly in this context reading the phrase as a subjective genitive makes better sense than the objective genitive.[50] If God is making manifest God's righteousness, when Paul says that righteousness comes through the *pistis iesou christou*, can Paul mean that God's righteousness would come through people having faith in Jesus? It makes little sense to say that God's righteousness is revealed in the world because of what human beings do. If we translate *pistis iesou christou* as "faith in Christ," then Paul is asserting a cause-and-effect relationship between the faith of human beings and God's righteousness, where the former causes the latter. Would it not make more sense that Paul is saying Jesus is the manifestation of God's righteousness?

Interpreting *pistis christou* as an objective genitive and translating it as "faith *in* Christ" leads the unsuspecting reader to believe there is no other interpretive possibility. Scholars who argue most strongly for translating *pistis christou* as "faithfulness *of* Christ" typically advocate reading the phrase as a subjective genitive.[51] In other words, they understand the phrase as referring to Christ's faith, not the faith of believers. Other scholars disagree that the phrase is necessarily a subjective genitive in all cases, but they support rendering the phrase "faith *of* Christ" in order to signal to readers there is ambiguity in the Greek. In any case, a growing number of scholars have become outspoken advocates for translating the phrase "faithfulness of Christ." It is likely that a majority of New Testament scholars all along the theological spectrum now favor this translation.[52] The point is that, technically speaking, the Greek equivalent of the phrase "faith in Christ" never occurs in the undisputed Pauline letters (even though it appears seven times in English translations). If Paul did not ever speak of having faith in Christ, that is, having faith in Christ on a par with having faith in God, then Paul's monotheism remained uncompromised.

Chapter

11

On a Mission from God

As we have already discussed, aniconic monotheism was the signature mark of Judaism in the Roman world. Jewish monotheism in Greco-Roman antiquity may be simply defined as the belief in one supreme God who creates and sustains the universe and who cannot be represented by any visible form. The most obvious public expression of this belief in the context of the Greco-Roman world was Jews' refusal to perform any acts of devotion to any other gods or godlike beings. This distinctive intellectual posture and the way it was embodied in the worship practices of Jews was noted by Greek and Roman writers, sometimes with admiration, sometimes with derision. But Jewish intellectuals of antiquity consistently express passion and pride whenever they write about the Jews' exclusive devotion to the one and only God. "Let us, then, engrave deep in our hearts this as the first and most sacred of commandments, to acknowledge and honour one God Who is above all, and let the idea that gods are many never even reach the ears of the man whose rule of life is to seek for truth in purity and righteousness," proclaims Philo of Alexandria.[1]

There were inherent tensions in ancient Jewish conceptions of God as God of the universe and also God as God of Israel. One of the most common ways in which Hellenistic Jews reconciled the universal and particular aspects of God was to understand Israel as mediating knowledge of the divine mind to the rest of the world—this idea can be found in Josephus and Philo, and earlier in writers like Ben Sira. But it is essentially an appropriation of the classic idea of election. In other words, the biblical and postbiblical understanding of Israel's election did not constitute a contradiction to the claim of universal monotheism. On the contrary, says Dahl, "The tension between the monotheistic faith in God as Creator of all mankind, and the specific, covenantal relationship between YHWH and his people, was resolved by means of the doctrine of election, which received its classical formulation in the book of Deuteronomy and the oracles of Second Isaiah."[2] What Dahl means is that Israel plays the role of God's specially designated servant who mediates between God and the Gentile nations.

Too often Pauline scholars have pitted Christian universalism against Jewish particularism. Ernst Käsemann provides the classic example: He takes Paul in Romans 3 to be speaking polemically against Jews who have so boasted in their own relation to God that they have compromised the true meaning of the *Shema*.[3] But as Dahl rightly shows, when Paul poses the question "Does God belong to Jews alone?" he is confident that there is only one answer and that it is self-evident: "Of course not!" Paul's question is intended for rhetorical effect, namely, to remind Paul's hypothetical dialogue partner and the audience of Romans of certain indisputable premises that they share in common. No Jew of Paul's time would deny that God is God of all peoples.[4]

Paul's mission must be understood as a synthesis between the image of God as universal Creator and Sustainer and the image of God whose portion is Israel. Paul's emphasis on God as the God of all peoples should not be taken as evidence that Paul embraced a universalistic vision of God *only after* he came to be a follower of Jesus. To be sure, the apostle's transformative experience of Jesus radically changed Paul's priorities. The difference, however, is not that Jesus signaled to Paul a kind of religious universalism that he had never known as a Pharisee. The difference is that Paul's vision of the risen Jesus meant the end of the world was near.

For Paul this signals that it is time to reach out to Gentiles. This is the moment for Israel to shine as the light to the nations. Paul understands his role as Apostle to the Gentiles to be a microcosm of Israel's role as God's servant to the nations. Recall how Paul describes the inauguration of his mission: he has been "called" by God, who has "set him apart" for the purpose of bringing "the gospel" to the nations (Rom 1:1; Gal 1:15–16). As the prophet Isaiah repeatedly stresses, God chose Israel as his servant. "You are my servant, Israel, in whom I will be glorified" (Isa 49:3). Paul is facilitating the turning of the nations to Zion.

Because Paul's brand of monotheism resembles the aniconic monotheism so common in Jewish writings of the Hellenistic and Romans periods, one may rightly ask how monotheism can be the reason Paul undertook a lifelong commitment to a mission to Gentiles. If most other Jewish contemporaries of Paul believed so passionately in the importance of God's universal sovereignty, why didn't they undertake a mission to save Gentiles from the horrors of idolatry, which, as we saw in chapter 5, Jews regarded as the sin that leads to all other sins, the mother of all evil. So, why didn't other Jews undertake a program to eradicate idolatry from the world?[5]

The primary difference between Paul and other diaspora Jews, Jews who either knew nothing of Jesus or attached no real significance to him, lies more with a different understanding of time and history than with theology. To be more precise, Paul's experience of Jesus led him to believe he was witnessing the first manifestations of the eschaton, the culmination of the history that began with Adam, and the beginning of a new and glorious era. The reason seeing the risen Jesus made such a huge difference to Paul was not because Paul now believed in resurrection (whereas before he didn't), nor was it because he suddenly realized that Jesus was the key to salvation (whereas before it was Torah), but because Jesus' resurrection signaled the eschaton. The resurrection communicated to Paul that the timeline of history lay very near its end, and this meant it was a critical moment, critical for all human beings, but especially critical for Israel who possessed special insight into the divine plan because the "oracles of God" had been entrusted to Israel, and because Israel had a special role to play at the culmination of history. Serving as a light to the nations, the people of Israel would facilitate the eschatological ingathering of the nations. The nature of the crucial "conversion" that resulted from Paul's experience of the risen Christ and that transformed Paul from a garden-variety Pharisee into the Apostle to the Gentiles was that Paul now felt a sense of urgency, an urgency that Jews like Philo and Josephus never felt. Of course, Josephus and Philo never claimed to have had a direct mystical revelation pointing toward the world's imminent doom of the kind Paul claims to have had.

Josephus and Philo, however, along with most other Hellenistic Jewish writers, display a large conceptual vision of God, in which God is Creator and Sustainer of the world and the God who appeared to Moses at Sinai and entered into a covenant with Israel. Although Hellenistic Jewish writers had different ways of reconciling how and why the God of the universe would reveal to one small nation special divine teachings and mandates, they never compromised the image of God as the God of the cosmos, the highest God, above which there is no other, and which has also maintained a unique relationship with Israel since the time of Abraham. Josephus and Philo believed that the Torah, Israel's constitution (its *politeia*), embodied God's universal laws, and thus Israel functioned as an example to the other nations about how to live in accordance with the divine will. But without any apocalyptic fervor, Josephus and Philo did not perceive any urgent need to devote themselves to the task of persuading all the Gentiles of the world to foreswear their idols in favor of exclusive devotion to the one and only true (but invisible) God. Josephus and Philo publicly advocated for the universal truth of Jewish monotheism in their writings. They spoke with respect and admiration of Gentiles who embraced Jewish monotheism and encouraged the equal treatment of proselytes, but they also encouraged a respectful tolerance of Gentiles, even in their worship of other gods.[6]

Ultimately, Hellenistic Jewish writers like Philo and Josephus hoped that one day God would be recognized by all peoples, but they were content simply to wait for that day. It was a far-off utopian vision. In the meanwhile, the difference between the present and the future accounted for the tension between God's particular connection to Israel and God's universal sovereignty over all of creation. In Paul's case, present and future have conflated because of his apocalyptic orientation. Moreover, his apocalyptic expectations did not allow him the luxury of the kind of religious tolerance exemplified by Josephus and Philo. The shortness of time compelled Paul to proclaim to the nations that they must abandon their idols, they must give up their various gods and lords.

Of course, a critical component of Paul's apocalyptic, and that which distinguishes him from other apocalyptically oriented Jews (such as those responsible for the Dead Sea Scrolls), is Jesus. Paul is apocalyptically oriented in two distinct but closely related senses: he believes the end is near, and he himself has experienced an *apocalypsis*, literally a "revelation" of the risen Christ. Precisely because Paul interprets this *apocalypsis* as signaling the first fruits of the general resurrection, it caused Paul to recalibrate his sense of time—he now experienced time as hurtling toward a final cataclysm.[7]

Abraham and the Gentiles[8]

Throughout the biblical canon and postbiblical literature, Abraham is consistently remembered as the founding father of the Jewish people, and it is the privilege of a Jew to be able to call Abraham father. The importance to Jewish identity of claiming descent from Abraham is evident in several New Testament texts. Early in the gospel of Matthew, John the Baptizer is preaching a fiery sermon in which he threatens, "Do not presume to say to yourselves 'We have Abraham as our ancestor'; for I tell you, God is able from these stones to raise up children to Abraham" (Matt 3:9).[9] Abraham's reputation as the one God chose from the mass of humanity to be the progenitor of God's people meant that a Jew could expect a share of the inheritance promised to Abraham by virtue of being a descendant of Abraham. John's statement is intended as a warning to Jews who may not have lived up to what God expects—Jews should not be presumptuous about counting on their kinship to Abraham to make up for their bad behavior. While the tone in Matthew apparently reflects internal hostilities between different groups of Jews, the general attitude it reflects is typical of many Jews in antiquity. As discussed in chapter 6, the vast majority of Jews of the late Hellenistic and Roman periods recognized that a claim to Jewish identity did not rest on birthright, but on belonging to the Jewish *politeia*, a shared "way of life" rooted in common customs and traditions and most tangibly represented by the Torah. Conversion and marriage were both ways in which non-Jews could become integrated into the Jewish community. Although there were some sectarian groups who adamantly condemned these practices, the evidence is overwhelming that conversion and intermarriage were a reality and that Jews found creative ways to give these practices legitimacy. Genealogy was certainly a factor in determining one's Jewishness, but it was hardly considered a sufficient condition to guarantee one's standing in the Jewish community. Although it is unlikely there was a standardized ritual process for conversion to Judaism in Paul's time—as would become the case in the rabbinic period—Gentiles who chose to participate in the Jewish *politeia* became members of the Jewish community.

Paul is no different from his Jewish contemporaries in thinking of Abraham primarily as father Abraham. What appears less typically Jewish is that Paul emphasizes Abraham's divinely promised role as the father of a *multitude of nations,* instead of the father of the Jewish people in particular. This shift in emphasis is partly the result of Paul's apocalyptic orientation—the divine promise to Abraham that he would be the father of a multitude of nations is only now being realized, "now" being the eschatological ingathering of the nations. It is also partly the result of Paul's self-understanding as Apostle to the Gentiles. Paul's mission is focused on Gentiles, and Abraham is a particularly useful model for teaching and preaching to Gentiles. As we will discuss in greater detail in a moment, Paul devotes the bulk of his discussions of Abraham in both Galatians 3–4 and Romans 4 and 9 to demonstrating that Gentiles, along with Jews, may claim Abraham as their father, precisely because God's promises explicitly state that Abraham shall be the father of many "nations," *goyim* in Hebrew, *ethne* in Greek. The Hebrew and Greek words are variously translated in English as "nations" (or sometimes "peoples") and "Gentiles." Typically, biblical translators favor using "Gentiles" when there is an implied contrast between "Jews" and *goyim/ethne* and use "nations" when the implied context is inclusive of all the world's peoples, as in the promise to Abraham in Genesis 12:3 that "in you all the nations shall be blessed," which is also cited by Paul in Galatians 3:8.

It is crucial for understanding Paul's larger theological project to recognize that what is most important about Abraham for the apostle is that he is the father of both Jews and Gentiles. Paul positions himself as a new kind of Abraham, capable of producing the very multitude of nations originally promised to the patriarch. This multitude of descendants, however, will form one family linked by their devotion to the one God, through whom they all are blessed. Of course, Paul creates Abrahamic descendants not through biological reproduction but through his preaching and teaching. He frequently speaks of himself as "father" and his followers as "children." As he says to the Corinthians: "I do not write this to you for shame, but as my beloved children for edification.

For, although you have myriad tutors in Christ, you do not have many fathers. It is I who became your father in Christ Jesus through [my preaching of] the gospel" (1 Cor 4:14–15). Paul is a verbal progenitor, struggling to form "Christ" in his Gentile children, so that they might become Abraham's heirs (see Gal 3:14; 4:19). Through his preaching, Paul makes willing Gentiles legitimate members of Abraham's family, which is the equivalent of making them children of God. By informing Gentiles of the blessings promised to Abraham and his seed, they become heirs of the divine promises, and Paul, as the bestower of the inheritance, has become their father. Insofar as Paul establishes this newly constituted family of God, he functions as a founding father, just like Abraham.

Paul understands himself as having a divinely ordained mission that will finally fulfill the promises made to Abraham. However, because Paul believes he lives at the dawn of the new age, the fulfillment of those promises entails not the careful cultivation of a single line of descendants as with Abraham, Isaac, and Jacob—and which consequently necessitated the exclusion of other "descendants," like Ishmael and Esau—but the opposite: leveraging the remnant to expand membership in God's people. Paul's mission as the new Abraham—or the representative of Abraham living in the new age—is to overcome the chasm between God and the nations that characterized the old age. In other words, instead of cultivating an elect people, Israel, by means of distinguishing Israel from the other nations, the goal now is to bring all the peoples of the earth together as God's family, thus reconciling God and creation.

For centuries Pauline interpreters assumed Paul's discussions of Abraham were intended to show how the patriarch represents the exemplary model of faith. Jews, too, both of antiquity and beyond, perceived in Abraham the perfect embodiment of obedient faith. But traditional Christian interpreters of Paul have not seen Abraham merely as a figure whose exemplary faithfulness provided Paul with a model for Christians to emulate. Rather, the patriarch is taken to be the ultimate proof of Paul's most important theological postulate: that one is justified by faith. Moreover, it has been assumed, particularly by Reformation and post-Reformation scholars, that the Pauline doctrine of justification by faith was formulated in a polemical context. As one highly accomplished scholar of the twentieth century has said,

"Thus—in Paul's view—his contemporaries were seeking to establish a righteousness of their own (as Paul himself had done, Phil 3:6, 9) by doing works required by the law."[10] In other words, justification by faith constitutes an argument *against* (alleged) Jewish claims that one is justified by law (or works of law).[11] Because the figure of Abraham constitutes the ultimate proof for the theological legitimacy of justification by faith, scholars have seen Paul's appeal to Abraham as part of the polemic against the supposedly classical Jewish position that one is justified by doing works of the law. Of course, as discussed earlier, the doctrine that one is saved by one's works is largely a Christian chimerical projection of what Jews in antiquity believed. The grace and mercy of God are essential components in any "classically" Jewish theological equation. Any polemic embedded in the Pauline phrase "justification by faith" is a polemic about the efficacy of Jesus' faith and whether or not Jesus inaugurated the ingathering of the Gentiles—but more on that later!

Some recent interpreters, however, have come to recognize that the significance of Abraham in Paul's thinking lies with the great patriarch's identity as, well, a great patriarch. That is, Abraham's role as founding father is more critical to understanding Paul's theology than is seeing the way in which Abraham functions as an exemplary figure. "Abraham becomes the reason why Gentiles experience salvation, not the example of how an individual becomes saved."[12] To be sure, both Galatians and Romans introduce Abraham by appealing to a line from Genesis 15:6 made famous by Paul's use of it: "Abraham believed God and it was credited to him as righteousness" (Rom 4:3; Gal 3:6). But both texts connect this scriptural comment on Abraham to his status as patriarch.[13] Quite simply, Paul argues in Galatians and Romans that Gentile Christ-followers can now claim Abraham as their ancestor and, alongside Jews, are the heirs to the promises God made to the patriarch. Put another way, Abraham is not just the father of the Jews; he is the father of Gentiles also—and not just metaphorically or spiritually, as is sometimes thought. No. Abraham is just as much the father of faithful Gentiles as he is of faithful Jews.

To be sure, Paul likens Abraham to his Gentile followers, but in ways that are easily overlooked by the casual reader. For example, Paul alludes to the image of Abraham as former idolater and polytheist when in Romans 4:5 he calls the patriarch "ungodly," the same word he uses to describe idolatrous Gentiles in Romans 1:18.[14] Similarly, in Galatians 4:3, 9, Paul's mention of the "elemental spirits" to which Gentiles were formerly enslaved functions also as an allusion to Abraham's life before his conversion to monotheism, when he was merely a Chaldean star-gazer who looked to the movements of celestial bodies to find divine guidance.[15]

While scholars note the descriptive similarities between Abraham and the Gentiles, most assume that the function of these connections is for the purpose of making an analogy or for rhetorical expedience. Similarities between Abraham and Gentiles, in other words, assist Paul in his portrayal of Abraham as an example of faith for Gentiles to emulate. Most interpreters do not perceive these similarities as intended to illustrate the way in which Gentiles really are the descendants of Abraham. By contrast, I think the similar descriptions of Abraham and Gentile believers are there precisely to reinforce the kindred connection that Paul argues Gentiles have in Abraham. People who are kin are supposed to be similar to one another; those who belong to the same family are assumed to share important characteristics. The emphasis for Paul, however, both in Galatians and Romans, is not on the way Gentiles can be *like* Abraham if they emulate his faith; rather, it is on their existing relatedness to him, which they are now entitled to claim because of Christ. Once they recognize their relatedness, they will in fact display similar characteristics to their father Abraham; they will renounce idolatry and become monotheists.[16]

In English there is no etymological relationship between the verb "to believe" and the noun "faith," but in Greek they are the same word; the verb is *pisteuo* and the noun is *pistis*. Thus, another way to translate Genesis 15:6 is "Abraham had faith in God . . ." Moreover, "righteousness" can also be rendered "justification." So, it would be perfectly acceptable to translate Paul's citation of Genesis 15:6 as "Abraham had faith in God and it was credited to him as justification" or even "justice."[17] The words "faith" and "justification"—words so critical to the Reformation doctrine of justification by faith—were already embedded in a critical verse about Abraham from Genesis. While this may seem like nothing more than a trivial point about the technicalities of translation, it is essential to understanding the relationship between faith and justification and the relationship of these terms to others, like grace, works, and law in terms of *Paul's* logic. In other words, the "doctrine" of justification by faith is a product of the Reformation; it is not inherent in Paul's letters, even if Reformation theologians are indebted to Paul for the idea. Paul's use of the words "faith" and "justification" were not first or foremost elements in a theological formula; rather they were part of the scriptural "stuff" that informed Paul's mode of expression. However, it is difficult to perceive Paul's meaning as laid down in Romans and Galatians precisely because modern translations reflect the assumption that the doctrine of justification is the subject of which Paul is speaking and that the Abraham story and the various citations of Scripture are being presented as illustrations of the doctrine. That is why, unfortunately, one cannot depend on existing translations for quotations of the text; hence it is necessary for me to use my own translations.[18] Let's begin with an excerpt from Galatians:

> Because Abraham "believed God, and it was credited to him as righteousness," so you see, those descended of faith—they are the sons of Abraham. And scripture, foreseeing that God would justify the nations out of faith proclaimed the gospel beforehand to Abraham, saying "In you shall all the nations be blessed," so that those descended of faith are blessed with faithful Abraham. (Gal 3:6–9)

Paul utilizes an odd Greek phrase in this passage, *hoi ek pisteos*, which I have rendered "those descended of faith" and highlighted in Roman-face above. The NRSV and NIV translate the same phrase as "those who believe."[19] Literally, the phrase translates "those from faith" or "out of faith," depending on how one chooses to render the little Greek preposition *ek*. Unfortunately, a literal translation does not reveal much about how "those" relates to "faith." More interpretive work is necessary to make sense of what Paul is saying, which is what most translations do.

The rendering of the NRSV and NIV is typical of most English translations, which tend to gloss over the awkwardness of the phrase *hoi ek pisteos*. The gloss itself reflects the reigning assumption that the faith of individual believers is what Paul refers to in Galatians 3:6–9. Paul's point is then taken to be that, insofar as the faith of believers resembles the faith of Abraham, they can be called "sons of Abraham." The relationship between Gentiles and Abraham according to this view is one of affinity. The language of kinship constitutes merely the rhetorical or metaphorical means of making the point that Gentiles should have the same kind of faith that Abraham had.

In contrast, I translate *hoi ek pisteos* as "those descended of faith," because in the context of kinship relations, that is exactly what *ek* means. As already mentioned, virtually any dictionary of ancient Greek will tell you the preposition *ek* generally denotes separation from, out of, or away from something. Of course, in certain contexts *ek*, like any preposition, takes on certain connotations, and thus more specific meanings can be assigned to it. One rather common usage of *ek* is to denote "origin as to family, race, city, people, district, etc."[20] In describing genealogical relations, to take one example, it essentially means "born of." When Paul calls himself a "Hebrew born of Hebrews" (Phil 3:5), the only word in the Greek between "Hebrew" and "Hebrews" is *ek*.[21] Since the second half of Galatians 3:7 makes clear that Paul is making a claim about who constitute the "sons of Abraham" and, in v. 9, who has a share in the blessings promised to Abraham, the context of the passage provides a pretty good indicator that *ek* is here being used in the sense of origins or derivation. Paul is using the language of genealogical descent. To paraphrase Paul in v. 7: the descendants "of faith" are the true heirs of Abraham. (I will explain who exactly Paul refers to momentarily.) If Paul meant to say "those who believe" are the children of Abraham, surely he wouldn't have used the obtuse phrase *hoi ek pisteos* when there are so many common alternatives, which he uses whenever that is what he means.[22] Paul's choice of words in Galatians 3:7 and 9 indicates that he is not here speaking of the personal belief of individuals but of an external source of faith from which others derive benefit. It is not the believers' own faith to which Paul refers in this passage but most likely Abraham's faith. Being a descendant of Abraham entitles one to certain benefits, namely, receiving the blessings God promised to Abraham and his descendants, as Paul reminds his audience in v. 8. This interpretation is corroborated by Romans 4:16, in which the expression *to ek pisteos Abraam* appears, which means "those descended from the faith of Abraham."[23]

What does Paul mean when he speaks of people descended from the faith of Abraham? He means that Abraham's descendants possess membership in the lineage of Israel by virtue of the great patriarch's indefatigable trust in God's promise for a multitude of progeny, descendants as numerous as the stars in the sky and the grains of sand on the beach. The bulk of Abraham's saga in Genesis revolves around the long-anticipated birth of the divinely designated heir, Isaac. While the promise of numerous progeny is repeated over and over, most of a lifetime passes and still Sarah has produced no child, no son, no heir. If not even one is born, how can they expect the many God has promised? Hope fades as Abraham and Sarah grow old.

The promise to Abraham that he would become the father of many nations is not a pledge made just for Abraham's benefit. It is God's promise to those who read and retell the Abraham story—namely, those who consider themselves the children of Abraham—that the promised blessings belong to them because of Abraham. Abraham was legendary for his faithfulness to God, and that faithfulness resulted in what we might call ensured benefits for all the patriarch's future descendants.

The idea that the faithfulness of the ancestors benefits the descendants of those ancestors is known as the "merit of the fathers," as we discussed in our brief survey of Judaism in Paul's time. God bestowed blessings on the descendants of Abraham because of Abraham's extraordinary faith. The faith of the one benefits the many. God promises Abraham that the nations shall be blessed through him. Paul believes he is living at a time when those promises are going to be fulfilled, and Paul views himself as the prophetic agent charged with the mission of proclaiming the message that that time has come. Scripture foretold that Abraham would be the father of many nations and that the nations would be blessed through him. That means that ultimately the nations have to become part of the family of Abraham before the end of the world in order for God to fulfill God's promises. The purpose of Paul's mission is to integrate all these various non-Jewish peoples into the Abrahamic family. Like Abraham, Jesus' faithfulness benefits others, in this case, Gentiles in particular.[24] Jesus' great act of faithfulness enables the integration of Gentiles into the lineage of Abraham, so that now Jews and Gentiles are all the heirs of God's promises. Paul's mission is about helping God keep God's promises.

Chapter

12

"On the Contrary, We Uphold the Law!"

Up to this point I have argued that Paul's Jewish identity remained fully intact throughout his life. His embrace of Christ did not cause him to reject the fundamental tenets of Judaism. Nor do his teachings constitute an attack on Judaism per se. They are not anti-Jewish. But as scholars and experienced readers of Paul know, the real challenge to maintaining this assertion lies with explaining the apostle's attitude toward Torah. It is Paul's comments about the law that form the substance of the traditional reading of Paul grounded as it is in the readings of Augustine and Luther, especially Luther.

According to the traditional view, Paul rejected Torah once he embraced belief in Jesus. After all, isn't it Paul who proclaimed Christ "the end of the law" (Rom 10:4, NRSV)? Jesus reportedly said he came "not to abolish but to fulfill" the law (Matt 5:17), but Paul is on record as saying otherwise. In terms of traditional Pauline theology, Christ *fulfilled* the law only in the sense that he *superseded* it, and it is this view, attributed to Paul, that became the standard Christian view, even though Paul said in Romans 3:31, about as clearly as one can imagine, "Do we then render Torah void? God forbid! On the contrary, we uphold the Torah!" At best, Christ renders the law antiquated and unnecessary. At worst, Christ's supersession of the law means continuing adherence to it is an offense against God. Either way, Paul's message was clear: Christ replaced the Torah, and from this simple assertion virtually the entire theological matrix of Christian anti-Judaism follows. The new covenant replaces the law given to Moses at Sinai, which subsequently comes to be regarded as the old covenant. Christianity displaces Judaism and all the privileges to which Jews once laid claim. In effect, God has rejected the Jews because of their faithless disobedience and embraced the Gentiles instead. The church replaced Israel, and Christians replaced Jews as God's chosen people.

As I illustrated briefly in chapter 2, "Paul the Problem," there is no denying that Paul makes negative comments about the law, in which "law" obviously refers to Jewish law, the law given to Moses at Sinai, or, in my preferred terminology, "Torah." In addition to Paul's rather blunt assertion that Christ is the end of the law, there are several other "classic" texts in which Paul ostensibly denigrates Torah and Torah observance and which place Torah in opposition to Christ. No doubt readers who are familiar with Paul's letters have already called some of them to mind. But here are a few illustrative passages from the NRSV:[1]

Christ redeemed us from the curse of the law. (Gal 3:13)

If you let yourselves to be circumcised, Christ will be of no benefit to you. (Gal 5:2)

While we were living in the flesh, our sinful passions, aroused by the law, were at work in our members to bear fruit for death. But now we are discharged from the law, dead to that which held us captive, so that we are slaves not under the old written code but in the new life of the Spirit. (Rom 7:5–6)

Apart from the law, sin lies dead. I was once alive apart from the law, but when the commandment came, sin revived and I died. (Rom 7:8–10)

Now before faith came, we were imprisoned and guarded under the law until faith would be revealed. Therefore the law was our disciplinarian until Christ came, so that we might be justified by faith. But now that faith has come, we are no longer subject to a disciplinarian. (Gal 3:23–25)

This list is by no means exhaustive. It is rather illustrative of those Pauline passages describing the deleterious effects associated with

Jewish law according to the traditional reading of Paul. They also show why Paul's proclamation of Christ as the end of the law is taken as a declaration of liberation from the domination of the law.

In terms of the traditional interpretation, the cumulative picture of Paul's view of the law looks something like this: Before the advent of Christ, humans lived "under law," but they were unable to meet its demands. Instead, the law only exacerbated the problem of sin; it caused the arousal of "sinful passions," the very thing the law was supposed to prevent. As a result, the law did not teach people how to avoid sin; it merely convicted them of their status as sinners. The law imprisoned them in their own sin and thereby became a "curse" that would inevitably condemn them to death. Christ then becomes the solution to the plight the law inflicts on human beings. To put it in familiar terms, Paul's great insight was the realization that a person could only be justified *by faith*, and *not by works of the law*. Not surprisingly, many of those passages that put Torah and Christ in antithetical relation are the very same ones that contain Paul's teaching of justification by faith. Here are some more examples from the NRSV:

> For *"no human being will be justified in his sight"* by deeds prescribed by the law, for through the law comes the knowledge of sin. (Rom 3:20)

> For we hold that a person is justified by faith apart from works prescribed by the law. (Rom 3:28)

> We know that a person is justified not by the works of the law but through faith in Jesus Christ . . . because no one will be justified by the works of the law. (Gal 2:16)

Passages in Romans and Galatians that contain Paul's teachings on justification by faith were the signature texts of the Reformation, and they continue to be central to virtually all forms of Protestant Christianity. In the contemporary American context, justification by faith remains the cornerstone of Christian theology, both on the popular level and among Christian preachers, teachers, and university professors. To be sure, it is more heavily emphasized in the evangelical context, but it functions as an implicit theological assumption among mainline Protestants as well as Catholics. Precisely because justification by faith is often used by contemporary American Christians to teach the virtue of humility, and that God loves people in spite of their faults, it generates virtually no controversy between the Christian "right" and "left." Rather it is simply taken for granted as an integral part of Christian faith. Although Protestant and Catholic theologians once engaged in heady debates about the doctrine of justification by faith, there has been long-standing agreement that justification by faith is a central component of the apostle's teachings, that it refers to the fundamental way in which humans must relate to God, and that it is key to salvation.[2] It is therefore an essential part of Christian identity. And since Paul speaks of justification by faith in opposition to works of law, it follows that Christian faith implies the eschewal of (Jewish) law.

In other words, Paul's doctrine of justification by faith is understood as a polemic against the assumed alternative, namely, that one is (or could ever be) justified by works of law. The theological dichotomy between works and faith was taken by Protestant Christians as so self-evidently true that it became a kind of standard of measure for assessing the spiritual value of religion in general, as well as any particular religion. "True Christianity" as the Reformers presented it, understood itself as a religion of pure faith, stripped of all extraneous "works." Judaism, on the other hand, stands at the opposite end of the spectrum: it is a religion of nothing but works, and therefore could be used to represent the worst form of religious expression, exactly the opposite of faith in God.

Under the headings "Judaism" and "Christianity" we could place a whole host of closely related antitheses, whereby Judaism consistently represents the bad form of religion and Christianity the good form: Works and Faith, Law and Gospel, Flesh and Spirit, Sin and Righteousness, Judgment and Forgiveness, Condemnation and Grace, Death and Life. Moreover, the source of all these antitheses lies squarely in the tradition of Pauline theology that prioritizes Paul's teaching that a person is justified by faith and not works of law. It is no wonder that Paul's negative comments about law remain "the chief source of Christian anti-Judaism."[3] With great verve, Lloyd Gaston summarizes the traditional anti-Jewish framework within which Paul's comments about the law are read:

Paul seems able to proclaim his gospel of grace only against the dark foil of Jewish legalism. The Judaism which many see reflected in Paul's polemics is thus a joyless, hypocritical, nationalistic means of earning salvation by mechanically doing the works of the law. The God of the Jews is seen as a remote, gloomy tyrant who lays the burden of the law on people, and their response is twofold: they either become proud and self-righteous hypocrites who are scrupulous about food but ignore justice, or they are plunged into guilt and anxiety, thinking themselves accused for breaking a single commandment. . . . Against this background, the gospel of freedom from the law would be good news indeed, and it could only be a stiff-necked stubbornness which kept the Jews from welcoming it.[4]

What Gaston does not explicitly mention in the quotation but which is the assumption that gives rise to all other assumptions about Paul (and I suspect Gaston would agree), is that interpreters have read the apostle's teachings about law through the lens of his conversion. Readers have largely presumed that Paul's embrace of Christ necessarily involves a rejection of Torah, and so they have read his letters through this lens. Because a Christian is defined as someone who has faith in Jesus, while a Jew is defined as someone who puts their faith in Torah, Torah observance and faith in Jesus are assumed to be mutually exclusive. The choice between Torah and Jesus is the choice between being Jewish and being Christian. One must choose between these two options. Readers have therefore presumed that Paul's embrace of Christ required a rejection of Torah. Jesus replaces Torah; faith replaces works. That was Paul's personal experience, and that was the message Paul preached. The once self-righteous Pharisee "discovered" the futility of observing law when Jesus was revealed to him. Law condemns; Jesus saves. As one highly respected scholar once proclaimed, "Paul's negative assessment of 'works of the law' constitutes a denial of the orthodox Jewish (Pharisaic) doctrine of salvation."[5] Thus Paul's comments about Jewish law make perfectly good sense within the traditional Paul-the-convert, faith-versus-works framework.

However, as we have already discussed at some length, Paul did not convert from Judaism to Christianity; he did not reject Judaism in order to embrace something else. Paul's experience of Jesus occurs within the religious and theological matrix of ancient Judaism. There is no denying that Paul had some sort of profound religious experience through which he became a believer in Jesus (whereas previously he had been a skeptic) and, simultaneously, received a divine commission to become an apostle to the Gentiles. But this experience did not cause him to turn away from Judaism. As we have seen throughout this book, there is ample evidence in Paul's letters that the apostle maintained a robust sense of Jewish identity throughout his life.

Thus we come to the critical question before us: If Paul did not undergo a conversion from Judaism to Christianity, how do we explain Paul's denigrating remarks about the law? How do we explain the antithetical relationship Paul draws between Jesus and Torah? Why would Paul associate the law with sin and death, and Christ with redemption and eternal life if, as I have thus far maintained, Paul never rejected any of the core values of Judaism? How do we explain Paul's saying to the Galatians "Christ redeemed us from the curse of the law" (Gal 3:13)?

Nothing less than an entirely new framework is needed to interpret what Paul says about the law—and not simply because many well-meaning Jews and Christians would like to rid Christianity of its anti-Jewish legacy, important and necessary though that goal is, but also because the old framework left much of what Paul said unexplained or rendered it invisible. The majority of modern readers do not even realize that Paul makes as many positive statements about the law as negative ones, because scholars and religious leaders have largely ignored them. Early in this study I mentioned Romans 2:13, where Paul says it is the doers of the law who are righteous. Since the traditional construction of Pauline theology makes much of the law's inferiority relative to Christ, and since Christian identity is rooted in salvation by faith and *not works of the law*, Paul's affirmations of Torah have been either overlooked or explained away as irrelevant to Paul's main message.

Many scholars before me have attempted to construct a new paradigm for interpreting Paul. My own work builds on the work of new-perspective scholars, especially their interest in examining Judaism in the most historically plausible, less polemical way. But this work has also had its limits. Before I move on to articulate my view, let me very briefly share three other proposed solutions to the problem of Paul and the law that grow out of this scholarship.

The first proposed solution is to say that Paul is a phony. Put in other words, Paul really was ignorant of Jewish law. In this scenario, Paul is disingenuous about his claims to being a Pharisee; he is not well schooled in the study of Torah and the "traditions of the ancestors." He only made those claims to gain credibility and influence in his mission. (A less cynical solution similar to this one is that Paul didn't make any sense; his writings are full of contradictions, and interpreters have spent too much time trying to make Paul make sense. In this case, he's not a liar exactly but he is a boastful fool.)[6]

This proposal is a cynical one. While it is certainly possible that Paul lied, there is no reason he shouldn't be given the benefit of the doubt, at least as much as we give any other voice from the past. In addition, Paul does show skill in interpreting Scripture, often displaying Pharisaical reasoning. While there may be passages in Paul's letters that are difficult to understand, even rising to the level of interpretive mysteries, they are very limited in number once one understands the historical context and the logic of Judaism that informs his thinking.

The second proposal comes from E. P. Sanders, who understands Paul's perspective on the law to be completely out of keeping with the typical understanding evident in the mass of Jewish literature contemporary with Paul. Sanders finds no rational way to explain this disconnect, and, as a result, he concludes that Paul's logic works backward, "from solution to plight." In other words, Paul's experience of the risen Jesus causes the apostle to invent a "problem with Mosaic law" so as to rationalize his transformation. Christ is the solution to the plight of Torah, but only after the fact. There is no comprehensible cause and effect.[7]

A variation of this argument is to see Paul's embrace of Jesus and concomitant rejection of Jewish law through a psychological lens that says converts tend to develop a hatred and rejection of their old self. Thus Paul *had* to condemn his previous commitment to Torah.

Since we have established that Paul's experience of Jesus was not a conversion, this solution to the problem fundamentally does not work. The primary problem is that it doesn't explain anything at all—it's a punt. Paul's critical discussions of Torah are seen as making no sense because there isn't any way to account for Paul's negative assessment of law within the logic of Judaism, especially in relation to his laudatory claims about Jesus. One must give up and say that Paul's condemnations of Torah are just that—condemnations. The only difference between this view and the traditional view is that the former claims that Paul's comments are not fair. He just made them up to justify his newfound faith. This view is hardly fair in its assessment of Paul.

The third proposed solution originated with J. D. G. Dunn, but it has been adopted by numerous scholars who identify with the new perspective. Dunn explains that Paul's negative comments about law reflect not a critique of Torah per se but rather a particular abuse of the law. Dunn argues that the issue Paul is addressing is rooted in ethnic nationalism, a kind of Jewish arrogance that diminishes and excludes non-Jews. In extreme cases, it would constitute xenophobia, with the law becoming the way in which Jews could drive a wedge between Jews and non-Jews. The best example is *kashrut*, Jewish dietary laws. If people do not eat together, they do not socialize together, and the mixing of different kinds of people is prevented. Thus Dunn understands Paul's arguments about law, as well as his embrace of Christ, to be in the spirit of reform. Paul offers a reformist message, but he does so from within Judaism, much as Luther himself critiqued what he understood to be abuses and corruption of the Christianity of his day.[8]

While this proposal is more compelling than the others, it still falls short. It presupposes that ethnic nationalism is a severe problem when, as we saw in chapter 6, there was much more interaction between Jews and non-Jews. Of course, there were certain groups who were exclusivist, such as the Qumran community, but there is no reason to believe this problem extended generally to the Jewish population, and no reason to believe that Paul was a former member of this group. On the contrary, Hellenistic Jews were integrated with their Hellenistic Gentile neighbors, perhaps more so than Jews were in earlier periods in history. As we discussed earlier, writers like Josephus and Philo would seem to be in many ways more respectful and more tolerant of those Greeks and Romans who worship other gods than Paul was. Furthermore, it's hard to imagine that ethnic pride would get too out of control in the Diaspora without a specific provocation. Even though Dunn was partly motivated to pursue this new perspective on Paul and the law in order to address the anti-Semitism embedded in the standard reading of Paul, his explanation of Paul's issue with the law still rests implicitly on a stereotype of Jews as xenophobic.

In my experience of teaching Paul for the past fifteen years, it is difficult for readers to read Paul without the lenses of the Reformation, that is, without assuming that Paul is all about justification by faith and that justification by faith is the theological opposite of justification by (works of) the law. The new perspective has made progress toward seeing Paul differently, but its explanation of the problem as Jewish ethnocentrism still falls short.[9] Because the historical evidence points to the vast majority of Hellenistic Jews being well integrated into the larger society, it seems to me very unlikely that an extreme form of ethnic nationalism was the problem. That this was the issue seems even less likely if we consider that Paul's mission is out in the Diaspora.

Thus far in this book I have tried to locate Paul thoroughly in the world of ancient Jewish life and thought by showing that his own identity as a Jew was never compromised and that his mission and teachings were grounded in typical Jewish ways of theologizing. Having laid that groundwork, my goal now is to propose a new framework for understanding Paul's teaching about Torah, a framework that has already been under construction for about thirty years. I will call the scholars who have pioneered this new way of looking at Paul radical new-perspective scholars, or "the radicals" for short. I will articulate five principles to keep in mind as a kind of tool set to use when interpreting Paul. Four will be dealt with in this chapter, and the other one, where I address Paul's notion of justification by faith, will be dealt with in the next chapter.

I will illustrate these principles by appealing to specific Pauline texts, but of course only a sampling will be dealt with. That is why I hope the reader will think of these as interpretive tools they can use when they read Paul, so that when encountering perplexing comments Paul makes about law, the reader will be able to decode them with the help of these tools. Because of the entrenched nature of the traditional paradigm, it is very difficult to see Paul with a new set of eyes. Therefore I have formulated these principles largely in reaction to the standard reading of Paul's letters, so as to draw the contrast between this new framework and the old framework with as much relief as possible for the reader.

1) Paul's audience is made up of Gentiles, so everything he says about law applies to Gentiles, unless specified otherwise.
This is an extremely important point, because the vast majority of Paul's

negative statements about the law are easily explained by the fact that Paul is addressing a Gentile audience.[10] Although Paul explicitly writes his letters to Gentiles, interpreters of Paul have trouble keeping the Gentile audience in mind when actually reading him. The reason for this, once again, is the intractability of the traditional paradigm. When Paul says (according to most English translations) that one is justified "not by works of the law" but through "faith in Jesus Christ," it seems obvious to readers that Paul is condemning the observance of law as a legitimate religious practice. Since the signature mark of Judaism is Torah, Paul would seem to be condemning Judaism. Trapped in this perspective, one is forced to conclude that the apostle opposes—at times violently—Torah. The function and significance of Torah is finished. Christ has replaced Torah.

But this familiar interpretation takes no consideration of Paul's rhetoric. No thought is given to the audience. The traditional paradigm of reading Paul has so masked Paul's rhetoric that it is challenging even for astute readers to perceive any other way to read the apostle. As John Gager says, *"If you miss Paul's rhetorical strategies, you will get him wrong."*[11] Without any attention to the rhetorical context, interpreters assume Paul is speaking to a universal audience and making categorical statements about Judaism and law. However, if one only keeps in mind that Paul is consciously speaking to Gentiles, the force of his comments changes dramatically.[12] Of course, there are specific rhetorical circumstances that characterize each letter, but in general, awareness of the Gentile audience makes all the difference.

The introductory chapter of Romans illustrates how Paul addresses himself to Gentiles: Paul says that he was "called to be an apostle" (1:1) so that he might bring about the "obedience of faith among all the nations [=Gentiles] for the sake of his name" (1:5). He tells the Romans that he wants to come to them so that he might "reap some harvest" among them just as "among the rest of the nations, both to Greeks and barbarians" (1:13–14). Notice he says here "Greeks and barbarians," not "Greeks and Jews." Paul's attention is clearly directed at a non-Jewish audience.

In Galatians, too, Paul explains at length how he was commissioned to preach to Gentiles, while Peter and others had responsibility for preaching to Jews. He is motivated to recount this history in order to beef up his reputation as the authoritative voice to Gentiles in general and the Galatians in particular. Thus when Paul rails against circumcision, as he does in Galatians, it is not because circumcision is inherently bad. It is because he does not want *Gentiles* to get circumcised. There is no question he is adamantly opposed to it: "I, Paul, say to you that if you become circumcised, Christ will be of no benefit to you" (Gal 5:2). But *you* clearly means *Gentiles*, not Jews and not people in general. Paul makes clear that his concern lies specifically with the justification of Gentiles (Gal 3:8), and when he says that "Christ redeemed us from the curse of the law" (Gal 3:13), he means that Christ has removed the curse that Gentiles suffered under because, to paraphrase Deuteronomy, those who do not do what the Torah requires are cursed (27:26). Not surprisingly, Paul cites the very text from Deuteronomy in the same passage in which he says that Christ has redeemed those who have heretofore been cursed (see Gal 3:10).

It may seem to get complicated for the reader who knows this passage and who knows what Paul says in Galatians 3:11–12, that is, between Galatians 3:10 and 3:13, so let me clarify the in-between text as well. When Paul says, "It is clear that no one is justified before God by the law, for 'the righteous one shall live by the faithfulness'"(Gal 3:11, citing Hab 2:4), he does indeed mean all people—Jews and Gentiles alike—are made righteous by faithfulness, but his point is that Jews always stood righteous before God because of *God's* faithfulness to the covenant, not because Israel observed the law in perfect obedience. If Israel did not have to earn her way to righteousness, then surely Gentiles do not have to earn their way to righteousness either. Paul is not contrasting law and faith; he is arguing that God has acted in the same gracious manner to Gentiles as God did to Jews who had the long-standing benefit of a covenant with God.

Scholars agree that Galatians is prompted by rival teachers who came to Galatia sometime after Paul had gained a following there.[13] In Paul's opinion, their message constitutes a different gospel, and Paul is extremely agitated by the situation (see Gal 1:6). In centuries past these rival teachers were understood to be Jews preaching Judaism, and that they were threatening Paul's core message of justification by faith. Ostensibly they were promoting the "doing of works," understood as a shorthand for Judaism. In more recent years, the vast majority of scholars understand the context a little differently. The rival teachers are followers of Jesus just like Paul, but they have a more typically "Jewish" orientation (I say this of course with irony). For them, following Jesus requires at least circumcision, and possibly Torah observance more generally. In other words, following Jesus requires that one convert to Judaism.

Paul thinks otherwise. In fact, Paul draws the opposite conclusion about the significance of Jesus for Gentiles. This is most likely due to his sense that time is coming to a close. Prior to his experience of the risen Jesus—which led him to the realization that the resurrection of the dead and final judgment were coming, which led him to conclude that it was the end of the world as we know it—he would have had no use for this urgent message to Gentiles. If there was any conversion for Paul, it was a conversion about what time it was in history. The resurrection of Jesus has inaugurated the ingathering of the nations. That means they will be gathered together as nations in all their multiplicity. After all, that is really the point of the ingathering of the nations—that all the different peoples of the earth finally recognize the God of Israel.[14]

In short, Paul's comments about law come out of Paul's understanding of himself as a prophetic figure whose particular prophetic message is directed to the Gentiles. Paul is first and foremost the Apostle to the Gentiles, and this identity is the critical key to understanding virtually everything Paul says about law. Paul's intended audience is comprised of Gentiles who have recently come to believe in the God of Israel and in God's emissary on earth, Jesus Christ. Whatever Paul's comments about Jewish law are, they are meant to address the question of the way in which Torah relates to Gentiles. It is a perfectly logical agenda for Paul and his Gentile followers to have taken up. Now that Gentiles have come to know God and be known by God through Jesus Christ, what does Torah mean for them? To them?

2) Torah is for Jews but provides a standard for all.
As we saw in chapter 5, Torah did set Jews apart from the other nations. As God tells Israel in Exodus 19:6, "You shall be for me a priestly kingdom and a holy nation." Of course it is not just the physical possession of the Torah—though this was indeed understood to be a great privilege—but the observance of Torah that distinguished Jews from others. In the Roman era, it was particularly circumcision, Sabbath observance, and dietary laws that identified Jews as Jews—at least in theory. But there were Jews who were not observant and non-Jews who

took up these practices for whatever reason. The ancient world was as religiously complex as the modern one.

However, when Pauline scholars speak of how Jewish observance of Torah set the Jews apart from other peoples, they usually mean more than simply distinguishing Jews from others in practice—the way any culture might have mores and behaviors that distinguish them. They usually mean it in theological terms, and it is often meant negatively.[15] In many rants against Jews and Judaism from antiquity, through the medieval era, and right up to the modern period, the charge has been made that Jews were more sinful than any other people. Hence God placed the "yoke of the law" on them in order to tame their sinful nature. Consequently, this only made the Jews more sinful.

This view remains implicit in many modern commentaries and books on Paul. In the view of one modern scholar, Israel is marked off from others by her special sinfulness. God gave the law to Israel in order that she might be a "light to the nations" so that all humanity could be rescued from the sin of Adam. But Israel does not fulfill this role because of her persistent disobedience. This results in the "heaping up" of sin upon the people of Israel.[16] As Paul says, "sin was in the world before the law, but sin is not counted if there is no law" (Rom 5:13). The Torah caused an accounting for sin in a way that was not the case for others. God then punishes Israel severely, with exile and the occupation of the land for centuries, culminating with the Romans.[17]

Paul, however, never actually says that Israel bears the dubious honor of heaping up sin upon herself, explicitly or implicitly. In Romans 3:25, Paul says, "[Jesus] . . . whom God presented as a means of expiation through [Jesus' act of] faith with his blood in order to demonstrate [God's] righteousness, because, in his forbearance God passed over the sins previously committed" (Rom 3:25). It cannot be the case that Paul is speaking here of Israel's accumulated sin, as some commentators argue, and it seems highly unlikely that he is speaking of humanity in general. Paul is rather speaking in the same tradition as that expressed by 2 Maccabees:

> *For in the case of the other nations the Lord waits patiently to punish them until they have reached the full measure of their sins; but he does not deal in this way with us, in order that he should not take vengeance on us afterward when our sins have reached their height. Therefore he never withdraws his mercy from us. Although he disci-*

plines us with calamities, he does not forsake his own people (2 Macc 6:14–16)

Since Israel had the Torah but Gentiles did not, it is the latter who have suffered the accumulation of sin. Jews had a means of atonement, through sacrifices, prayer, and repentance. In fact, the punishments that Israel has suffered have served as a form of discipline similar to that of a parent toward a child. That God punished Israel for her wrongdoing reflects God's ongoing participation in the covenant. This kept God and the people of Israel in the covenantal relationship. Gentiles had no such covenant, no such special relationship. From Paul's perspective, *they* are the ones who have been disadvantaged.

The doctrine of election meant Jews understood Torah as the bestowal of a privilege and an honor that set them apart from other peoples, and the core of that election lay in God's giving Israel the Torah. But the majority of Jews of the Hellenistic era did not use these practices as a way to exclude and demean non-Jews, nor did Jews define themselves by ethnicity alone, as evidenced by the opportunity for Gentiles to convert to Judaism. There were also traditions that mitigated the doctrine of election. That is to say, there are biblical and postbiblical texts that said that Israel was no more deserving of special status than any other people. Although conversion was not an option in ancient Israel, it becomes one in the Hellenistic era. Indeed, Josephus claims that anyone who was willing to take on the customs of the Jews would be counted among the Jewish people, and Philo defends the rights of proselytes as full members of the Jewish community.[18]

Nor does Paul veer from this common understanding of the relation between Jews and Gentiles. Like most any Jew, Paul believes that Jews have a privileged place among the nations. As he says in Romans 3, "What is gained by being a Jew? What is the benefit of circumcision? Much in every way! To begin with, they [the Jews] were entrusted with the oracles of God" (vv. 1–2). In Galatians 2:15 Paul says, "We are Jews by nature and not Gentile sinners." Paul implies that it is Gentiles who hold the status of sinner, and not Jews. At the beginning of Romans 9 Paul lists several privileges that have been bestowed on Israel: "They are Israelites and to them belong sonship, glory, the covenants, the giving of the law, worship and the promises, to them belong the ancestors from whom came Christ according to the flesh" (vv. 4–5). There is no doubt that Paul assumes that Israel is elect, like virtually every other Jew of his day, and that the Torah, understood as the covenant between God and Israel, is what gives Israel her special status. This covenanted status meant that Israel's sin was kept in check. Sin did not accumulate because the covenant enabled her to make atonement for sin. Beyond this, the covenant itself meant that Israel enjoyed the grace of God; God bound Godself to Israel for eternity. Whatever the sins that Israel committed, God would always ensure that she righted herself so as to stay bound to God. All this is to say that in Romans 3:25, Paul cannot mean that Israel's sin has been accumulating. It is the sins of the Gentiles that have been "heaped up" upon them.

But also like every other Jew, Paul is trying to cope with a theological tension that became particularly acute in the Hellenistic era. How does one reconcile the notion that God is the God of Israel, specially chosen to be God's own possession, with the image of God as the one and only Creator God, the God of the cosmos? The God of Abraham, Isaac, and Jacob, the God who made a covenant with Israel, is also the God who created the entire world, including all the people who inhabit it. Paul addresses this tension directly: "Is God the God of Jews only? Is he not the God of Gentiles also—of course of Gentiles also!" (Rom 3:29).

The point has been made repeatedly: Paul is Apostle to the Gentiles, and this means he is particularly focused on the Gentile question: how does God relate to Gentiles? Interestingly, even though Paul sometimes speaks as if the Torah is the exclusive obligation of Jews, he also implies that Gentiles are accountable to the conduct it requires. The beginning chapters of Romans, in which Paul reflects on past history and how the state of humanity has become degraded, speak positively of those who live by the law: "When Gentiles who have not had the law do by nature what the law requires, they are a law to themselves even though they do not have the law" (Rom 2:14). Romans 2, along with the end of Romans 3, where Paul speaks of the accumulation of Gentile sin, implies that Gentiles were obligated to the law but did not accept it. In fact, the first chapter of Romans is a very serious indictment of the nations' sins—particularly their denial of the first and foremost commandment: to worship only the one, true, living God, forsaking all others.[19]

Of course, Romans 2 would seem to argue that there were "righteous Gentiles," a notion found not infrequently in ancient Jewish literature. Stories of the piety of specific Gentile persons, of respecters of the Jewish God, and even those who take on specific practices, abound in Jewish literature, from Genesis to Josephus. These Gentiles are, of course, the exception that proves the rule: Gentiles in general are sinners because they worship other gods.[20] Nevertheless, stories that cast Gentiles in a favorable light further reflect an understanding of Jewish society as based on Jewish practice and commitment to at least a core set of beliefs, not on a biologically inherited ethnicity. Paul's writings reflect that same understanding.

Now then, Paul's understanding of the relation between Gentiles and Torah is more subtle than at first it may seem. On the one hand, Gentiles are sinners because they have not lived according to God's law. As Romans makes so clear, "God shows no partiality" (Rom 2:11), so why would God have one standard for Jews and another for Gentiles? On the other hand, at this point in time—that is, in Paul's time—Torah is the possession of Jews (see Rom 3:2). The corollary to this is Paul's adamant position that Gentiles not take on the obligations of Torah observance.

Ironically, the traditional view of Paul portrays him as *favoring* Gentiles or at least seeing no difference between Gentiles and Jews. In my view, Paul reflects the various and sometimes contradictory aspects reflected among other Hellenistic Jewish authors. Gentiles, generally speaking, are considered inferior in Jewish eyes. At the same time, ancient Jewish authors of moderate persuasion recognized that people are people; there are bad Jews and good Gentiles. For Jewish thinkers, who pondered the nature of cosmic redemption, the status of Gentiles would eventually need to be solved. Typically this vision took one of two forms: either the nations would be condemned for their bad behavior— their worship of other gods and their persecution of Israel—or they would be reconciled to God in the final ingathering of the nations, as we discussed earlier.[21] Paul obviously subscribes to the latter vision. This may derive from his background as a Pharisee.[22] There were other apocalyptic thinkers besides Paul at this time, to be sure, but most of those envisioned the condemnation of the nations, not their salvation. Those who were more integrative in their approach to Gentiles tended not to be apocalyptic in their orientation. What makes Paul stand out is that his apocalyptic orientation leads him to view Gentiles inclusively. It is the time for the ingathering of the nations—that is what his mission is all about, gathering in the nations. Thus, God is no longer waiting for the Torah to do its work in the world more broadly. The kingdom of God is coming now. Since Gentiles have completely failed to meet this standard, the question is how shall they be forgiven?

It is at this point that Paul's Christology comes in. Christ is the sacrifice that atones for all those sins that have accumulated on all those Gentiles. For Gentiles to take up Torah observance now would be an act of faithlessness. It would be to deny the grace that God has extended to the Gentiles. As we shall see shortly, "justification by faith" refers to the divine "fix" for the problem that Gentiles suffer because of their accumulation of sin. Paul does not have a problem with Jewish law; the problem he is trying to solve entails the relationship of Gentiles—*specifically* Gentiles—to the law. Because the Gentiles are subject to God's judgment, the standard for which is the Torah, Gentile guilt has accumulated beyond measure without any means of atonement. Some sort of shortcut is needed for the nations to atone for their sins and thereby be incorporated into God's family.

In other words, Paul understands Torah to be God's provision for humanity to be in relationship with God. It is given to the Jews, due to their election, but because it is integral to the natural order of God's created universe, some Gentiles were able to follow it.[23] Torah thus was God's answer for how humanity could be in relationship with God. It was a divine system. Since Gentiles could not follow it, God had to find an extrasystemic means of incorporating Gentiles into God's family. That extrasystemic means was Jesus Christ.

The reader of Paul must realize that Paul never speaks against Jews' observance of Torah—never. He speaks strongly, however, against Gentile observance. Although he never explicitly says that Jews should continue the observance of law even though Christ has come, there is every indication that he assumes they will continue to observe the ordinances and commandments of the law. In Romans 9–11 Paul says most emphatically that God can never break God's promises. Thus the covenant between God and Israel necessarily remains in effect, which means that both God and Jews must abide by their parts in the covenant.

3) The law is not meant to condemn humanity; it serves a positive pedagogical function.

One scholar paraphrases Luther's position on the central purpose of the law as follows: "The law, like a mighty hammer, is meant to crush human self-righteousness and to drive human beings, made aware of their sinfulness, to the mercy of the Savior."[24] Even if we were to articulate this attitude in less severe terms, the claim is that the law serves to exacerbate the problem of sin. According to this view, law intensifies the desire to sin, and so humans become more sinful creatures as a result. The only teaching function of the law is, then, to enable humans to recognize how hopelessly sinful they are, which then results in such monstrous shame and guilt and desperation that one is completely beaten down into a worthless worm. This view of the law is rooted in the idea that human nature is totally depraved. Everyone is by nature a sinner.

But Paul does not share this cynical view of human nature in spite of the fact that Paul is credited with first developing this idea. According to ancient Jewish literature, just because all people sin does not mean that all people are *sinners,* meaning morally irredeemable. There were various ways in which Israel confessed her sins, both collectively and individually. The entire Levitical system of sacrifice assumes that everybody sins, and the Psalms provide numerous examples. "Happy are those who do not follow the advice of the wicked, or take the path that sinners tread, or sit in the seat of scoffers, but their delight is in the law of the LORD, and on his law they meditate day and night" (Ps 1:1–2). There is no doubt that biblical and postbiblical Jewish literature expresses the view that all people, including God's favorite people, sin. That same literature speaks also of the "wicked" and the "righteous." Both sin, but only the wicked hold the status of "sinner" in the sense of being morally irredeemable. The righteous are not morally perfect; they are not sin-free. The difference between the wicked and the righteous is largely a matter of orientation. The wicked are willfully sinful; they repeatedly do wrong and are without humility and never repent. The righteous want to live lives in accord with the will of God, but they recognize they are flawed; they sometimes go astray, but when they do, they repent and right themselves.

> *Have mercy on me, O God,*
> *according to your steadfast love;*
> *according to your abundant mercy,*
> *blot out my transgressions.*
> *Wash me thoroughly from my iniquity,*
> *and cleanse me from my sin.*

For I know my transgressions,
And my sin is ever before me. (Ps 51:1–3)

Neither biblical tradition in general nor Paul in particular understands human beings in general as depraved, unable on their own to do
anything good. The purpose of law is not condemnation. On the contrary, Torah provides the necessary guidance to live a righteous life.

To be sure, when we read Paul's saying, "But law came in, with the
result that transgressions increased, but where sin increased, grace extended further" (Rom 5:20), it sounds as if he is saying exactly what
Augustine and Luther thought he was saying: that the law only makes
things worse. It is more likely that Paul means simply that when the
Torah was given on Mount Sinai, there was accountability that there had
not been before. One cannot transgress the law if no law is in place.

But there are other reasons to doubt the traditional understanding
of the law as designed to increase the problem of sin. The most obvious
way to rebut this position is to reveal the unnamed theological assumption on which it rests. If the giving of the law to Moses exacerbated sin,
then God *caused* the exacerbation of sin! This would be a most bizarre
theology to attribute to Paul (or any other Jew in antiquity or, for that
matter, at any other time), especially since Paul is famous for his proclamations of the "righteousness of God." Why in the world would a
righteous God cause wickedness to increase? Is this not to accuse God
of malevolence?

Interpreters bury this problem by explaining it in terms of human sin.
God's law is good, but humans simply have a natural inclination toward
sin. One typical illustration of this is to imagine a young child. As this
child grows and possesses more understanding, her parents articulate
rules she must follow—she is told not to touch fragile things, not to
take things that belong to others, not to play when chores or homework
must be done, etc. These rules are intended to ensure that the child is
well behaved and to enable the child to become a responsible, ethical
adult. But, so the theory goes, the very imposition of these rules causes
the child to want to break them. While the child was ignorant of these
rules, there was no desire to break them, but now that they have been
imposed, the child desires to transgress these boundaries. The problem
with this illustration from human psychology is that it doesn't apply to

most adults. For most well-adjusted people, rules, laws, and ordinances are what keep human beings from acting out, and if they break the rules, it is usually for their own personal gain, not because of some innate desire to break rules for the sake of breaking them.

This psychological assumption is grounded in an extremely pessimistic anthropology. It holds that human nature is essentially bad. To be human is to be a sinner. This may sound reminiscent of the popular adage "to err is human." But there is a critical difference. Luther and the Reformers believed that human beings *desire* to do evil, and, without the grace of God, human beings will inevitably do evil. This is none other than the doctrine of original sin, which was understood by Augustine, Luther, and Calvin to be rooted in Paul's letter to the Romans. Even when a person does something good, it's for the wrong reasons— conceit, pride, or self-satisfaction. When Paul says "Just as sin came into the world through one person, and through sin death, so death spread to all people, because all sinned" (Rom 5:12), most readers assume that Paul is articulating the doctrine of original sin.

Once one believes that human beings are irredeemably depraved, it follows that law isn't going to help alleviate the situation. Sinning becomes inevitable. Law can neither curb the desire to sin nor is it effective in stopping evil acts. All the law can do is help humans recognize how bad they really are and that it is impossible for them to be any different.

One way to defeat this dark view of humanity that Paul allegedly taught, and the concomitant negative view of the law that follows from it is to look at Romans 7:7–13 directly, where we find that famous dialogue Paul has with himself:

What then shall we say? Torah is sin? God forbid! Rather, if it had not been for Torah, I would not perceive sin. Indeed, if Torah had not said, "You shall not desire," I would not have recognized desire. But sin found the occasion to work all manner of desire in me by using this commandment. For, without Torah, sin is dead.[25] I was once living without Torah, so when the commandment came [to me], sin sprang to life, and I died, and the very commandment that is meant for life spelled death for me. For sin found the occasion to deceive me with this commandment and by its means kill me. Thus indeed, the Torah is holy, so is the commandment holy and just and good.

*Then what is good brought death to me? God forbid! Rather it was
sin, so that sin would be exposed—by using what is good to produce
death in me, thus could sin become manifestly sinful by means of this
commandment.*

According to the standard reading, Paul is describing his own personal struggle with law and sin. With the usual lenses, this text ostensibly implies that his very knowing about the commandment against
desiring caused him to start desiring, whereas before he would not have
given it a thought. He was blissfully ignorant and well behaved. But the
law ruined everything. "The very commandment that is meant for life
spelled death for me" (v. 10).

And the text ostensibly continues in the same vein. Indeed the next
part of Romans 7 is even more famous:

*I do not understand what I do. For I do not do what I want, rather
I do what I hate. . . . For I know that nothing good dwells within me,
that is, within my flesh. I can will what is right, but I cannot do it.
For I do not do the good I want, but the evil I do not want is what I
do. . . . I am a wretched man! Who will rescue me from this body of
death? (Rom 7:15–24)*

If there is any single passage that sounds like it reinforces Luther's
reading, this is it.

But the debates about this text over the centuries indicate that its
meaning is not as obvious as it might seem to a modern reader. There
is already some ambiguity when Paul says he "would not perceive sin"
if it had not been for the law. Although it has sometimes been taken to
mean that Paul would not have sinned if the law had not been imposed
on him, Paul's point is most likely that he did not understand that he
was sinning by desiring until there was a law forbidding it. As Robert
Jewett describes what Paul is saying, "Without the presence of a law, he
would have been unaware of sin."[26] Put in Paul's words, "where there
is no law, there is no violation" (Rom 4:15). Reading the text this way
is reinforced by 7:12, where Paul says emphatically that the law is holy,
just, and good. Paul did not know he was doing anything wrong until
there was a law to teach right from wrong. One may not live up to the

standards of the law, but that does not make the law the cause of one's failure. The law serves the positive function of teaching one right from wrong, even if the end result is also a lesson in humility.

In order to understand Romans 7, and thus understand how the law serves as teacher, it is essential that we consider the identity of the speaker in this passage. Paul shifts from speaking in the first common plural voice of "we" (7:7a) to speaking in the first singular voice of "I." Following the traditional paradigm, modern readers typically assume Paul is speaking autobiographically. The text ostensibly provides a window into Paul's own moral and spiritual development, specifically the process by which he came to realize that sin is an intractable force and inextricably linked with human nature and how the law does not so much mitigate sin as magnify it. He was a Torah-observant Jew and, being a Pharisee, a zealous one at that. But scrupulous observance of the law ultimately did not work to achieve the moral perfection he was seeking. If anything, it made things worse; it drew attention to the fact that he could not do the good he wanted to do. Hence Paul's reflections in Romans 7 are seen as an exploration of the struggle of a troubled conscience and a divided self.

The autobiographical orientation to Romans 7 can be traced back to Augustine, who became convinced that the internal struggle of the divided self represents the experience of every Christian.[27] Martin Luther followed Augustine and saw in this text support for his famous slogan *simul iustus et pecattor,* one is "at the same time justified and a sinner." That is to say, even though Christians are justified by their faith in Christ, they remain unchanged in terms of their nature. Christians do not improve their moral status by being in Christ, but their being justified is no less important a transformation. The main difference between the "before" and the "after" is the psychological peace that results from the knowledge of God's justifying verdict (even if it is a legal fiction), which brings with it the hope of salvation. In sum, Romans 7:7–25 is taken to be Paul's recounting of his conversion experience, which then becomes the model for future conversions.

But there is another way to understand the identity of the tortured speaker in Romans 7, namely that Paul is speaking as someone else. In other words, the move to the first person singular is Paul imagining himself as a character for the purpose of rhetoric. This rhetorical feature has a name, *prosopopeia*, "speech in character," and it is not uncommon in antiquity. Early Christian authors knew that speakers could assume the voice of an imagined other in order to convey a different perspective on a topic. It is much harder for modern readers to spot because they are reading the text in translation and have different rhetorical conventions.

There are good reasons to assume that Paul is using speech-in-character. First, several ancient commentators on Romans read the text this way, including those whose native language was Greek and/or who were well educated in elevated Greek rhetorical style. The great third-century biblical scholar Origen took it as obvious that Paul is speaking in another's voice.[28] Origen believed Paul is reflecting the progressive stages of faith a Christian would experience. Second, when Paul switches voice from the first person plural to the singular, he also shifts the identity of the audience. Instead of addressing the Romans, the voice represents an internal dialogue with a divided self, which itself was characteristic of speech-in-character.[29] Third, Paul says that he was once "alive apart from the law" (Rom 7:9). As Origen pointed out, it makes no sense that Paul would say such a thing. Since we know he was a Jew from birth, there is no time when he was "alive apart from the law." Finally, given what we've seen so far, there is no reason to believe that Paul himself had any kind of struggle with the Torah. He says in Philippians that he was "blameless as to the law." The idea that Paul realized it was impossible for him (or anyone else) to keep the law, which meant he was an irredeemable sinner in the eyes of God, which then caused him an unbearably guilty conscience, which then led him to cast off the "yoke of the law" for Christ, derives from the traditional conversion portrait of Paul. As Krister Stendahl has said, "The Pauline awareness of sin has been interpreted in light of Luther's struggle with his conscience."[30] Rather, in contrast to Luther, Paul himself had what Stendahl calls a "robust conscience."[31] In other words, he felt confident about his ability to act in accord with the will of God.

There is near consensus among modern scholars that Paul is using speech-in-character in Romans 7, but there is dispute about who the identity of the character is. Many still think the text is autobiographical, reflecting an earlier time in Paul's life, before his conversion, when he speaks as a "Jew."[32] Some have suggested he is speaking in the voice of Adam—who is "alive apart from the law" prior to receiving the first commandment—because God told Adam not to touch the tree of the knowledge of good and evil. If Adam violates this commandment, God says, he will surely die. A very short while after receiving this commandment, Adam does eat from the tree, and the consequences are grave. (Oddly, Adam does not die, though God inflicts serious punishments. Later tradition had it that Adam was previously immortal and became mortal only after violating the commandment.) Adam's condemnation means the condemnation of all. Ultimately, none of these suggestions are completely satisfying, which is why interpreters keep revisiting the issue.

Recently, however, a new proposal has been made. Stanley Stowers has proposed that Paul speaks as a Gentile, and this seems to me a likely option if we take seriously Paul's Jewish identity together with his mission as Apostle to the Gentiles.[33] The first advantage to this interpretation is that it follows through on reading Paul as speaking to Gentiles. Gentiles are Paul's concern, not Jews, and, as already discussed, law is not a problem in general; the problem is how to deal with Gentiles who have not had the benefit of God's law. Thus we would have a clear reason why he suddenly has this dialogue with himself in the context of the letter—one that is not rooted in Augustine, Luther, and modern psychology, but in an understanding of the self that is rooted in the first-century world of Hellenistic Judaism.

We know Paul opposes Gentiles observing Jewish law. Thus, he wants to talk the Romans out of this practice. Romans 7 is part of his strategy for doing that. Paul becomes a mouthpiece for the Gentile whose encounter with Jewish law occurs in adulthood, which is why he says he was "once alive apart from the law." The audience in Rome to whom Paul writes is most likely comprised of Judaizing Gentiles, that is, Gentiles interested in Jewish observance as part of their commitment to Jesus. Perhaps they were initially God-fearers and subsequently became followers of Jesus who believed this meant they needed to practice Jewish law. Perhaps it was other Jewish missionaries who taught them that. It does not matter which it is. What matters is that the character Paul portrays encounters Jewish law later in life; he is not a Jew from birth.

Furthermore, Paul does not pick just any commandment or the Ten Commandments collectively; he picks the commandment against "coveting," what I have translated as "desire." "This prohibition was given a special significance by Jews who wanted to show the correspondence of Jewish teaching and the Greco-Roman ethic of self-mastery."[34] Self-mastery is the Greco-Roman human ideal, and Hellenistic Jews assimilated the idea to their own traditional ethic. We saw earlier how Jews stereotyped Gentiles as unable to control their sexual appetites, while Jews saw themselves as those who conducted their bodies appropriately, crediting Torah observance as the means by which they accomplished this. Like other Hellenized people around the Mediterranean basin, Jewish writers argued that their way of life was the way to address the problem of desire, so it is no surprise that Paul would too. We may then assume that many Gentiles who were drawn to Jewish observance were likely attracted to it because it helped them live up to this ideal of self-mastery.

The condition that Paul describes in Romans 7 is known in Greek as *akrasia*, which may be translated "uncontrolled desire." Paul may fault other Jews for some things, but uncontrolled desire is not one of them. Instead, Paul imagines here what it must feel like to be a Gentile who tries to take on the mantle of Torah.[35] While it brings knowledge of how to behave rightly, it does not solve the problem of *akrasia*. Rather, it makes one acutely aware of the failure to control oneself. Now the Gentile is plagued not only with *akrasia* but with the awareness of moral failing. Paul demonstrates his empathy by portraying the emotional angst one would feel at the knowledge of one's failure to control oneself. Thus we see the dialogue of a self divided: "I can will what is right, but I cannot do it" (v. 18). "I take delight in the law inside myself but I see another law in my members that wages war on the law of my mind and makes me captive to the law of sin that exists in my members" (v. 22–23).

For the Gentile, the law brings knowledge, but it does not bring relief. Escape from this tortuous condition comes from "the Spirit of life in Christ Jesus" (8:2). Therefore the law can be described as serving an "indicting" function, but it is better described as having a teaching function (cf. Gal 3:24: "the law was our teacher"). It creates awareness, bringing knowledge of what is right and wrong and an understanding of human desire as a problem, but it cannot fix the problem, partly because Gentiles are incapable of mastering their desires, and partly because it is too late to fix the problem—God's judgment is imminent.

The law was not given by God in order to be an agent of condemnation, not for Jews, not for Gentiles, not for anybody. It was given as a guide to living in accord with the law of God, as is obvious from Hebrew Scripture. Paul's position, however, is that it effectively acts as condemnation *now* for Gentiles because the world is coming to an end, which means the time has come for God's judgment. The nations, having worshipped other gods, have not lived in accord with the divine law, so their sins have heaped up upon them. They have not accounted for their sins, and therefore God's wrath is coming. It is too late for the law to be their salvation. Thus the law does constitute an indictment for Paul, but that indictment applies only to idolatrous Gentiles. It is not an indictment of humanity in general.

4) The doing of good works is not the opposite of having faith.
According to the tradition, the contrast that Paul articulates between "faith" and "works" is shorthand for the essential Christian theological contrast between the doing of works of the law and faith in Jesus Christ. Speaking of faith and works implies a host of other oppositions: Law increases one's sins before God; Christ alleviates them. Law makes the human condition worse; Christ makes it better. Law causes distance from God; Christ enables access to God. Torah means absolute accountability with no forgiveness; Christ means grace. Torah leads to condemnation; Christ leads to salvation.

From the perspective of traditional Christianity and its view of Pauline theology, Jews believe they can *work* their way to salvation. "Paul means deeds of obedience to formal statutes done in a legalistic spirit with the expectation of thereby meriting and securing divine approval and award."[36] For Jews it's a matter of earning enough merit points so as to gain God's approval, so as *to be justified*, or, in other words, *to be righteous in God's sight*. Christians believe this attitude is foolish or arrogant or both. One can never be righteous before God. Any attempt to strive for moral or ritual perfection is either the result of hubris, believing oneself capable of such perfection, or the result of a lack of faith, an inability to trust in God and instead to place one's trust in oneself and one's achievements. One cannot work one's way toward the requisite state of righteousness needed to attain salvation. It's given as a gift—all one has to do is *believe* (in Christ). While good works may be the manifestation of faith, they at best remain theologically extraneous, irrelevant to establishing one's ultimate relationship to God; at worst the doing of good works is a prideful attempt to manipulate God into granting rewards in return for good behavior. That, in sum, is the critical core not just of Pauline theology but of Protestant Christianity as well. The message of justification by faith, defined in absolute contrast to justification by works of law, is the gospel!

Interpreters of Paul do not usually go to great lengths to explain the expression "works of law" because the assumption is that the meaning is obvious. For the most part, commentators assume the expression "works of law" refers to the actual practice of keeping the precepts of law, or, put more simply, living by the law. But because of the generalized theology that has derived from the reading of Paul, readers often take "works" as a stand-in to mean any kind of human effort or achievement, which is viewed negatively because it cannot save you; only faith can do that.

To be sure, Paul always uses the expression "works of law" in a negative sense and in contrast to faith, grace, or the Spirit. The phrase *ergou nomou*, "works of the law," appears only eight times;[37] the singular "work of law" appears once (Rom 2:14, translated by the NRSV "what the law requires"—discussed below). Of the eight appearances of *ergou nomou*, seven of them occur with the preposition *ex* (translated by the NRSV in this context as "by"), the other with the preposition *choris* meaning "without," and the sense is negative in all of them. As readers would expect, the majority of the apostle's uses of this phrase appear when Paul is claiming that one is not justified by works of law, *ex ergou nomou*, as in "no one will be justified by the works of the law" (Gal 2:16, NRSV).

It is possible, however, that by "works of the law" Paul does not speak of human activity, but of how the Torah affects Gentiles. To capture this meaning, the Greek phrase *ex ergon nomou* is probably best translated "from the workings of the Torah" or perhaps even "from prescriptions of the Torah."[38] When Paul claims that justification cannot come from works of the law, it means that the Torah does not benefit Gentiles, at least not in the way it benefits Jews. Whereas once it surely would have been of benefit to them, that is no longer the case because the final judgment is imminent. Put in simple terms, it is too late. So that *now*, because Gentiles are outsiders to the Torah, it cannot provide the grace they need to stand before God, righteous, at the final judgment.

Let us consider Romans 3:19–20: "We know that whatever the Torah says it says to those in the law, in order that every mouth may be stopped and the whole world be accountable to God. For no human being will be justified before him from the workings of the Torah, for through law comes knowledge of sin."[39] This passage is typically viewed as the conclusion of Paul's description (in Rom 1:18–3:20) of how utterly depraved human beings are and how the law is completely helpless to do anything about the situation. According to the traditional reading, Paul provides a string of quotations from Scripture in Romans 3:10–18 so as to illustrate the wickedness of humanity—no one stands righteous before God, and the purpose of the law is to point this out, not to enable anyone's justification.

Although the foundation of that view is dependent on the opening chapters of Romans, the standard Augustinian-Lutheran lens is where the idea truly originates, not with Paul. As we discussed, Paul does not literally see in humanity hopeless depravity. Not everyone is the same kind of evildoer. Not everyone has fallen into such moral turpitude as to be incapable of doing anything good. Paul is exaggerating the situation in Romans 3:10–18 much as the psalmists (whom he's quoting) did. It is no revelation that human beings sin. The fact that Paul relies on the psalms to make his point makes that clear. Furthermore, Paul later will say to the Romans "sin will have no dominion over you" and encourage them to become "slaves of righteousness," so it cannot be the case that human beings cannot act for the good (see Rom 6:12–23). Paul's speech about there being no one who is righteous is largely for rhetorical effect. People do not always live up to moral standards; they often do not even live up to the standards they set for themselves. But Paul's point also goes beyond this. As mentioned several times, Paul's view is rather that humankind is unraveling as time draws to a close.[40] The current age is in decline; creation has become more and more corrupt—this is one of the reasons that things are coming to an end and a new age is about to dawn. All people will need to give account for themselves and their failures as they stand before God at the final judgment. Paul's apocalyptic perspective must be kept in mind.

It is important to understand that Paul is not literally condemning all of humanity as hopelessly mired in sin—although, according to the traditional paradigm, that is supposedly the reason people cannot do any good works. From within this paradigm, readers must assume that Paul is arguing for the depravity of humanity if they are to understand Paul as saying that no one can be justified by works. To be sure, if everyone is wicked by nature, everyone by definition acts wickedly, so the pursuit of good works is a hopeless endeavor.

Augustine and Luther, however, haven't completely missed the mark. Paul believes that, on the whole, Gentiles are depraved on account of idolatry. They are driven by uncontrollable passion. As Paul says in Romans 1:24, "God gave them up through the lusts of their hearts to impurity and the degrading of their bodies among themselves," and in 1:28–29, "to a confused mind and to things that should not be done. They were filled with every wickedness." He then provides a long list of all those many sinful acts in which they engaged: murder, strife, deceit, gossip, etc. But, as we saw earlier, the subject of this whole diatribe is Gentiles. Romans 1 is not a description of the corruption of humanity; it's a description of the corruption of Gentiles, as made clear by the fact that Paul begins his description with the ungodly behavior of idolatry (1:18–19). Whatever issues Paul may have had with other Jews, idolatry was not one of them. Idolatry and its attendant moral corruption is one of the features that distinguishes Gentiles from Jews. It cannot therefore be the case that Paul speaks of all humanity, inclusive of Jews and Gentiles. The problem is with Gentiles.

There is no good reason why Paul and so many other Jewish writers held such a damning view of the Greeks, Romans, Egyptians, and others, except to say that it was a stereotype, one that also served to articulate Jewish identity. Since aniconic monotheism is so central in ancient (and modern) Judaism, it was important to elevate this aspect to the highest virtue and to construct the worship of many gods in the form of idols as the opposite, the lowest vice. (I want to stress that I am in no way endorsing Paul's damning view of Gentiles. It is important to realize that this is just a bias of Paul's.) Paul's perspective is not revolutionary; it's typical of Hellenistic Jewish writers. The idea did not come to him because of his alleged conversion to Christianity. His view of Gentile morality was the same before and after his encounter with the risen Jesus.

At the same time, like other Jewish writers, Paul believes there are exceptions. There are Gentiles who live exemplary lives as well as Jews who live lives of moral turpitude. That's why Paul can say that if certain Gentiles, the "uncircumcised," observe the law, then they will be regarded as if they are Jews, "circumcised," and they will judge certain Jews who, in spite of having possession of the law, break it (Rom 2:26–27). In other words, what you do matters, whether you are Jew or Gentile, even if the expectation is that Jews will behave appropriately and Gentiles will not.

Indeed, in Romans 2, Paul has some very good things to say about the doing of good works. In 2:6, Paul says that God will "repay according to each one's works" (*erga*, the same Greek word used for works in Romans 3:20 but in a different form), and he goes on to say "to those who by patiently doing good seek for glory and honor and immortality, he will give eternal life; while to those who pursue wickedness out of selfish ambition and ignore the truth, there will be wrath and fury" (2:7–8). The question is, if Paul's point is to show that doing works is useless for proving one's righteousness because people are hopelessly sinful, why would he distinguish between those who do good works and those who do evil and, moreover, say that God rewards those who do good and punishes those who do evil? Moreover, faith in Christ is nowhere in view in Romans 2.[41]

Romans 2:12–13 may be the most puzzling verse of all for those who adhere to the traditional paradigm. Even the usual translations cannot manipulate this verse to mesh with Pauline theology: "All who have sinned apart from the law will also perish apart from the law, and all who have sinned under the law will be judged by the law. For it is not the hearers of the law who are righteous in God's sight, but the doers of the law who will be justified" (NRSV).[42] I have sometimes asked students to read this text in my introductory course on the New Testament, and, on one occasion, the student reader thought she had a typo in her Bible because she did not believe that Paul could say that the doers of the law would be justified.

Then what is Paul saying? If a person's deeds matter, how do we account for Paul's saying that one cannot be justified by "works of law"? The broad answer is that Paul thought about faith, works, and grace as part of an integrated theological vision for how one relates to God. Ancient Judaism typically combined the idea that one's moral status before God derives from ethical behavior (which, according to Jewish tradition, means following the Torah) and that God judges people with grace and mercy. One is responsible and accountable to God for one's own actions, but God is also merciful, gracious, and willing to overlook one's sins. As Rabbi Akiba said, "All is foreseen, but freedom of choice is given; and the world is judged by grace."[43] From the perspective of systematic theology, of course, this is problematic, but neither Paul nor other ancient Jewish writers were systematic theologians. Rather, Paul reflects the same covenantal theology we would expect of any other Jew of his day. The expectation is that individuals lead ethical lives, lives that are consistent with worship of the one, true, living God—one's life should in fact *be* the way one worships God.

The fact is that covenantal theology does not set faith and works in opposition, and neither does Paul. Trusting in God, being faithful to God—what Christians today would typically call having faith in God— that *is* obedience. And being obedient to God's commandments is the embodiment of faithfulness.[44] Faith is not some separate and distinct thing, and it is certainly not the opposite of performing acts pleasing to God. Hence it should not come as a surprise when Paul acclaims Torah observance or the doing of good works. It only seems like a contradiction because of the traditional lens. When Luther chose to add the word "alone" to Romans 1:17, so that it read "the one who is righteous shall live by faith *alone*," he imposed an opposition between works and faith into the theology of Paul that is not otherwise there.[45] Ironically, once we remove the faith-versus-works glasses, we can recognize that living one's life in accord with the will of God is integral to the statement: "the one who is righteous shall live by faith."[46] As we already noted, living one's life in accord with God's commandments is the expression of one's devotion to God. As Paul says in 1 Corinthians 7:19, "Keeping the commandments of God means everything!"[47]

Paul does turn to law when he is looking for ethical guidance. As Stowers says, "Paul assumes that . . . good works are both proper and essential."[48] In addition to Paul's affirmation of Jews' observance of the law, as well as the observance of the law generally in the early chapters of Romans, Paul turns explicitly to the teachings of Torah in Romans 13:8–10, naming four of the ten commandments. Paul's point there is not that each and every commandment must be observed to be good. Rather, he turns to these commandments as illustrative of the way in which following the teachings of Torah means that one is acting in love toward another, and "love is the fulfilling of the law" (Rom 13:10). There is no reason to think that Paul thought that any failure to act in accord with the will of God meant one was condemned to hell for all eternity. Faithfulness encompassed a whole disposition toward God; it is the sum of one's life and whether it was lived in service to God and others or not. Repentance and forgiveness are part of the picture. Paul takes it for granted that people are not perfect; they will make mistakes and they will sin, but if they orient themselves with love toward others and God, they fulfill the Torah. Paul is not worried about every little prescription of Torah, especially when speaking to his Gentile audience, because Paul understands many of the commandments as being binding only on Jews, the obvious case here being circumcision. Gentiles do not need to be circumcised in order to be in accord with Torah. But they *are* obligated to be in accord with Torah. However—and this is the problem—the nations have not fulfilled the Torah. They've been vicious, violent, licentious idolaters, and moreover they have no covenantal relationship with God. How can this situation be resolved? Either God is going to condemn all the nations save Israel, or the nations must somehow be reconciled. Paul envisions the latter. This is where faith comes in.

Chapter
13

Justification Through Jesus Christ

The reader may now be persuaded—at least encouraged to consider—that Paul does not have the negative theological view of "works" that is typically ascribed to him. Yet, if I am to demonstrate that Paul ultimately does not oppose human action to human faith, it is critical to explain what Paul means by "justification by faith," since Paul does say that one is "justified by faith" and not "works of the law." How can I possibly claim that Paul is not setting the two in opposition?

The answer is relatively simple: The Pauline notion of justification by faith does not mean that one is justified by one's own faith in Jesus; rather, Jesus' faithfulness puts right Gentiles and incorporates them into the family of God.[1] The closest there is to a description of Jesus' faithful obedience in Paul's letters appears in a hymn that Paul quotes in Philippians:

> *In Christ Jesus,*
> *who, though he was in the form of God,*
> *did not regard equality with God*
> *as something to be exploited,*
> *but emptied himself,*
> *taking the form of a slave,*
> *being born in human likeness.*
> *And being found in human form,*
> *he humbled himself*

and became obedient to the point of death—
even death on a cross. (Phil 2:5–8, NRSV)[2]

This for Paul is what Jesus did to atone for the sins of Gentiles and restore the relationship between the whole human family and God. It must remain something of a mystery exactly why Paul (and presumably other followers of Jesus) came to understand this particular act by this particular individual as able to achieve this profound reconciliation, but it is what Paul believed, and it is what he preached. Jesus' death was evidently seen as effecting atonement, and part of this atonement was achieved by the fact that Jesus was *obedient to the point of death,—even death on a cross.* In going to his death, Jesus is the primary actor. Obedience to God requires him to make a sacrifice of himself. It is this great act of faithfulness that works to extend God's grace to the Gentiles. Just as Abraham and the patriarchs' great acts of faithfulness enabled Israel to enjoy God's grace through the merit of the fathers, so, too, Jesus' faithfulness means that God will look favorably upon the nations and not hold them accountable for their accumulated sin. It was not Israel's faith *in* Abraham that allowed her to enjoy God's favor, but the faith *of* Abraham. The same kind of theological system is at work with Jesus and the Gentiles.[3]

At the same time, Jesus' obedience is a model for others, as was the case with Abraham. It is not as if a follower of Jesus has nothing to do in response to God's grace. But that response is one of emulating the same kind of faithfulness that Jesus demonstrated, not having faith *in* Jesus the way that would later become essential for Christians.[4] For Paul, emulating Jesus' faithfulness meant not just trusting in God's promises; it meant acting in such a way as to realize those promises. Paul's mission was all about working to bring about those promises of God, and that was what he wanted others to do. God promised that all the nations would be blessed in Abraham, which Paul interpreted in light of the eschatological traditions about the ingathering of the nations—which Paul thought was imminent—and this in turn is why his message has such urgency. God's kingdom is coming. God's justice is coming. The Roman imperial order will be overturned. The faithful response is to act in accord with God's will in bringing about the kingdom. Just as the gift of Torah required a faithful response from Israel, the gift of Jesus required a faithful response from Gentiles. Belief, insofar as it is a kind of mental assent to a particular theological doctrine, is not what Paul meant by faith, and it was not simply belief that would ensure one's justification.

Paul contrasts faith and works in order to demonstrate that Gentiles are off the hook for law observance. Like Israel, they are the beneficiaries of God's grace. The observance of Torah is not required of Gentiles in order for them to be righteous before God, in order for them to become part of God's family, in order for them to be part of the world to come, "saved" in Christian language. The death and resurrection of Jesus has achieved the reconciliation between Gentiles and God that was envisioned by Israel's prophets. To put it boldly, Jesus saves, but he only saves Gentiles. By that I do not mean that Paul believed that Jesus is irrelevant for Jews. Paul hoped his fellow Jews would eventually recognize the cosmic significance of Jesus as marking the beginning of the messianic age. But the significance was not that Jews needed to be saved from their sins. The efficacy of Jesus' sacrificial death was for the forgiveness of the sins of the nations. The Gentiles, who were once idolaters, are forgiven for their sins, which have been building up (see Rom 3:25). They now stand righteous (=justified), ready to become children of God, heirs to the Abrahamic promises, possessed of the same status as Israel, heirs according to the promise (see Rom 4:20).

It may help the reader to grasp the significance of this interpretation of justification by faith by restating the traditional view. The starting assumption is that human beings must be righteous in God's sight in order to be saved. God does not save unrighteous people, for that would compromise the notion that God is just. Luther came to believe that a human being could not do anything to achieve the righteousness necessary to be saved, *except* having faith in Jesus Christ.[5] The Christian believer in Jesus is completely passive. For Luther, humans "are not capable of initiating, or collaborating with, the process leading to justification."[6] Justification is bestowed upon the Christian through God's grace and mercy.[7]

There is no question that grace plays a critical role in Paul's thinking. But the position advocated in this book is markedly different from the traditional interpretation. The best way to begin to differentiate my position from the traditional understanding is to clarify the way in which the Pauline expressions "faith in Christ" and "the righteousness of God" mean very different things in the interpretation being put forward here from the standard Protestant position.

We have already discussed in chapter 10 the debate over whether the expression *pistis christou* means "faith in Christ," as it is typically translated, or "faith (or faithfulness) of Christ."[8] Following the important work of Sam Williams, Lloyd Gaston, Richard Hays, and others, I argued for the latter interpretation and translate the phrase "faithfulness of Christ." This means that the term "faith" in the phrase "justification by faith" refers not to the believers' faith, but to Jesus' own faith. To put it another way, the phrase "justification by faith" says nothing about what believers must do; if only refers to what Jesus already did. It is Jesus' own act of faith that makes others righteous.

A similar kind of issue affects the interpretation of the phrase "the righteousness of God," although the issue is not as obvious. Unlike *pistis christou*, the phrase *dikaiosyne theou* is almost always translated "righteousness of God." Luther came to believe that the phrase did not refer to God's own righteousness, but rather to righteousness that God imputes to humanity, and thus what humans possess if they believe in Jesus Christ. Romans 3:22 is critical here; the NRSV reads "the righteousness of God through faith in Jesus Christ for all who believe." In this context and with this translation, the phrase ostensibly implies that the righteousness of God is something ascribed to humans through their belief in Jesus. If we translate *pistis christou* as "faith in Christ," then Romans 3:22 requires that the "righteousness of God" not refer to God's own righteousness, but to the righteous status of human beings that God has bestowed on the believer because of his or her faith. In other words, traditional interpreters understand Romans 3:22 as just another way of saying that a person is justified by his or her faith in Jesus. The phrase, however, is better understood as referring to God's own righteousness.[9] Thus, when Paul tells us that "the righteousness of God has been made manifest through the faithfulness of Jesus Christ," he means it is through the faithful act of Jesus that God's righteousness has been made known. Grammatically, both should be understood as subjective genitives (discussed in chapter 10). The "righteousness of God" means God's own righteousness, and the "faithfulness of Jesus Christ" refers to Jesus' faithful act of obedience in willingly going to his death on the cross.

Whether these two phrases should be considered objective or subjective genitives may seem like a minor, technical issue of translation, but a great deal is at stake for understanding justification by faith, for understanding how it relates to law, and ultimately for understanding Christianity's relationship to Judaism. If justification by faith points to Jesus' faithfulness, then the centuries-long understanding of the opposition between Christ and the law no longer stands. For that opposition was predicated on the person's attitude toward these things. "Faith" meant a person's faith in Christ, and "law" meant a person's observance of Torah. Furthermore, each of these represented a theological extreme used to evaluate any religion. Christianity represented faith and was of course at the top; Judaism represented law and was at the bottom. Any form of religion that advocated the performance of certain actions as a way of becoming righteous was a bad form of religion. Sixteenth-century Roman Catholicism, in the eyes of Luther, was just that sort of bad religion, but Judaism remained the ultimate paradigm of bad religion.

What then is the distinction between faith and law? First, we should note that Paul never puts faith and law in direct opposition; the contrast is stated as "faith" versus "works of law," where "works of law" refers to the requirements of the law.[10] Second, and more important, Paul is speaking to Gentiles. One must always keep this in mind: Gentiles, Gentiles, Gentiles! Paul's point is simply that while Jews' possession of Torah enabled them to stay in good stead with God, this is not true of Gentiles. What the Torah does for Jews, Jesus does for Gentiles. The significance of the opposition that Paul describes is not an ontological difference between faith in Jesus and observance of Torah, but rather the differing situations of Jews and Gentiles as history comes hurtling to a close.

While Torah has been the unique possession of Jews, it represents the standard to which everyone is accountable, at least theoretically. Gentiles should have known enough to live by God's law, even if they weren't there when God handed the Torah to Moses. We have already seen that in Paul's view human nature is not hopelessly depraved. Everyone, Jew and Gentile alike, has the same capacity to do good or to do evil (see Rom 2:20). Jews may have been "entrusted with the oracles of God" (Rom 3:2), but all people are morally accountable—that is, accountable to God's law, and God's law *is* Torah. Jews do not have any special moral nature that sets them apart from Gentiles; both they and Gentiles are held morally accountable. As Paul says in Romans, "God shows no partiality" (2:11), by which Paul means that God has the same moral standard for both Jews and Gentiles. But Israel enjoys a covenantal relationship with God that has enabled Jews to maintain the appropriate moral status. That is not to say that Israel did not behave badly at times, sometimes very severely and arguably often, as we know from numerous biblical stories and the indictments against the people by prophets like Jeremiah. But because of God's eternal commitment to Israel—exemplified by divine promises made to Abraham, David, and others—God has ensured that Israel will always be put right. Gentiles, on the other hand, have not been "in" the covenant with God, and thus Torah has not "worked" for Gentiles; they're outside the system. That is why the expiating death of Jesus is necessary. So when Paul says that the law does not justify Gentiles, it is not because humans are, in principle, incapable of observing law and being righteous thereby, or that the obligations of Torah in a general sense do not apply to Gentiles. In theory, Gentiles are capable of observing Torah, as Paul explains in Romans 2–3. But because they have been outside the system for so long, there is now a huge chasm that must be bridged (see Rom 1:20). Up to this point, there has been no atonement, no rectification for Gentiles. That is why God's wrath has been building up against them. Now it's time to pay. In other words, as the end of history approaches and all the nations are gathering together in peace and harmony to worship the one God, the issue of accountability is much greater for Gentiles, collectively speaking, than it is for Jews. What God has done in Jesus resolves the predicament of Gentiles.

Here is where grace comes in, and it plays a critical role in Paul's thinking. Paul's emphasis on grace in his letters to the Romans and Galatians is due to his emphasis on Gentiles, though Paul relies on traditional Jewish theology for his concept of grace. Indeed, in order to grasp the role of grace for Gentiles, one first needs to understand the role of grace for Israel. From Paul's point of view (as for any other Jew of the day), Israel has had the long-standing advantage of being chosen as God's "treasured possession," which put her in a position of privilege vis-à-vis the other nations.[11] To put the matter concretely, God made a covenant with Israel that was unique, and that covenant was manifest in the Torah. By manifest I mean more than just that the Torah was the physical document that contained the regulations to which Israel was obliged. The Torah expressed the nature of the relationship between God and Israel, and that relationship was characterized by love and an eternal bond on the part of both parties. Once Israel and God made the covenant, the requirements of the Torah that God asked of Israel and that Israel pledged to keep were an expression of Israel's devotion to God. And God's promises, that Israel would never be abandoned and that she would eventually be redeemed, were the expression of God's love for Israel. The perfect performance of each and every command- ment was not a requirement for each individual member of Israel to be a beneficiary of God's promises. Atonement, on the other hand, *was* an integral part of the covenant. That the people should demonstrate their faithfulness to God through the observance of Torah was of course expected, but this was their *response* to God in light of their possession of the covenant. As E. P. Sanders said, "the covenant was not earned, but . . . obedience to the commandments is the consequence of the prior election of Israel by God." He goes on to cite a passage from the Talmud:

> R. Joshua b. Karha said: "Why does the section, *Hear, O Israel* (Deut 6:4–9) precede the [section] *And it shall come to pass if ye shall hearken [diligently to my commandments]*?—so that a man may first take upon him the yoke of the kingdom of heaven and afterward take upon him the yoke of the commandments. (*Bera- koth* 2.2)[12]

In other words, one is first a subject in the kingdom of heaven, and then one is subject to the commandments. Faith first, works second. It's classic Jewish theology, which makes Paul's argument about faith something less than unique.

To be sure, this did not mean that each and every person, no matter their behavior, was guaranteed redemption. For persistent faithlessness would mean that one was no longer participating in the covenant. But Israel as a people was guaranteed redemption. If a majority of Israel became faithless, then God would retain a remnant so as to ensure the continuation of the covenant and the fulfillment of promises. Sanders put it this way:

> Although God would punish disobedience and although inten- tional rejection of God's right to command implied rejection of the covenant, the Rabbis did not have the view that God's covenant

with Israel was conditional on obedience in the sense that the covenantal promises would be revoked by God because of Israel's sin. The covenant is, in this sense, unconditional, although it clearly implies the obligation to obey.[13]

My point in rehearsing the relationship between the election of Israel, the covenant, and the observance of commandments is to demonstrate that Israel belongs to God on the basis of grace, not because of obedience. Paul knows that, and that theological reality is a critical part of his argument that Gentiles will now be reconciled to God through grace. Exactly why God did choose Israel was as much a mystery to ancient Jewish writers—who imagine a variety of different midrashic explanations—as it is to modern readers. But the very mysteriousness of the reason points to its being an act of grace—for no one really knows why God chose Israel; God just did.

Moreover, Paul's working assumption is that Jews are already benefiting from grace. I said before that Paul's problem was not the inherent theological inadequacy of the law, but what to do about the nations who had not had the benefit of it. But my point in saying this is not that Jews knew the rules and Gentiles didn't, but that Jews already enjoyed God's grace while Gentiles did not. Jews could be confident of their status as righteous before God. Individual wrongdoing does not matter as long as one remained faithful to God as a matter of principle (not as a matter of details). God has committed to forgive Israel her sins. Jews are "justified" by virtue of the covenant. On the other hand, since Gentiles have been outside the covenant, *their* wrongdoings will count against them at the final judgment without some kind of divine intervention.

Paul's message is that God has now extended grace to Gentiles. The apostle's pounding on about grace is not because he himself had never experienced God's grace as a Pharisee and he found it in his experience of Jesus. Paul knew of grace firsthand as a member of Israel, and now that history was coming to its cataclysmic end, Paul wanted to extend the same grace Israel had enjoyed to Gentiles. It was time for the ingathering of the nations, and Jesus, in his obedience, had accomplished what was necessary for Gentiles to participate; their sins would be forgiven, and they would be ready to stand before their Maker and Judge.

The most important passage for understanding Paul's message to Gentiles—arguably the most important passage in Paul's letters—is Romans 3:21–30. Many if not most interpreters of Paul see this as the thesis or the center of Paul's argument in Romans.[14] It is certainly the case that in this one passage the reader may see in the text the interpretation of Paul's message being put forward here in all its aspects: that the "faithfulness of Christ" and "the righteousness of God" are subjective genitives, that Paul's message of justification by faith is targeted specifically to Gentiles, because they are the ones in need of it, and that God's action through Jesus was a gift that enables Gentiles to experience that same grace Jews already enjoyed. Here is my translation:

> Now, however, apart from Torah, the righteousness of God has been made manifest to which the (same) Torah and the prophets gave witness; [namely,] the righteousness of God (which has come) through the faithfulness of Jesus Christ for all those who are faithful. For there is no distinction. For all have sinned and lack the glory of God. But they are justified as a gift by his grace through the redemption that is in Christ Jesus whom God presented as a means of expiation through [Jesus' act of] faith with his blood in order to demonstrate his righteousness, because, in his forbearance God passed over the sins previously committed, for the sake of demonstrating his righteousness at this very moment, that he may be shown to be just, and that he justifies the one who is (born) of the faithfulness of Jesus. Whence comes boasting? It is excluded. Through which law? Of works? Of course not! Rather, through the law of faithfulness. For we maintain that a person is justified by faithfulness, without works of Torah. Or does God belong to Jews alone? Does God not also belong to Gentiles? Indeed, to Gentiles also. Since God is one, it is he who justifies the circumcised out of [his] faithfulness [to the covenant] and the uncircumcised through faithfulness [of Jesus]. Do we then render Torah void through faithfulness? God forbid! On the contrary, we uphold the Torah![15]

Building on my translation, I offer a paraphrase of this passage below, one which I hope will bring together all the elements necessary to the understanding of Paul's message that I have argued for throughout this book. Remember, the letter is addressed to Gentiles. Paul makes comparisons to the status of Israel and the role of Torah, but the point he is making concerns the salvation of Gentiles. In essence, he is describing the ingathering of the nations at the culmination of history, assuring his Gentile audience that they will be part of redemption, while clarifying for them the ongoing inclusion of Jews in this same redemption:

> The righteousness of God has been made manifest outside of the covenant between God and Israel, though this righteousness was foretold in the Scriptures. Specifically, this righteousness has been made manifest through the faithfulness of Jesus Christ and is available to anyone who demonstrates faithfulness themselves. For ultimately there is no distinction between people. All have sinned and lack the glory God intended for humans. But now all the Gentiles are righteous by the gift of God's grace. That is to say, they have redemption through Christ Jesus, whom God presented as a means of expiation (through Jesus' faithfulness evident in his obedience unto death) in order to prove his righteousness. In forbearance God held back from punishing the nations for their accumulated sin, for the sake of demonstrating that now, at the end of time, he is righteous, proving that he is just and that he justifies those who have been reborn through their baptism in Jesus.
>
> No one has the right to boast of having the advantage over the other. Were Jews ever made righteous before God merely by fulfilling the requirements of Torah? Of course not! Rather it's been through our trusting in God. For we know that for anyone to be righteous in God's sight, that one must be faithful above all else—must trust in God's promises—and this is true whether or not the person fulfills the requirements of Torah. Or does God belong exclusively to Jews? Isn't God the God of Gentiles also? Of course! For God is one. Therefore God justifies Israel because of God's faithfulness to the covenant, and God also justifies the Gentiles by means of Jesus' faithfulness.
>
> Has Jesus' act of faith rendered the covenant between God and Israel meaningless? God forbid! On the contrary, we who are members of Israel are fulfilling the prophesies of Torah by acknowledging God's redemption of the whole world.

Chapter

14

It's the End of the World as We Know It

Making sense of Paul's letters is a tricky business. Paul is complicated, and Pauline scholarship is even more complicated. There is much more that could be said, and I am confident the conversation about Paul will continue long after this book. I look forward to participating in that continuing conversation. Even the scholars who have most influenced my work—Krister Stendahl, Lloyd Gaston, John Gager, Stanley Stowers, Neil Elliott, and Mark Nanos—will disagree with me on many of the details of my reading of Paul. What we share, however, is the same basic orientation toward Paul, and that orientation involves more than a new perspective; it's a radical new perspective. Indeed, it's a new paradigm.[1]

As longtime students of Paul know, I have left unexplained many statements in Paul's letters that still need explaining. Put another way, even those who have been convinced to step into this new paradigm or who are at least sympathetic to it will ask, What about this text? How do you explain that verse? I admit that there remain a few stubborn passages, but really very few. What is more, there were stubborn texts in the old paradigm, like "the doers of the law will be justified." In fact, I would say there were more of them. In my experience of reading Paul with students, most of the texts that befuddle them befuddle them because they're not really inside the new paradigm. In most cases, they're willing and open to it, but nearly two thousand years of reading Paul in the traditional Christian paradigm gets in the way. It is very hard to change paradigms; it usually takes a long time.

One of the texts that remains to be addressed is Romans 9–11. It is the *locus classicus* for most of us who have adopted this radical new perspective on Paul, but it's also a text that presents challenges. One reason I did not treat it in this book is because there are several good discussions of it already.[2] Another is that it would have required another book. For the sake of manageability, I have tried to stick with more narrowly defined units of texts. Paul's argument in Romans 9–11 is very complicated, with many twists and turns, and to do justice to it would have required a lot more discussion. Nevertheless, some would say that I have cheated by not addressing these very important chapters of Romans.

Therefore, before I let the reader go, I feel compelled to answer a question that has been raised by the radical-new-perspective interpretation of Romans 9–11 and that will no doubt be asked of me by colleagues and others who have followed the developments in the new ways of reading Paul. It is the question of "two-ways salvation." Two-ways salvation is a designation used to critique the interpretation of Romans 9–11 offered by some radical-new-perspective scholars. It refers to the view that interprets Paul as saying there are two different ways to salvation, Torah for Jews, Jesus for Gentiles. The charge of "two-ways salvation" is meant to suggest incredulity that Paul would have ever envisioned more than one way to salvation. Paul's commitment to Christ is so all-encompassing that he never would have intended to say any such thing. The implication of the charge is that if this is the logical conclusion of this radically new way of looking at Paul, then it cannot be right, because Paul couldn't possibly be saying that there are two ways to salvation.

In the previous chapter, "Justification Through Jesus Christ," I said that Jesus saves, but he saves only Gentiles. By making that claim, many will read this book as an endorsement of the view that Paul is saying there are two different ways to salvation. So for those who want an answer to the question, Does Paul really think there are two ways to salvation? my answer is yes, for those who see Paul from within the traditional paradigm; it is no for those in the new paradigm.

The problem is the question itself. It presupposes the old way of looking at things. The question that underlies the question of two-ways salvation is, How can I be saved? Since the "I" in this question must necessarily be either Jew or Gentile—or to translate it into later Christian language, Jewish (or some other religion) or Christian—then it follows that there must be two ways to salvation if one accepts the radical new perspective. The traditional interpreters look at the new interpreters and say, "Are you serious? You think Paul thought the answer to this question is Torah if I'm a Jew and Jesus if I'm not?" When put in these terms, it sounds as though God had two entirely different plans for how to reconcile each group, two different standards for achieving their salvation, and two independent means for each of them to get there. Seemingly, they are on two parallel, nonintersecting tracks to heaven and, to take it to the absurd, two distinct spaces in heaven when they get there.

The starting assumption of the new paradigm is that it is not about personal salvation. Paul's letter to the Romans is not an answer to the question, How can I be saved? Rather, it is his answer to the question, How will the world be redeemed, and how do I faithfully participate in that redemption? For Paul the question had great urgency, since God had already initiated the process of redemption.

People should not be passive recipients of salvation; they need to be participants in the process. There is no doubt that Paul envisions the world's being redeemed as one world. And redemption certainly includes putting the whole world right, Jews, Gentiles, everybody. But part of being put right means faithfully participating in the redemption under way, and there is no reason why the participants all need to have the same role to be faithful participants. Paul sees his own mission as his participating in redemption, but not everyone has to do what he is doing.

The rabbis did not think non-Jews needed to observe all the commandments of the Torah to be redeemed—in fact, they are decidedly not to observe many of them. The rabbis envisioned the Gentiles' adhering to a small subset of law, known as the Noahide code. Yet the rabbis did not think this counted as two separate ways to salvation. Both groups are supposed to be in concord with the will of God, both are called to obedience, and in their different roles, both are being faithful to the Torah. There are different components that encompass redemption and different stages in realizing it, and those different stages may affect people differently or require them to play different roles, but that does not mean there are two different systems of redemption. As Krister Stendahl said in response to the question of two-ways salvation, it is God's "traffic plan" for how redemption is realized.[3]

Moreover, Paul's description of the culmination of history is not a description of how each and every individual person gets "saved." Paul speaks corporately. Luther, and millions of Christians since, may have seen Romans as the answer to the question, How can *I* be saved? But that is not Paul's question. Paul's question is, Now that the end of time is at hand, how will God reconcile all people, Jews and Gentiles, collectively? Romans 9–11 is evidence that Paul believes the answer to this question lies in the prophetic tradition of the ingathering of the nations, and the imagery of that tradition is of the nations coming together in harmony and living in peace, "the lion lies down with the lamb." It is a vision of the world redeemed as a whole. To be sure, there will be a judgment, an accounting of sin—that is why Jesus is necessary for the Gentiles. But it is not at all clear that the final judgment for Paul involves each and every person accounting for each misstep. It is the big sins of the world that need to be accounted for. The nations will stand before God as nations, not as individual persons. In modern terms, we may think of these as the sins of oppression, racism, pollution, corporate greed, to name just a few. The Roman Imperial order in which Paul found himself certainly committed the same kinds of sins.

Romans 9–11 is the narrative version of Paul's vision of redemption that he articulates in abstract form in Romans 3:21–26, and it looks something like this: Israel was chosen by God through grace, not because she did anything to earn it. God chooses whomever God chooses to carry out God's purposes, and in that sense, Israel's election was no different, but it was for a special purpose: that she be a light to the nations (see Isa 49:6). That Israel would be a light to the nations meant that Israel would play a critical role in God's plan for redemption. Paul's understanding of himself as the Apostle to the Gentiles is his interpretation of God's commissioning to be a light to the nations. God had promised that all the nations would be blessed through Abraham. That promise had to be fulfilled in order for redemption to be realized, because God always fulfills God's promises.

The problem that emerged, and the reason Paul has critical things to say about Israel in Romans 9–11, is that Israel had failed to live up to her appointed role as the light to the nations. The lack of faith he refers to on Israel's part is not a lack of faith in God but a failure to recognize that God has initiated the process of redemption. Paul's critique of

Israel is not that Torah observance has prevented her from having faith in Christ (as the critical comments of Israel are usually interpreted). The problem is that Israel is not heeding the words of the Torah carefully enough. God declared "the end from the beginning" (Isa 46:10). The death and resurrection of Jesus signaled the start of the divine plan for redemption. It was time for the ingathering of the nations, when the Gentiles would foreswear their false gods and turn to the God of Israel. Unfortunately, Israel did not perceive that the time for salvation had come. Unlike Gentile followers of Christ in Rome to whom Paul wrote his letter, Israel did not realize what time it was. And because Israel did not recognize what God was doing, she was not functioning as the light to the nations that Isaiah had prophesied.

Although Israel failed to recognize the significance of Christ and fulfill her role as light to the nations, Paul interprets it as a part of God's plan for achieving the ingathering of the nations after all. Just as God hardened Pharaoh's heart in order that God's name would be known throughout the world, so now God is hardening Israel's heart in order to protract the timetable for redemption, thus giving more time for the nations to respond to God's call for redemption through Jesus. Israel's failure means greater mercy for Gentiles. In the meantime, Paul and others proclaiming the good news of Jesus are the faithful remnant enabling God to carry out God's plan.

The hardening of the heart is temporary, of course, for God has promised Israel her redemption, and God's promises are irrevocable (see Rom 11:29). Once the full number of the Gentiles has come in, as Paul tells us, then "all Israel will be saved" (Rom 11:26). Indeed, Paul's language becomes more and more inclusive as he approaches the culmination of his argument, and it would be hard to deny that Paul's vision of redemption is expansive, if not universal. It is not only I and other modern scholars interested in interfaith dialogue who have highlighted this language in Romans 11; the church fathers Origen and Abelard and the modern theologian Karl Barth also saw in Paul's words a vision for universal salvation.[4]

Interestingly, Paul never seems to give up on the language of Jew and Gentile, in spite of this vision. He envisions all the various nations coming together to dwell in the new creation as children of God, but they are included in their variety as different peoples. In other words, Paul does not collapse Jew and Gentile into one generic mass of humanity.[5] All will be kin; none will be strangers, but the Gentile will not become Jew, and the Jew will not become Gentile. "God created a multiplicity of nations, and a multiplicity of nations God will redeem."[6]

To be sure, I have not here worked through the nuances of the text to argue my case, but this reading is not far-fetched or dismissive of the complexity of the text; it does, however, require the reader to adopt a new paradigm. There is nothing that forces a reader to understand Paul as saying Israel—that is, Jews—must convert to Christianity to be saved. There is no reason why one must interpret Paul's statement that "all Israel will be saved" to mean that all Israel will convert, as has traditionally been the case. For that matter, there is no reason to interpret Paul's description of the "full number of Gentiles" as meaning just some people. It seems to me a plainer reading of the text to say that when Paul says "all" he means all.

I think everyone can agree that Paul's message was about grace. Why is it necessary to put limits on this grace? Let's let Paul's message of grace stand as it is. It seems to me a great start for thinking about religious pluralism. But that is for another book.

Glossary

aniconic monotheism—belief in one God whose identity cannot be represented in images

apocalyptic/apocalypse—from the Greek word "revelation," a type of literature in which the heavens are opened to a human figure and an eschatological reality is revealed

Apocrypha—sometimes used as a general term to refer to ancient texts excluded from the Bible but which had authority for some Jews and/or Christians; it is also the term used to refer to those works that became part of the Greek Bible that became authoritative for Christians but which were excluded from the Hebrew canon, authoritative for Jews

Christology—an understanding of the nature and purpose of Christ

codex—an ancient book with pages sewn together on one side (as opposed to a scroll)

Diaspora—Jewish communities (in antiquity in the context of this book) outside the land of Israel, mainly spread around the Mediterranean basin and parts East

eschatology/eschaton—an expectation of what happens at the end of the world

halakhah—a rabbinic term for Jewish law

Hasmoneans—a priestly family originally from the town Modein, who become known as the "Maccabees" and who came to dominate the Jerusalem temple establishment in the second century BCE

Hellenistic Judaism—Judaism during the Greco-Roman period that has been influenced by Greek language, thought, and culture

Josephus—first-century Jewish historian who wrote in Greek

justification—traditionally used to translate the Greek word *dikaisune,* "righteous," in Paul's letters

midrash—a rabbinic term for biblical interpretation

Mishnah—the first book of rabbinic literature, it consists of six orders, each of which contain several tractates, most of which address *halakhic* issues

new perspective on Paul—a term coined by J. D. G. Dunn referring to a trend in scholarship that recognizes the anti-Semitism connected to the traditional reading of Paul and in reaction takes seriously the need to locate Paul in his Jewish context using Jewish sources

Philo—first-century Jewish philosopher and biblical commentator who wrote in Greek

politeia—Greek word meaning "constitution" or the notion of belonging to a particular constitution, thus sometimes translated "citizenship"

proselyte—a convert to Judaism

pseudepigrapha—nonbiblical texts written between the second century BCE and the second century CE pseudonymously attributed to famous biblical figures

purity/impurity—purity is a state that allows one to be in the divine presence; impurity is its opposite; there are two kinds of impurity discussed in the book: ritual and moral, each with different properties

soteriology—an understanding of salvation

Septuagint—translation of the Hebrew Scriptures into Greek by Alexandrian Jews of third and second centuries BCE

Talmud—a collection of rabbinic writings produced between the second and sixth centuries CE

Torah—a Hebrew word meaning "instruction," refers to the first five books of the Bible or the Jewish Bible as a whole; may also be used as a translation of the Greek word *nomos,* usually translated into English as "law"

Notes

Introduction

1. Krister Stendahl, *Paul Among Jews and Gentiles* (Philadelphia: Fortress, 7–23).

Chapter 1: Was Paul Really Jewish?

1. See also Rom 9:3, 11:1; Phil 3:5.
2. Some Christians regard the Bible as more authoritative than do others. Evangelical Christians give the Bible a very high status, and many regard the biblical text as the perfect, inerrant Word of God, while many mainline Christian denominations ascribe lesser status to the biblical text. Nevertheless, every Christian denomination of which I am aware treats the Bible with reverence and respect, recognizing its foundational role in Christian tradition.
3. Graydon Snyder, *Ante Pacem: Archaeological Evidence of Church Life before Constantine* (Macon, GA: Mercer Univ. Press, 1985). See also Daniel Boyarin, *Border Lines: The Partition of Judaeo-Christianity*, Divinations: Rereading Late Ancient Religion (Philadelphia: Univ. of Pennsylvania Press, 2004). Boyarin argues that Judaism and Christianity were one amalgamated religious complex.
4. Bar Kokhba, also known as Bar Cosiba, led a revolt against the Romans in 132–135 CE.

Chapter 2: Paul the Problem

1. A perusal of five study Bibles randomly chosen from my own bookshelves revealed that four out of five contained the identical three-frame map of Paul's

three missionary journeys. It is Map 14 in three Bibles, all of which are published by Oxford Univ. Press: *The New Oxford Annotated Bible* (2001); *The Access Bible* (1999); and *The Catholic Study Bible* (1990). It is Map 7 in *The New Jerusalem Bible: Reader's Edition* (New York: Doubleday, 1990). The *HarperCollins Study Bible* contains no official map of Paul's missionary journeys in the Map Appendix, but several maps appear in the notes that accompany Acts, and two of them correspond to Paul's missionary travels as narrated in Acts (New York: HarperCollins, 1993), 2084, 2090.

2. There are three separate accounts in Acts of Paul's experience of the risen Jesus: Acts 9:1–31; 22:6–16; 26:12–18.

3. The episode with Eutychus appears in Acts 20:7–12. Herod makes an appearance in ch. 12, which recounts Herod's execution of James, brother of John, the imprisonment (and miraculous escape) of Peter, and Herod's own bizarre death. Cornelius appears in ch. 10. Important officials, sometimes named, sometimes not, seem to play a role in nearly every episode; sometimes they assist Paul and his companions (often becoming believers); other times they are among the persecutors, but their motivations derive more from fulfilling the duty of their office than malice toward Paul. The story of the shipwreck, which is quite lengthy, can be found in ch. 27.

4. The only place Acts explicitly labels Paul, as well as his companion Barnabas, "apostles" occurs in 14:14, although certain important early manuscripts do not include the word "apostles" here. In Acts 14:4 the word "apostles" is used generically in a context that implicitly ascribes it to Paul. Except for these two instances, the author of Acts understands the designation "apostle" to refer to the twelve apostles whom Jesus chose as his official emissaries (see Luke 6:13–16).

5. For a classic study on the difference between the image of Paul in Acts and the image Paul projects of himself in his letters, see P. Vielhauer, "On the 'Paulinisms' of Acts," in *Studies in Luke-Acts*, eds. Leander Keck and J. Louis Martyn (Nashville: Abingdon, 1966), 35–50.

6. There is a scholarly consensus that the same person who wrote the Gospel of Luke also wrote Acts, thus the author of both texts is commonly referred to as Luke. This designation, however, is merely a convenience. Like most ancient Christian narrative texts, the Gospel of Luke and Acts circulated anonymously. Titles such as "The Gospel According to Luke" or "Acts of the Apostles" were added later when the individual texts were gathered into collections.

7. Leander E. Keck, "Images of Paul in the New Testament," *Interpretation* 43, no. 4 (1989): 351. As Keck says, Paul's role in Acts is designed not to tell us so much about Paul, but rather to demonstrate that "Paul marks the turning point in salvation history when the mission to Israel comes to an end."

8. A minority of scholars assigns Acts to the genre of the ancient novel. This view is represented in the work of Richard Pervo, *Profit with Delight: The Literary Genre of the Acts of the Apostles* (Philadelphia: Fortress, 1987); and Dennis Ronald MacDonald, *The Legend and the Apostle: The Battle for Paul*

in Story and Canon, 1st ed. (Philadelphia: Westminister, 1983). The dominant view of Acts as history is represented by Martin Hengel, *Acts and the History of Earliest Christianity*, trans. J. Bowden (Philadelphia: Fortress, 1980). For an introductory explanation of Acts as ancient history and a critique of the ancient-novel theory, see Bart D. Ehrman, *The New Testament: A Historical Introduction to the Early Christian Writings* (New York: Oxford Univ. Press, 2007; reprint, 4th ed.), 143.

9. Thucydides, *History of the Peloponnesian War*, I.22. A handy English translation is found in Steven Lattimore, *The Peloponnesian War* (London: Hackett Publishing, 1998).

10. Modern readers tend to overestimate the "factuality" of both ancient and modern history. This faith in historical writing derives from the long-standing ideal of objectivity, which itself comes from the modern emphasis on facts. See Peter Novick, *That Noble Dream: The "Objectivity Question" and the American Historical Profession* (Cambridge: Cambridge Univ. Press, 1988), 31–46, and Hayden White, *Tropics of Discourse: Essays in Cultural Criticism* (Baltimore: Johns Hopkins Univ. Press, 1978), 121–34.

11. David Trobisch, *Paul's Letter Collection: Tracing the Origins* (Minneapolis: Fortress, 1994), 8–9.

12. Virtually all textbooks raise the issue of pseudonymity, though they do not agree on what is and what is not pseudonymous.

13. Raymond Brown estimates that 80 percent of scholars believe Ephesians is pseudonymous. See Raymond Edward Brown, *Introduction to the New Testament*, Anchor Reference Library (New York: Doubleday, 1997), 620.

14. The majority of scholars not only agree that Paul did not write the Pastoral Epistles, but they also believe that the same person wrote all three.

15. See 1 Tim 3:1–12; 5:17–22; Titus 1:5–16.

16. Ignatius of Antioch, *Letter to Smyrneans*, 8–9, in Ehrman, *The Apostolic Fathers I* (Cambridge: Harvard Univ. Press, 2003), 303–5.

17. See esp. 1 Tim 4:11–16; 2 Tim 2:2; Titus 1:5.

18. See Rom 12:3–8; 1 Cor 12:4–31; 14:37–40.

19. The great Christian teacher and scholar Origen did not believe Paul was the author of Hebrews, though he did suggest it was authored by one of Paul's disciples. By the fifth century, dispute about Pauline authorship virtually disappeared, due largely to the claims of Jerome and Augustine that Hebrews was authentic.

20. Hebrews came to be associated with Paul primarily because it circulated with early collections of Paul's letters, including Chester Beatty Biblical Papyrus II. Chester Beatty not only includes Hebrews, it places Hebrews immediately after Romans, but, like other ancient Greek manuscripts of Hebrews, Paul's name does not appear anywhere in the text. Although we do not know who chose to bind it in a collection of Paul's letters or why, doing so created a perceived link between Paul and Hebrews.

21. Terry Eagleton, *Literary Theory: An Introduction*, 2nd ed. (Minneapolis: Univ. of Minnesota Press, 1996), 6.

22. A significant part of 1 Corinthians contains answers Paul provides to ques-

tions that the Corinthians have sent to him through letters (see esp. 7:1). Paul often received news, inquiries, or well-wishes from his followers, but it is not clear if this information came to him from oral reports, including perhaps secondhand information, or whether it came from letters congregants sent him. One reason for the lack of clarity is that, since there was no federal Roman postal system, letters were sent through messengers. Thus, when Paul sent Timothy to visit the Thessalonians and Timothy returned with a "report of good news" (1 Thess 3:6), it is quite possible that Timothy carried a letter from the Thessalonians to Paul, but it is difficult to know with certainty whether it was a letter or a report Timothy had made on behalf of the Thessalonians.

23. See, for example, the explanatory notes by Carl Holladay in *The Access Bible* (New York: Oxford Univ. Press), 285. In commenting on Galatians 3:19–20, Holladay calls attention to the serious enigma of the text when he says, "*Because of transgressions*: This is a very difficult phrase: as a way of dealing with transgressions that could be dealt with no other way? As a way of naming our transgressions?" (Italics in original.) Holladay offers no answers. Cf. N. T. Wright, who lists a selection of divergent English translations and says that Galatians 3:15–22 may be the most difficult in the entire Pauline corpus: *The Climax of the Covenant* (Minneapolis: Fortress, 1992), 157–58.

24. See for example, Hans Dieter Betz, *Galatians*, Hermeneia (Minneapolis: Fortress, 1979), 161–80.

25. This view is represented by J. L. Martyn, who translates Galatians 3:19 as "Why, then, the Law at all? It was added *in order to provoke transgressions*, until the seed should come to whom the promise had been made" (italics mine). J. Louis Martyn, *Galatians: A New Translation with Introduction and Commentary*, Anchor Bible (New York: Doubleday, 1997), 352.

26. Though other persuasive options have been put forward. N. T. Wright, for example, argues that the single offspring refers to a single family; *Climax of the Covenant*, 162–74.

27. Martyn, who pushes the notion in his commentary that Paul is saying the law was given by God precisely to provoke sin more than any other modern English language commentator I know, seems utterly unbothered by the perverse notion of God that his reading of Galatians requires Paul to hold.

28. The translation for these texts comes from the NRSV. Later I will provide my own translations for these verses.

29. Cf. John G. Gager, *Reinventing Paul* (New York: Oxford Univ. Press, 2000), who also illustrates Paul's conflicting statements about law by similar means.

30. Translation from NRSV.

31. In my view, Paul's overall attitude toward women is positive. Most of the negative comments about women that are associated with Paul come from the disputed letters. See Neil Elliott, *Liberating Paul: The Justice of God and the Politics of the Apostle* (Sheffield: Sheffield Academic, 1995).

Chapter 3: How Paul Became a Christian

1. See the study by Margaret M. Mitchell, *The Heavenly Trumpet: John Chrysostom and the Art of Pauline Interpretation* (Louisville, KY: Westminster/John Knox, 2002). Mitchell demonstrates how John Chrysostom, among the most important of the Greek church fathers from the fourth century and a passionate devotee of Paul, was able to weave together various traditions about Paul into a remarkably vivid and compelling figure who became the model human being for Christianity.

2. 1 Clement 5.5–7 in Bart D. Ehrman, ed. and trans., *The Apostolic Fathers*, Loeb Classical Library, 2 vols. (Cambridge, MA: Harvard Univ. Press, 2003), vol. 1, 45.

3. Codex Alexandrinus, one of the most important manuscripts of the Christian Bible (dated to the fifth century) includes 1 Clement. For discussion of the significance of 1 Clement, including its scriptural status, see Bart D. Ehrman, *Lost Christianities: The Battle for Scripture and the Faiths We Never Knew* (New York: Oxford Univ. Press, 2003), 141–43.

4. The Acts of Paul and the Acts of Paul and Thecla, together with the pseudonymous 3 Corinthians, were likely originally composed as a single text by a second-century author. Translations of these texts are handily available in Bart D. Ehrman, ed., *Lost Scriptures: Books That Did Not Make It into the New Testament* (New York: Oxford Univ. Press, 2003).

5. François Bovon, "Paul Comme Document Et Paul Comme Monument," in *Chrétiens En Conflit: L'epître De Paul Aux Galatians, Essais Bibliques no. 13* (Genève: Labor et Fides, 1987).

6. Ernst Dassmann, *Der Stachel Im Fleisch: Paulus in Der Frühchristlichen Literatur Bis Irenaeus* (Münster: Aschenmdorff, 1979).

7. Karlfried Froehlich, "Which Paul? Observations on the Image of the Apostle in the History of Biblical Exegesis," in *New Perspectives on Historical Theology: Essays in Honor of John Meyendorff*, ed. Bradley Nassif (Grand Rapids: Eerdmans, 1996), 289.

8. Harry Y. Gamble, "The Pauline Corpus and the Early Christian Book," in *Paul and the Legacies of Paul*, ed. William S. Babcock (Dallas: Southern Methodist Univ., 1990).

9. See 1 Corinthians 7, where Paul engages in an extended discussion about marriage and celibacy. It is especially illuminating precisely because Paul compares the two life-style choices. Paul affirms the legitimacy of marriage and sexuality, especially if one is married at the time one became a believer—such a person should not seek a divorce. At the same time, he says, "Just as the one who marries his virgin does well, the one who refrains from marrying will do better" (7:38). Paul also affirms the right of individuals to choose sexual abstinence within marriage, as long as both parties agree to it (7:5–7, 29). Cf. 1 Timothy, where the celibate life is apparently forbidden, unless one is of very advanced age (5:9, 14). Marriage is listed as a requirement for men seeking church office (3:2, 9) and for all nubile women, whose salvation depends upon childbearing (2:15).

10. Acts of Thecla 9 in Ehrman, *Lost Scriptures*, 115.

11. Acts of Thecla 41 in Ehrman, *Lost Scriptures*, 121.

12. *On Baptism*, ch. 17 in Roberts, et al., *The Ante-Nicene Fathers: Latin Christianity: Its Founder, Tertullian* (New York: C. Scribner's Sons, 1903), 53.

13. This is the argument of MacDonald in *The Legend and the Apostle*.

14. Cf. the comments of Mitchell, *Heavenly Trumpet*, 381.

15. References to Paul's having persecuted the church occur in the following places in the undisputed epistles: Gal 1:13, 23; 1 Cor 15:9; and Phil 3:6. In Gal 1:13 and 1 Cor 15:9, Paul specifically calls the church "the church of God."

16. See also Titus 3:3.

17. *Confessions* 8.12.29. Translation from Henry Chadwick, *St. Augustine's Confessions* (New York: Oxford, 1998).

18. See the discussion in Stanley K. Stowers, *A Rereading of Romans: Justice, Jews, and Gentiles* (New Haven: Yale Univ. Press, 1994), 39.

19. Augustine did not hold a consistent view about who the "I" of Rom 7 was. Initially Augustine thought Paul was speaking in the persona of someone who has not yet chosen to respond to God with faith and thus had not yet received grace. According to Augustine's early view, the "I" belongs to Paul only in so far as it reflects Paul's experience before the receipt of grace, that is, prior to his conversion. See Paula Fredriksen, "Paul and Augustine: Conversion Narratives, Orthodox Traditions, and the Retrospective Self," *Journal of Theological Studies* 37 (1986):3–34.

20. *Propositions*, 13–18. Translation from Paula Fredriksen Landes, *Augustine on Romans: Propositions from the Epistle to the Romans, Unfinished Commentary on the Epistle to the Romans* (Chico, CA: Scholars Press, 1982), 7.

21. See Paula Fredriksen, "Paul and Augustine: Conversion Narratives, Orthodox Traditions, and the Retrospective Self," *Journal of Theological Studies* New Series 37, no. 1 (1986), 20–26.

22. Augustine did, however, see in Paul's words in Rom 11:26—"all Israel will be saved"—the possibility of eschatological conversion.

23. This rendering comes from the Septuagint.

24. The phrase "living letters of the law" comes from Bernard of Clairvaux. See Jeremy Cohen, *Living Letters of the Law: Ideas of the Jew in Medieval Christianity* (Berkeley: Univ. of California Press, 1999).

25. Gavin I. Langmuir, *History, Religion, and Antisemitism* (Berkeley: Univ. of California Press, 1990), 297–301.

26. Markus Wriedt, "Luther's Theology," in *The Cambridge Companion to Martin Luther*, ed. Donald McKim (Cambridge: Cambridge Univ. Press, 2003), 88.

27. Heiko Augustinus Oberman, *Luther: Man Between God and the Devil* (New Haven: Yale Univ. Press, 1989). Oberman says that we must read Luther "in the shadow of the chaos of the Last Days and the imminence of eternity" (12).

28. Cited in Oberman, *Luther*, 153–54.

29. Wriedt, "Luther's Theology," 90.

30. Oberman, *Luther*, 102–6.

31. Krister Stendahl, "Paul and the Introspective Conscience of the West," in *Paul among Jews and Gentiles* (Philadelphia: Fortress, 1976), 83.
32. Oberman, *Luther*, 151, emphasis in original.
33. Oberman, *Luther*, 153, emphasis in original.
34. Martin Luther, *Preface to the Old Testament*, translated text from Timothy F. Lull, ed. *Martin Luther's Basic Theological Writings* (Minneapolis: Fortress, 1989), 127.
35. Stephen Westerholm, *Perspectives Old and New on Paul: The "Lutheran" Paul and His Critics* (Grand Rapids: Eerdmans, 2004), 23.

Chapter 4: Reading Paul as a Jew—Almost

1. This discussion is adapted from my essay, "Following in the Footnotes of the Apostle Paul" in *Identity and the Politics of Scholarship in the Study of Religion*, eds. José Ignacio Cabezón and Sheila Greeve Davaney (New York: Routledge, 2004), 77–97. There are several other important Jewish scholars who wrote influential works on Paul that there is not room to discuss, but there are good treatments elsewhere. The most thorough discussion of the history of Jewish scholarship on Paul can be found in Stefan Meissner, *Die Heimholung des Ketzers: Studien zur juedischen Auseinandersetzung mit Paulus* (Tuebingen: J.C.B. Mohr (Paul Siebeck, 1996). Alan Segal extends Meissner's work into the most recent scholarship in "Paul et ses exégètes juifs contemporains," *Recherche de science religieuse* 94 (2006): 413–44.
2. The 1938 essay was actually a revised form of an earlier essay. The essay was originally published in 1922 as "Romantische Religion. Ein erster Abschnitt aus einem Werke über Klassische u. romantische Religion," in *Festschrift zum 50 jährrigen Bestehen der Hochschule für die Wissenschaft des Judentums*, 1–48 (Berlin). The English edition used here is "Romantic Religion," in *Jewish Perspectives on Christianity*, ed. F. Rothschild (New York: Crossroad, 1990), 59–91.
3. Baeck, "Romantic Religion," in *Jewish Perspectives*, 66–67.
4. See Ekkehard Stegemann, "Introduction to Martin Buber," in *Jewish Perspectives*, 111–21, esp. 119.
5. Martin Buber, *Two Types of Faith*, trans. Norman Goldhawk (New York: Macmillan, 1951), 145.
6. In addition to Josephus, Buber gives the example of the Apocalypse of Ezra, which is also usually dated to the first century CE; see Buber, *Two Types of Faith*, 146–47.
7. Richard L. Rubenstein, *My Brother Paul* (New York: Harper & Row, 1972).
8. See, for example, A. N. Wilson, *Paul: The Mind of the Apostle* (New York: Norton, 1997); Gerd Lüdemann, *Paul: The Founder of Christianity* (New York: Prometheus Books, 2002).
9. Joseph Klausner, *From Jesus to Paul*, trans. William F. Stinespring (New York: Macmillan, 1943), 581–82.
10. Klausner, *From Jesus to Paul*, 591.

11. The early modern tradition of seeing Paul as the true founder of Christianity and as a man who betrayed Judaism continues among many Jewish readers today. The most polemical version of this position can be found in Hyam Maccoby, *The Mythmaker: Paul and the Invention of Christianity* (New York: Harper & Row, 1986).
12. See Eisenbaum, "Paul, Polemics, and the Problem of Essentialism," in *Biblical Interpretation* 13, no. 3 (2005): 224–38. Some have argued recently that Jews are using Paul to work out some intra-Jewish polemics as well. See Jonathan Blumberg-Kraus, "A Jewish Ideological Perspective on the Study of Christian Scripture," *Jewish Social Studies* 4 (1997): 121–52; and Daniel R. Langton, "Modern Jewish Identity and the Apostle Paul: Pauline Studies as an Intra-Jewish Ideological Battleground," *Journal for the Study of the New Testament* 28 (2005): 217–58.
13. Stendahl, "Introspective Conscience," in *Paul Among Jews and Gentiles*, 86–87.
14. J. D. G. Dunn, *Jesus, Paul, and the Law: Studies in Mark and Galatians* (Louisville: Wesminster/John Know, 1990), 202.
15. Romans is an exception—as Paul himself tells us in the letter, he has not been to Rome and is not the founder of the community there. Nevertheless, Paul is prompted to write Romans by specific circumstances.
16. E. P. Sanders, *Paul and Palestinian Judaism: A Comparison of Patterns of Religion* (Philadelphia: Fortress, 1977).
17. See the discussion in Sanders, *Paul and Palestinian Judaism*, 81–85. Sanders illustrates the understanding of fulfilling the commandments as an expression of Israel's love and devotion (as opposed to a system of requirements necessary for salvation) with the following excerpt from a rabbinic midrash on Deuteronomy 6:6: "'And these words which I command you this day shall be upon your heart.' Rabbi says: Why is it said? Because it says 'And thou shalt love the Lord thy God with all thy heart' (Deut 6.5). I do not know how one should love God, and so scripture says, 'And these words which I command you this day shall be upon your heart.' Place these words upon your heart so that through them you will come to know the one who spoke and the world came into being, and cleave to his ways." (*Sifre Deuteronomy* 33; also cited by Sanders, *Paul and Palestinian Judaism*, 83)
18. E. P. Sanders, *Paul, the Law, and the Jewish People* (Minneapolis: Fortress, 1983), 192. Sanders's comment that "What must be noted in Paul's critique of Judaism is that it is a critique of his native religion as such, and it is a critique which covers what is Judaism by definition" is indicative of the antithesis that remains between Paul and Judaism in Sanders's view.
19. Sanders, *Paul and Palestinian Judaism*, 552.
20. J. D. G. Dunn, *The Theology of Paul the Apostle* (Grand Rapids: Eerdmans, 1998), 717.
21. Dunn, *Theology of Paul the Apostle*, 5.
22. Mark Nanos, *The Mystery of Romans: The Jewish Context of Paul's Letter* (Minneapolis: Fortress, 1996), 6.

23. Brumberg-Kraus, "A Jewish Ideological Perspective on the Study of Christian Scripture," *Jewish Social Studies 4* (1997): 121–52.

24. Perhaps the most significant study that reflects this perspective is Daniel Boyarin, *A Radical Jew: Paul and the Politics of Identity*, Contraversions: Critical Studies in Jewish Literature, Culture and Society 1 (Berkeley: Univ. of California Press, 1994). Boyarin's is an appreciative reading, but, like Buber, sees Paul's interest in Hellenism as having so impacted the apostle's perspective on Judaism that it became something else, something beyond Judaism. See also Alan F. Segal, *Paul the Convert: The Apostolate and Apostasy of Saul the Pharisee* (New Haven: Yale Univ. Press, 1990). Segal emphasizes continuity but in spite of their different conclusions about Paul from mine, both of these works have been influential in my study of Paul.

25. This new paradigm is represented in the work of Krister Stendahl, John Gager, Stan Stowers, Lloyd Gaston, Mark Nanos, Neil Elliott, and W. S. Campbell. See also the volume by Magnus Zetterholm, *Approaches to Paul: A Student's Guide to Recent Scholarship* (Minneapolis: Fortress, 2009).

Chapter 5: Paul's Jewish Inheritance

1. For an explanation of the periodization of ancient Jewish history, see Shaye D. Cohen, *From the Maccabees to the Mishnah* (Philadelphia: Westminster/ John Knox, 1987), 6–8.

2. See G. W. Bowersock, *Hellenism in Late Antiquity* (Ann Arbor: Univ. of Michigan Press, 1990).

3. See Seth Schwartz, *Imperialism and Jewish Society 200 B.C.E. to 640 C.E.* (Princeton: Princeton Univ. Press, 2001). Schwartz argues persuasively that scholars have overemphasized the sectarianism of Second Temple Judaism.

4. Some scholars working in this period use the terminology of "Judeans" to translate the Greek word *Ioudaios* in order to underscore the ethnic identity embedded in the term. See for example, Caroline Johnson Hodge, *If Sons, Then Heirs: A Study of Kinship and Ethnicity in the Letters of Paul* (New York: Oxford Univ. Press, 2007) and Philip F. Esler, *Conflict and Identity in Romans: The Social Setting of Paul's Letter* (Minneapolis: Fortress, 2003). While there may be some value in doing this, I will translate the same term as "Jews," partly because it is the more familiar and partly because "Judeans" is too restricted in its meaning and has problematic implications. See the critique by Amy-Jill Levine, *The Misunderstood Jew: The Church and the Scandal of the Jewish Jesus* (San Francisco: HarperSanFrancisco, 2006), 160–65.

5. I have adopted this term from John Dominic Crossan and Jonathan L. Reed, *In Search of Paul: How Jesus's Apostle Opposed Rome's Empire with God's Kingdom* (San Francisco: HarperSanFrancisco, 2004).

6. Take, for example, Strabo: "For he [Moses] said, and taught, that the Egyptians were mistaken in representing the Divine Being by the images of beasts and cattle, as were also the Libyans; and that the Greeks were also wrong in modeling gods in human form; for, according to him, God is the

one thing alone that encompasses us all and encompasses land and sea—
the thing which we call heaven, or universe, or the nature of all that exists.
What man, then, if he has sense, could be bold enough to fabricate an image
of God resembling any creature amongst us? Nay, people should leave off
all image-carving, and, setting apart a sacred precinct and a worthy sanctuary, should worship God without an image . . ." (*Geographica* 16.2.35;
Stern, 1.299–300). See also Cassius Dio, *Historia* 35.17.2 (Stern, 2.351),
and Varro (preserved in Augustine, *City of God* 4.31, Stern 1.209).

7. Here is Josephus (*Contra Apion* 2.166–167) on the subject: "The universe
   is in God's hands; perfect and blessed, self-sufficing and sufficing for all, He
   is the beginning, the middle, and the end of all things. By his works and
   bounties He is plainly seen, indeed more manifest than ought else; but his
   form and magnitude surpass our powers of description. No materials, however costly, are fit to make an image of Him, no art has skill to conceive and
   represent it. The like of Him we have never seen, we do not imagine, and
   it is impious to conjecture. We behold His works: the light, the heaven, the
   earth, the sun, the waters, the reproductive creatures, the sprouting crops.
   These God created, not with hands, not with toil, not with assistants of
   which he had no need; He willed it so, and forthwith they were made in all
   their beauty. Him we must worship by the practice of virtue; for that is the
   most saintly manner of worshipping God. We have but one temple for the
   one God . . . common to all as God is common to all. The priests are continually engaged in His worship, under the leadership of him who for the time
   is head of the line. With his colleagues he will sacrifice to God, safeguard the
   laws, adjudicate in cases of dispute, punish those convicted of crime."

8. Josephus, *Contra Apion* 2.242–54.

9. Josephus, *Contra Apion* 2.190–94.

10. See, e.g., 2 Maccabees 4–6, which recounts the depredations of two rather
    nasty rival high priests, Jason and Menelaus, and the early chapters of Jose-
    phus' *Jewish War* recount numerous instances of a similar type.

11. See especially the documents known as the *Community Rule*, cols. 5–8 (also
    known as 1QS) and *Some Matters Concerning Religious Law* (4QMMT).
    The most accessible English translations of these texts can be found in Géza
    Vermès, *The Complete Dead Sea Scrolls in English* (New York: Penguin,
    1997).

12. See Tobit 1:6–8.

13. Interestingly, Jews' horror of images does not merit mention as a peculiar
    Jewish practice in Roman sources as often as circumcision, observance of
    the Sabbath, and abstaining from pork.

14. Philo, *Special Laws*, 65.

15. "In return for their foolish and wicked thoughts, which led them astray to
    worship irrational serpents and worthless animals, you sent upon them a mul-
    titude of irrational creatures to punish them, so that they might learn that
    one is punished by the very things by which one sins" (Wis 11:15–16).

16. Only fragments of Artapanus work have been preserved, but they are avail-
    able in English translation in Carl Holladay, comp. and trans., *Fragments*

from Hellenistic Jewish Authors (4 vols.; Chico, CA: Scholars Press, 1983), vol. 1, 189–243.

17. *Antiquities* 19.328–31.
18. *Contra Apion* 2.237.
19. Philo, speaking with special reference to proselytes in *Special Laws* 1.53, says they should not "deal in idle talk or revile with an unbridled tongue the gods whom others acknowledge, lest they on their part be moved to utter profane words against Him who truly is."
20. See the discussion by George W. E. Nickelsburg, *Ancient Judaism and Christian Origins: Diversity, Continuity, and Transformation* (Minneapolis: Fortress, 2003), 90–108.
21. Of course, there is biblical precedent for using the term "god(s)" of angelic beings; see, e.g., Deuteronomy 33:2; Psalm 82.
22. Text originally published by Carol Newsom, *Songs of the Sabbath Sacrifice: A Critical Edition* (Atlanta: Scholars, 1985). A convenient English translation can be found in Vermès, *Complete Dead Sea Scrolls*, 321–30. Vermès calls the work "Songs for the Holocaust of the Sabbath."
23. Sometimes only four archangels are named: Gabriel, Michael, Raphael, and Sariel. Other times there are seven, adding the names Uriel, Re'uel, and Remiel. In Enoch they are known as "the holy watchers." See Nickelsburg, *Ancient Judaism and Christian Origins*, 99.
24. Tobit 12:15 lists Raphael as one of seven angels, but other sources count only four (e.g., 1 Enoch 10, though cf. 1 Enoch 20–36 where seven are presumed).
25. For the priests' requirements to maintain a greater degree of holiness, see Exod 29:33; 39:30; Lev 6:8–30; 21. The story of Nadab and Abihu in Leviticus 10 is a frightening illustration of the exceptional care required of the priests in their sacred duties.
26. See for example Leviticus 15:31: "Thus you shall keep the people of Israel separate from their uncleanness, so that they do not die in their uncleanness by defiling my tabernacle that is in their midst" (NRSV).
27. Jonathan Klawans, *Impurity and Sin in Ancient Judaism* (New York: Oxford Univ. Press, 2000).
28. Evidence that moral impurity is incumbent upon all can be found, for example, in Leviticus 18:26–27: "You must keep my laws and my rules, and you must not do any of the abhorrent things, neither the citizen nor the stranger who resides among you; for all those abhorrent things were done by the people who were in the land before you, and the land became defiled" (JPS). As Christine Hayes has pointed out, the understanding of Gentiles as exempt from the obligations of ritual impurity and thus as inherently *pure*, is only recently coming to light in scholarship. In the past, scholarship has simply assumed that Jews considered Gentiles to be inherently *impure*. See Christine E. Hayes, *Gentile Impurities and Jewish Identities: Intermarriage and Conversion from the Bible to the Talmud* (New York: Oxford Univ. Press, 2002), 4–5, 224 and the discussion below on Gentiles.
29. *Mekhilta Behodesh* 5 (219; II 229ff) cited by Sanders, *Paul and Palestinian Judaism*, 86.

30. Both Josephus and Philo generally avoid the topic of election and instead emphasize the piety of the Jews. Thus they imply the Jews are more deserving of God's favor. See for example Philo, *Special Laws* I.51, and Josephus, *Contra Apion* II, 291–95.

31. 1QH^a 15.26–31. The Psalms of Thanksgiving are often known as the *Hodayot*, meaning "Thankgiving" in Hebrew, so named because they often begin with an invocation of thanks. Translation from Garcia Martinez, vol. 2, p. 897.

32. See, for example, Josephus, *Contra Apion* II.154; 173.

33. Solon, for example, is remembered as lawgiver to the Athenians. Historically, Solon was preceded by Draco, who seems to have been the first Athenian to formulate a set of written laws. Thus, Solon's legislation was probably a campaign of legal reform and expansion, rather than the initial establishment of a constitution. In any case, it is Solon, not Draco, who was seen as the founding lawgiver by the Athenians.

34. Only fragments of Aristobulus have survived, but they are accessible in English translation in Holladay, comp. and trans., *Fragments from Hellenistic Jewish Authors*, see vol. 3. The fact that the Hebrew writings that comprise the Torah were not translated into Greek until the late third century BCE at the earliest—that is, long after the time of Plato and Pythagoras—did not seem to present a problem for Aristobulus. He surmises that the Scriptures must have circulated in earlier translations, because the writings of Moses historically precede the writings of the philosophers and because Greek philosophy is so obviously dependent on Torah that there can be no other plausible explanation.

35. Erich S. Gruen, *Diaspora: Jews Amidst Greeks and Romans* (Cambridge, MA: Harvard Univ. Press, 2002), 222.

36. See the notes on the passage in the *Oxford Access Bible* (p. 1131—Old Testament) and the *HarperCollins Study Bible, Revised Edition* (p. 1170), all of which mention that the observance of distinctly Jewish dietary laws is at stake. L. F. Hartman and A. A. Dillela in their highly regarded commentary on Daniel surmise that this opening story of the book is meant to encourage Jews to remain steadfast in their commitment to the dietary laws in the face of exile and persecution. They also make observations that reveal a partial awareness of the weakness of this interpretation: "Since Daniel and his companions believed that with good conscience they could eat only vegetables . . . , it seems that they feared that any meat or fish they received as royal rations might include forbidden species or might have been prepared in an 'unclean' way. It is not as easy, however, to say why they abstained also from wine, since wine as such was not forbidden by any Jewish law. Perhaps they acted as Nazirites, who abstained from all alcoholic beverages, or perhaps they thought that part of the wine had been poured out in libation to pagan gods and thus became ritually unclean for Jews" (*The Book of Daniel: A New Translation with Notes and Commentary on Chapters 1–9* [Anchor Bible; Garden City, NY: Doubleday, 1977], 133).

37. See, e.g., the note on Daniel 1:8 on p. 1304 of the *HarperCollins Study Bible*.

38. First Samuel 14, where Jonathan eats honey on the battlefield in direct contradiction to Saul's oath, might be cited as one such example, but, in fact, this is not a violation of the dietary laws, because the issue is the oath Saul took before the battle, which involves food.

39. See esp. Esther 2:9. Because Esther is said to have not betrayed her Jewish identity to anyone in the palace (2:10), she apparently receives and consumes the food portions she is given. The text records no pangs of conscience by Esther, neither does it imply judgment or condemnation. Greek Esther, however, does show some anxiety about the lack of anxiety manifest in the Hebrew version of the story. Thus, in a Greek addition to the text inserted later in the story, in which Esther prays to God for aid, she says the following: "Your servant has not eaten at Haman's table, and I have not honored the king's feast or drunk the wine of libations" (Addition C: 14:17).

40. See 2 Kings 25:27–30 and its parallel in Jeremiah 52:31–34.

41. The most oft-cited examples are Tob 1:10–11; Jdt 10:5; 12:1–2; 1 Macc 1:62–63; 2 Macc 5:27; 6:8, 18–31; 7:1. In other sources of the period, however, there is frequent mention of abstaining from pork, but this practice stands virtually alone as a specific reference to Jewish food laws.

42. Josephus, *Contra Apion* 2.193.

43. Nickelsburg, *Ancient Judaism and Christian Origins*, 44.

44. *Sifre Deuteronomy* 41 (87).

45. The two exceptions usually cited are Isaiah 26:19 and Daniel 12:2. Both of these texts, however, are considered late biblical texts. Certainly Daniel is firmly dated to the second century BCE.

46. Sirach 17:30, 41:10–11; 44:14.

47. Paula Fredriksen, "Judaism, the Circumcision of Gentiles, and Apocalyptic Hope: Another Look at Galatians 1 and 2," *Journal of Theological Studies* New Series 42, no. 2 (1991): 544. Texts that illustrate this attitude are Isa 49; Joel 3:1–17; Mic 7, 4:11–14; Zeph 2.

48. Sanders, *Paul and Palestinian Judaism*, 147–82.

49. R. H. Charles, *The Apocalypse of Baruch* (London: A. and C. Black, 1896), lxxxiif., also cited in Sanders, *Paul and Palestinian Judaism*, 39.

50. Sanders, *Paul and Palestinian Judaism*, 141.

51. *Mishnah Sanhedrin* 10.1.

52. *Mishnah Sanhedrin* 10.1. The text continues: "R. Akiba says: Also he that reads the heretical books [i.e., books excluded from the canon], or that utters charms over a wound and says, I will put none of the diseases upon thee which I have put upon the Egyptians: for I am the Lord that healeth thee (Exod 15:26). Abba Saul says: Also he that pronounces the Name with its proper letters."

53. Fredriksen, "Judaism, the Circumcision of Gentiles, and Apocalyptic Hope," 544.

54. A similar sentiment appears in 1 Enoch 91.11–14.

55. *Siddur haShalem*, ed. P. Birnbaum (New York, 1949), quoted in Fredriksen, "Judaism, the Circumcision of Gentiles and Apocalyptic Hope," 547.

56. Fredriksen, "Judaism, the Circumcision of Gentiles, and Apocalyptic Hope," 547.

Chapter 6: Who Is and Who Isn't a Jew?

1. Hayes, *Gentile Impurities*. As Hayes says in the introduction to her book, "I argue that different views on the access of Gentiles to Jewish identity, deriving from diverse conceptions of Gentile impurity, played a central role in the formation of Jewish sects in the Second Temple period and in the separation of the early church from what would later be rabbinic Judaism" (p. 4). Although Hayes's book discusses different conceptions of the Jew-Gentile boundary, I believe she would support the thrust of the argument I lay out here that a majority of ancient Jewish texts, including the Torah itself and later rabbinic texts that became definitive, did not perceive or construct an impermeable boundary between Jew and Gentile.

2. Dunn, *Jesus, Paul, and the Law*, 142.

3. Hayes, *Gentile Impurities*, 21.

4. Hayes uses the phrase "Torah law" to refer to laws explicitly stated in the (written) Torah, in distinction to rabbinic laws made by inference. In later strata of rabbinic tradition, the rabbis in some very limited cases consciously articulate ways in which Gentiles contract or convey impurity, but they demonstrate awareness that legal stipulations regarding the ritual impurity of Gentiles do not derive from Torah law, but are considered "rabbinic law," which is a broad term covering all teachings that derive from texts that are not, properly speaking, *Torah* (i.e., the five books), like the prophets, as well as ancestral traditions passed down through Joshua and the elders and the rabbis themselves. While teachings of this category are given great respect, their authoritative status is secondary to that of the Torah and cannot in theory contradict any Torah law. In any case, the way in which Gentiles communicate impurity is not the usual way—not through menstrual blood or semen, but spittle! See Hayes, *Gentile Impurities*, 107–8, 21–33. See also Jonathan Klawans, "Notions of Gentile Impurity in Ancient Judaism" in *Association for Jewish Studies Review* 20 (1997): 286–312.

5. Hayes, *Gentile Impurities*, 109, 256 n. 9.

6. The opposite view is taken by Gedalia Alon, *Jews, Judaism and the Classical World: Studies in Jewish History in the Times of the Second Temple and Talmud*, trans. Israel Abrahams (Jerusalem: Magnes, 1977). Alon argues that the exclusion of Gentiles from purity regulations indicates that Gentiles are regarded as inherently impure, but his argument has been thoroughly refuted by both Hayes, *Gentile Impurities*, and Klawans, "Notions of Gentile Impurity."

7. *Mishnah Miqwa'ot* 8.4.

8. Hayes, *Gentile Impurities*, 111. The translation of *Mishnah Miqwa'ot* 8.4 comes from Hayes. For texts illustrating the same principle with regard to

menstrual blood, see *Mishnah 'Eduyyot* 5.1; *Mishnah Niddah* 4.3, 7.3, the last of which reads as follows: "All bloodstains [on women's garments] that come from Rekem are levitically clean and R. Yehudah declares them unclean because they are converts and are in error. Those from Gentiles are clean. Those from Israelites and Samaritans, R. Meir declares them unclean and the sages declare them clean because they are not suspected in regard to stains" (Hayes's translation, p. 111). It is important to note that the rabbis create some forms of ritual impurity that Gentiles can potentially convey to Jews. In so doing, they are aware that they go beyond Torah law; see n. 4.

9. For a discussion of ancient historians' and ethnographers' reports of circumcision practices, see John M. G. Barclay, *Jews in the Mediterranean Diaspora: From Alexander to Trajan (323 BCE–117 CE)* (Edinburgh: T&T Clark, 1996), 438.

10. Shaye D. Cohen, *The Beginnings of Jewishness: Boundaries, Varieties, Uncertainties* (Berkeley: Univ. of California Press, 1999), 39.

11. Cohen, *Beginnings of Jewishness*, 25–68.

12. Cohen, *Beginnings of Jewishness*, 26.

13. James H. Charlesworth, ed., *The Old Testament Pseudepigrapha*, 2 vols. (New York: Doubleday, 1985), vol. 2, 98.

14. Texts named as reflecting this attitude include 4QMMT, 4QFlorilegium, and a smattering of lines from a few other texts.

15. Leviticus 21 articulates two sets of marriage laws for priests: vv. 7–9 and vv. 13–15. Only the latter, which pertain to the high priest's family, specify the requirement of endogamy. However, the distinction in marital requirements was for the most part lost in Second Temple times. It is generally assumed that all priests should marry women from priestly families.

16. For example, the story of Moses and Zipporah in Exodus. See also Cohen, *Beginnings of Jewishness*, 241–62.

17. See, for example, Jub 16:17–18: "From the Sons of Isaac one should become a holy seed, and should not be reckoned among the Gentiles. For . . . and all his seed had fallen into the possession of God, that it should be unto the Lord a people for [his] possession above all nations and that it should become a kingdom of priests and a holy nation." Of course Jubilees is reading Exodus 19:5–6 in conjunction with other key texts, like Gen 34; Lev 18:21 and 20:2–3, the last two understood by the author of Jubilees to be a ban on all sexual relations with Gentiles. See the discussions in Cohen, *Beginnings of Jewishness*, 253–55, and Hayes, *Gentile Impurities*, 73–81.

18. According to James Kugel, Jewish identity in the Second Temple period could no longer rely on geography and thus had to create other kinds of "borders" to preserve a sense of Jewish identity. Jubilees and 4QMMT represent one strategy for creating those borders: namely, understanding membership in Israel as being part of a holy seed that is different in kind from the rest of humanity. James L. Kugel, "The Holiness of Israel and the Land in Second Temple Times," in *Texts, Temples, and Traditions: A Tribute to Menahem Haran*, ed. M. V. Fox, et al (Winona Lakes, IN: Eisenbrauns, 1996).

19. Cohen, *Beginnings of Jewishness*, 140–74.

20. *Contra Apion* 2.121–23.
21. *Contra Apion* 2.210.
22. See e.g., *Contra Apion* 2.221–31.
23. *Panegyricus* 50, in George Norlin, trans. *Isocrates, Volume I*, Loeb Classical Library (Cambridge: Harvard Univ. Press, 1980).
24. Tiberius Julius Alexander, Philo's nephew and notorious enemy of Josephus, evidently renounced his Jewish identity and became fully "romanized." See Barclay, *Jews in the Mediterranean Diaspora*, 105.
25. Cohen, *Beginnings of Jewishness*, 134.
26. Erich S. Gruen, *Diaspora: Jews Amidst Greeks and Romans* (Cambridge, MA: Harvard Univ. Press, 2002), 126–32; and *Heritage and Hellenism: The Reinvention of Jewish Tradition* (Berkeley: Univ. of California Press, 1998), 292–97.
27. Jerusalem and the land retain a special significance, as evidenced by diaspora Jews' support of the Jerusalem temple. Genealogy or what Cohen calls "ethnicity" continued to play a role as well without being definitive. For example, certain exclusions and limitations pertained to proselytes—in other words, certain privileges enjoyed by Israelites were denied to proselytes—but these restrictions were dissolved within three generations (at most). See Cohen, *Beginnings of Jewishness*, 308–40.
28. Cf. Josephus's comments that Jews can hold citizenship in the cities within which they reside and still be considered Jews. For example, Jews who live in Alexandria can appropriately be called "Alexandrians," or Jews who reside in Antioch are "Antiochenes." Whether or not Jews actually held all the rights and privileges of citizenship in cities like Alexandria is a matter of scholarly debate and should not be taken for granted. Nevertheless, the evidence is unequivocal that Jews did participate in the civic and political life of many Greek cities around the Mediterranean and that both Greek and Roman imperial authorities sometimes granted special political privileges to Jews. Josephus argues that the process by which Jewish communities became part of the fabric of local civic life is analogous to the process of Roman colonization. See *Contra Apion* 2.38–41; cf. *Antiquities* 19.278–91. For a fuller discussion of the political integration of Jews in the Greco-Roman world, see Barclay, *Jews in the Mediterranean Diaspora* and Gruen, *Diaspora*.
29. *Contra Apion* 2.280–84.
30. Philo, *Moses*, 2.17–27. Philo goes on at much greater length than Josephus about the influence of Jewish law among non-Jews. Philo uses the topic to segue into recounting how and why the Torah was translated into Greek, an enterprise that was sponsored by Ptolemy III and thus involved the cooperation of Jews and non-Jews. After recounting the now famous story of the origins of the Septuagint, Philo then reports that there is a major festival held on the island of Pharos (where the translators performed their work) and that Jews and "a multitude of others cross the water" (from Alexandria) each year to commemorate this great event (2.41–43).
31. Cf. Wolf Liebeschuetz, "The Influence of Judaism among Non-Jews in the Imperial Period," *Journal of Jewish Studies* 52, no. 2 (2001): 134–52. See

also E. Leigh Gibson, *The Jewish Manumission Inscriptions of the Bosporus Kingdom*, vol. 75, Texts and Studies in Ancient Judaism (Tübingen: Mohr Siebeck, 1999). It is also important to remember that the Herodian family had close ties to Rome: There were Herodian family members who lived in the Imperial household for periods of time, and there were significant liaisons (the most significant being Bernice, who was the daughter of Herod Agrippa I and who had an affair with Titus (39–81 CE) before he became emperor.

32. The excerpt of Juvenal is taken from *Saturae* 14.96–106. Other Roman writers of the first and second centuries CE who express hostility toward Judaism almost invariably include derisive remarks about Sabbath observance and abstention from pork. Two such Roman writers make mention of the widespread practice of lighting lamps on the Sabbath. One is Seneca, an immediate contemporary of Paul; the other is a satirist named Persius. See Barclay, *Jews in the Mediterranean Diaspora*, 307.

33. Because Joseph resisted the attempted seduction by Mrs. Potiphar (Gen 39), he is proudly and frequently remembered by later Jewish interpreters as the paragon of sexual continence. See the discussion by James L. Kugel, *In Potiphar's House: The Interpretive Life of Biblical Texts*, 1st ed. (San Francisco: HarperSanFrancisco, 1990). An English translation of *Joseph and Asenath* can be found in J. H. Charlesworth, *Old Testament Pseudepigrapha*, vol. 2, 177–247. A reliable date for the text is admittedly a challenge, though it must postdate the Septuagint and thus can hardly be any earlier than the late third century BCE. Most scholars have placed it in the second century BCE–first century CE range, though one scholar has recently made a case for a third-century CE date and a Christian provenance; see Ross Shepard Kraemer, *When Aseneth Met Joseph: A Late Antique Tale of the Biblical Patriarch and His Egyptian Wife, Reconsidered* (New York: Oxford Univ. Press, 1998).

34. *Special Laws* 1.51.

35. It is especially noteworthy that Philo does not mention circumcision in connection with proselytes in *Special Laws* I, because it begins with an extended explanation of the significance of circumcision before segueing into a discussion of the special laws concerning proper worship.

36. Philo, *Questions and Answers on Exodus* 2.2.

37. Equivalent expressions include *sebomenos* and *phoboumeno ton theon*. The Hebrew equivalent *yire shamayim* appears in rabbinic literature. Use of *theosebes* appears in Josephus; see, e.g., *Antiquities* 14.110; and 20.189–196; in which Josephus calls Poppaea, the wife the emperor Nero *theosebes*! Philo does not use the term *theosebes* in reference to Gentiles, but he does use *epelus*. John North, Judith Lieu, and Tessa Rajak, eds. *The Jews among Pagans and Christians: In the Roman Empire* (London: Routledge, 1992), 62.

38. For example, Joseph in *Joseph and Asenath* is repeatedly called *theosebes*, though, interestingly, it is never used of Asenath, even after her conversion. For references to other examples from Jewish Hellenistic literature see the discussion by Judith M. Lieu, "The Race of the God-fearers," in *Neither Jew*

nor Greek? Constructing Early Christianity, Studies of the New Testament and Its World (Edinburgh: T&T Clark, 2002), 60–64.

39. Tessa Rajak, "The Jewish Community and Its Boundaries," in *The Jewish Dialogue with Greece and Rome: Studies in Cultural and Social Interaction* (Leiden: Brill, 2002), 347.

40. Lieu, "Race of the God-Fearers" in *Neither Jew nor Greek?*, see esp. 63.

41. The Aphrodisias inscription is dated to the early third century. The original location of the column remains a mystery. Most archeologists and epigraphers who have studied the inscription believe it likely marked the threshold to a Jewish building of some sort, but it is not clear that it was a synagogue.

42. Philo, *Special Laws* 2.15.62–63; *Embassyto Gaius* 156–57.

43. See the discussion in Barclay, *Jews in the Mediterranean Diaspora*, 292–98.

44. The term *theosebes* does not appear in Acts, but synonymous terms appear in Acts 10:2, 22, 35; 13:16, 26, 43, 50; 16:14; 17:4, 17; 18:7.

45. I have modified the NRSV here, which adds the words "to Judaism," even though they are not in the Greek, which simply reads *sebomenon proseluton,* "pious proselytes."

46. Gruen, *Diaspora*, 241–43. Gruen cites Philo, *On Flaccus* 46.

47. *Contra Apion* 2.38–39.

Chapter 7: The Flexible Pharisees

1. The late Second Temple period would be approximately 200 BCE to 70 CE, when the temple was destroyed by the Romans.

2. One example is the Therapeutae, whom we know only from Philo (*Contemplative Life* 2); another is the "fourth philosophy" mentioned by Josephus (*Antiquities* 18.9). For descriptions of the "big three," namely, Sadducees, Pharisees, and Essenes, scholars depend primarily on Josephus in *Jewish War*, 2.119–66, and *Antiquities*, 13.171–73; 18.11–25.

3. Shaye Cohen offers the simple but useful following definition: "A sect is a small, organized group that separates itself from a larger religious body and asserts that it alone embodies the ideals of the larger groups because it alone understands God's will." Cohen, *Maccabees to the Mishnah*, 125.

4. Jonathan Klawans, while not denying the priestly identity of the Sadducees, downplays the significance of that identity for understanding the Sadducees and argues that they are best understood in terms of Wisdom literature, particularly the Wisdom of Ben Sira; see Jonathan Klawans, "Sadducees, Zadokites, and the Wisdom of Ben Sira," in *Israel's God and Rebecca's Children: Christology and Community in Early Judaism and Christianity; Essays in Honor of Larry W. Hurtado and Alan F. Segal*, ed. David B. Capes, et al (Waco: Baylor Univ. Press, 2007).

5. Josephus says they are the most precise interpreters of the laws (*Jewish War* 2.162).

6. Josephus, *Antiquities* 13.288–98.

7. Josephus, *Jewish War* 1.107, and *Antiquities* 13.399–400.

8. The account in the *Jewish War* runs from 1.107 to 114; in the *Antiquities* from 13.400 to 432.

9. Few realize that there are a number of gospel stories that feature Pharisees who are favorably disposed to Jesus. For example, Jesus is invited to dine with Pharisees in Luke 7:36–50 and Luke 14:1, and the Pharisees warn Jesus about Herod in Luke 13:31. Nicodemus, a Pharisee, seems particularly amenable to Jesus in John 3:1–21. To be sure, these are the minority compared to negative portrayals. Nevertheless, they should not be overlooked.

10. Steve Mason, "Pharisaic Dominance Before 70 CE and the Gospels' Hypocrisy Charge (Matt 23:2–3)," *Harvard Theological Review* 83, no. 4 (1990): 363–81.

11. I make this claim on the assumption that the Essenes lived at the Dead Sea. The ancient sources about whether the Essenes lived separately or not is mixed. Moreover, Josephus says that not all Essenes eschewed marriage. See *Jewish War* 2.160–61.

12. The derivation of the label "Pharisee" is disputed, but it is usually assumed to derive from the Hebrew or Aramaic root verb *prs*, which can mean "to separate, distinguish, or interpret." In addition to Josephus and New Testament texts, the term appears in rabbinic literature, especially when the rabbis contrast the teachings of the Pharisees and Sadducees, but the rabbis typically call them *hakamim*, "sages." For discussion of the ways in which the Pharisees may have distinguished themselves while not separating themselves from larger Jewish society, see Anthony J. Saldarini, "Pharisees," in *Anchor Bible Dictionary*, ed. David Noel Freedman (New York: Doubleday, 1992).

13. The label "Pharisee" does not appear in Scroll texts, but scholars identify certain other designations with Pharisees, namely "the seekers of smooth things" and "the builders of the wall." See James C. VanderKam and Peter Flint, *The Meaning of the Dead Sea Scrolls: Their Significance for Understanding the Bible, Judaism, Jesus, and Christianity* (San Francisco: HarperSanFrancisco, 2002), 276–79.

14. The text from Genesis is a conflation of Genesis 1:27 and 2:24. The parallel to the Markan debate on divorce is found in Matthew 19:3–9.

15. The Covenant of Damascus 4.18–21. Translation mine based on Hebrew text in Florentino García Martínez and Eibert J. C. Tigchelaar, *The Dead Sea Scrolls Study Edition* (Leiden: Brill, 1997).

16. Cf. also the comment by Josephus that "the Pharisees are naturally lenient in the matter of punishments" (*Antiquities* 13.297–98).

17. I necessarily generalize about the Pharisees' perspective. There were different opinions on various matters. The schools of Hillel and Shammai are remembered in rabbinic sources as representing the "liberal" and the "conservative" points of view, respectively. The rabbis, however, tend to favor the views of Hillel.

18. *Mishnah Eduyyot* 8.4. I follow Neusner for the spelling of "Yosi," rather than that of Danby, which is "Jose." Otherwise, this text and all other

citations from the Mishnah are from Danby's translation (unless otherwise indicated).

19. *Mishnah Hagigah* 2.2.

20. The ruling is addressing the teaching that contact with a corpse causes defilement, but it is not clear exactly what this ruling means. The relevant texts are Leviticus 21:11; 22:3–7 and Numbers 19:11–21. For a discussion of the problematic nature of the text, see David Weiss Halivni, *Midrash, Mishnah, and Gemara: The Jewish Predilection for Justified Law* (Cambridge, MA: Harvard Univ. Press, 1986), 27–30.

21. *Mishnah Yadayim,* 4.7 reads "The Sadducees say, We cry out against you, O ye Pharisees, for ye declare clean an unbroken stream of liquid. The Pharisees say, We cry out against you, O ye Sadducees, for ye declare clean a channel of water that flows from a burial ground." To "declare clean" means in this case the liquid is inherently clean and thus not susceptible to uncleanness. The Pharisees' retort to the Sadducees makes the point that the Sadducees are logically inconsistent in this opinion, because they do not apply the same principle in the reverse situation: liquid flowing from an unclean source that makes contact with something clean does not then render the unclean source clean.

22. 4QMMT, lines 5–8.

23. Jacob Neusner, *From Politics to Piety: The Emergence of Pharisaic Judaism*, 2nd ed. (New York: Ktav, 1979).

24. *Antiquities* 13.296.

25. See *War* 1.110–111; 2.162–166; *Antiquities* 18.11–17.

26. *Antiquities* 18.16–17.

27. See *War* 2.162–163; *Antiquities* 18.13–14. Interestingly, Josephus describes this belief differently in the *Antiquities* than he does in the *War*. In *War*, it sounds like he is describing reincarnation; in *Antiquities*, like a new kind of life. In neither case, however, does he describe the reward for a good life as eternal, whereas he does describe the punishment of the wicked as eternal.

28. On this last point, see Acts 23:8–9. While the question of free will does not come up directly in the New Testament in reference to the Pharisees, texts such as Acts 23:8–9 imply a similar position on the matter as that described by Josephus.

29. For those who were Pharisees, being so was probably not their primary identity. Saldarini, "Pharisees," 302.

30. Neusner, *Politics to Piety*, 83.

31. Klawans, *Impurity and Sin in Ancient Judaism*, 108–9. Here, Klawans discusses the differences between *haberim* and Pharisees—for it may have only been some Pharisees who engaged in such eating practices.

32. Though it does seem to reflect the tendency of Jews in this age to transform the concept of temple sanctity by expanding it to communal gatherings (for study, prayer, or Sabbath observance, etc.) in which the presence of holiness is experienced.

33. Since tithing involved setting aside a portion of agricultural produce before it could be consumed, Pharisees were concerned to see that such food had

been properly tithed before consuming it. Tithing applied only within the land, where social and political structures were in place to ensure its systematic practice. (Tithing was connected to an understanding of property division that obtained only in the land of Israel: Unlike the other tribes, no portion of the land was given to the Levites. As landless priests, they were dependent on the other tribes' offerings and tithes for sustenance. See Num 18:8–32; Deut 8:1–8.) For more on tithing and purity and their function as dietary laws for the Pharisees, see Neusner, *Politics to Piety*, 83–90.

Chapter 8: Paul the (Ex?)-Pharisee

1. Robin Griffith-Jones, *The Gospel According to Paul: The Creative Genius Who Brought Jesus to the World* (San Francisco: HarperSanFrancisco, 2004), 1.
2. Seyoon Kim, *The Origin of Paul's Gospel*, 2nd ed., Wissenshaftliche Untersuchungen (Tübingen: Mohr, 1981). Kim sees Paul's conversion implicit in dozens of places in Paul's letters.
3. Stendahl, *Paul Among Jews and Gentiles*, 7–23.
4. The traditional English translations of Galatians 1:15 typically render it something like "God, who was pleased to reveal his Son *to* me . . ." rather than "*in* me," as I translate it. The choice of "in" to render the Greek preposition *en* reflects my desire to capture the ambiguity of Paul's description of this experience. The traditional translation presupposes knowledge of information from Acts and the long-standing Christian tradition that Paul received a vision of Jesus, and that that is what Paul is describing in Galatians 1. As virtually all Pauline scholars acknowledge, if Paul simply wanted to say that God revealed Jesus *to* him, he chose a very awkward manner of expression. At the very least, scholars would agree that my choice of "in" to translate the Greek *en* has the advantage of being the more literal translation.
5. Cf. the critique by John G. Gager, *The Origins of Anti-Semitism: Attitudes toward Judaism in Pagan and Christian Antiquity* (New York: Oxford Univ. Press, 1983). Gager argues that the emphasis on "call" as opposed to "conversion" does not really get to the heart of the issue, namely accounting for what Paul has claimed to repudiate. I hope to do this in the discussion that follows.
6. The RSV renders the phrase "former life in Judaism," but the 1990 revision of that translation, the NRSV, renders it "earlier life." Other translations that use "former" are the NASB, which reads "former manner of life"; the Amplified Bible, which reads "earlier career and former manner of life"; and the NKJV, which reads "former conduct in Judaism."
7. Cf. Acts 18, where, during one of Paul's trials, the Roman proconsul dismisses the charges as an intramural debate. From the proconsul's perspective, there is no essential difference between Jesus-followers and other Jews.
8. Elsewhere Paul refers explicitly to gospel traditions that were handed down to him by other apostles and which he then passed on to his followers (see 1 Cor 15:1). In both cases, Paul's authority and credibility are at issue, but

different circumstances dictate different kinds of responses. In Galatians Paul obviously feels that emphasizing the direct revelation of Jesus will bolster his credibility, while in 1 Corinthians he finds his best source of authority lies in stressing the knowledge he acquired from the other apostles.

9. The NRSV and most other English translations usually translate Galatians 2:15 "We are Jews by birth . . ." The Greek word *phusei* literally means "by nature," though "by birth" is a perfectly acceptable reading. I have chosen not to render it "by birth" because modern readers too readily assume that Paul is trying to distinguish his ethnic identity from his religious identity. Unlike modern people, Paul does not have such neat categories.

10. Cf. Acts 15:5, which mentions "believers who belonged to the sect of the Pharisees . . ."

11. Luke Timothy Johnson, "The New Testament's Anti-Jewish Slander and the Conventions of Ancient Polemic," *Journal of Biblical Literature* 108 (1989), 419–41.

12. Cf. Segal, whose book, *Paul the Convert*, does argue Paul's conversion is critical to interpreting Paul, but he recognizes the limits of historical data, as well as the cultural variations in the idea of conversion (see 299–300).

13. There are other texts that contain autobiographical references, as, for example, mention of his having persecuted the church (see 1 Cor 15:9), or being a member of the tribe of Benjamin (see Rom 11:1), but these texts do not include mention of the Damascus road encounter with Jesus as religiously transformative. Two other times Paul refers to Jesus' appearing to him (see 1 Cor 9:1; 15:8), but it is again for the purpose of proving his apostolic credibility. In both instances Paul stresses how the appearance of the risen Jesus to him is the same as what the other apostles experienced. Since Jesus' appearance to Peter, James, and the others is not regarded as a conversion (because they were already followers of Jesus in his earthly form), it is clear that Paul does not refer to his encounter with Jesus so as to highlight a personal religious transformation.

14. Cf. Segal, who cites the following texts as critical to understanding Paul's experience of conversion: Rom 8:29, 2 Cor 3:18, Phil 3:21, and 1 Cor 15:29.

15. For a recent proponent of this view, see Martin Hengel, *The Pre-Christian Paul* (Philadelphia: Trinity Press International, 1991), 83–84.

16. Fredriksen, "Paul and Augustine," 10–13.

17. Fredriksen, "Paul and Augustine," 12. As Fredriksen says, "It is, moreover, counter-intuitive to hold that Jews generally would consider compatriots executed by an oppressive occupying force to be anything other than victims, if not heroes."

18. Crossan and Reed call the competition for pagan converts by Paul or other Pauline-type Christians "convert poaching," as a way to describe the threat it would have posed to synagogue authorities who needed and desired the support of pagan sympathizers and God-fearers. Crossan and Reed, *In Search of Paul*, xi–xii, 214. See also John G. Gager, "Paul, the Apostle of Judaism," in *Jesus, Judaism, and Christian Anti-Judaism: Reading the New Testament after the Holocaust*, ed. Paula Fredriksen and Adele Reinhartz (Louisville: West-

minster/John Knox, 2002); Terence L. Donaldson, *Paul and the Gentiles: Remapping the Apostle's Convictional World* (Minneapolis: Fortress, 1997).

19. Fredriksen, "Judaism, the Circumcision of Gentiles, and Apocalyptic Hope," 253–55.

20. That Josephus assesses the Pharisees positively in his works and counts himself among them would certainly seem to indicate that the Pharisees were not openly hostile to Roman authorities. For more discussion of the Pharisees, see chapter 7.

21. Richard Horsley, *Jesus and Empire: The Kingdom of God and the New World Disorder* (Minneapolis: Fortress, 2003); Neil Elliott, *The Arrogance of Nations: Reading Romans in the Shadow of Empire* (Minneapolis: Fortress, 2008); Elliott, "The Apostle Paul and Empire." *In the Shadow of Empire: Reclaiming the Bible as a History of Faithful Resistance* (Louisville: Westminster/John Knox, 2008), 97–116; Davina Lopez, *Apostle to the Conquered: Reimagining Paul's Mission* (Minneapolis, Fortress, 2008); Crossan and Reed, *In Search of Paul*.

22. Crossan, *In Search of Paul*, 6. Italics in original.

23. For a compelling argument about how the issue of Gentiles in the church only becomes an issue as a result of the delay of the apocalypse and the second coming of Jesus, see Fredriksen, "Judaism, the Circumcision of Gentiles, and Apocalyptic Hope."

24. Boyarin, *Radical Jew* (50–53; 152–57), argues something similar, but there is a critical difference between his point of view and mine. Boyarin argues that Paul was bothered by Jewish "ethnocentrism" and wished to bring Jews and Gentiles together into one community by erasing the distinctive practices of Judaism. The goal is to make everyone one and the same. In my view, Paul's goal is to bring Jews and Gentiles into one community while maintaining difference.

Chapter 9: A Typical Jew

1. Boyarin, *Radical Jew*, also calls Paul a "cultural critic" (52).

2. In four letters (Romans, 1 and 2 Corinthians, and Philippians), Paul addresses his audience as "holy ones" in the opening salutation of the letter.

3. Calvin J. Roetzel, *Paul: The Man and the Myth*, Studies on Personalities of the New Testament (Columbia: Univ. of South Carolina Press, 1998), 34.

4. Cf. 1 Corinthians 14:33, where Paul similarly refers to "*all* the churches" as "holy ones."

5. Jonathan Klawans, "Interpreting the Last Supper: Sacrifice, Spiritualization, and Anti-Sacrifice," *New Testament Studies* 48 (2002): 1–17.

6. Klawans, "Interpreting the Last Supper," 14.

7. The word I have rendered "body" in Greek literally means "vessel," which is a euphemism for body, though some English translations take it as a euphemism for "wife."

8. The word "sanctification" in 1 Thessalonians 4:3 is the same Greek noun (*hagiosmos*) as the word translated "holiness" in vv. 4, 7.

9. Klawans, *Impurity and Sin in Ancient Judaism*.

10. Klawans, *Impurity and Sin in Ancient Judaism*, 26. See also the discussion in chapter 7.

11. Klawans, *Impurity and Sin in Ancient Judaism*, 151.

12. Cf. the discussion by Nanos, *The Mystery of Romans*, 192–201. See also Peter Tomson, *Paul and the Jewish Law: Halakha in the Letters of the Apostle to the Gentiles*. Compendia Rerum Iudaicurum ad Norum Testamentum, Section 3: Jewish Traditions in Early Christian Literature, Vol. 1. (Assen: Van Gorcum; Minneapolis: Fortress, 1990), 151–86.

13. Most modern English translations render *ethne* in 1 Corinthians 5:1 as "pagans." See, e.g., NRSV; NIV; NASB. As with 1 Thessalonians 4:5, Paul uses the Greek term *ethne*, which I have rendered "Gentiles," explicitly in reference to those who are outside the community at Corinth.

14. As stated explicitly in Leviticus 18:8: "You shall not uncover the nakedness of your father's wife."

15. The quotation in v. 13 is from Deuteronomy 17:7, which is the climax of the legal instructions concerning what to do with a person who commits idolatry (stone them).

16. Paul uses the first person plural throughout this section. However, while he speaks of "your *bodies*" in v. 15 and then describes the defilement of a single body that is united with a prostitute in vv. 15–18, when Paul says "your *body* is a temple of the Holy Spirit," the pronoun "your" is plural, but "body" is singular. The tendency of English translators to render the Greek *en humin* in v. 19 as "within you" rather than "among you" misleads the reader into thinking Paul regards the individual body of the believer as the temple of God. But this is highly unlikely. In all the relevant passages, it is clear that Paul understands the corporate body as analogous to the temple. Cf. 1 Cor 3:16–17; 12:12–31; 2 Cor 6:16. Individual bodies are, of course, part of the corporate body and thus also have an impact on its well-being.

17. Klawans, *Impurity and Sin in Ancient Judaism*, 151.

18. By contrast, 2 Corinthians 6:14–7:1 expresses an extremely negative view of marriage between believers and unbelievers: "Do not be mismatched with unbelievers. For what partnership is there between righteousness and lawlessness? Or what fellowship is there between light and darkness? What agreement does Christ have with Beliar? Or what does a believer share with an unbeliever?" (vv. 14–15, NRSV). One cannot, however, rely on this text as evidence of Paul's own views because a large number of scholars regard it as an interpolation, and there are some good reasons to be wary of its authenticity. The authenticity of 2 Corinthians 6:14–7:1 has been debated for over a century. The debate intensified after the discovery of the Dead Sea Scrolls because of the eerily similar language of dualism and the mention of Beliar (=Belial in the DSS). For a brief and balanced discussion of the arguments for and against seeing the text as an interpolation, see Raymond Edward Brown, *An Introduction to New Testament Christology* (New York: Paulist, 1994), 550–51. For another brief but insightful analysis of this text, including how and why it became inserted into 2 Corinthians, see Nils Alstrup Dahl, *Stud-*

ies in Paul: Theology for the Early Christian Mission (Minneapolis: Augsburg, 1977), 62–69. So uncharacteristically Pauline is this passage that some have argued it actually constitutes an anti-Pauline fragment inserted into Paul's letter to combat what was perceived to be Paul's accommodationist attitude.

19. Segal, *Paul the Convert*, 169–71, sees a role for purity in Paul's thinking similar to mine.

20. Paul's attitude toward genealogy reflects virtually the same pattern of thought as found among non-Christian Jews who accepted proselytism. Jewish writers frequently affirmed the proselyte as fully Jewish, as Jewish as any native-born Jew. At the same time, a proselyte was called "proselyte," not "*ioudaios*," which clearly indicates a classificatory distinction. Furthermore, proselytes had certain disabilities (priests may not marry them) owing to having a different parentage. However, their genealogical alterity was remedied in a generation or two, for the children of proselytes are not called "proselytes" but "Jews."

21. See Cohen, *Beginnings of Jewishness*, 272 n. 32 and Hayes, *Gentile Impurities*, 159. Hayes has this to say: "[B]oth Paul and the early church fathers, on the one hand, and the Palestinian rabbis . . . on the other, were reckoning with and responding to the same cultural problem—the need or desire to redefine Israel along other than genealogical lines. Both Paul and the rabbis reject (to greater and lesser degrees and for different reasons) the zeal for genealogical purity characteristic of Ezra, Jubilees, and Qumranic sources. . . . The rigid and highly impermeable group boundary established by Ezra and intensified among some Second Temple Jewish groups represented by texts like Jubilees and 4QMMT were in tension with other strands of the tradition (a permeable group boundary is seen in the Torah) and contemporary reality, which increasingly included the dual phenomena of conversion and marriage with converts. I venture to suggest that this tension became nothing less than a cultural identity crisis to which Paul and the rabbis found it necessary to respond."

22. To get a sense of just how steeped, see Richard B. Hays, *Echoes of Scripture in the Letters of Paul* (New Haven: Yale Univ. Press, 1989).

23. While various pagan festivals entailed the reading or retelling of foundational myths and legends, they were not regarded as the embodiment of the people's *politeia*, "constitution," in the way Torah was for Jews.

24. Jews of all varieties by this time considered the Torah proper, that is, the five books of Moses, also known as the Pentateuch, as being not only of divine origin but also the central foundation of Jewish Scripture. The prophetic writings also enjoyed widespread esteem and were considered to be divine oracles. The same is true about Psalms and several other texts later known to Christians as wisdom literature (e.g., Proverbs, Job, Ecclesiastes). Although a lesser status was sometimes claimed for the prophetic writings and wisdom literature—that is, in relation to the Torah—many of these books were studied with the same care and attention as the five books and were cited as divine word in the same way texts from Torah were cited. Nevertheless, the boundaries of the canon are fuzzy, such that some texts may have

been considered authoritative Scripture for some Jews but not for others. This is likely the case for Enoch, for example, of which four copies have been found at Qumran.

25. Readers who know Paul's letters well may be wondering about a passage in 2 Corinthians in which Paul seemingly compares the "new covenant" to "written code." This is the only passage in the undisputed Pauline letters in which Paul seems to explicitly disparage the Torah. "For the letter kills, but the spirit gives life," says Paul in 2 Corinthians 3:6. And in 3:14 Paul refers to the "old covenant," which surely refers to the covenant given at Sinai, that is, the Torah. An extended exegesis of this text is beyond the scope of this discussion, but a few basic points of information on Paul's language here should suffice to assure readers of my basic point that Paul remained reverent toward Torah throughout his life. There is no reason to read Paul's contrast between the "new covenant" and "written code" as a contrast between the new covenant wrought in Christ, which brings life, and the old covenant of Torah, which brings death. That reading is rooted in the assumptions of later Christian interpreters who themselves were informed by the reality of a New Testament and an Old and an awareness that Jews belonged to the "Old" and rejected the "New." In actuality, Paul is contrasting two different modes of interpretation, not two different and incompatible covenants, and certainly not two different collections of sacred texts. That Paul is arguing about the proper way to interpret texts is especially evident in vv. 14–16. After Paul gives his own spin about the veil of Moses in Exodus 34, he critiques those who effectively are still "veiled" when they "read Moses." Paul is criticizing those who do not grasp the true meaning of Torah, and in this case, he is mostly speaking of Jews who do not believe in Jesus (to whom there are very few references in Paul). Without the aid of the spirit, the writing is meaningless. It lies dead on the page (or the stone).

26. For the most accessible argument for Paul's directing his critical comments about law to Gentiles, see Gager, *Reinventing Paul.* Other scholars who have emphasized this point, and to whose work I am especially indebted, are Lloyd Gaston, *Paul and the Torah* (Vancouver: Univ. of British Columbia Press, 1987), Neil Elliott, *The Rhetoric of Romans: Argumentative Constraint and Strategy and Paul's Dialogue with Judaism* (Sheffield: JSOT, 1990), Nanos, *The Mystery of Romans,* and Stowers, *A Rereading of Romans.*

27. Fredriksen, "Judaism, the Circumcision of Gentiles, and Apocalyptic Hope."

Chapter 10: A Radical Jewish Monotheist

1. Dahl, *Studies in Paul,* 70–94.
2. This is the argument of Krister Stendahl, *Final Account: Paul's Letter to the Romans* (Minneapolis: Fortress, 1995).
3. See Calvin J. Roetzel, *The Letters of Paul: Conversations in Context,* 4th ed. (Louisville: Westminister/John Knox, 1998).

4. Johan Christiaan Beker, *Paul the Apostle: The Triumph of God in Life and Thought* (Edinburgh: T&T Clark, 1989), 17.

5. However, Paul did not see presiding over baptisms as an essential part of his mission (see 1 Cor 1:14–17).

6. Here I am in full agreement with Nanos, *The Mystery of Romans*, 166–238.

7. The story of Abraham's purchase of Machpelah is told in Genesis 23. References to some of Abraham's various sojourns appear in Gen 12:10; 13:1–7; 20:1; 21:34; and 22:19. The pattern of sojourning continues through the lives of Isaac and Jacob.

8. Jubilees 11:16–17. Jubilees is an extracanonical text that appears to have enjoyed fairly wide circulation. Copies of Jubilees were found among the Dead Sea Scrolls, though scholars knew of its existence long before the discovery of the scrolls. Translation taken from James L. Kugel, *The Bible as It Was* (Cambridge, MA: Belknap, Harvard Univ. Press, 1997), 133–48.

9. Kugel argues that the tradition of Abraham as the first to believe in God derives partly from the need to account for another verse, namely, Joshua 24:2–3: "And Joshua said to all the people, 'Thus says the Lord, the God of Israel: "Your ancestors lived of old beyond the Euphrates, Terah, the father of Abraham and of Nahor; they served other gods. Then I took your father Abraham from beyond the River and led him through all the land of Canaan."'" See Kugel, *Bible as It Was*, 133–34.

10. *Antiquities* 1.154–57.

11. This is especially true of Jubilees, Pseudo Philo and, to a certain extent, Philo.

12. For discussion of the role astronomy plays in Abraham's "conversion" to monotheism in postbiblical tradition, with special attention to Josephus's account, see Annette Yoshiko Reed, "Abraham as Chaldean Scientist and Father of the Jews: Josephus, *Ant.* 1.154–168, and the Greco-Roman Discourse About Astronomy/Astrology," *Journal for the Study of Judaism* 35 (2004): 119–58.

13. Pamela Eisenbaum, "Paul as the New Abraham," in *Paul and Poltics: Ekklesia, Israel, Imperium, Interpretation*, ed. Richard A. Horsley (Harrisburg, PA: Trinity, 2000).

14. Dunn, *Theology of Paul the Apostle*, 28–29.

15. Some scholars have argued that Jesus was not unique, that early devotion to Jesus was no different from the veneration of angels in ancient Judaism, or that Jesus was originally conceived of as a redeemer figure, but a fully human one, and that such a figure would have been fully consistent with Jewish monotheism. The deification and attendant worship of Jesus is then explained as the result of the influence of Hellenistic culture, particularly of pagan religious practice and belief. This understanding of the evolution of Christology is usually credited to Wilhelm Bousset, *Kyrios Christos: A History of Belief in Christ from the Beginnings of Christianity to Irenaeus*, trans. J. E. Steely (Nashville: Abingdon, 1970). While some early believers might well have thought of Jesus in terms similar to angels or demigods, I am convinced

by those scholars who argue that the veneration of angels or other semidivine beings in ancient Judaism does not amount to a kind of devotion comparable to that found among early believers in Jesus. See Larry W. Hurtado, *One God, One Lord: Early Christian Devotion and Ancient Jewish Monotheism*, 2nd ed. (Edinburgh: T&T Clark, 1998), 26–35, Loren Stuckenbruck, *Angel Veneration and Christology*, (Tübingen: Mohr, 1995).

16. Larry W. Hurtado, *Lord Jesus Christ: Devotion to Jesus in Earliest Christianity* (Grand Rapids: Eerdmans, 2003), 52.

17. Hurtado, *Lord Jesus Christ*, 71–72.

18. Hurtado, *Lord Jesus Christ*, 72.

19. Nanos, *Mystery of Romans*, also stresses Paul's emphasis on monotheism.

20. Dunn, *Theology of Paul the Apostle*, 28. The number could be even higher, as some Greek manuscripts have "God" in certain verses where others read "Christ" and where the standard critical edition of the Greek New Testament follows the latter reading. It is possible that as the church became more christocentric, Christian scribes replaced the word "God" with the word "Christ."

21. Dunn counts six instances of "gospel of God" and eight of "gospel of Christ," along with one instance of "gospel of his son" (Rom 1:9). Dunn, *Theology of Paul the Apostle*, 166.

22. See 1 Cor 1:2; 10:32; 11:16, 22; 15:9; 2 Cor 1:1; Gal 1:13; 1 Thess 2:14. Paul uses the phrase "church of Christ" only rarely. In the case of Galatians 1:22, where Paul refers to "the churches in Judea who are in Christ," he likely needs to distinguish between Jews who do not believe in Jesus and those who do.

23. As Dunn notes, "the God who quickens the dead" appears also as the second of the "Eighteen Benedictions" (Hebrew: *Shemonah Esrai*), an ancient Jewish prayer that still forms part of traditional Jewish liturgy today. Dunn, *Theology of Paul the Apostle*, 40.

24. For references to particular Pauline texts, see Dunn, *Theology of Paul the Apostle*, 38–41. Dunn observes how this aspect of Paul's monotheism is, however, in contrast to Greek philosophical monotheism.

25. See also 1 Thess 1:2; 3:9; Rom 1:8; 1 Cor 1:4.

26. See Rom 6:17; 7:25; 10:1; 2 Cor 8:16; 9:11–12; Phil 4:6; 1 Thess 3:9.

27. I have used the NRSV translation for 2 Corinthians 1:20, which admittedly is a bit of a paraphrase. But the verse is almost impossible to translate literally into English, and I believe the NRSV has certainly captured the meaning of the verse. More literal renderings can be found in the KJV and the NASB.

28. For other examples, see the opening greetings of each letter; typical is "Grace to you and peace from God the Father and the Lord Jesus Christ."

29. Dunn, *Theology of Paul the Apostle*, 245.

30. Hurtado, *Lord Jesus Christ*, 108–10, especially n. 73. See Dunn, *Theology*, 249, for citations from Philo and Josephus.

31. Walter H. Wagner, *After the Apostles: Christianity in the Second Century* (Minneapolis: Fortress, 1994), 106.

32. N. T. Wright, *The Climax of the Covenant: Christ and the Law in Pauline Theology* (Minneapolis: Fortress, 1993), 128.

33. Hurtado, *Lord Jesus Christ*, 114. Hurtado calls it an "astonishingly bold association of Jesus with God."

34. *Logos* essentially figures as an equivalent to *Sophia* in Philo. See *Allegorical Interpretation* 1.63. For discussion of the relationship between Sophia, Logos, and early Christology, see James D. Dunn, *The Christ and the Spirit: Collected Essays of James D. G. Dunn*, vol. 1 (Edinburgh: T&T Clark, 1998), 341.

35. Richard A. Horsley, "The Background of the Confessional Formula in 1 Kor 8:6," *Zeitschrift für die neutestamenliche Wissenschaft* 69 (1978), and "Gnosis in Corinth: 1 Corinthians 8:1–6," *New Testament Studies* 27 (1980): 32–51.

36. For elaboration on the use of the term *doxa* and its cognates, see Claudia Camp, "Understanding a Patriarchy: Women in Second Century Jerusalem through the Eyes of Ben Sira," in *Women Like This: New Perspectives on Jewish Women in the Greco-Roman World*, ed. Amy-Jill Levine, *Society of Biblical Literature: Early Judaism and Its Literature 1* (Atlanta: Scholars Press, 1991), and Pamela Eisenbaum, "Sirach," in *Women's Bible Commentary, Expanded Edition*, ed. Carol Newsom and Sharon Ringe (Louisville: Westminster/John Knox, 1998), 300.

37. There is only one text where the application of *theos* to Jesus is even a possible interpretation of the text. That text is Romans 9:5. The wording is awkward in Greek, and thus there is room for debate about the translation. A reader of English would not necessarily know there was any issue here since the NRSV and many other standard translations render the text in such a way as to make it clear that Paul is referring to God here, properly speaking, and Dunn defends that interpretation: Dunn, *Theology of Paul the Apostle*, 255–56.

38. Dunn, *Theology of Paul the Apostle*, 254. "*Kyrios* is not so much a way of *identifying* Jesus with God, but if anything more a way of *distinguishing* Jesus from God" (italics in original).

39. See Dunn, *Theology of Paul the Apostle*, 260.

40. Pamela Eisenbaum, "A Speech Act of Faith: The Early Proclamation of the Resurrection of Jesus," in *Putting Body and Soul Together: Essays in Honor of Robin Scroggs*, ed. Virginia Wiles, et al (Valley Forge, PA: Trinity, 1997).

41. See Beker, *Paul the Apostle: The Triumph of God in Life and Thought*, 362–63; Dunn, *Theology of Paul the Apostle*, 258–59. Both look comprehensively at the language of glorification and other types of worship language in Paul and conclude that Paul is notably consistent in reserving such language for God and avoiding the application of such language to Christ. Out of dozens of passages, there are only a couple that are ambiguous.

42. Dunn, *Theology of Paul the Apostle*, 259. Italics in original. Cf. Hurtado, *Lord Jesus Christ*; he labels the type of devotional practice found in Paul

"binitarian," by which Hurtado means that, while devotion is still within a monotheistic framework, the pattern of devotional practice in Paul's letters already represents a radical innovation in Jewish monotheism, because Jesus so frequently appears in prayers, hymns, and petitions alongside God in so highly exalted a position. At the same time, like Dunn, Hurtado acknowledges that Paul's devotional language is consistent in its being addressed *to* God *through* Jesus. Thus I do not disagree with Hurtado's analysis of the relevant Pauline texts. But I'm not sure the label of "binitarian" is helpful for capturing Paul's theological disposition. It seems to me that the label should be reserved for those writers who begin to speak of Jesus in a way virtually interchangeable with God but do not yet think in Trinitarian terms.

43. For example, while Paul directs his doxologies (praise hymns traditionally devoted to the glory of God) to God (e.g., Rom 11:36; Gal 1:5), some doxologies found in later New Testament writings (e.g., Rev 1:4–5; 2 Pet 3:18) are directed to Jesus. See Hurtado, *Lord Jesus Christ*, 152. On the other, cf. the study by Ian G. Wallis, *The Faith of Jesus Christ in Early Christian Traditions* (Cambridge: Cambridge Univ. Press, 1995).

44. Sometimes, technically speaking, Paul's exhortation to faith is directed to the resurrection of Jesus as the definitive act of God. See, e.g., Rom 10:9: "If you profess with your lips Jesus as Lord and *believe* in your heart *that God raised him from the dead*, you will be saved."

45. Eisenbaum, "A Speech Act of Faith."

46. As the reader will see in the following discussion, a few interpreters would agree that faith is absolutely central, but they believe the Pauline concept of faith has been sorely misunderstood. One such interpreter is Richard B. Hays, *The Faith of Jesus Christ: The Narrative Substructure of Galatians 3:1–4:11*, 2nd ed. (Grand Rapids: Eerdmans, 2002).

47. The Greek phrase *pistis iesou christou*, that is, "faith of Jesus Christ" occurs with minor variations (e.g., "faith of *Jesus*," "faith of *Christ*") seven times in the undisputed Pauline letters: Rom 3:22, 26; Gal 2:16 (twice), 20; 3:22; and Phil 3:9.

48. The NRSV, NIV, NASV, CEV, NAB, and ESV are all popular translations that translate these passages "faith in Jesus Christ."

49. William Tyndale, who was greatly influenced by Luther, and whose translation has been so influential in the history of English translation, translated *pistis christou* as "fayth of Christ" except in one instance where it is translated "him who belivith on Jesus" (Rom 3:26).

50. The phrase "righteousness of God" is the same kind of grammatical construction and has the same issue as "faith of Christ." Thus, it is arguable whether this is a subjective or objective genitive. Luther took the phrase as an objective genitive, meaning that the righteousness here does not refer to God's own righteousness; it refers to the righteousness that God *imputes* to the believer, righteousness that the believer receives from God. But more recently scholars have argued that the phrase does refer to God's righteous-

ness. See Sam K. Williams, "The 'Righteousness of God' In Romans," *Journal of Biblical Literature* 99 (1980): 241–90.

51. Sam K. Williams, "Again Pistis Christou," *Catholic Biblical Quarterly* 49 (1987): 431–47.

52. L. T. Johnson recently claimed that the debate has now shifted in favor of the subjective genitive reading. See his Foreword to the second edition of Hays, *The Faith of Jesus Christ*, xiii. Johnson credits Hays's work with initiating that shift. For a defense of the objective genitive reading, see James D. G. Dunn, "Once More, ΠΙΣΤΙΣ ΧΡΙΣΤΟΥ" in E. Elizabeth Johnson and David M. Hay, *Pauline Theology, Volume IV: Looking Back, Pressing On* (Atlanta: SBL Press, 1997), 61–81.

Chapter 11: On a Mission from God

1. *Special Laws* 65.
2. Dahl, *Studies in Paul*, 180–81.
3. Ernst Käsemann, *Commentary on Romans*, trans. Geoffrey W. Bromiley (Grand Rapids: Eerdmans, 1980), 102–4. "Paul turns Israel's own presuppositions against itself" says Käsemann in reference to Romans 3:29–30 (p. 104).
4. Dahl, *Studies in Paul*, 189. See also Nanos, *Mystery of Romans*, 179–97. Nanos's views about the significance of the Shema in Romans have been very influential on my own interpretation of Romans.
5. There is some debate about whether Jews at this time actively proselytized non-Jews, and, therefore, whether Paul's mission to Gentiles was an extension of that missionary program. At this point, most scholars think that Jews did not actively try to recruit Gentiles to Judaism, though they were open to those who showed interest. See Martin Goodman, *Mission and Conversion: Proselytizing in the Religious History of the Roman Empire* (Oxford: Oxford Univ. Press, 1996), and B. J. Lietaert Peerbolte, *Paul the Missionary* (Leuven: Peeters, 2003), 19–53.
6. For a discussion of Philo's and Josephus's tolerance of Gentile worship, see Louis H. Feldman, *Jew and Gentile in the Ancient World: Attitudes and Interactions from Alexander to Justinian* (Princeton: Princeton Univ. Press, 1993), 132–48.
7. Paul speaks of the "first fruits" of the new age in 1 Corinthians 15:20 and Romans 8:28.
8. This discussion is adapted from my essay: Pamela Eisenbaum, "Paul as the New Abraham," in *Paul and Politics: Ekklesia, Israel, Imperium, Interpretation,* Richard Horsley, ed. (Harrisburg, PA: Trinity Press International, 2000), 130–45.
9. Cf. the vehemently polemical exchange about Abrahamic descent between Jesus and his Jewish auditors in John 8:31–47.
10. C. K. Barrett, *Paul: An Introduction to His Thought* (Louisville: Westminster/John Knox, 1994), 83.
11. Pamela Eisenbaum, "A Remedy for Having Been Born of Woman: Jesus,

Gentiles, and Genealogy in Romans," *Journal of Biblical Literature* 123 (2004): 686 n. 48.

12. Michael Cranford, "Abraham in Romans 4: The Father of All Who Believe," *New Testament Studies* 41 (1995): 73.

13. The NRSV translates Romans 4:3: "Abraham believed God and it was reckoned to him as righteousness." There is not too much difference between the word "reckoned" and "credited." I chose the latter primarily because it better captures what Paul is saying in this context. The Greek verb, *logizomai,* literally means to "count" something.

14. Cf. Romans 5:6. On the connections between Romans 1 and 4, see Edward Adams, "Abraham's Faith and Gentile Disobedience: Textual Links Between Romans 1 and 4," *Journal for the Study of the New Testament* 65 (1997): 47–66; and James D. G. Dunn, *Romans 1–8,* vol. 38a, Word Biblical Commentary (Dallas: Word, 1995), 205.

15. See Martyn, *Galatians,* 399–400; Yoshiko Reed, "Abraham as Chaldean Scientist"; and Cranford, "Abraham in Romans 4."

16. Stowers, *Rereading of Romans,* 227–28.

17. Elliott, *Arrogance of Nations,* 75.

18. Cf. the comments of Gaston: "If there is one attitude which underlies all of these assumptions, it would be the religious attitude which predisposes a certain way of construing the Greek when it is ambiguous, particularly with respect to certain genitives." Gaston, *Paul and the Torah,* 11.

19. In a similar vein, the NASB has "Therefore, be sure that it is those who are of faith who are sons of Abraham." More literal renderings of *hoi ek pisteos* can be found in the RSV, which has "men of faith," and the KJV, which has "they which are of faith." Interestingly, the NKJV renders Galatians 3:6 less literally: "therefore know that *only* those who are of faith are sons of Abraham." The addition of the word "only" betrays the translators' desire to eliminate any ambiguity in the text.

20. Frederick William Danker, et al., eds., *A Greek-English Lexicon of the New Testament and Other Early Christian Literature,* 3rd ed. (Chicago: Univ. of Chicago Press, 2000), 295–96; and Henry George Liddell and Robert Scott, eds., revised and augmented by Sir Henry Stuart Jones, *A Greek-English Lexicon* (Oxford: Clarendon, 1996), 499.

21. The phrase "Hebrew born of Hebrews" in Philippians 3:5 reads in Greek *Hebraios ex Hebraion.* The preposition *ek* is spelled *ex* when the next word begins with rough breathing, the equivalent of an 'h' in English. Other examples where *ek* means "born of" can be found in Matt 1:3, 5, 16; John 1:13; Luke 1:27; 2:4; 23:7; Acts 4:6; Rom 1:3; 9:6; Gal 4:4, 22.

22. For example, he sometimes uses the participle *hoi pisteuontes,* which is the literal equivalent of "those who believe." See e.g., Gal 3:22; Rom 3:22; 4:11; 10:9, 14.

23. The phrase *to ek pisteos* in Romans 4:16 is essentially the same construction as *hoi ek pisteos* in Galatians 3:7 and 9 but in the singular in Romans 4:16, literally then, "the one descended from faith." Nevertheless, Paul is using a generic example in the Romans verse. In the latter half of Romans 4

Paul vacillates between singular and plural forms and yet employs the same grammatical construction using *ek*.

24. Stowers, *Rereading of Romans*, 72.

Chapter 12: "On the Contrary, We Uphold the Law!"

1. I intentionally cite the NRSV at this point. When discussing some of these verses later in the chapter I will use my own translation.
2. See the *Joint Declaration on the Doctrine of Justification* (1999) made by the Lutheran World Federation and the Catholic Church. See also Anthony N. S. Lane, *Justification by Faith in Catholic-Protestant Dialogue: An Evangelical Assessment* (London: Continuum, 2002) for a balanced account.
3. Gaston, *Paul and the Torah*, 18.
4. Gaston, *Paul and the Torah*, 16. For another accessible analysis and critique of the traditional view, see Neil Elliott, *Liberating Paul: The Justice of God and the Politics of the Apostle* (Sheffield: Sheffield Academic, 1995).
5. Betz, *Galatians*, 16.
6. For the view of Paul as a liar and a phony, see Maccoby, *Mythmaker*. For the view of Paul as an inconsistent thinker, see Heikki Räisänen, *Paul and the Law*, 2nd ed. (Tübingen: Mohr, 1987).
7. Sanders, *Paul and Palestinian Judaism*, 442–43.
8. This understanding is found throughout Dunn's works. Easy access to many of Dunn's new-perspective essays can be had in the recent volume *The New Perspective on Paul: Collected Essays* (Tubingen: Mohr Siebeck, 2005). N. T. Wright argues similarly in *What Saint Paul Really Said: Was Paul of Tarsus the Real Founder of Christianity?* (Grand Rapids: Eerdmans, 1997). Boyarin, too, *Radical Jew*.
9. See the critique by Hodge, *If Sons, Then Heirs*, 8.
10. For a good discussion of this, see Gager, *Reinventing Paul*, 43. Understanding Paul's audience as Gentile is fundamental to the work of Stendahl, Stowers, Gaston, and thus to the radical new perspective generally.
11. Gager, *Reinventing Paul*, 13. Italics in original.
12. Among the strongest interpreters of Paul who give attention to rhetoric, especially the audience question, are Elliott, *Rhetoric of Romans*, and *Arrogance of Nations*; John G. Lodge, *Romans 9–11: A Reader-Response Analysis* (Atlanta: Scholars, 1996); Stowers, *Rereading of Romans*.
13. See the discussion in Martyn, *Galatians*.
14. Fredriksen, "Judaism, the Circumcision of Gentiles, and Apocalyptic Hope," 546–47.
15. In antiquity, Justin Martyr had claimed that God commanded Jews to circumcise so that it would be easier to condemn Jews at the time of the last judgment. See *Dialogue with Trypho*, 16.36–37.
16. Wright, *Climax of the Covenant*, 198, 202–3.
17. Wright, *Climax of the Covenant*.
18. For a more detailed discussion, see chapter 5, the section titled "Torah and Election," and chapter 6.

19. Stowers, *Rereading of Romans*, 83–125. In contrast to the radical new perspective, the vast majority of commentators see Romans 1 as an indictment of humankind more generally, even those sensitive to the Gentile rhetoric of Romans, see Robert Jewett, *Romans: A Commentary* (Minneapolis: Fortress, 2007), 152.

20. Räisänen, *Paul and the Law*, 94–109. Räisänen argues that Paul contradicts himself between Romans 1 and 2, arguing that in Romans 1 Paul paints a picture of universal sinfulness and then in Romans 2 claims that some Gentiles keep the law. But Räisänen fails to take account of Paul's Jewish framework as well as the forms of Hellenistic rhetoric Paul is following. Paul is not writing systematic theology, nor is he writing with the rigor of a scholastic philosopher. Paul's logic is not too different from saying, "Germany fell under the spell of a brutal and psychotic dictator" and then mentioning those Germans who resisted Hitler.

21. Fredriksen, "Judaism, the Circumcision of Gentiles, and Apocalyptic Hope."

22. Segal, *Paul the Convert*, 269.

23. Segal, *Paul the Convert*, 200; Stowers, 109–18.

24. Westerholm, *Perspectives Old and New on Paul*, 27.

25. I have preserved the literal translation "dead," but I think Paul speaks euphemistically here; he means something closer to "invisible." It is another way of saying what he has just said: without Torah, one cannot even perceive sin. However, because the next sentence uses terms for "life," I want Paul's rhetorical use of metaphor to be apparent. Cf. Danker, *Greek-English Lexicon*, 667, who confirms this understanding and offers Romans 5:20 and 8:10 in support.

26. Jewett, *Romans: A Commentary*, 446.

27. Augustine originally believed that Paul was not speaking autobiographically, but then later in fact he did think he was speaking autobiographically. See Fredriksen, "Paul and Augustine," 25.

28. Stowers, *Rereading of Romans*, 264–69.

29. I do not mean to imply that Romans 7 is not part of the letter addressed to the Romans; I speak rather of the audience as rhetorically constructed—what Stowers calls the "encoded reader" or "audience" (Stowers, *Rereading of Romans*, 21–33).

30. Stendahl, *Paul Among Jews and Gentiles*, 79.

31. Stendahl, *Paul Among Jews and Gentiles*, 80.

32. See the discussion in Jewett, *Romans: A Commentary*, 444.

33. Stowers, *Rereading of Romans*, 258–84.

34. Stowers, *Rereading of Romans*, 278.

35. Stowers, *Rereading of Romans*, 52, 273–84.

36. Gaston, *Paul and the Torah*, 100, citing E. DeWitt Burton, *A Critical and Exegetical Commentary on the Epistle to the Galatians* (Edinburgh: T. and T. Clark, 1921), 120.

37. Gal 2:16 (3 times); 3:2, 5, 10; Rom 3:20, 28.

38. Here I am following the suggestion of Gaston, *Paul and the Torah*, 100–106.

39. Some believe that Romans 3:20 is paraphrasing Psalm 143:2.

40. Stowers, *Rereading of Romans*, 85–100.

41. Jesus is only mentioned as judge in Romans 2:16.

42. A word about the translation of Romans 2:12: While the NRSV renders 2:13 well, the same is not true of 2:12. Although I do not have time to discuss it in detail, I prefer the following translation: "Whosoever has sinned lawlessly will also perish lawlessly, and whosoever has sinned by the law will be judged by the law." In place of "apart from the law" I have translated the word "lawlessly" (following Stowers, *Rereading of Romans*, 138–42). The terminology of Romans 2:12 is usually understood as meant to differentiate between Jews and Gentiles. In the standard translation, "those who are apart from the law" refers to Gentiles—for they did not have the Torah, while Jews did; thus, "those who have sinned by the law" refers to Jews. To be sure, Paul is undoubtedly discussing Jews and Gentiles in Romans—dare we say, it is the main subject—the way they have each had a different fate, a different historical path, and the way God relates to each group and the way they relate to each other. But it is likely that in this passage Paul literally distinguishes between those who live in accord with God's law, whether Jew or Gentile, and those who do not, whether Jew or Gentile.

43. *Mishnah Aboth* 3:16.

44. Rom 1:5; 15:18. See Paul Sevier Minear, *The Obedience of Faith; the Purposes of Paul in the Epistle to the Romans* (Naperville, IL: Allenson, 1971).

45. This verse is the basis for the doctrine of *sola fide*, by faith alone. Although Origen seems to have also made a similar reference regarding Rom 1:17, he never constructed the faith-works opposition that Luther did. See Reasoner, *Romans in Full Circle*, 17.

46. Admittedly, Paul's emphasis here is probably not on a life lived in devotion to the commandments. Although there is debate about exactly how we should interpret Paul's message here, we must acknowledge that the word "live" in this verse is Paul's way of affirming eternal life, or at least life as the reward for living faithfully. Cf. Deut 30:15–20.

47. First Corinthians 7:19 in full reads "Circumcision is nothing and uncircumcision is nothing; but obeying the commandments of God is everything!" (NRSV). The first part of the verse sounds like Paul is undermining the commandment to circumcise, but Paul's assumption is most likely that God commanded only Jews to circumcise, thus implying that God excluded Gentiles from this commandment. Therefore, when Jews circumcise, they are following the commandments, and when Gentiles do not, they are also following the commandments.

48. Stowers, *Rereading of Romans*, 188. Stowers provides the following examples: 1 Cor 15:58, 16:10, Phil 2:12; Gal 6:4.

Chapter 13: Justification Through Jesus Christ

1. I have argued elsewhere that Paul's vision for an integrated community of Jews and Gentiles is of one family, not where everyone becomes the same

and differences are erased, but where those differences are respected. See Eisenbaum, "Is Paul the Father of Misogyny and Anti-Semitism?" *Cross Currents* 50 (2000–01), 506–24.

2. The hymn continues in vv. 9–11 with a description of the exaltation.
3. Stowers, *Rereading of Romans*, 227–50.
4. Sam K. Williams, *Jesus' Death as Saving Event: The Background and Origin of a Concept* (Cambridge: Harvard Univ. Press, 1975).
5. In a scholian on Galatians 2:16, Luther quite literally said this, "Righteousness is faith in Jesus Christ." See Alister E. McGrath, *Iustitia Dei: A History of the Christian Doctrine of Justification*, 3rd ed. (Cambridge: Cambridge Univ. Press, 2005), 223.
6. McGrath, *Iustitia Dei*, 220.
7. That is why the doctrine of justification by faith in Lutheran tradition is actually stated as "justification by grace through faith."
8. The following English translations have "faith in Christ": NRSV, NIV, NJB, CEV, Good News. Strangely, the KJV translates the phrase "faith in Christ" in Galatians, and "faith of Christ" in Romans.
9. Williams, "The 'Righteousness of God' in Romans."
10. Gaston, *Paul and the Torah*, 100–106. See also the earlier discussion in the previous chapter.
11. See Deut 7:6; 14:2; Exod 19:5.
12. Sanders, *Paul and Palestinian Judaism*, 85.
13. Sanders, *Paul and Palestinian Judaism*, 97.
14. See W. S. Campbell, "Romans III as a Key to the Structure and Thought of Romans," in *The Romans Debate*, ed. Karl Donfried (Peabody, MA: Hendrickson, 1991), 251–64.
15. Although the translation is mine, I have been influenced by the translation of Gaston, *Paul and the Torah*, 172. Words in parentheses represent words that do not have an equivalent in the Greek but may reasonably be inferred. Words in brackets are words I have added for clarification.

Chapter 14: It's the End of the World as We Know It

1. Gager, *Reinventing Paul*, 145.
2. Lodge, *Romans 9–11*; Nanos, *Mystery of Romans*; Gaston, *Paul and the Torah*, to name a few.
3. Stendahl, *Final Account*, 7.
4. Mark Reasoner, *Romans in Full Circle: A History of Interpretation* (Louisville: Westminster/John Knox, 2005), 55–66.
5. J. Christiaan Beker, "The Faithfulness of God and the Priority of Israel in Paul's Letter to the Romans," in *The Romans Debate*, Karl P. Donfried, ed. (Peabody, MA: Hendrickson, 1991), 327–32.
6. Eisenbaum, *Invitation to Romans* (Nashville: Abingdon, 2006), 88.

Bibliography

Adams, Edward. "Abraham's Faith and Gentile Disobedience: Textual Links Between Romans 1 and 4." *Journal for the Study of the New Testament* 65 (1997): 47–66.

Alon, Gedalyahu. *Jews, Judaism, and the Classical World: Studies in Jewish History in the Times of the Second Temple and Talmud.* Translated by Israel Abrahams. Jerusalem: Magnes, 1977.

Augustine. *Augustine on Romans: Propositions from the Epistle to the Romans, Unfinished Commentary on the Epistle to the Romans.* Translated by Paula Fredriksen Landes. Chico, CA: Scholars, 1982.

Barclay, John M. G. *Jews in the Mediterranean Diaspora: From Alexander to Trajan (323 BCE–117 CE).* Edinburgh: T&T Clark, 1996.

Barrett, C. K. *Paul: An Introduction to His Thought.* Louisville: Westminster/John Knox, 1994.

Beker, Johan Christiaan. "The Faithfulness of God and the Priority of Israel in Paul's Letter to the Romans." In *The Romans Debate*, edited by Karl Donfried, 327–32. Peabody, MA: Hendrickson, 1991.

———. *Paul the Apostle: The Triumph of God in Life and Thought.* Edinburgh: T&T Clark, 1989.

Betz, Hans Dieter. *Galatians: A Commentary on Paul's Letters to the Churches in Galatia.* Minneapolis: Fortress, 1979.

Bousset, Wilhelm. *Kyrios Christos: A History of the Belief in Christ from the Beginnings of Christianity to Irenaeus.* Translated by J. E. Steely. Nashville: Abingdon, 1970.

Bovon, François. "Paul Comme Document Et Paul Comme Monument." In *Chrétiens En Conflit: L'Épître De Paul Aux Galates*, 54–65. Genève: Labor et Fides, 1987.

Bowersock, G. W. *Hellenism in Late Antiquity.* Ann Arbor: Univ. of Michigan Press, 1990.

Boyarin, Daniel. *Border Lines: The Partition of Judaeo-Christianity*. Philadelphia: Univ. of Pennsylvania Press, 2004.

———. *A Radical Jew: Paul and the Politics of Identity*. Berkeley: Univ. of California Press, 1994.

Brown, Raymond Edward. *An Introduction to New Testament Christology*. New York: Paulist, 1994.

———. *An Introduction to the New Testament*. New York: Doubleday, 1997.

Brumberg-Kraus, Jonathan, "A Jewish Ideological Perspective on the Study of Christian Scripture," *Jewish Social Studies* 4 (1997): 121–52.

Buber, Martin. *Two Types of Faith: A Study of the Interpretation of Judaism and Christianity*. Translated by Norman Goldhawk. New York: Macmillan, 1951.

Camp, Claudia. "Understanding a Patriarchy: Women in Second Century Jerusalem Through the Eyes of Ben Sira." In *Women Like This: New Perspectives on Jewish Women in the Greco-Roman World*, edited by Amy-Jill Levine. Atlanta: Scholars, 1991.

Campbell, W. S. "Romans III as the Key to the Structure and Thought of Romans." In *The Romans Debate*, edited by Karl Donfried. Rev. ed. (Peabody, MA: Hendrickson, 1991), 251–64.

Charles, R. H. *The Apocalypse of Baruch*. London: A&C Black, 1896.

Charlesworth, J. C., ed. *The Old Testament Pseudepigrapha*. 2 vols. New York: Doubleday, 1983.

Cohen, Jeremy. *Living Letters of the Law: Ideas of the Jew in Medieval Christianity*. Berkeley: Univ. of California Press, 1999.

Cohen, Shaye J. D. *The Beginnings of Jewishness: Boundaries, Varieties, Uncertainties*. Berkeley: Univ. of California Press, 2001.

———. *From the Maccabees to the Mishnah*. Philadelphia: Westminster/John Knox, 1987.

Cranford, Michael. "Abraham in Romans 4: The Father of All Who Believe." *New Testament Studies* 41 (1995): 71–88.

Crossan, John Dominic and Jonathan L. Reed. *In Search of Paul: How Jesus's Apostle Opposed Rome's Empire with God's Kingdom*. San Francisco: HarperSanFrancisco, 2004.

Dahl, Nils Alstrup. *Studies in Paul: Theology for the Early Christian Mission*. Minneapolis: Augsburg, 1977.

Dassmann, Ernst. *Der Stachel Im Fleisch: Paulus in Der Frühchristlichen Literatur Bis Irenäeus*. Münster: Aschenmdorff, 1979.

Donaldson, Terence L. *Paul and the Gentiles: Remapping the Apostle's Convictional World*. Minneapolis: Fortress, 1997.

Dunn, James D. G. *The Christ and the Spirit: Collected Essays of James D. G. Dunn*. Vol. 1, *Christ and the Spirit*. Edinburgh: T&T Clark, 1998.

———. *Jesus, Paul, and the Law: Studies in Mark and Galatians*. Philadelphia: Wesminster, 1990.

———. *The New Perspective on Paul: Collected Essays*. Tubingen: Mohr Siebeck, 2005.

————. *Romans 1–8,* Word Biblical Commentary. Vol. 38a. Dallas: Word, 1995.

————. *The Theology of Paul the Apostle.* Grand Rapids: Eerdmans, 1998.

Eagleton, Terry. *Literary Theory: An Introduction.* 2nd ed. Minneapolis: Univ. of Minnesota Press, 1996.

Ehrman, Bart D. *The Apostolic Fathers.* 2 vols. (Cambridge, MA: Harvard Univ. Press, 2003).

————. *Lost Christianities: The Battle for Scripture and the Faiths We Never Knew.* New York: Oxford Univ. Press, 2003.

————. *Lost Scriptures: Books That Did Not Make It Into the New Testament.* New York: Oxford Univ. Press, 2003.

————. *The New Testament: A Historical Introduction to the Early Christian Writings.* 4th ed. New York: Oxford Univ. Press, 2007.

Eisenbaum, Pamela. *Invitation to Romans.* (Nashville: Abingdon, 2006).

————. "Is Paul the Father of Misogyny and Anti-Semitism?" *Cross Currents* 50 (2000–2001), 506–24.

————. "Paul as the New Abraham." In *Paul and Politics: Ekklesia, Israel, Imperium, Interpretation,* edited by Richard A. Horsley. Harrisburg, PA: Trinity, 2000.

————. "A Remedy for Having Been Born of Woman: Jesus, Gentiles, and Genealogy in Romans." *Journal of Biblical Literature* 123 (2004): 671–702.

————. "Sirach." In *Women's Bible Commentary: Expanded Edition,* edited by Carol Newsom and Sharon Ringe, 298–304. Louisville: Westminster/John Knox, 1998.

————. "A Speech Act of Faith: The Early Proclamation of the Resurrection of Jesus." In *Putting Body and Soul Together: Essays in Honor of Robin Scroggs,* edited by Virginia Wiles, Alexandra Brown, and Graydon Snyder. Valley Forge, PA: Trinity, 1997.

Elliott, Neil. "The Apostle Paul and Empire." In *In the Shadow of Empire: Reclaiming the Bible as a History of Faithful Resistance,* edited by Richard A. Horsley, 97–116. Louisville: Westminster/John Knox, 2008.

————. *The Arrogance of Nations: Reading Romans in the Shadow of Empire.* Minneapolis: Fortress, 2008.

————. *Liberating Paul: The Justice of God and the Politics of the Apostle.* Sheffield: Sheffield Academic, 1995.

————. *The Rhetoric of Romans: Argumentative Constraint and Strategy in Paul's Dialogue with Judaism.* Sheffield: JSOT, 1990.

Esler, Philip F. *Conflict and Identity in Romans: The Social Setting of Paul's Letter.* Minneapolis: Fortress, 2003.

Feldman, Louis H. *Jew and Gentile in the Ancient World: Attitudes and Interactions from Alexander to Justinian.* Princeton: Princeton Univ. Press, 1993.

Fredriksen Landes, Paula. *Augustine on Romans: Propositions from the Epistle to the Romans; Unfinished Commentary on the Epistle to the Romans.* Chico, CA: Scholars Press, 1982.

Fredriksen, Paula. "Judaism, the Circumcision of Gentiles, and Apocalyptic

Hope: Another Look at Galatians 1 and 2." *Journal of Theological Studies* 42 (1991): 532–64.

———. "Paul and Augustine: Conversion Narratives, Orthodox Traditions, and the Retrospective Self." *Journal of Theological Studies* 37 (1986): 3–34.

Froehlich, Karlfried. "Which Paul? Observations on the Image of the Apostle in the History of Biblical Exegesis." In *New Perspectives on Historical Theology: Essays in Honor of John Meyendorff*, edited by Bradley Nassif and John Meyendorff, 279–99. Grand Rapids: Eerdmans, 1996.

Gager, John G. *The Origins of Anti-Semitism: Attitudes Toward Judaism in Pagan and Christian Antiquity*, 56–76. New York: Oxford Univ. Press, 1983.

———. "Paul, the Apostle of Judaism." In *Jesus, Judaism, and Christian Anti-Judaism: Reading the New Testament After the Holocaust*, edited by Paula Fredriksen and Adele Reinhartz, 56–76. Louisville: Westminster/John Knox, 2002.

———. *Reinventing Paul.* New York: Oxford Univ. Press, 2000.

Gamble, Harry Y. "The Pauline Corpus and the Early Christian Book." In *Paul and the Legacies of Paul*, edited by William S. Babcock, 265–80. Dallas: Southern Methodist Univ., 1990.

García Martínez, Florentino, ed. *The Dead Sea Scrolls Translated: The Qumran Texts in English.* Translated by W. G. E. Watson. New York: Brill, 1994.

Gaston, Lloyd. *Paul and the Torah.* Vancouver: Univ. of British Columbia Press, 1987.

Gibson, E. Leigh. *Texts and Studies in Ancient Judaism.* Vol. 75, *The Jewish Manumission Inscriptions of the Bosporus Kingdom.* Tübingen: Mohr, 1999.

Goodman, Martin. *Mission and Conversion: Proselytizing in the Religious History of the Roman Empire.* New York: Oxford Univ. Press, 1996.

Griffith-Jones, Robin. *The Gospel According to Paul: The Creative Genius Who Brought Jesus to the World.* New York: HarperSanFrancisco, 2004.

Gruen, Erich S. *Diaspora: Jews Amidst Greeks and Romans.* Cambridge, MA: Harvard Univ. Press, 2002.

———. *Heritage and Hellenism: The Reinvention of Jewish Tradition.* Berkeley: Univ. of California Press, 2002.

Halivni, David Weiss. *Midrash, Mishnah, and Gemara: The Jewish Predilection for Justified Law.* Cambridge, MA: Harvard Univ. Press, 1986.

Hayes, Christine E. *Gentile Impurities and Jewish Identities: Intermarriage and Conversion from the Bible to the Talmud.* New York: Oxford Univ. Press, 2002.

Hays, Richard B. *Echoes of Scripture in the Letters of Paul.* New Haven: Yale Univ. Press, 1989.

———. *The Faith of Jesus Christ: The Narrative Substructure of Galatians 3:1–4:11.* 2nd ed. Grand Rapids: Eerdmans, 2002.

Hengel, Martin. *Acts and the History of Earliest Christianity.* Translated by John Bowden. Philadelphia: Fortress, 1980.

———. *The Pre-Christian Paul.* Translated by John Bowden. Philadelphia: Trinity, 1991.

Horsley, Richard A. "The Background of the Confessional Formula in 1 Kor 8:6." *Zeitschrift für die neutestamenliche Wissenschaft* 69 (1978): 130–35.

———. "Gnosis in Corinth: 1 Corinthians 8:1–6." *New Testament Studies* 27 (1980): 32–51.

———. *Jesus and Empire: The Kingdom of God and the New World Disorder* Minneapolis: Fortress, 2003.

———. *Paul and Empire: Religion and Power in Roman Imperial Society.* Harrisburg, PA: Trinity, 1997.

———, ed. *Paul and Politics: Ekklesia, Israel, Imperium, Interpretation.* Harrisburg, PA: Trinity, 2000.

Hurtado, Larry W. *Lord Jesus Christ: Devotion to Jesus in Earliest Christianity.* Grand Rapids: Eerdmans, 2003.

———. *One God, One Lord: Early Christian Devotion and Ancient Jewish Monotheism.* 2nd ed. Edinburgh: T&T Clark, 1998.

———. "The Origin of the Nomina Sacra: A Proposal." *Journal of Biblical Literature* 117 (1998): 655–73.

Isocrates. *Isocrates, Volume I.* Transl. George Norlin. Loeb Classical Library. Cambridge: Harvard Univ Press, 1980.

Jewett, Robert. *Romans: A Commentary.* Minneapolis: Fortress, 2007.

Johnson, E. Elizabeth, and David M. Hay, eds. *Pauline Theology, Volume IV: Looking Back, Pressing On.* Atlanta: SBL Press, 1997.

Johnson, Luke Timothy. "The New Testament's Anti-Jewish Slander and the Conventions of Ancient Polemic," *Journal of Biblical Literature* 108 (1989): 419–41.

Johnson Hodge, Caroline. *If Sons, Then Heirs: A Study of Kinship and Ethnicity in the Letters of Paul.* New York: Oxford Univ. Press, 2007.

Josephus, Transl. H. St. J. Thackeray, et al. 10 vols. Loeb Classical Library. New York: G. P. Putnam, 1926–1965.

Juvenal. *Juvenal and Persius.* Transl. Susan Morton Braund. Loeb Classical Library. Cambridge, MA: Harvard Univ. Press, 2004.

Käsemann, Ernst. *Commentary on Romans.* Translated by Geoffrey W. Bromiley. Grand Rapids: Eerdmans, 1980.

Keck, Leander E. "Images of Paul in the New Testament." *Interpretation* 43 (1989): 341–51.

Kim, Seyoon. *The Origin of Paul's Gospel.* 2nd ed. Tübingen: Mohr, 1984.

Klausner, Joseph. *From Jesus to Paul.* Translated by William F. Stinespring. New York: Macmillan, 1943.

Klawans, Jonathan. *Impurity and Sin in Ancient Judaism.* New York: Oxford Univ. Press, 2000.

———. "Interpreting the Last Supper: Sacrifice, Spiritualization, and Anti-Sacrifice." *New Testament Studies* 48 (2002): 1–17.

———. "Notions of Gentile Impurity in Ancient Judaism." *Association for Jewish Studies Review* 20 (1995): 285–312.

———. "Sadducees, Zadokites, and the Wisdom of Ben Sira." In *Israel's God and Rebecca's Children: Christology and Community in Early Judaism and Christianity: Essays in Honor of Larry W. Hurtado and Alan F. Segal*, edited by David B. Capes, April D. DeConick, Helen K. Bond, and Troy Miller, 263–76. Waco, TX: Baylor Univ. Press, 2007.

Kraemer, Ross Shepard. *When Aseneth Met Joseph: A Late Antique Tale of the Biblical Patriarch and His Egyptian Wife, Reconsidered.* New York: Oxford Univ. Press, 1998.

Kugel, James L. *The Bible as It Was.* Cambridge, MA: Belknap, Harvard Univ. Press, 1997.

———. "The Holiness of Israel and the Land in Second Temple Times." In *Texts, Temples, and Traditions: A Tribute to Menahem Haran*, edited by M. V. Fox et al, 21–32. Winona Lakes, IN: Eisenbrauns, 1996.

———. *In Potiphar's House: The Interpretive Life of Biblical Texts.* San Francisco: Harper, 1990.

Langmuir, Gavin I. *History, Religion, and Antisemitism.* Berkeley: Univ. of California Press, 1990.

Langton, Daniel R. "Modern Jewish Identity and the Apostle Paul: Pauline Studies as an Intra-Jewish Ideological Battleground," *Journal for the Study of the New Testament* 28 (2005): 217–58.

Levine, Amy-Jill. *The Misunderstood Jew: The Church and the Scandal of the Jewish Jesus.* San Francisco: HarperSanFrancisco, 2006.

Liebeschuetz, Wolf. "The Influence of Judaism Among Non-Jews in the Imperial Period." *Journal of Jewish Studies* 52 (2001): 235–52.

Lietaert Peerbolte, L. J. *Paul the Missionary.* Peeters: Leuven, 2003.

Lieu, Judith M. *Neither Jew nor Greek?: Constructing Early Christianity.* Edinburgh: T&T Clark, 2002.

Lieu, Judith, John North, and Tessa Rajak, eds. *The Jews Among Pagans and Christians: In the Roman Empire.* London: Routledge, 1992.

Lodge, John G. *Romans 9–11: A Reader-Response Analysis.* Atlanta: Scholars, 1996.

Lopez, Davina. *Apostle to the Conquered: Reimagining Paul's Mission.* Minneapolis, Fortress, 2008.

Lüdemann, Gerd. *Paul: The Founder of Christianity.* New York: Prometheus Books, 2002.

Lull, Timothy F., ed. *Martin Luther's Basic Theological Writings.* Minneapolis: Fortress, 1989.

Luther, Martin. *A Commentary on St. Paul's Epistle to the Galatians.* Cambridge: James Clark, 1953.

Maccoby, Hyam. *The Mythmaker: Paul and the Invention of Christianity.* New York: Harper & Row, 1986.

MacDonald, Dennis Ronald. *The Legend and the Apostle: The Battle for Paul in Story and Canon.* Philadelphia: Westminister, 1983.

Martyn, J. Louis. *Galatians: A New Translation with Introduction and Commentary.* New York: Doubleday, 1997.

Mason, Steve. "Pharisaic Dominance before 70 CE and the Gospels' Hypocrisy Charge (Matt 23:2–3)." *Harvard Theological Review* 83 (1990): 363–81.

McGrath, Alister E. *Iustitia Dei: A History of the Christian Doctrine of Justification.* 3rd ed. Cambridge: Cambridge Univ. Press, 2005.

Meissner, Stefan. *Die Heimholung des Ketzers: Studien zur juedischen Auseinandersetzung mit Paulus.* Tuebingen: J. C. B. Mohr (Paul Siebeck), 1996.

Minear, Paul Sevier. *The Obedience of Faith: The Purposes of Paul in the Epistle to the Romans.* Naperville, IL: Allenson, 1971.

Mitchell, Margaret M. *The Heavenly Trumpet: John Chrysostom and the Art of Pauline Interpretation.* Louisville: Westminster/John Knox, 2002.

Nanos, Mark. *The Mystery of Romans: The Jewish Context of Paul's Letter.* Minneapolis: Fortress, 1996.

Neusner, Jacob. *From Politics to Piety: The Emergence of Pharisaic Judaism.* 2nd ed. New York: Ktav, 1979.

Newsom, Carol. *Songs of the Sabbath Sacrifice: A Critical Edition.* Atlanta: Scholars, 1985.

Nickelsburg, George W. E. *Ancient Judaism and Christian Origins: Diversity, Continuity, and Transformation.* Minneapolis: Fortress, 2003.

North, John, Judith Lieu, and Tessa Rajak, ed. *The Jews among Pagans and Christians: In the Roman Empire* (London, Routledge, 1992).

Novick, Peter. *That Noble Dream: The "Objectivity Question" and the American Historical Profession.* Cambridge: Cambridge Univ. Press, 1988.

Oberman, Heiko Augustinus. *Luther: Man Between God and the Devil.* New Haven: Yale Univ. Press, 1989.

Pervo, Richard. *Profit with Delight: The Literary Genre of the Acts of the Apostles.* Philadelphia: Fortress, 1987.

Philo, *Works.* Transl and ed. F. H. Colson and G. H. Whitaker. New York: Loeb Classical Library, 1929–62.

Räisänen, Heikki. *Paul and the Law.* 2nd ed. Tübingen: Mohr, 1987.

Rajak, Tessa. *The Jewish Dialogue with Greece and Rome: Studies in Cultural and Social Interaction.* Leiden: Brill, 2002.

Reasoner, Mark. *Romans in Full Circle: A History of Interpretation.* Louisville: Westminster/John Knox, 2005.

Reed, Annette Yoshiko. "Abraham as Chaldean Scientist and Father of the Jews: Josephus, *Ant.* 1.154–168, and the Greco-Roman Discourse About Astronomy/Astrology." *Journal for the Study of Judaism in the Persian, Hellenistic and Roman Period* 35 (2004): 119–58.

Roetzel, Calvin J. *The Letters of Paul: Conversations in Context.* 4th ed. Louisville: Westminister/John Knox, 1998.

———. *Paul: The Man and the Myth.* Columbia: Univ. of South Carolina Press, 1998.

Rubenstein, Richard L. *My Brother Paul.* New York: Harper & Row, 1972.

Saldarini, Anthony J. "Pharisees." In *Anchor Bible Dictionary*, edited by David Noel Freedman, 289–303. New York: Doubleday, 1992.

Sanders, E. P. *Paul and Palestinian Judaism: A Comparison of Patterns of Religion.* Philadelphia: Fortress, 1977.

———. *Paul, the Law, and the Jewish People.* Minneapolis: Fortress, 1983.

Schwartz, Seth. *Imperialism and Jewish Society 200 B.C.E. to 640 C.E.* Princeton: Princeton Univ. Press, 2001.

Segal, Alan F. *Paul the Convert: The Apostolate and Apostasy of Saul the Pharisee.* New Haven: Yale Univ. Press, 1990.

———. "Paul et ses exégètes juifs contemporains," *Recherche de science religieuse* 94 (2006): 413–44.

Snyder, Graydon. *Ante Pacem: Archaeological Evidence of Church Life Before Constantine.* Macon, GA: Mercer Univ. Press, 1985.

Stendahl, Krister. *Final Account: Paul's Letter to the Romans.* Minneapolis: Fortress, 1995.

———. *Paul Among Jews and Gentiles.* Philadelphia: Fortress, 1976.

Stern, Menachem. *Greek and Latin Authors on Jews and Judaism.* 3 vols. Jerusalem: Israel Academy of Sciences and Humanities, 1974–84.

Stowers, Stanley K. *A Rereading of Romans: Justice, Jews, and Gentiles.* New Haven: Yale Univ. Press, 1994.

Stuckenbruck, Loren. *Angel Veneration and Christology: A Study in Early Judaism and the Christology of the Apocalypse of John.* Tübingen: Mohr, 1995.

Tomson, Peter. *Paul and the Jewish Law: Halakha in the Letter of the Apostle to the Gentiles.* Compendia Rerum Iudaicurum ad Novum Testamentum. Section 3: Jewish Traditions in Early Christian Literature, Vol. 1. Assen: Van Gorum; Minneapolis: Fortress, 1990.

Trobisch, David. *Paul's Letter Collection: Tracing the Origins.* Minneapolis: Fortress, 1994.

VanderKam, James and Peter Flint. *The Meaning of the Dead Sea Scrolls: Their Significance for Understanding the Bible, Judaism, Jesus, and Christianity.* San Francisco: HarperSanFrancisco, 2002.

Vermès, Géza. *The Complete Dead Sea Scrolls in English.* New York: Penguin, 1997.

Wagner, Walter H. *After the Apostles: Christianity in the Second Century.* Minneapolis: Fortress, 1994.

Wallis, Ian G. *The Faith of Jesus Christ in Early Christian Traditions.* Cambridge: Cambridge Univ. Press, 1995.

Westerholm, Stephen. *Perspectives Old and New on Paul: The "Lutheran" Paul and His Critics.* Grand Rapids: Eerdmans, 2004.

White, Hayden. *Tropics of Discourse: Essays in Cultural Criticism.* Baltimore: Johns Hopkins Univ. Press, 1978.

Wiles, Virginia, Alexandra R. Brown, Graydon F. Snyder, eds. *Putting Body and Soul Together: Essays in Honor of Robin Scroggs.* Valley Forge, PA: Trinity, 1997.

Williams, Sam K. "Again *Pistis Christou*." *Catholic Biblical Quarterly* 49 (1987): 431–47.

———. *Jesus' Death as Saving Event: the Background and Origin of a Concept.* Cambridge: Harvard Univ. Press, 1975.

———. "The 'Righteousness of God' in Romans." *Journal of Biblical Literature* 99 (1980): 241–90.

Wriedt, Markus. "Luther's Theology." In *The Cambridge Companion to Martin Luther,* edited by Donald McKim, 86–119. Cambridge: Cambridge Univ. Press, 2003.

Wright, N. T. *The Climax of the Covenant: Christ and the Law in Pauline Theology*. Minneapolis: Fortress, 1993.

———. *What Saint Paul Really Said: Was Paul of Tarsus the Real Founder of Christianity?* Grand Rapids: Eerdmans, 1997.

Zetterholm, Magnus. *Approaches to Paul: A Student's Guide to Recent Scholarship*. Minneapolis: Fortress, 2009.

Index

318   *Index*

Torah, Paul's attitude toward *(continued)*
  solutions to, 213–15
  standard to which everyone is accountable, 244–45
  works of law and, 234–39
tradition, Scripture and, 167–71
transformative spiritual events. *See* conversion; conversion of Paul
translations, 55–60, 134–35, 168, 190, 191–95, 243–44
Trobisch, David, 261n11
Two Types of Faith (Buber), 57, 265n6
Tyndale, William, 288n49

VanderKam, James C., 277n13
Vielhauer, P., 260n5

Wagner, Walter, 286n31
Wallis, Ian, 288n43
Wesley, John, 54
Westerholm, Stephen, 52, 265n35, 292n24
What Is Christianity? (Harnack), 56
Williams, Sam, 243, 288–89nn50–51, 294n4, 294n9
Wilson, A. N., 265n8

Wisdom (divine knowledge as woman), 185, 186
Wisdom of Solomon, 72–73, 152, 185, 186
women
  evangelical views on, 30, 33
  as members of Pauline circle, 37
  Paul's views on, 29–30, 262n31
  Tertullian and teaching and baptizing of, 37–38
works. *See* faith in Christ versus good works
works of law, 234–39
worship, 68–74
  idolatry and, 72
  and monotheism, 68–69, 74
  in Second Temple Judaism, 71–72
Wriedt, Markus, 264n26, 264n29
Wright, N. T., 183, 262n23, 262n26, 287n32, 291n8, 291nn16–17

xenophobia, 215

Yoezer, R. Yosi b., 123–24

Zechariah, 96
Zetterholm, Magnus, 267n25